R00025 29181

DUE DATE	RETURN DATE	DUE DATE	RETURN DATE
MAY 05 1987			
JUN 05 1987			

D1275726

Psychotherapy Process

Current Issues and Future Directions

Psychotherapy Process

Current Issues and Future Directions

Edited by

Michael J. Mahoney

The Pennsylvania State University
University Park, Pennsylvania

PLENUM PRESS · NEW YORK AND LONDON

Library of Congress Cataloging in Publication Data

Main entry under title:

Psychotherapy process.

Includes index.
1. Psychotherapy. 2. Cognitive therapy.
I. Mahoney, Michael J. [DNLM: 1. Psychotherapy. WM420.3 P974]
RC480.5.P775   616.8'914   79-9134
ISBN 0-306-40244-0

© 1980 Plenum Press, New York
A Division of Plenum Publishing Corporation
227 West 17th Street, New York, N.Y. 10011

All rights reserved

No part of this book may be reproduced, stored in a retrieval system, or transmitted, in any form or by any means, electronic, mechanical, photocopying, microfilming, recording, or otherwise, without written permission from the Publisher

Printed in the United States of America

492316

To
Guy T. Pilato

Contributors

Merrill P. Anderson • Division of Social Sciences, University of Minnesota, Morris, Minnesota

Diane B. Arnkoff • Department of Psychology, The Pennsylvania State University, University Park, Pennsylvania

Theodore X. Barber • Proseminar Institute, Research Division, Cushing Hospital, Framingham, Massachusetts

Aaron T. Beck • Department of Psychiatry, The University of Pennsylvania, Philadelphia, Pennsylvania

Richard C. Bedrosian • Department of Psychiatry, The University of Pennsylvania, Philadelphia, Pennsylvania

Kenneth S. Bowers • Department of Psychology, University of Waterloo, Waterloo, Ontario, Canada

Lynda Butler • Department of Psychology, University of Waterloo, Waterloo, Ontario, Canada

Gerald C. Davison • Department of Psychology, University of Southern California, Los Angeles, California

James Fadiman • Mechanical Engineering Department, Stanford University and California Institute of Transpersonal Psychology, Menlo Park, California

Jerome D. Frank • Department of Psychiatry, The Johns Hopkins University School of Medicine, Baltimore, Maryland

Susan R. Glaser • Department of Speech, University of Oregon, Eugene, Oregon

Marvin R. Goldfried • Department of Psychology, State University of New York at Stony Brook, Stony Brook, New York

Yolanda F. Hall • Department of Preventive Medicine, Rush–Presbyterian–St. Luke's Medical Center, Chicago, Illinois

Eric Klinger • Department of Psychology, University of Minnesota, Morris, Minnesota

Terry J. Knapp • Department of Psychology, University of Nevada, Las Vegas, Nevada

A. W. Landfield • Department of Psychology, University of Nebraska, Lincoln, Nebraska

Richard S. Lazarus • Department of Psychology, University of California, Berkeley, California

Michael J. Mahoney • Department of Psychology, The Pennsylvania State University, University Park, Pennsylvania

Grover Maxwell • Minnesota Center for Philosophy of Science, University of Minnesota, Minneapolis, Minnesota

Mary Lou Maxwell • Department of Psychology, University of Minnesota, Minneapolis, Minnesota

Donald Meichenbaum • Department of Psychology, University of Waterloo, Waterloo, Ontario, Canada

Walter Mischel • Department of Psychology, Stanford University, Stanford, California

Ulric Neisser • Department of Psychology, Cornell University, Ithaca, New York

Linda Whitney Peterson • Department of Pediatrics, Medical School, University of Nevada, Reno, Nevada

Victor Raimy • 6770 Hawaii Kai Drive, Honolulu, Hawaii

William J. Ray • Department of Psychology, The Pennsylvania State University, University Park, Pennsylvania

Robert N. Sollod • Department of Psychology, The Ferkauf Graduate School, Yeshiva University, New York, New York

Paul L. Wachtel • Department of Psychology, The City College of the City University of New York, New York, New York

Walter B. Weimer • Department of Psychology, The Pennsylvania State University, University Park, Pennsylvania

G. Terence Wilson • Graduate School of Applied and Professional Psychology, Rutgers University, Piscataway, New Jersey

Joseph Wolpe • Department of Psychiatry, Temple University, Eastern Pennsylvania Psychiatric Institute, Philadelphia, Pennsylvania

Preface

Whatever else it may be, psychotherapy offers a clear form of human compassion channeled through myriad assumptions about the causes and solutions of human distress. There has, of course, been a longstanding debate about whether the psychotherapist is best described (and trained) as an artisan or a scientist. Volumes of scholarly argument have also addressed such themes as the essential ingredients of psychotherapy, the role of technique, the importance of client characteristics, and the significance of the therapist's personality. Experts have defended a wide range of opinions on these issues and have mustered evidence to support their individual claims.

The purpose of the present volume is neither to defend nor to expand any specific claim about psychotherapy. Rather, it is intended to be a heuristic compendium of contemporary views on this humane endeavor. At the most basic level of analysis, the field of psychotherapy research now faces three fundamental questions:

1. Is psychotherapy effective?
2. When and why is it effective?
3. How should psychotherapists be trained?

The latter two questions obviously presume that the first can be answered affirmatively. Although I would hardly defend the generalization that all forms of psychotherapy are effective for all clients, it is equally clear that there is now ample warrant for the contention that some of the things we do in our fifty-minute hours seem to have positive effects. This cautious optimism is clearly reflected in Garfield and Bergin's second edition of their classic *Handbook of Psychotherapy and Behavior Change.* Cautious optimism is (fortunately) a far cry from zealous dogmatism, however, and we have many issues to address in our continuing refinement of psychotherapeutic services.

This book is an attempt to pull together a wide range of opinions on the *process* of psychotherapy. In doing so, it does not imply or endorse a dichotomous distinction between psychotherapy process and outcome. These two pragmatically inseparable issues can, however, be segmented in terms of their theoretical significance. One of the cardinal assumptions of past psychotherapy research has been that *what the therapist does makes a difference*. This notion has been cogently challenged at one level of analysis by such writers as Jerome D. Frank who argue that the technical content of therapy is much less important than its metastructure and form of delivery. Contributors to this volume present and defend these two extremes—along with a host of other interpretations and conjectures. Because its explicit purpose is heuristic, I have invited contributors to submit speculative and impressionistic chapters rather than dry and conservative reviews of the available literature. The result is, I think, an exciting collection of scholarly diversity and a valuable amalgam of research-worthy conjectures.

To further stimulate and illustrate the wide range of expert opinions in the field, I have employed a quasi-dialectical format in that each chapter is followed by a brief commentary from a recognized expert in the field. These commentaries range from cautious endorsements to energetic rebuttals and they add an important dimension to the issues under discussion. Controvery and dialectical exchange are the lifeblood of scientific progress. By presenting divergent views in close juxtaposition, I hope that the book will offer further impetus to the growing body of research on psychotherapy process.

MICHAEL J. MAHONEY

Contents

xiii

Chapter 1

A Structural and Transactional Approach to Cognition in Clinical Problems

ROBERT N. SOLLOD AND PAUL L. WACHTEL

The study of cognition by psychologists has been largely isolated from the study of either action or desire. In most of the dominant models and approaches in the area of cognition, man is viewed as a kind of information-processing machine that transforms and organizes perceptual input. In pursuing such models, contemporary cognitive psychologists have achieved a good deal of sophistication, and the efforts by an increasing number of psychotherapists to incorporate these new developments into their clinical approach are likely to prove quite productive. But in applying these models to clinical problems, it will be necessary to pay a good deal of attention to the continuous interplay between cognitive processes and other activities of the organism.

For a period in the late 1940s and 1950s, such a research program was widely pursued. The studies, which were frequently described under the rubric of the "new look" in perception and cognition, attempted to examine how cognitive functioning interacted with the individual's motivational

ROBERT N. SOLLOD • Department of Psychology, The Ferkauf Graduate School, Yeshiva University, New York, New York 10003.   PAUL L. WACHTEL • Department of Psychology, The City College of the City University of New York, New York, New York 10031.

states and enduring motivational dispositions. For more than a decade this kind of work was pursued by a great many researchers, including some of the most prominent names in psychology. Then, within a few years, this research largely dropped out of sight, and references to it today are rare.

The reasons for the decline and abandonment of the "new look" work are complex and fascinating. Some of the early work on "perceptual defense," (e.g., comparisons of perceptual thresholds for supposedly neutral and taboo words) was methodologically rather naive, and criticisms tended to be both abundant and cogent. In response to this early criticism, however, the work became increasingly sophisticated. In a certain sense, so too did the criticisms. But—unnoticed apparently by either the critics or the defenders of this work—the criticisms became increasingly irrelevant to the clinical concerns that stimulated this line of inquiry in the first place. More and more debate began to be concerned with fine points of definition in distinguishing between "perceptual" and "response" effects, while leaving untarnished the clear demonstrations—still not successfully refuted—that motivational factors could influence people's *experiences* (Wolitzky & Wachtel, 1973). Whether one called the processes *response processes* or *perceptual processes*, it was clear that in ambiguous situations—as so many of the important interpersonal and affective matters of concern to the clinician are—people's motives and expectations influenced how they categorized and labeled what they encountered, and hence how they proceeded to deal with life events. As in clinical practice, so too in experimental research there exists a sound foundation for inquiring further into the link between motives and cognitive processes, but of late there has been relatively little fruitful work along these lines.

One of the prime reasons for the derailment of this line of inquiry was the reliance on methods like the tachistoscope, which are generally more suited to examining the fine points of perceptual theory in the motive–perception relationship than to exploring the issues of concern to the clinician.[1] In most tachistoscopic studies, acts of perception, or the cognitive processes involved in evaluating a stimulus, are treated as end points, rather than as part of a *sequence* of events in which cognitive processes lead to actions by the person (based on his appraisal of the situation), which in turn influence and change the situation that is to be appraised (and further acted upon). Such a continuous series of feedback-governed processes is characteristic of most of the problems dealt with by the clinician. Some problems, such as certain simple phobias, do seem to involve appraisals of events that are essentially nonreactive in the patient's behavior (e.g., the danger inherent in

---

[1] A notable exception is the work of Silverman (e.g., 1976), who has used tachistoscopic methods to explore matters of great clinical relevance and has reported some rather extraordinary findings.

a small room or on a high floor of a building). Such problems may perhaps be fairly well understood in terms of a model which looks at the mediating processes *per se*. But in most clinical problems, the faulty mediating processes are influenced not only by motivational factors (as noted above) but also by feedback from the consequences of actions taken on the basis of the appraisal. For such problems the isolated study of cognitive processes can be not only incomplete, but at times misleading. One of us has discussed how lack of attention to such issues has limited the clinical relevance of research on cognitive style (Wachtel, 1972a,b) and has led to misleading conclusions about a whole range of experimental studies on personality processes and psychopathology (Wachtel, 1973a,b).

To a substantial degree, the overreliance on such methods as the tachistoscope by the "new look" researchers reflected their incorporation of the dominant trends in psychodynamic thought, which were largely intrapsychic in their emphasis. Like academic researchers on cognition, intrapsychically oriented psychodynamic thinkers tend to focus upon the internal mediating processes *per se* or on how they are activated by particular kinds of environmental input. They do not stress cyclical processes (Wachtel, 1977a), or what Bandura has called "reciprocal determinism" (Bandura, 1978).

As noted above, the broad psychodynamic assumptions of the "new look" work (e.g., regarding defensive processes that alter awareness) were validated to a much greater degree than is generally recognized. But the intrapsychic emphasis placed limits on the kinds of questions that were asked. Following the lead of clinical theorists such as Sullivan, Horney, and Erikson, it is possible to incorporate the clinical observations from which predominantly intrapsychic theories derive into a framework that is more interpersonal or transactional. Attending to the full implications of such a conceptual strategy suggests new models for research (Wachtel, 1977a) and for therapeutic intervention (Wachtel, 1977b). Of particular importance are the possibilities such a conceptual strategy offers for integrating psychodynamic and behavioral approaches to clinical problems.

Such an integration is further facilitated by the greatly increased interest in cognitive processes by behavior therapists in recent years. Though labeled as "cognitive," this trend seems to us to reflect more generally an interest in internal mediating processes, and thus potentially to open the way for behavior therapists to consider the full range of processes that have been of concern to psychodynamic theorists for many years. The initial impressively trim, spare lines of models derived from laboratory experimentation have had to be modified to accommodate the complexities encountered by behavior therapists in their increasingly diverse clinical practices. We do not expect cognitive behavior therapists to "rediscover" psychoanalysis. Coming from a different tradition—both substantively and epistemologically—we expect that they will bring the particular strengths and perspectives of their origins to bear on their approach to clinical issues. They will see and add things that analysts—viewing things from a different vantage point—have long missed. But they are also likely, it seems to us, to find that their concerns about covert self-statements, constructs, and images dovetail to a substantial degree with the concerns of psychodynamic thinkers.

A number of prominent behaviorally oriented clinicians and researchers have already made important contributions to the analysis of complex mediating processes in personality and behavior change (e.g., Bandura, 1969; Goldfried & Davison, 1976; Lazarus, 1971; Mahoney, 1974; Meichenbaum, 1977; Mischel, 1973). Since several of these individuals are contributors to the present volume and can therefore elaborate it themselves for the reader, this chapter will have relatively little to say about this work directly. But the emphasis we will place on the importance of viewing cognition transactionally—on recognizing that cognitive structures are formed, maintained, and changed in relation to the individual's actions on the environment—does constitute in places an implicit critique of (or at least a friendly reminder regarding) aspects of the emerging tradition of cognitive behavior therapy.

In general, we regard this work as highly promising, but we see a danger that in its "rediscovery" of cognition, some of the virtues of the *behavioral* perspective from which it began will be lost. Of particular concern is the necessity to retain the emphasis on *action* that has characterized the behavioral approach to clinical problems. We suspect, for example, that future research will reveal that far more of the success of Ellis's (1962) rational-emotive therapy—which has been so attractive to cognitively oriented behavior therapists—is due to its emphasis on structured real-life tasks and to the therapist's vigorous urging that the patient do things differently than to the rationalistic analysis of the patient's "irrational" ideas. We are heartened by the increasing interest of behavior therapists in their patients' internal processes, and agree strongly that the underlying assumptions and attributional tendencies that people bring to situations are crucial. But we regard a lot of the current work as holding a far too rationalistic model of how people make sense of their world and reach conclusions about what is going on and what they should do.

We suspect that cognitive behavior therapy will go through an evolution similar to that which occurred in psychoanalysis: Freud, too, started with efforts to *persuade* his patients and to rely on insights of a rather cognitive sort. Increasingly, however, psychoanalytic work revealed the limitations of such an approach (while highlighting its value as a *part* of how change occurs). Saying the right words was not enough. Intellectual insight alone produced little change.

From the beginning, of course, Freud recognized to some extent that insight must be accompanied by affect, that it could not be effective if it was coldly rational. But it took many years of clinical work to develop fully the implications of this recognition and to find ways to prevent lifeless intellectualization from draining the process of its efficacy.[2] In a parallel way, contemporary practitioners of cognitive behavior therapy and rational-emotive approaches are aware of the need for insights to be put into action in the person's daily life, but still seem to us to be at a point where they overvalue cognitive clarity *per se*, as Freud did. The truth shall make us free—but only if we not only *know* it, but also *feel* it and *act* upon it.

A TRANSACTIONAL PERSPECTIVE ON COGNITION AND PERSONALITY STRUCTURES

We have stressed thus far that cognitions must be understood in relation to other aspects of psychological functioning. Cognitive processes can appropriately be viewed as either cause or effect. Cognitions influence our emotional reactions, as Ellis (1962), Beck (1976), and others have pointed out, and cognitions are *influenced by* emotional processes, as indicated by psychoanalytic observations, "new look" perceptual research, research on hormonal influences on thought, etc. Cognitions play a major role in determining how we will behave, and our actions and their consequences feed back to influence our cognitions. Cognitions are influenced by environmental input, and they actively shape the environment we encounter, both by interpreting and giving meaning to it, and by leading to actions that select among alternative environments and alter environmental conditions that are encountered. Cognitive processes are neither epiphenomena (or mere "way stations") nor the absolute center of the causal nexus of behavior. They are an essential and integral part of a quite complex set of chains of causal events in which feedback loops and repeated cycles of events figure prominently (Wachtel, 1977a).

A generally similar perspective has recently been offered by Bandura (1978), though it is hardly the exclusive province of social-learning theory. Among theorists beginning from a broadly psychoanalytic perspective, Shapiro (1965)[3] and Klein (1970) have been particularly concerned with cognitive processes, and with how the individual's way of organizing perceptual input and construing the events of his life both determine and are

[2] And of course the task is still far from complete, and the critical distinction between "intellectual" and "emotional" insight still far from fully understood.

[3] Shapiro (1970, 1975) has subsequently clarified ways in which his "holistic" approach *differs* from a psychodynamic approach, but his original starting point was clearly that of psychoanalytic ego psychology.

determined by his behavior and his experiences. Shapiro, for example, notes that the neurotic person

> seems to think in such a way and his attitudes and interests are such as to continue to sustain the neurotic process and to make the characteristic neurotic experiences inevitable. . . . [His] attitudes and interests will be of a sort that guarantees that the next neurotic act—which from an objective standpoint may sustain and continue the neurotic process—will appear as the only plausible next thing to do. (pp. 18–19)

> The neurotic person is no longer merely a victim of historical events . . . his way of thinking and his attitudes—his style, in other words—have also been formed by that history, are now integral parts of that neurotic functioning and move him to think, feel, and act in ways that are indispensable to it. (p. 21)

For Klein,

> the behavioral unit appropriate to the study of cognitive attitudes is the patterned sequence of behavioral events that eventuate in an experienced attainment. The child's creeping after a toy exemplifies such a complex yet integrated unit of responses; back actions from objects en route provoke new stimulations, inhibit some, facilitate others, and finally produce a terminal experienced attainment. (p. 213)

He notes that motor response

> does not necessarily *follow* perception. Neither is it necessarily the executor of perception, although it is an indispensable component of a more comprehensive adaptive effort. . . . In the Object Assembly test of the Wechsler–Bellevue test, trial-and-error movements may provide opportunities for *perceptual* restructuring; the subject may move a block and *then* see the crucial relation. . . . The role of perception and motor activity in reflecting the adjustive requirements of intention is lost when we rigidly adhere to the older model of stimulus, followed by perception, followed by motor response. (p. 212)

A potentially even more thoroughly cyclical or reciprocal view of the role of cognition in clinical problems can be derived from the interpersonal theory of Sullivan (1954), from Horney's (e.g., 1939, 1945) descriptions of vicious circles in neurosis, White's (1959) concept of efficacy, and from a variety of related views. Wachtel (1977a,b) has discussed how the cognitive and motivational structures that have been of interest to psychodynamic theorists and clinicians can be understood in a thoroughly transactional way as both the cause and the product of the person's way of living. On the basis of particular assumptions about the likely consequences of various ways of interacting with others, the individual engages in interpersonal transactions which are very likely to yield feedback that confirms the original assumptions and makes the whole process likely to occur again. Thus, the shy young man who tells himself that women are not likely to be interested in him, that he is not handsome enough, or dynamic enough, is likely to approach women in an awkward, hesitant manner that evokes responses that seem to confirm his view that he is not sufficiently appealing. Or the hostile, hard-driving man-on-the-make, who tells himself that everyone is out for himself and no one can be trusted with confidences is likely to find that experience confirms this—without clearly realizing that it is his own behavior toward others that evokes such an antagonistic and competitive attitude on their part (or that the same people who, in his experience, do try always to top him and to take advantage of every weakness or even of simple openness on his part, are capable of acting quite differently with others who have established a different relationship with them and evoke a different set of responses).

Recognition of the role of such cyclical transactions has important clinical implications. It allows the clinician to recognize that the patient's erroneous assumptions about the world are not so erroneous for his particular idiosyncratic slice of life. In the patient's world, the things he (seemingly wrongly) anticipates often *do* in fact happen, at least to some degree. Efforts to help the patient examine and correct his assumptive world must take into account how its behavioral implications make it more accurate than it would otherwise seem. Such an analysis is still relevant and important but must be presented to the patient in a broader, transactional context. If you explain your therapeutic strategy in a way that makes clear to the patient that you do understand what kind of experiences he has been having, you are likely to elicit greater cooperation with the therapeutic work.

The above should not be taken to imply, however, that the patient's assumptions are necessarily "correct." *Some* distortion or error most often does play a role in maladaptive behavior patterns. Some clarification is introduced, we think, by applying the Piagetian notion of schema to interpersonal transactions. As Wachtel (1977b) has noted in applying this concept to phenomena labeled as transference by analysts, the notion of schema

> implies that not only do we assimilate new experiences to older, more familiar ways of viewing things (as is implicit in the concept of transference), we also do eventually accommodate to what is actually going on.
>
> Thus, as in transference phenomena, new people and new relationships tend to be approached in terms of their similarity to earlier ones; and frequently, particularly in the special conditions of the psychoanalytic situation, one sees what appear to be quite arbitrary assumptions and perceptions occurring. But in principle, I would suggest, accommodation is always proceeding apace and would, with non-reactive sources of stimulation, eventually lead to a fairly accurate picture of what one is encountering. The problem is that other people are *not* non-reactive. How they behave toward us is very much influenced by how we behave toward them, and hence by how we initially perceive them. Thus,

our initial (in a sense distorted) picture of another person can end up
being a fairly accurate predictor of how he or she will act toward us;
because, based on our expectation that the person will be hostile, or
accepting, or sexual, we are likely to act in such a way as to eventually
draw such behavior from the person and thus have our (initially inaccurate) perception "confirmed." Our tendency to enter the next relationship with the same assumption and perceptual bias is then strengthened,
and the whole process likely to be repeated again. (pp. 53–54)

THE CLINICAL RELEVANCE OF PIAGET'S MODEL OF COGNITION

The utility of a concept borrowed from Piaget for explicating and
developing the point of view we have been stressing is far from a casual
accident. Piaget's developmental and cognitive perspective has a good deal
in common with the point of view we have been advocating. Piaget's
approach is very centrally concerned with how the developing person's
cognitive structures at once shape and are shaped by his actions on and in
the world. The dual functions of assimilation and accommodation reflect
this continuing interaction. Neither can occur alone. One always finds some
molding of the person to the shape of the world he encounters and some
changing, selecting and redefining of what is encountered to make it fit the
available structures that the person brings to bear. Piaget's integrative
theoretical orientation always views cognitive functioning within the context
of the individual's biological development and maturation, the activity of
the individual, his or her interaction with other people, and the qualities of
the physical environment.

Only recently has the potential clinical relevance of Piaget's work
begun to be tapped. No doubt the stylistic difficulty of Piaget for American
readers, as well as the divergence between the underlying philosophical and
methodological assumptions of structuralism and those of American
psychology, have contributed to the limited use of Piaget's ideas by
clinicians on this side of the Atlantic. Even in the areas of education and
developmental psychology—where Piaget's work seems more directly
applicable—American psychologists began to show a substantial interest
only decades after the publication of Piaget's early works. In clinical areas,
receptivity has been even slower in developing.

Piaget himself was strongly inclined, except very early in his career, *not*
to study abnormal or pathological phenomena. In an autobiographical
statement Piaget (1952) indicated that as a consequence of his mother's
poor mental health he always detested any "departure from reality." At
first, he says, "it was this disturbing factor which ... made me intensely
interested in questions of psychoanalysis and pathological psychology.

Though this interest helped me to achieve independence . . . I have never since felt any desire to involve myself deeper in that particular direction, always much preferring the study of normalcy." Largely as a result of this attitude on Piaget's part, rather than on the basis of any theoretical necessity, the Geneva School has, with few exceptions, avoided clinical areas.

In attempting to spell out the implications of Piaget's work for understanding clinical problems, it should be noted that Piaget has had rather little to say concerning the relationship of cognition to emotion. In fact, Piaget recently wrote, "nor have I been interested in affective life (except to live it!)" (1975). Nonetheless, Piaget's framework has much of value to the clinician. It is important to recognize that, although Piaget is widely viewed in America as primarily a child psychologist, his interests have ranged far more broadly. Though he did devote much effort to mapping out and describing the stages of normal cognitive development, his was not just a descriptive theory. He was especially interested in the *process* of cognitive development, and thus in evolution and change. His work is firmly rooted in an understanding of biological adaptation, and thus is, in principle, quite applicable to maladaptation as well, and to its correction.

Piaget's approach shares with behavioral approaches an emphasis on understanding the individual's actual behavior in response to environmental stimulation. But he stresses far more the particular adaptive demand that is experienced in relation to the stimulation encountered, and the way in which the individual's present mode of understanding both defines and informs the response required to meet the challenge of external change. Piaget's approach presumes the presence of underlying cognitive structures and he sees behavior and interaction with the environment as a function of these structures and also as leading to change and development in them. Like the behaviorists, Piaget sees learning as integrally related to the individual's actions in the world, rather than rising out of an internal mental process. But behavior and interaction with the environment lead to significant learning, in Piaget's view, only when there is already present a readiness of the individual, reflected in the existence of sufficiently developed cognitive structures and the ability to perform certain cognitive operations. The ability to master the concept of conservation, for example, occurs in children who—in other ways—show the potential for operational thought. The clearly preoperational child, when exposed to a conservation problem, is unable to answer it correctly. Even if taught the correct answer (as a discrete response) in training sessions, the child proves unable to generalize to different problems involving the same concept. Mastery of conservation involves the ability to consider more than one aspect of a situation. Development of conservation requires not only suitable experience and behavior but also a certain preexisting level of cognitive functioning.

Similar behaviors, in Piaget's view, have different significances for individuals with different cognitive levels. Piaget is thus very careful in his studies of cognitive development in children not only to observe whether an individual solves a given problem (the actual behavior) but also to inquire as to the underlying rationale for the solution. In the conservation example, the ability is considered fully attained when the child gives the correct answer and also indicates a suitably logical basis for the answer.

The more recent cognitive-behavioral approaches have much in common with the Piagetian approach in their emphasis on the importance of cognitions and the relation of such cognitions to behavior and adjustment. Compared to most current cognitive-behavioral theorists, however, Piaget places more stress on the overall cognitive level and organization or the total set of cognitive operations of which an individual is capable. Cognitive-behavioral theorists tend to emphasize *specific* cognitions or thoughts and the consequences of such cognitions for either the individual's behavior or emotional experience. They either do not emphasize or fully elaborate the concept of cognitive framework or structure in which the specific cognition is embedded. The therapeutic focus of Beck (1976) and Ellis (1962), for example, is on changing specific irrational thoughts; Meichenbaum (1977) has focused on specific statements of internal dialogue. Therapeutically they aim at changing the specific irrational thoughts or on modifying statements of internal dialogue. Piaget's complementary emphasis is on the more general cognitive framework, the cognitive structure of an individual and the kinds of cognitive operations in which an individual can engage. The irrational thought "I must be perfect" or "Everything must happen exactly as I wish" may be changed without necessarily implying any enhancement of the more general ability to look at oneself from a variety of perspectives that would be emphasized in a clinical approach incorporating Piaget's concepts.

APPLICATIONS TO CLINICAL WORK WITH CHILDREN

Perhaps the most direct and obvious area of application of Piaget's work is in clinical work with children. In order to work effectively with children it is necessary not only to empathize with their feelings but also to have some appreciation of the model of reality which they have constructed and also some understanding of the kinds of cognitive operations they can perform. Children are not merely smaller versions of adults. The Piagetian tests of cognitive functioning are explicitly developed to indicate how the child actually goes about apprehending reality rather than the particular facts or specific skills he has attained or the speed and persistence with which he functions. For example, the conservation tests assess whether or not a child comprehends the fact, say, that the weight or mass of a piece of clay remains the same regardless of how its shape may be modified, or that a quantity of water remains constant when poured from a cup to a flat dish.

A child who attains conservation has not merely learned a new piece of information but is able to use his mind in a qualitatively different way from the preconservation child. In order to attain conservation, a person must be able to reflect on or have the ability to disengage from the immediate perceptual given. Without this ability, a person is absorbed in the immediate perception. The preconservation child, when asked to compare two equal quantities of water—one spread out in a flat dish and the other in a cup—after having watched the water in the flat dish being poured from an identical cup, may be so impressed by the vastness of the water in the flat dish that he will say that there is more water in the dish, or may be so struck that the water in the cup is "higher" that he thinks that the cup contains more water. The child who has attained conservation will be able to step back from the immediate perception of a single aspect of the situation (say, the perceived vastness of the water in the dish). He will be able to realize that the water there could be poured back into the cup from which it came, or that no water had been added or subtracted in the manipulation there. Such a child has a different way of making sense of reality and dealing with it than the preconservation child.

There is some evidence that the ability to conserve in children does have more general implications for overall functioning. Goldschmid (1968) has shown that children who achieved conservation earlier were more mature emotionally and more popular than others. In addition, he demonstrated that children rated as neurotic achieved conservation later than normal children. It has also been found (Dudek, 1972; Dudek & Dyer, 1972) that children who showed regression on Piaget's conservation tests—after having first attained conservation—were more concrete, cautious, careful, and unimaginative than other children as evidenced by their Rorschach responses.

Piaget's fundamental understanding that children have a variety of levels of ordering their experience and ways of using their minds is a rich source of insight for the clinician. This perspective is often complementary to (or an elaboration of) perspectives already important in traditional clinical approaches, though at times it can point to rather novel considerations. Consider, for example, how Piaget's view can add to our understanding of the special difficulty children can have in dealing with parental conflict, separation, or divorce. Guilt and self-recrimination is a common outcome for such children. Their sense of responsibility for what has happened is often quite disproportionate to their actual role in the events. Traditionally, clinicians have frequently attempted to understand this phenomenon by focusing upon the child's *wishes* and his limited ability to distinguish between the consequences of wishes and those of actions. When there is a (largely coincidental) congruence between what the child wished and what actually occurred, the child feels responsible. Such a view includes both motivational and cognitive-developmental considerations. It is not only the particular content of the child's wish that is relevant, but his tendency to erroneously estimate the impact of his wishes on events. Piaget's concept of egocentrism, with its focus on the child's tendency to see *all* events as centrally concerned with him, and on his difficulty in understanding the point of view of others and their broader range of concerns, nicely complements the more traditional focus.

The Piagetian concept of egocentrism is applicable in understanding a fairly broad range of characteristics of child behavior and cognition. Egocentrism, as Piaget uses the term, does not mean narcissism or selfishness and has no moralistic connotations, but is rather as Looft (1972) has stressed, "an embeddedness in one's own point of view." There are different levels of egocentrism. In the earliest stages of infancy, there is presumed to be a total lack of subject–object differentiation, which gradually yields to the formation of the object concept as something apart from the child's own ego. At a more advanced level of growth out of egocentrism, the child learns to distinguish between his own viewpoint and that of others. Laurendeau and Pinard (1970) have studied the development of growth out of egocentrism in the area of spatial perspectives. In the earliest stage, the child is unable to imagine a three-dimensional scene from any but his own point of view. Next, the child is able to indicate awareness that other points of view exist, but is not able to imagine accurately how the three-dimensional scene might appear to them. The higher stages of this ability involve greater degrees of accuracy in imagining exactly how the scene might appear from other viewpoints.

The ability to imagine with some accuracy what the viewpoint of another might be is based on the cognitive capacity to decenter, that is to be able to step back from one aspect of what is perceptually given and to consider other aspects. As we have indicated, the same ability to step back from what is immediately given is required to pass a test of conservation.

Chandler (1976) has developed a test of egocentricity in which a child is shown a series of picture sequences and asked to make up stories to accompany them. The egocentric child is unable to imagine the existence of more than one viewpoint (of a child protagonist in the sequences) and cannot understand that the behavior of the child might seem inexplicable to another (who has a different perspective because he is not privy to all the child's experiences). For example, in one of Chandler's picture sequences, a child is shown as being sad after her snowman melts. She runs to a nearby street where she is drawn to the smells coming from a bakery. The friendly baker offers her gingerbread-men cookies which remind her of the melted snowman. She becomes sad again and suddenly runs out of the bakery; the baker is puzzled by her behavior.[4] The egocentric child assumes that the baker is aware that the child ran out of the bakery because of her experience with the snowman melting. Thus, such a child cannot account for the baker's puzzled expression. The child who has grown out of this degree of egocentrism is aware that the baker and the child have two separate viewpoints, and he thus is able to understand why the baker is puzzled that the child suddenly left the bakery.

The concept of egocentrism can be useful in understanding why a child is so often vulnerable to the role of "identified patient." The child's being chosen as identified patient serves a purpose in the family, as therapists operating from a family systems perspective have frequently pointed out; but in addition to the *family* dynamics, the child's accepting and playing into the role is made more likely by the general tendency toward egocentricity in his cognitive functioning. In such an egocentric stance, the child is unable objectively and accurately to assess the nature of family interactions and to sort out the relative role and weight of each family member in such interactions. As a result, he is likely to assign excessive responsibility to his own role in family conflict, to feel guilty and responsible for the family's behavior, and thus to accept readily the family's belief of his responsibility for their behavior.

For therapy with young children, egocentrism is a normal aspect of the child's functioning in the session. For example, preschool children often do not explain their thoughts and feelings because they assume that the therapist views the world the way they do. It is necessary for the therapist to probe quite thoroughly in order to elicit their thoughts and feelings. In addition, they are often very concerned that anything they tell the therapist will automatically be known by the parents. In one case, an egocentric but nonpsychotic five-year-old boy expressed some negative thoughts about his parents and then immediately left the therapy room to see if his parents in the waiting room were angry over what he had said. It is thus difficult for young children, who are normally egocentric, to form open, trusting relationships with therapists; in addition, their explanations of both internal and external phenomena are almost exclusively self-referential.

The areas of play and social interaction with others are both clarified and emphasized by Piagetian concepts. In any therapeutic work with children, it is necessary for clinicians to have a clear sense of what is age-appropriate behavior. Parents often have unrealistic expectations for the functioning of children at different ages. The Piagetian cognitive-developmental approach provides a clear conceptual framework which can guide

---

[4] The sequence of events is represented only by pictures, and the child must explain what has happened.

clinicians in their appreciation of the quality of play and interaction with others appropriate for children at different ages. There is, furthermore, an emphasis on the encouragement of social interaction to facilitate cognitive development. In Piaget's (1950) view, it is social interaction with others—especially in the early concrete operational period—that leads to a diminution of egocentrism. Flavell (1963) has indicated that the child, through interaction with others (particularly through conflicts and arguments), is forced to examine his own percepts and concepts from other viewpoints and thus gradually divests himself of cognitive egocentrism. This approach would support the clinician's working not only in a direct symptom-focused way with children who fail to show certain age-appropriate reciprocity or who show deficits in other aspects of social interaction, but also by a more indirect encouragement of social interaction generally. Selman, Newberger, and Jaquette (1977) have described a quasi-educational therapeutic program which specifically focused on the encouragement of structured social interaction as a means of changing the qualitative nature of cognitive functioning.

APPLICATIONS TO ADULT PSYCHOTHERAPY

The applications of Piagetian concepts to psychotherapy of adults rest on a number of considerations. If adults' cognitive functioning were both monolithic and uniformly complete, there might be little application of Piaget to adults. But in fact the complete attainment of formal operational thinking in adults has been found not to occur universally. Adults show a wide range of levels of cognitive functioning. A recent study by Kuhn, Langer, and Kohlberg (1977) indicated that 15% of normal adults gave no evidence of formal operations and 55% showed only partial or incomplete acquisition of formal operational thinking. Formal operational thought had been completely attained by only 30%. Thus, with regard to the development of those abilities specifically pinpointed by Piaget, there is a wide range of individual variation among adults, with many displaying significant deficits in functioning.

In addition, there is much evidence for wide variation of cognitive functioning within an individual. Even though Piaget used emotionally neutral tasks in his studies, he was aware that a person might perform differently on tasks of a similar type but involving different content. For example, a child may be able to attain conservation of weight but not conservation of number. Such intraindividual differences appear to be a function not only of the intrinsic difficulty of a task, but also of the person's history of experience with a given area, as well as the emotional significance of the task. As we have learned in recent years (e.g., Mischel, 1968), conceptions of personality that assume a monolithic consistency do not stand up very well in clinical or real-life situations removed from the experimental laboratory.

Even though a person may, in general, perform at a formal operational level, such a level of functioning cannot be assumed to be invariant across all situations. Weiner (1975) has reported several cases in which anxiety and conflict in particular areas led to regressions in cognitive functioning.

Childhood modes of construing, experiencing and behaving are thus not entirely eradicated in adults. Adult thought and behavior arise from long experience in more childlike modes. Piaget has shown that such development is dependent not merely on biological maturation alone, but also on the nature of interaction with the environment. Lack of sufficient experience or experience of a limiting kind in a certain area may impede full cognitive development in that area. The concept of horizontal decalage refers to the fact that the level of cognitive functioning may be higher in one area of application than another. For example, a girl who has been taught that playing with mechanical devices is unfeminine may carry into adulthood rather oddly magical or global notions of the working of an automobile or of household devices; in this area she may have an incapacity to see the relationship of the workings of one part of a device to another even though in other respects she is quite capable of such analytic thinking. Piaget's approach emphasizes that such a deficit is not simply one involving lack of knowledge about the working of machines, but involves the way the person construes reality and thus influences her perception of mechanical devices and the nature of her interaction with them, as well as her thinking about them. Similarly, a withdrawn or shy person or one who has grown up in an environment with insufficient opportunity for interpersonal interaction can be viewed not merely as having an impoverished repertoire of social behavior and little information about social reality but also as having an inadequately developed construction of social reality with many egocentric and childlike features present.

In addition to gaps from lack of experience in certain areas of cognitive-developmental growth, certain types of upbringing may actively prevent cognitive growth more generally. Lidz (1973) has pointed out, for example, that many types of disturbed families actively encourage egocentric thinking in the adolescent. In fact, egocentric thinking is a plausible way for the adolescent to explain the constant overreaction of the family to his most trivial behaviors. Such a person is likely to carry the same type of egocentric thinking to other situations. Lidz has pointed to this process particularly in the families of young schizophrenics and, like Feffer (1967), has considered many forms of schizophrenic symptomatology, including ideas of reference and certain delusional patterns, in terms of an underlying cognitive egocentricity.

In addition to the appreciation that all adults do not always function uniformly at the highest level of formal operational thinking, Piagetian concepts have further relevance to understanding what occurs in psychotherapeutic work with adults. Inasmuch as psychotherapy may be seen as a process of cognitive development, general Piagetian concepts such as egocentrism, schema, cognitive structure, and the processes of assimilation and accommodation, as well as Piaget's ideas about the growth and transformation of structure through new interaction and experience, are applicable to understanding the psychotherapeutic process.

An interesting perspective is provided, for example, by viewing psychotherapy as a social interaction encouraging growth out of egocentrism. In a wide variety of therapies, the patient becomes aware of and gradually learns to imagine the viewpoint of the therapist regarding his behavior and experience. Regardless of the particular theoretical stance of the therapist, the very process of learning to consider one's behavior and experience from different viewpoints represents growth out of cognitive egocentrism, with implications, as Looft (1972) has pointed out, for more effective and wider-ranging social interaction. Watzlawick (1976) has developed the technique of reframing, which he defines as changing "the conceptual and/or emotional setting or viewpoint in relation to which a situation is experienced and to place it into another frame that fits the facts of the same concrete situation equally well or even better, and thereby changes its entire meaning." Even short of such explicitly emphasized techniques, the very process of a patient speaking to a therapist about his thoughts and feelings and listening to the therapist's theories, views and interpretations concerning such thoughts and feelings encourages decentering. This is particularly true when those thoughts and feelings revealed during the therapeutic process have been kept out of discussions with others.

As noted earlier the view of transference as the employment of schemata in which assimilation predominates is another example of the application of Piagetian concepts to psychotherapy. These concepts lead to an appreciation of why, from a purely cognitive point of view, change in psychotherapy may be difficult and slow. Kuhn (1962), informed by a Piagetian approach, has discussed scientific paradigms and indicated that they change only with great difficulty and only after much contrary evidence has accumulated. A given paradigm assimilates many facts or findings and thus its proponents are reluctant to abandon it even though it may not explain *all* the relevant data. It is precisely those facts which cannot be explained by a given scientific theory—but which can be incorporated into a new theoretical framework—which are most crucial for change in scientific paradigms. The shift from Newtonian to Einsteinian physics, for example, was marked by an emphasis on those few areas of physical phenomena—such as the motion of the planet Mercury—which were not adequately accounted for in the Newtonian framework. An analogy can be drawn between the historical development of scientific theory and individual progress in psychotherapy. The individual has certain schemata which assimilate many facts. One therapeutic task is to draw the patient's attention to facts which cannot so easily be assimilated into these extant schemata and by so doing encourage accommodation of extant cognitive structures to these facts. In this view, certain aspects of resistance to psychotherapeutic change can be seen as due to insufficient accommodation or too ready assimilation.

To return to a prior theme, it may also be noted that as the patient learns to attend to discrepancies between his view of the world and what actually goes on in his life, he may not only correct specific errors in his prior view but also develop a fuller awareness and appreciation of the nature of his actual organizing cognitions about others. This process may be considered as one of helping the patient to move away from cognitive egocentrism. Rather than being embedded in his view of others (regardless of its accuracy or adequacy), the patient can develop a growing awareness of the relativistic nature of that point of view.

PIAGETIAN PERSPECTIVES ON SCHIZOPHRENIA

One emerging area of application of Piaget's ideas is a reconceptualization of schizophrenic functioning (Blatt & Wild, 1976; Sollod, 1979). Strauss and Carpenter (1978) have recently concluded that the functioning of schizophrenics may be thought of not only in terms of pathological symptomatology but also in terms of the quality of the patient's thinking as well as his or her social adjustment. This emphasis on the level of thought organization as well as symptomatology has origins in the work of Hughlings Jackson (1887) who referred to both the "negative mental element" and the "positive mental element" in insanity. He concluded, "we have to consider not only the absurdity but also the elaborateness of the mentation remaining possible" in the insane. Since that time, a number of investigators including Vigotsky (1934) and Werner (1957) emphasized the salience of looking at cognitive and/or perceptual organization in schizophrenia in addition to symptoms of psychopathology. Piagetian approaches follow in this tradition of the application of developmental-cognitive considerations in understanding schizophrenia. They add to these more traditional approaches a more refined articulation of stages of development, a series of well-defined empirical tests to measure such development directly, and a comprehensive theory indicating the relation of functioning at various levels of cognitive functioning to areas of adaptation.

Piaget's elaborate and highly articulated model of cognitive development has recently begun to be operationalized with standardized empirical tests (Goldschmid & Bentler, 1968; Laurendeau & Pinard, 1963, 1970).

These tests very generally indicate qualitative stages of cognitive functioning. Schizophrenic thinking has been explored using a variety of Piagetian tests—including a study by Piaget (1923) himself—and it has been established that there are differences between schizophrenics and normal adults, with the performance of schizophrenics being structurally similar to those of normal children (Trunnell, 1964, 1965). In addition to nosological differences, Kilburg and Siegel (1973) found that reactive schizophrenics performed better than process schizophrenics on tests of formal operational thinking.

Sollod (1976) reported that 21% of the chronic paranoid inpatients ($N = 28$) and 39% of other chronic schizophrenic inpatients tested ($N = 23$) did more poorly on tests on conservation than the average 7-year-old child as reported by Goldschmid and Bentler (1968). The poor functioning of schizophrenics on Piagetian tests did not appear in these studies to be primarily a function of low IQ. Trunnell (1964), for example, reported similar IQs in the normal and schizophrenic groups. Sollod (1976) found that Wechsler Adult Intelligence Scale vocabulary scores were much more highly correlated with years of formal education than were scores on concrete operational thinking.

In addition to the exploration of differences between diagnostic groups (Sollod and Lapidus, 1977), the determination of a level of cognitive functioning in schizophrenics appears to have some utility in predicting adaptive capacity of subjects both within and between diagnostic groupings. Sollod (1976) found that of a group of chronic hospitalized schizophrenics, patients who, regardless of assigned diagnosis, had achieved at least day-pass status were all successful on a series of tests of concrete operational thinking. Patients not on day pass were mixed with regard to concrete operations. Thus, success on these tests was found to be a necessary but not sufficient condition for day-pass status. Such a finding was consistent wtih Piaget's theoretical emphasis that the ability to solve conservation problems was not an isolated aspect of mental functioning but reflected a qualitative level of mental organization with consequences for the nature of the person's functioning in daily life.

Functioning on Piagetian tasks was also found to predict particular aspects of symptomatology. For example, patients at the preoperational level were found to be largely free of significant delusional ideation, fear–worry or anger–hostility as measured by the Structured Clinical Interview (Burdock & Hardesty, 1969). Suchotliff (1970) has reported that schizophrenic subjects with difficulty in decentering shared communication deficiencies both in comparison to normals and to schizophrenics without comparable deficiencies.

Such findings strongly suggest the salience of cognitive functioning in schizophrenics as measured by Piagetian tests both as an outcome variable and as a criterion variable in a variety of studies. The use of level of cognitive functioning to categorize schizophrenics would reduce the high variance typical of this area of research. Investigations of cognitive functioning in schizophrenics make it clear that the conventional diagnostic groups, though different in their mean cognitive scores, each contain subjects at many different levels of cognitive functioning. In spite of similarities based on pattern of pathology or course of illness, such subjects—one for example functioning at a preoperational level and another at a formal operational level (equivalent in some respects to the difference between a normal five-year-old and a normal sixteen-year-old)—would be expected to respond very differently to a variety of both clinical situations and experimental stimuli.

In exploring, for example, the question of the efficacy of psychotherapy for schizophrenics, the patient at the formal operational level might be expected to respond differently to a variety of therapeutic modalities than a patient functioning at the concrete operational level. Putting both of these patients in the same group in a study should lead to a great deal of response variability to a specified therapeutic modality. The patient able to function at the formal operation level is able to reflect on his or her own thinking, and thus should be more amenable to an insight-oriented approach than a patient unable to engage in such thought.

Such cognitive differences should be salient not only in response to psychotherapy, but in treatment and discharge planning within the hospital. Consider, for example, two patients who are being prepared for a community-care home. Although both have about the same degree and type of manifest psychopathology, it is found that one is markedly egocentric, unable to understand or imagine the possible impact of his behavior on others or to be responsive to more subtle interpersonal cues; the other is sociocentric, able rather accurately to imagine a variety of viewpoints other than his own and to be aware of the impact of his behavior on others. The former patient, even though trained or programmed for a community home, is lacking in the ability to adjust sensitively to the requirements of others. It is possible that an impasse in regard to his adjustment to others might arise; for example, he might engage in a routine unpleasant to the other occupants of the home and appear rather intransigent to their expressed displeasure. A worthwhile predischarge endeavor in such a case would be not only to see to what extent the patient could be "programmed" to engage in appropriate daily behavior but to encourage him to engage in sociocentric thinking. Should such efforts be without success, a greater emphasis on rule-following would appear in order as well as working with the staff of the home to be extremely direct and emphatic in necessary communications with the patient. Such an approach would not be required in the case of the more sociocentric patient, who could function quite well on the level of normal social interaction.

APPLICATIONS TO THE AGED

Considerations of the level of effective cognitive functioning appear to be relevant as well to psychogerontology. Deficits in both formal and concrete operational thinking in the aged have been found in many studies (Papalia, 1972; Papalia & Bielby, 1974). Ajurieguerra and Richard (1966) found that the loss of cognitive abilities occurs in reverse of the order of acquisition in normal development. The differing levels of effective functioning in the aging seem to be salient (in much the same way as previously discussed for schizophrenics) as a predictor variable for both daily adjustment—in particular the quality of social interaction—and for experimental studies of cognition. Jackson (1974), for example, studied cognitive functioning in elderly subjects from private nursing home facilities on a battery of Piagetian tasks. He found that the subjects who were successful at conservation had more social interaction and were institutionalized for shorter periods than the nonconservers.

One area of possible application for the elderly is in the area of person–environment fit and the choice of appropriate residences or nursing homes. A person with a high degree of sociocentric thinking, or more generally, with the ability to engage in decentered thought, is able to engage in diverse and complex social interactions such as games, conversations and the like, the significance of which will be lost on the more regressed elderly patient.

Although there certainly are important motivational and interpersonal factors that contribute to the difficulties the elderly have in functioning, a sensitive understanding of their predicament requires as well an accurate assessment of their cognitive abilities and limitations. Piagetian tests and concepts are likely to enhance the cognitive capacity of elderly patients.

Saccuzzo (1977) has discussed similarities between the functioning of the aged and schizophrenics and has suggested that the common feature of cognitive regression could well explain these findings. It has not yet been determined how much of this regression in the elderly is due to a biologically programmed deterioration and how much to the nature of the physical and social enviroment in which they are found. It seems likely that both of these interact in a vicious circle. The initial reduction in activity and lapses of cognitive functioning due to aging lead slowly and inexorably to an environment increasingly lacking in the kind of stimulation that is required for the maintenance of effective cognitive functioning and the motivational support to implement it. Particularly in hospitals and nursing homes—but frequently even when living alone or with their families—the elderly are often given few responsibilities and little opportunity for challenge, stimulating social interaction, or the exercise of their mental capacities. The monotonous conditions under which many elderly people live can at times approximate the conditions of a sensory deprivation experiment, in which the efficacy of cognitive functioning is sharply reduced.

Thus there is present in the elderly a combination of biological deficit or deterioration, withdrawal from social interaction, and reduced interaction with the physical environment. These factors are the reverse of the biological maturation, social interaction, and active exploration of the world that Piaget has described in normal cognitive development. A view of cognitive regression in the elderly most consistent with Piaget's approach would emphasize the interaction of these factors rather than assigning a unique causal importance to any one alone.

DISPROPORTIONATE DISABILITY

Another area in which cognitive functioning has recently been connected with a clinically significant phenomenon is disproportionate disability, a syndrome in which there is catastrophic disability as a result of minimal residual physical impairment from a work-related injury. This phenomenon has long been observed by clinical workers. Ellenberger (1970) reports that Freud studied a number of cases of railroad workers who suffered a catastrophic reaction to injury termed "railway spine." Freud did not address the quality of cognitive functioning in considering these cases.

The adaptive significance of the quality of cognitive functioning was highlighted in a recent study of disproportionate disability by Shands and Meltzer (1975). A group of subjects were chosen who, in spite of the most minimal physiological impairment, evidenced severe psychological reaction characterized in many cases by extreme disorganization, withdrawal, and isolation. In one typical case, a saleswoman who fractured her leg in a fall and developed some residual swelling and stiffness in her leg, became depressed and suicidal, gained 15 pounds, and was subject to weeping spells and anxiety attacks. She was preoccupied with her condition, repetitively expressed the wish that the accident had never occurred, and checked and rechecked her leg to see if it had completely returned to normal. She felt that she had become a "different person" since the accident.

When compared with a matched group of psychiatric patients, the disproportionate-disability patients showed marked difficulty on the Verbal Similarities subtest of the Wechsler Adult Intelligence Scale. Although their overall measured IQ was similar to the psychiatric controls, they demonstrated an inability to engage in abstract thinking. The explanation provided by Shands and Meltzer is that those patients' self-concepts reflects their inability to disengage from the most concrete aspects of reality. Swelling of a leg, loss of a digit, or the development of a noticeable scar would represent irremediable damage to their self-concept. The concept "I am a person with a damaged leg or finger" becomes for them the equivalent of "I am a damaged person." Whereas from a psychoanalytic perspective their reaction might be viewed as displacement of castration anxiety, for Shands and Meltzer the patients' concrete and global thinking is seen as most salient.

Although the findings of this study are far from conclusive, they suggest that level of cognitive ability may be an important indicator of adaptive capacity for a wide range of stresses involving threats to bodily integrity. Such threats might include injury, reconstructive or cosmetic surgery, rapid weight change, or serious illness. In addition, the quality of cognitive functioning may prove to be a predictor of ability to adjust effectively to a variety of stresses other than physical impairment.

IMPLICATIONS FOR PSYCHOLOGICAL ASSESSMENT

Assessment of intellectual functioning is another area in which Piagetian concepts and approaches have clinical relevance (Phillips, 1975). In place of a quantitative score, Piaget's tests indicate a qualitative level of functioning (Pinard & Laurendeau, 1964). Items in standard intelligence tests are chosen to differentiate between children at specified ages, with the score expected of a given age determined empirically. In Piagetian testing, the items are chosen to reflect certain types of cognitive processes with the age of attainment determined after the construction of the test. The conventional test is designed to score whether an answer is right or wrong, whereas the Piagetian tests explore the reasoning behind both right and wrong answers. Among the merits of a Piagetian approach to intelligence testing is a somewhat greater generality of application, as the stages are not as closely linked to the content of traditional schooling as are the Wechsler and Stanford-Binet. In spite of reported intercultural similarities at the concrete operational level (Voyat & Silk, 1970) there do appear to be substantial differences between cultures with regard to these tests, particularly at the formal operational level (Dasen, 1973).

Using Piagetian approaches to assessment, it might be determined that a culturally deprived, lower-class child, with an IQ score in the retarded range, was merely demonstrating a measured lack of certain specific skills and abilities associated with a middle-class environment or classroom learning. Such a child might, however, evidence operational thought, even though he scored lower on the WISC than a highly motivated and well-socialized middle-class child who was preoperational. The Piagetian tests, more clearly than the WISC, would point to environmental and motivational explanations for the poor performance of the ghetto child in more conventional tests and might rule out a diagnosis of retardation suggested by the results of the WISC.

Christ (1977, 1978) has described his work with both psychotic and brain-damaged children and adolescents and indicated that assessment of the level of effective cognitive functioning—rather than IQ alone—is necessary to determine the most effective therapeutic intervention. Emotionally disturbed adolescents with near normal IQ scores may have a pre-operational level of cognitive functioning. In the brain-damaged population, Christ has noted that two fifteen-year-olds with about the same IQ may function at different cognitive levels. According to Christ, insight-oriented psychotherapy can be used with brain-damaged youngsters who have attained concrete and formal operational thinking, but children who function at the sensorimotor and preoperational level require supportive and instructional approaches.

Sollod (1977) has explored the integration of Piagetian tests with a standard psychological battery in adult schizophrenic patients. He suggested that Piagetian tests usefully complement the more structured intelligence tests, as well as the projectives. In the case of the WAIS, the Piagetian concept of level of cognitive organization provides a framework within which the intelligence test results can be understood. The comparison of results on projectives with those of Piagetian tests indicates the relation of emotions, feelings, and fantasy in a variety of thematic areas to the more abiding cognitive-structural aspects of personality. An adult patient at a low cognitive-developmental level, on the basis of structural considerations alone, should be expected to demonstrate many areas of regressed and primitive thought in projective tests; in a patient with a higher cognitive-developmental level, equivalently regressed projective responses would have a primarily dynamic rather than a structural significance.

CONCLUDING COMMENTS

We have emphasized the importance of understanding cognitive functioning in context—as part of a continuing interplay between cognition, overt behavior, and environmental input and feedback. In exploring the implications of such a perspective for clinical research and practice, we have noted some important convergences (though also differences) between the work of cognitive-behavior therapists, particular versions of psychodynamic theory, and the psychological theories of Piaget. Piaget's work has not been heavily relied upon by clinicians thus far, but we have tried to indicate some important potential areas of applicability. Even as the importance of internal mediating processes has been increasingly stressed by clinicians who previously played down such processes, the importance of the individual's actions in the world has continued to be stressed by a wide range of clinicians and theorists. Piaget's theories provide a particularly well-developed perspective on how to integrate internal cognitive structure, overt action, and interaction. Indeed, in Piaget's terms, it is impossible to even speak of one without the other. We have emphasized some of the transactional implications of Piaget's work, in which cognitive structures are viewed as the result of a continuing series of transactions between extant structures and the events that are encountered by them (and, to a substantial degree, brought about by them). In our view, further progress in developing a cognitive perspective for clinicial psychology depends greatly on the degree to which it is understood that cognitive structures are developed and modified by real-world actions that are in turn constrained and guided by extant structures; on the integraton of affective and motivational considerations into such a perspective; on an understanding of the wide range of levels of cognitive organization that underlies people's attitudes and belief systems; and on the development and selection of intervention methods that are suited to the particular way in which the individual goes about making sense of the world.

Finally, a note of caution: We have emphasized Piaget's approach in this chapter more than some other perspectives because we feel that it has been particularly underutilized and that little effort has been made to integrate it with other perspectives on clinical phenomena. But it is essential that the reader not take this as a starting point for treating Piaget's approach as a new "answer" or "system." Even in this chapter we stress other perspectives as well, and in our work generally the potential contribution of Piaget's concepts is just beginning to be explored. We do think that concepts such as cognitive structure, egocentrism, equilibrium, accommodation, and assimilation have significant potential for clinical thinking; but that potential will be quickly eroded if one's gaze is fixed too exclusively on Piaget, without the "decentering" that will permit a more useful and balanced understanding of his contribution.

REFERENCES

Ajurieguerra, J., & Richard, J. *Quelques aspects de la désintégration des praxies idéomatrices dans les démences du grand age. Cortex cerebral*, 1966, *27*, 438–462.

Bandura, A. *Principles of behavior modification.* New York: Holt, Rinehart and Winston, 1969.

Bandura, A. The self system in reciprocal determinism. *American Psychologist*, 1978, *33*, 344–358.

Beck, A. *Cognitive therapy and the emotional disorders.* New York: International Universities Press, 1976.

Blatt, S., & Wild, C. *Schizophrenia: A developmental analysis.* New York: Academic, 1976.

Burdock, E., & Hardesty, A. *Structured clinical interview manual.* New York: Springer, 1969.

Chandler, M. *Egocentrism and childhood psychopathology: The development and application of measurement techniques.* Paper presented at the biennial meeting of the Society for Research in Child Development, Minneapolis, 1976.

Christ, A. Cognitive assessment of the psychotic child: A Piagetian framework, *Journal of the American Academy of Child Psychiatry*, 1977, *16*, 227–238.

Christ, A. Psychotherapy of the child with true brain damage. *American Journal of Orthopsychiatry*, 1978, *48*, 505–515.

Dasen, P. Biology or culture? Interethnic psychology from a Piagetian point of view. *Canadian Psychologist*, 1973, *14*, 149–166.

Dudek, S. A longitudinal study of Piaget's developmental stages and the concept of regression: II. *Journal of Personality Assessment*, 1972, *36*, 468–478.

Dudek, S., & Dyer, G. A longitudinal study of Piaget's developmental stages and the concept of regression: I, *Journal of Personality Assessment*, 1972, *36*, 380–389.

Ellenberger, H. *The discovery of the unconscious.* New York: Basic Books, 1970, pp. 438–439.

Ellis, A. *Reason and emotion in psychotherapy.* New York: Lyle Stuart, 1962.

Feffer, M. Symptom expression as a form of primitive decentering. *Psychological Review*, 1967, *74*, 16–28.

Flavell, J. *The developmental psychology of Jean Piaget.* Princeton, N.J.: Van Nostrand, 1963.

Goldfried, M., & Davison, G. *Clinical behavior therapy.* New York: Holt, Rinehart and Winston, 1976.

Goldschmid, M. The relation of conservation to emotional and environmental aspects of development. *Child Development*, 1968, 579–589.

Goldschmid, M., & Bentler, P. *Concept assessment kit—conservation: Manual and keys.* San Diego, Calif.: Educational and Industrial Testing Service, 1968.

Horney, K. *New ways in psychoanalysis.* New York: Norton, 1939.

Horney, K. *Our inner conflicts.* New York: Norton, 1945.

Jackson, D. Relationship of residence, education, and socialization to cognitive tasks in normal adults of advanced old age. *Psychological Reports*, 1974, *35*, 423–426.

Jackson, H. Remarks on the evolution and dissolution of the nervous system. *Journal of Mental Science*, 1887, *33*, 25–48.

Kilburg, R., & Siegel, A. Formal operations in reactive and process schizophrenics. *Journal of Consulting and Clinical Psychology*, 1973, *40*, 371–376.

Klein, G. *Perception, motives, and personality.* New York: Knopf, 1970.

Kuhn, D., Langer, L., & Kohlberg, L. Attainment of formal operations. *Genetic Psychology Monographs*, 1977, *1*, 97–188.

Kuhn, T. *The structure of scientific revolutions.* Chicago: University of Chicago Press, 1962.

Laurendeau, M., & Pinard, A. *Causal thinking in the child.* New York: International Universities Press, 1963.

Laurendeau, M., & Pinard, A. *The development of the concept of space in the child.* New York: International Universities Press, 1970.

Lazarus, A. *Behavior therapy and beyond.* New York: McGraw-Hill, 1971.

Lidz, T. *The origin and treatment of schizophrenic disorders.* New York: Basic Books, 1973.

Looft, W. Egocentrism and social interaction across the life span. *Psychological Bulletin*, 1972, *78*, 73–92.

Mahoney, M. *Cognition and behavior modification.* Cambridge, Mass.: Ballinger, 1974.

Meichenbaum, D. *Cognitive-behavior modification: An integrative approach.* New York: Plenum, 1977.

Mischel, W. *Personality and assessment.* New York: Wiley, 1968.

Mischel, W. Toward a cognitive social learning reconceptualization of personality. *Psychological Review*, 1973, *80*, 252–283.

Papalia, D. Status of several conservation abilities across the life span. *Human Development*, 1972, *15*, 229–243.

Papalia, D., & Bielby, D. Cognitive functioning in middle and old age: Review of research based on Piaget. *Human Development*, 1974, *17*, 295–301.

Philips, J. *The origins of intellect: Piaget's theory*. San Francisco: Freeman, 1975.

Piaget, J. *La pensée symbolique et la pensée de l'enfant. Archives de Psychologie*, 1923, *18*, 273–304.

Piaget, J. *The psychology of intelligence*. New York: Harcourt, Brace, 1950.

Piaget, J. Jean Piaget (autobiographical sketch). In E. Boring (Ed.), *A history of psychology in autobiography* Vol. 4). Worcester, Mass.: Clark University Press, 1952, pp. 237–256.

Piaget, J. In foreword to Weiner, M., *The cognitive unconscious. A Piagetian approach to psychotherapy*. Davis, Calif.: International Psychological Press, 1975.

Pinard, A., & Laurendeau, M. A scale of mental development based on the theory of Piaget. *Journal of Research in Science Teaching*, 1964, 253–260.

Saccuzzo, D. Bridges between schizophrenia and gerontology: Generalized or specific deficits? *Psychological Bulletin*, 1977, *84*, 595–600.

Selman, R., Newberger, C. M., & Jaquette, M. *Observing interpersonal reasoning in a clinic/educational setting: Toward the integration of developmental and clinical-child psychology II*. Paper presented at the Biannual Convention of the Society for Research in Child Development, New Orleans, 1977.

Shands, H., & Meltzer, J. Disproportionate disability: The Freud–Charcot syndrome rediscovered. *Journal of Psychiatry and Law*, 1975, *3*, 25–37.

Shapiro, D. *Neurotic styles*. New York: Basic Books, 1965.

Shapiro, D. Motivation and action in psychoanalytic psychiatry. *Psychiatry*, 1970, *33*, 329–343.

Shapiro, D. Dynamic and holistic ideas of neurosis and psychotherapy. *Psychiatry*, 1975, *38*, 218–226.

Silverman, L. Psychoanalytic theory: "The reports of my death are greatly exaggerated." *American Psychologist*. 1976, *31*, 621–637.

Sollod, R. A Piagetian approach to psychopathology: Concrete operational thinking and adjustment in hospitalized schizophrenics. (Doctoral Dissertation, Columbia University, 1974). *Dissertation Abstracts International*, 1976, *37B*. (University Microfilm No. 76-29309).

Sollod, R. *Piagetian tests in psychological assessment*. Paper presented at the 7th Annual Symposium of the Jean Piaget Society. Philadelphia, 1977.

Sollod, R. *A Piagetian perspective on schizophrenia*. Paper presented at the 9th Annual International Interdisciplinary UAP–USC Conference on Piagetian Theory and the Helping Professions, Los Angeles, 1979.

Sollod, R., & Lapidus, L. Concrete operational thinking, diagnosis, and psychopathology in hospitalized schizophrenics. *Journal of Abnormal Psychology*, 1977, *86*, 199–202.

Strauss, J., & Carpenter, W. The prognosis of schizophrenia: Rationale for a multidimensional concept. *Schizophrenia Bulletin*, 1978, 4, 56–67.

Suchotliff, L. Relation of formal thought disorder to the communication deficit in schizophrenics. *Journal of Abnormal Psychology*, 1970, *76*, 250–257.

Sullivan, H. *The psychiatric interview*. New York: Norton, 1954.

Trunnel, T. Thought disturbance in schizophrenia. *Archives of General Psychiatry*, 1964, *11*, 126–136.

Trunnel, T. Thought disturbance in schizophrenia: Replication study utilizing Piaget's theories. *Archives of General Psychiatry*, 1965, *13*, 9–18.

Vigotsky, L. Thought in schizophrenia. (J. Kasanin, trans.) *Archives of Neurology and Psychiatry*, 1934, *31*, 1062–1077.

Voyat, G., & Silk, S. Cross-cultural study of cognitive development on the Pine Ridge Indian Reservation. *Pine Ridge Research Bulletin*. Washington, D.C.: Dept. of Health, Education, & Welfare, 1970, *11*, 52–73.

Wachtel, P. Cognitive style and style of adaptation. *Perceptual and Motor Skillls*, 1972, *35*, 779–785. (a)

Wachtel, P. Field dependence and psychological differentiation: A re-examination. *Perceptual and motor skills*, 1972, *35*, 179–189. (b)

Wachtel, P. Psychodynamics, behavior therapy, and the implacable experimenter: An inquiry into the consistency of personality. *Journal of Abnormal Psychology*, 1973, *82*, 324–334. (a)

Wachtel, P. On fact, hunch, and stereotype: A reply to Mischel. *Journal of Abnormal Psychology*, 1973, *82*, 537–540. (b)

Wachtel, P. Interaction cycles, unconscious processes, and the person–situation issue. In D. Magnusson & N. Endler (Eds.) *Personality at the crossroads: Towards an interactional psychology*. Hillsdale, N.J.: Lawrence Erlbaum, 1977. (a)

Wachtel, P. *Psychoanalysis and behavior therapy: Toward an integration*. New York: Basic Books, 1977. (b)

Watzlawick, P. The psychotherapeutic technique of "reframing." In J. Claghorn (Ed.), *Successful psychotherapy*. New York: Bruner Mazel, 1976, pp. 119–127.

Weiner, M. *The cognitive unconscious: A Piagetian approach to psychotherapy*. Davis, Calif.: International Psychological Press, 1975.

Werner, H. *Comparative psychology of mental development*. New York: International University Press, 1957.

White, R. Motivation reconsidered: The concept of competence. *Psychological Review*, 1959, *66*, 297–333.

Wolitzky, D., & Wachtel, P. Personality and perception. In B. Wolman (Ed.), *Handbook of general psychology*. Englewood Cliffs, N.J.: Prentice-Hall, 1973.

Egocentrism and Evidence

Making Piaget Kosher

DONALD MEICHENBAUM AND LYNDA BUTLER

In such a brief response to so rich a chapter as offered by Sollod and Wachtel it is worthwhile to put our sentiments up front, especially if we are to heed their call for the need to tie cognition and motivation together. First, we are in sympathy with their attempt to invite Piaget into the nest of clinical problems (although Piaget was perhaps wise in avoiding such problems, as Sollod and Wachtel have described). We are, however, deeply concerned, as we will make evident below, about the blanket application of a small set of concepts to a wide range of clinical problems. Is it "kosher" to accuse Sollod and Wachtel of perhaps being too egocentric in their attempt to assimilate such diverse clinical phenomena as schizophrenia, age-related deficits, disproportionate reactions to physical disability, and so forth, into Piaget's concept of egocentrism?

While you are mulling over the "kosher" aspects of this concern, let us quickly note that we are in sympathy (translate this to mean that we have said the same or similar things elsewhere—see Meichenbaum & Butler, in press; Meichenbaum, Butler, & Joseph, 1978) with Sollod and Wachtel's position about the complex interaction of cognitive, affective, and be-

DONALD MEICHENBAUM AND LYNDA BUTLER • Department of Psychology, University of Waterloo, Waterloo, Ontario, Canada N2L 3G1.

havioral processes as the individual negotiates his or her social environment. In fact, theorists, researchers, and practitioners of very different persuasions seem to be offering a similar explanatory model for behavior and behavior change. The chapter by Sollod and Wachtel makes a further contribution, couched in Piagetian terms, to this emerging trend. The basic elements of the emerging model include:

1. A "transactional" approach to behavior, where the individual is active in engendering environments (see also Bowers, 1973; Lazarus & Launier, 1978; and others).
2. The notion of psychological functioning as an ongoing sequential process that involves the interaction of the individual's cognitions and behavior with environmental and intrapersonal consequences. Bandura (1978), for example, has characterized this interactive process as "reciprocal determinism," a process of continuous reciprocal interaction between behavioral, cognitive, affective, and environmental influences.

Meichenbaum and his colleagues (Meichenbaum & Butler, 1978; Meichenbaum et al., in press) have spoken of an *evidential* model of change. This model involves three basic elements, namely, the individual's cognitive structures, cognitive processes, and overt behavior. Let us start with the simplest element, which is overt behavior—those actions which the individual emits that usually have some intrapersonal and/or interpersonal consequence. Here we once again concur with Sollod and Wachtel in their highlighting of behavior enactments as a key feature of all forms of psychotherapy. Sollod and Wachtel's suggestion, that therapeutic change, in the case of rational-emotive therapy, for example, may be mediated as much by the client's engaging in structured real-life tasks as by the challenging of the client's irrational beliefs, is consistent with our clinical experience and theoretical formulations, and with the empirical findings summarized by Bandura (1977).

The question remains, however, as to why cognitive-behavioral approaches work better than solely cognitively based interventions. We would argue that such behavioral enactments or graded task assignments provide the client with *evidence* (intrapersonal and interpersonal consequences of their overt behavior) that is inconsistent with their prior expectations, self-statements, or images (what we call cognitive processes). Moreover, the repeated collection of such contradictory evidence permits the client to engage in even more bold experiments (the transactional nature of change), that provide more evidence that may eventually have an impact on one's cognitive structures. By cognitive structures we are referring to the meaning systems or affective concerns that engender particular cognitive processes and overt behavior. A more detailed presentation of the model is beyond the scope of this commentary. But it is appropriate to juxtapose this model of change with the Piagetian view as presented by Sollod and Wachtel.

The recognition of the role of cognitive factors in behavior modification has led therapists to suggest that change occurs sequentially and at different levels. Not only do clients behave differently but, if therapy is successful, new behaviors and new experiences result in alterations in how environmental and intrapersonal consequences are appraised and in the "schemata" or cognitive structures that gave rise to those behaviors. For example, Kovacs and Beck (1978) in discussing cognitive-behavioral intervention with depressives indicate the need to modify maladaptive cognitive structures. By cognitive structures Kovacs and Beck are referring to relatively enduring characteristics of a person's cognitive organization or organized representatives of prior experience. Sollod and Wachtel's emphasis on Piaget's potential contribution to clinical problems is consistent with the emerging recognition of the need to consider something beyong the client's maladaptive behavior, environmental consequences, or even the client's internal dialogue. Something more is needed to explain the nature of psychopathology as well as the nature of competence (see Meichenbaum et al., in press). That something else is captured by the perennial concern with the concept of cognitive structures as described by Kovacs and Beck (1978), Meichenbaum et al. (in press), by Sollod and Wachtel, and by numerous others.

Although we concur with the importance of including some construct such as cognitive structure, with the accompanying processes of assimilation and accommodation operating to change such structures, there is a real danger in being seduced by the belief that we now understand the nature of the change process because we have a label for it. Reification and translation, whether in the form of Piagetian concepts or concepts derived from some other theory, do not help to explain the change process. For example, to say that assimilation and accommodation are invariant processes that are operating in each of the clinical cases offered by Sollod and Wachtel, or to say that egocentrism can be called upon to explain (or at least to describe) the diverse clinical problems that they enumerate is a tour de force of translation, but raises some concern about the adequacy of the explanation.

Let us take two examples offered by Sollod and Wachtel. The first is the example of the impact of disability on an individual. Sollod and Wachtel attribute the disproportionate reaction that sometimes follows such disabilities to egocentric processes. But this is a great burden for one concept to carry. Can one construct such as egocentrism be used to explain the sequence of intrapersonal and interpersonal reactions and changes that follow from such a disability? Several alternative constructs and processes have been offered in the literature; for an example, see the recent study by

Bulman and Wortman (1977) on attributional reactions to disabilities. Similarly, in Sollod and Wachtel's application of egocentrism to the problems of aging, they fail to consider the complexity of other processes which may be operating to mediate adjustment to this life circumstance. One such process is the role of a sense of control (see, for example, Langer & Rodin, 1976; Rodin & Langer, 1978).

The point simply is that psychologists have a penchant for finding one concept, one construct, and then pushing it to its limits across phenomena and across populations. This applies to Piaget's concepts as well as to other concepts. We would offer the same criticism, for example, in relation to Bandura's (1977) concept of self-efficacy as a means to explain behavior change. It is not that egocentrism or self-efficacy are irrelevant in explaining change, but rather that they are asked to do too much. They cover up a sequential change process that involves both intrapersonal and interpersonal processes, and on occasion societal processes, that are also undergoing change.

What is needed, instead, is a descriptive account of the wide variety of potential change mechanisms and alternative ways to view such change. When it comes to the case of Piaget, we feel that alternative explanations are readily available (see, for example, Siegel & Brainerd, 1978). It is not that Sollod and Wachtel would disagree that there are alternatives available, it is just that they fail to consider them. This is most apparent in the last section of their chapter in which they briefly summarize a host of studies employing a group-comparative approach to assess the performance of clinical versus nonclinical populations, or two clinical groups who presumably differ in level of pathology, on Piaget-based tasks. Here it is not the tasks *per se* that we would take issue with, but rather the research strategy that has been adopted. Elsewhere, Meichenbaum (1977) has questioned the validity and usefulness of such group-comparative and group-specific deficits approaches. Alternative research strategies are beginning to emerge which permit us to begin to describe more fully not only inadequate performance but also the mechanism involved in such performance. Meichenbaum (1977) has characterized this as a cognitive-functional approach to understanding inadequate performance. Similar suggestions for such a sequential task analytic approach to assessment have been offered by Brown (1978) and Belmont and Butterfield (1977). The thrust of these approaches, if translated to Sollod and Wachtel's concerns, is to determine exactly what a process such as egocentrism interfered with in terms of the individual's cognitive and behavioral repertoire. Exactly what does it mean to be egocentric? Can we do a situational analysis to determine when such behavior is most evident? What would be the nonverbal and interpersonal evidence for such behavior? Are such processes the same across the various clinical populations covered by Sollod and Wachtel? The answer to these and similar questions will make us less egocentric and make the entire enterprise of understanding human psychological functioning more "kosher."

REFERENCES

Bandura, A. Self-efficacy: Toward a unifying theory of behavioral change. *Psychological Review*, 1977, *84*, 191–215.

Bandura, A. The self-system in reciprocal determinism. *American Psychologist*, 1978, *33*, 344–358.

Belmont, J., & Butterfield, E. The instructional approach to developmental cognitive research. In R. Kail & J. Hagen (Eds.), *Perspectives on the development of memory and cognition*. Hillsdale, N.J.: Lawrence Erlbaum, 1977.

Bowers, K. Situationism in psychology: An analysis and critique. *Psychological Review*, 1973, *80*, 307–336.

Brown, A. Permissible inference from the outcome of training studies in cognitive development research. *Quarterly Newsletter of the Institute for Comparative Human Development*, 1978, *2*, 46–53.

Bulman, R., & Wortman, C. Attributions of blame and coping in the "real world": Severe accident victims react to their lot. *Journal of Personality and Social Psychology*, 1977, *35*, 351–363.

Kovacs, M., & Beck, A. Maladaptive cognitive structures in depression. *American Journal of Psychiatry*, 1978, *135*, 525–533.

Langer, E., & Rodin, J. The effects of choice and enhanced personality responsibility for the aged: A field experiment in an institutional setting. *Journal of Personality and Social Psychology*, 1976, *34*, 191–198.

Lazarus, R., & Launier, R. Stress-related transactions between person and environment. In L. Pervin & M. Lewis (Eds.), *Perspectives in interactional psychology*. New York: Plenum, 1978.

Meichenbaum, D. *Cognitive-behavior modification: An integrative approach.* New York: Plenum, 1977.

Meichenbaum, D., & Butler, L. Toward a conceptual model for the treatment of test anxiety: Implications for research and treatment. In I. Sarason (Ed.), *Test anxiety: Theory, research and applications*. Hillsdale, N.J.: Lawrence Erlbaum, 1978.

Meichenbaum, D., & Butler, L. Cognitive ethology: Assessing the streams of cognition and emotion. In K. Blankstein, P. Pliner, & J. Polivy (Eds.), *Assessment and modification of emotional behavior* (*Vol. 6*). New York: Plenum, in press.

Meichenbaum, D., Butler, L., & Joseph, L. Toward a conceptual model of social competence. In J. Wine & M. Smye (Eds.), *The identification and enhancement of social competence*. Washington, D.C.: Hemisphere, in press.

Rodin, J., & Langer, E. Long term effects of a control-relevant intervention with the institutionalized aged. *Journal of Personality and Social Psychology*, 1978, *35*, 897–902.

Siegel, L., & Brainerd, C. *Alternatives to Piaget: Critical essays on the theory.* New York: Academic, 1978.

Chapter 2

The Transpersonal Stance

JAMES FADIMAN

> *Today the idea of a personal self appears as an indispensable assumption of existence. Actually, like other views of human nature, it is in large measure a cultural idea, a fact within history, the product of a given era.*

> —Rosen (1969)

INTRODUCTION

Transpersonal psychology is the newest facet of American psychology—a self-proclaimed "fourth force" (after the Freudian, behavioristic, and humanistic forces). Transpersonal psychology is equally concerned with the gifted, the retarded, the saint, and the psychotic. It utilizes insights of such traditional systems of thought as Hinduism, Buddhism, Christianity, Sufism, and others.

The major journal in the field, the *Journal of Transpersonal Psychology*, defines the domain of transpersonal psychology as follows:

JAMES FADIMAN • Mechanical Engineering Department, Stanford University and California Institute of Transpersonal Psychology, Menlo Park, California 94025.

meta-needs, transpersonal process, values and states, unitive consciousness, peak experiences, ecstasy, mystical experience, being, essence, bliss,
awe, wonder, transcendence of self, spirit, sacralization of everyday life,
oneness, cosmic awareness, cosmic play, individual and species-wide
synergy, the theories and practices of meditation, spiritual paths, compassion, transpersonal cooperation, transpersonal realization and ac-
tualization; and related concepts, experiences and activities.

A person who practices psychotherapy within this general context can
be labeled a transpersonal therapist. Transpersonal psychotherapy may
include the treatment

of the full range of behavioral, emotional, and intellectual disorders as in
traditional psychotherapies, as well as uncovering and supporting strivings
for full self-actualization. The end state of psychotherapy is not seen as
the successful adjustment to the prevailing culture but rather the daily
experience of that state called liberation, enlightenment, individuation,
certainty or gnosis according to various traditions. (Speeth & Fadiman,
1979)

DEVELOPMENT OF TRANSPERSONAL THEORIES

*Learn your theories as well as you can, but put them aside when you
touch the miracle of the living soul.*

—C. G. Jung

Major theories of personality and therapy best fit their own creators
and to a lesser extent have general applications to others. Anyone who
wonders why Jung and Skinner came to different conclusions about the
nature of consciousness should look to their personal histories in *Particulars
of My Life* by B. F. Skinner (1976) and *Memories, Dreams, Reflections* by
C. G. Jung (1963) for the answer. The expression of their different ideas is
reflected in different experiments, deductions, conclusions, and extrapola-
tions, but the world view underlying these more objective formulations
arises out of their personal history.[1]

A school of thought in psychology, economics, art history, or any other
field, can be described as the work and writings of a number of people who
share the same subjective orientation and whose areas of concern partially
duplicate each other. In the case of the emerging transpersonal orientation,
the communality of ideas arose out of a common set of experiences with
nonhabitual states of consciousness and unconventional educational
experiences. One effect of these shared experiences was that the individuals

[1] While this essay may appear to be objective, it should be understood that objective writing is
a literary form and is designed to lend a patina of authority to what is fundamentally subjective opinion.

felt a pressing need to find some body of literature or research which could clarify, codify, interpret, and resolve the questions raised by what were emotionally important and yet bizarre occurrences.

The initial searching within mainstream psychology (with the exception of William James and a few others) proved to be barren. The result was a realization of the inadequacy of current theories. While there were models of consciousness, awareness, perception, and even models of unusual states of mind, none were inclusive or even fully explanatory. Missing from the psychological literature were adequate descriptions and clarifications of the prevalence and utility of transcendent experience, religious experience, psychotic experience and parapsychological data. Adding to the confusion were the experiences resulting from widespread use of psychoactive chemicals.

The search for information which would explain these experiences expanded to the older psychologies. The writings of Yogananda (1972), Suzuki (1956), and Gurdjieff (1950, 1968), all from different traditions, provided important insights. As these writings became acceptable and were read by persons trained in Western psychology, various connections were seen and the foundations for a confluence of older ideas with Western needs and values began to emerge. The positions that developed can be seen in the work of an experimental psychologist, Charles Tart; a psychoanalytically trained clinician, Stanislav Grof; and a western biochemist–philosopher, Ken Wilber.

Tart (1969, 1975a, 1975b) established the term "altered states of consciousness" as an aspect of transpersonal psychology, and developed both a theoretical structure and a scientific rationale for the study and explication of these states. It is clear from Tart's work, that it is scientifically respectable to assert alternate views of reality that are as substantial, consistent, and functional as the ones that are accepted within traditional Western psychology. Tart underscored the value of specialized training for researchers. His edited works, as well as his own extensive research, have helped bridge gaps between historical and clinical reports of unusual mental states and abilities, and also their replication in standard laboratory settings.

Grof (1975) provided relevant clinical data on altered state phenomena. While using psychedelic drugs in individual therapy sessions, he observed similarities in his patients' experiences. These observations led him from his initial psychoanalytic position to his current transpersonal perspective. Grof believes that personality is shaped by a combination of early experiences, the birth itself being a major factor. He suggests that basic personality types can be described by relating later behaviors to difficulties experienced during passage down the birth canal. Grof also suggests that predispositions to certain kinds of neurotic defenses are established during those first few minutes, and that it is possible in psychedelic therapy to reexperience those initial moments and to free the adult personality from their more crippling effects.

More important for schools of psychotherapy, Grof observed that as patients experienced repeated psychedelic sessions, they displayed a characteristic shift in the kind and content of problems that emerged. He reported that a severely disturbed individual would first grapple with issues best described by Freud, then work with psychodynamic concerns usually associated with the writings of Rank, and then begin to have therapeutic sessions which would confront issues most clearly discussed by Jung. This developmental sequence—from issues of lust and aggression, through concerns with power and interpersonal relationships, to experiences of a transcendent, archetypical, or mystic nature—is in accord with the developmental sequence of personal growth described in both Buddhist and Sufi thought.

What Grof proposes is that different schools of psychotherapy are, in fact, dealing with different aspects of experience. Evidence that supports a developmental notion can be sought from the cases of mental health professionals who took LSD-25 as part of a research and training project. The same sequence was observed. It did not begin with the more Freudian events, but in the middle of the sequence. The kinds of sessions reported, however, were indistinguishable from those reported by patients who had initially been highly disturbed at the commencement of treatment. One goal of psychedelic therapy, as practiced by Grof and others, is to encourage people to move along this sequential track without focusing either on insightful reorganizations of past memories or the establishment of new, more functional behaviors, although both of these are observed side-effects of the therapeutic process (Fadiman, 1965).

Another theorist who has provided useful clarification of the transpersonal perspective is Wilber (1977). He is the first person since William James to successfully describe an overview of the entire range of consciousness. What Wilber suggests is that consciousness should be viewed as a continuum with unity at one end (there is no real differentiation between any two things in the universe), and total dualism at the other (everything is separate and independent of everything else). From this grand overview one observes that most systems of psychology fall into one part or another of this spectrum, i.e., each deals with resolving one level of dualism. Wilber observes that rarely does a theory from either a psychological or spiritual discipline describe more than one aspect of the continuum.

This idea of different aspects of consciousness helps to add clarity where there are actual disagreements between theories. For example, both psychoanalysis and behaviorism describe the same area of psychological functioning, while Buddhism and psychoanalysis describe different portions of the continuum. From this systematic point of view, the value of psychotherapy is to allow a person to be comfortable with a larger and larger portion of the spectrum, rather than being fixated on any single point of awareness.

The confluence of the ideas of Tart, Grof, and Wilber demonstrates that there are different, yet equally valid, aspects to awareness. Also, it is a more flexible, healthier, more liberated, or more skilled individual who experiences more of these levels rather than less of them. What these contemporary transpersonal theorists have created is a systematic delineation of the possible scope of the mind.

THE OLDER PSYCHOLOGIES

> *Western consciousness is by no means consciousness in general, but rather a historically conditioned and geographically limited factor, representative of only one part of humanity.*

—C. G. Jung

Each of the previously discussed theorists, and transpersonal psychologists in general, draw heavily on the accumulated psychological literature outside the American mainstream. Examples of the ideas influencing current transpersonal therapists can be drawn from Buddhism, Sufism, and Yoga. For instance, in Buddhism there is a fundamental assertion and agreement about the nature of the self:

> In Buddhist thought there is a distinction made between the lesser self and the greater self. The lesser self is the ego, the consciousness of one's mind and body. The lesser self remains focused on the limitations of the individual, the consciousness of separateness between the individual and the rest of the world. This level of consciousness must be transcended in order to develop a real sense of unity with other beings and with nature.
>
> It is possible to identify oneself with one's greater self, which is as large as the entire universe, embracing all beings and all creation. This level of understanding is an essential element in the experience of enlightenment.
>
> However, identification with the greater self does not mean that the lesser self must be done away with. Training brings about a transcending of the lesser self, so that one is no longer dominated by it. Nirvana is not annhilation of the ego or smaller self, but transcendence of ego orientation. (Fadiman & Frager, 1976)

In the writings of the Islamic Sufis there is a distinction made between adjustments to external conditions versus alignment to an inner source of correct action. This alignment can be arrived at with the help of a teacher. The teacher encourages the development beyond the limits of reason so that a person may perceive what reason alone cannot accept. There is a distrust of rational processes and a continual emphasis on reaching conclusions experimentally—to know oneself not merely with clarity and insight, but with what is called "certainty."

Certainty is immediate; it is knowledge that you know with your whole being. For example, imagine that you wish to know about active volcanoes. You might start by reading about them, hearing talks about them, seeing slide shows and even films about them; or you might hike up to the cone of an active volcano, experience the steam and smoke swirling around you, your feet burning through your boots, and sounds and colors of the churning, boiling lava filling your ears. . . . In both cases you would know about volcanoes. In the second case, your knowledge could be compared to certainty (adapted from Siraj el-Din, 1970).

In the Yogic tradition there is the repeated suggestion that if you work to clarify the contents of your consciousness, there will be changes in how you relate to external things. What might be termed therapeutic progress proceeds from this point of view, i.e., therapeutic progress occurs not from confrontation or substitution, but from attrition or a growing disinterest in the neurotic aspects of one's life. Inappropriate habits and excessive desires seem to fade away as a person finds them to be less satisfying than the more transpersonal experiences. As one writer put it: "When does the attraction of the pleasure of the senses die away? When one realizes the consummation of all happiness and all pleasure in God—the indivisible, eternal ocean of bliss" (Ramakrishna, 1965, p. 93).

In summary, there is a considerable and sophisticated background of transpersonal theory. This extensive body of literature has encouraged the development of transpersonal therapy. The utility of a theory rests not on its internal elegance, but upon its applications. In the practice of any form of psychotherapy, the underlying theory is critical in determining the initial scope, goals, and processes that define that therapy.

PRACTICAL CONSIDERATIONS

> *Stop talking about satori, but first seek and discipline yourself with your body and soul.*
>
> *For years I suffered in snow and frost, now I am startled at pussy willows falling.*
>
> —Zen Master Mumon

The issue of therapeutic gains or improvement is fundamental to the practice of any form of therapy. Improvement, however, differs from therapy to therapy, and from patient to patient. A look at a few of the critical issues that concern transpersonal therapists may be the most straightforward way to explore this area.

Personality—A Subsystem of the Self [2]

A basic assumption of transpersonal psychology is that there is more to you than your personality. Your personality is your sense of a separate, different, unique identity. Your personality is but one facet, however, of the self—the total identity—and perhaps not even a central facet. The very word "transpersonal" means through or beyond the personality. To be totally identified with one's personality may be evidence of psychopathology. One therapeutic goal is to align the personality within the total self so that it functions appropriately.

These ideas fly in the face of the commonly accepted idea that the be-all and end-all of life is to improve your personality. Personal privacy, personal integrity, personal freedom are touted as desirable goals and correlated with mental health. There is nothing wrong with improving one's personality, but there is remarkably little evidence to support the notion that it can be done. The most telling criticism of psychoanalysis is that it produces so few *useful* results for such a great expenditure of time and effort. There are many results that emerge from psychoanalysis but most of these are confined to redefining and remembering past events and patterns while creating new patterns of beliefs within the personality.

It is as if you went to a health spa and they gave the whole treatment—exercise, steam bath, sauna, and massage—just to your arms. If you ask why they neglected to work on the rest of you, you are told, "The arms are the only parts that matter. They do all your interacting with the world. The rest of your body has limited value. In fact, there are some schools of massage that consider the body a myth made up to explain the origin of the arms. Don't worry yourself about the rest; just appreciate the health and vigor of your arms." Schools of psychotherapy which are exclusively focused on the personality or on the more narrow focus of manifest and covert behaviors are self-limiting. The only criticism of them is that they often appear unaware of their specialized arena of effectiveness.

A goal, within the context of transpersonal therapy, is to encourage and develop those tendencies which allow an individual to disidentify from the restrictions of the personality and to apprehend their identity with the total self. (See Assagioli, 1965, and *Synthesis*, 1974, for a full discussion.) An example drawn from therapeutic practice may clarify this. (Note: *This is not a transpersonal technique*, but has been helpful in some therapeutic situations. It has been utilized in early transpersonal counseling sessions to

[2] Theoretical constructs such as ego, id, or super-ego are subsystems of the personality and are not discussed here.

introduce the possibility of disidentifying from the limitation of the personality.) The questions are asked: "How much of your body has ever heard of you?" "What percentage of your body has ever had any interest in or concern for what you call your personality? Your ideas? Your attitudes? Your speculations? Your memories? Your aspirations?" The obvious answer is, "only a very small percentage."

The implication that arises in this discussion is that, given that most of our visible, material body is not concerned with personality, it is a truism to assert that an individual is more than his or her personality. When a client works with that consideration, his or her experience makes it increasingly evident that there is a considerable amount of daily activity that occurs without the intervention of personal consciousness.

A variation of the above example looks more directly at emotional upset. To a patient who reports uncontrollable anger, one might ask, "What parts of your body are angry; what parts are not?" Should the reply be along the lines of "I'm angry, all of me, my whole being," a therapist can highlight the obvious inaccuracy of the statement by asking, "Are your kneecaps angry? Are your toenails upset? Are your wrists enraged?" Once the client and the therapist can agree that perhaps only 10 percent of the body is dominated by emotion, then the patient is free to develop strategies that the other 90% of the body–mind can utilize during times of anger.

The method just described originated from a personal insight of Aldous Huxley. He was looking in the mirror one morning and congratulated his image on being the image of the famous and distinguished writer Aldous Huxley. Suddenly the thought came to him, "What part of my brain has ever heard of me?" His reply, "only small portions of the frontal lobes," left him pondering on the distinction between the personality and the totality of the person. As a person comes to accept the possibility that his or her personality is merely one aspect of the self, he or she becomes more open to the research, ideas, attitudes, capacities, and states of consciousness that are the core of transpersonal psychology.

Personal Drama

> When I have seriously ill patients who are obsessive—seriously ill people are obsessive by definition; they become obsessed with the significance of their internal drama, and reify it, crystallize it, stabilize it, as if the drama has no alternatives—I put them in contact with a real scenario.
>
> —Minuchin, cited in Malcolm (1978)

An alternative way to begin redefining the importance of personality is to describe it as a personal drama. For example, in a therapy group one person begins: "You know, what I'm feeling right now is . . ." With that opening line the group knows that the person is about to begin one of his personal dramas. If the group is new, the speaker is listened to intently, perhaps without interruption; he or she may be encouraged, confronted, gestalted, or whatever is the game plan within the group. If the group has been together a long time, it is likely that the members have heard or experienced this personal drama before so there is less attention, even some pressure to finish the particular version of the drama quickly so the group may respond and go on.

Personal dramas are predictable, repetitive, and complex patterns of behavior performed either with or without the presence or participation of others. Their repetitive nature is often not appreciated. A different way of viewing the kind of personal drama performed in therapy groups might be the following: "It is my turn to perform a personal drama, as is my right as a member of this group. I wish the rest of the group to stop their concerns with themselves and give me a lot of attention while I run through it. I will now do 'my mother really loved my sister more than me' followed by a chorus of 'my sexual feelings are frozen up inside me' and a final riff of 'some times I wish I were a lesbian, but if I were, I'd kill myself.'"

We all have a storehouse of personal dramas and most of us know our own as well as those of our friends. During political seasons we have friends who warn us, "Don't bring up politics." What they mean is that if we do, we'll be forced to listen to their personal drama on the issue; they are unable to stop the drama once it starts. Personal dramas are an unnecessary luxury and interfere with full functioning. They are part of our emotional baggage. It is usually beneficial for a person to gain some detachment from his or her own dramas, as well as learn to become detached from the personal dramas of others.

The behavior modifiers suggest a detached but compassionate approach to this problem. They suggest that since listening is one reward for behavior, if one wishes to extinguish a behavior, one method is to ignore it. Thus, for a child given to temper tantrums, the behavioral solution (and a very effective one) is to leave the child to scream and kick his heart out without an audience. When one does this, the child may rapidly learn to disidentify himself from the personal drama (since it has become useless) and to return quickly to the normal range of behaviors needed to rejoin the family unit. There has been some success reported with adult chronic pain patients where the staff repeatedly ignores all the pain-oriented behaviors. Many patients stop focusing on that aspect of themselves and show an overall improvement.

A more inclusive (dare I say more sophisticated) method of identifying personal dramas is to let the person know that you are watching his or her personal drama and that you are not confusing the writer with the actor. With children this might take the following form: When a tantrum begins, you draw your chair closer; you say to the child that you are impressed with their temper, their violence, but you would like to see the tantrum again with more kicking or perhaps with breath holding, like last week. This deflates the child's purpose in performing the tantrum. Initially, when you confront a person with the possibility that a behavior is only a personal drama, you may find the response to be fury and excitement. This quickly passes. If you are genuine in your appreciation of the person, the drama will often end with laughter and the relief that comes from being unmasked. Following is a story that demonstrates the point:

Once a young man came to see me. He was on a quest, he said, to explore, reconcile, and unite the current developments in physics, creativity, and consciousness. As his story unfolded, it was apparent that his life had been a series of almost successes: impressive undergraduate record but lost interest in his field; Rhodes scholar but it led nowhere; medical school but didn't finish. . . . On it went, more and more depressing in its content. I began to react with more and more interest and with more and more pleasure as each act in his life drama was recalled. Finally as he started to describe his marriage, I broke in, "It was a wonderful marriage but she left you and you don't know why."

He nodded but sat back miffed, as if I had come in with the last line of a long and complicated shaggy dog story.

"And your quest," I continued, "it isn't working either." Again, he was startled but grudgingly acknowledged my point. I began to applaud. I told him what a fine job he had done in constructing his life and how much I enjoyed listening to a real artist. He looked at me as if I'd gone crazy and tried to pick up his story again. "I'm now in the Bay Area and looking for a job but. . . ." "I can't find a good one," we both said in unison.

Again I applauded and told him that as much as I enjoyed him and his story I wondered why he always set it up to lose. Had he considered the alternative?

He mulled over the question in silence. Finally, I said, "Why don't you get a *bad* job?"

His grim, depressing countenance clouded and then cleared. He smiled; I smiled. He laughed and I laughed with him. We sat and laughed together about the story of his life. For a few minutes he seemed radiant. His posture changed, his speech strengthened and he reflected on some of the past incidents of his life as if he were the author, not the victim. I wished him well and sent him off job-hunting.

Is this the tale of a cure? A Milton Erikson-like turn-around of a human being? Not likely. It is more likely that he soon recovered from the giddy feelings of disidentification and returned to his former gloomy role reinforced with the total failure of his visit as the next bead on his string. Yet for a moment, there was a way of relating, of self-acceptance, of self-esteem that is the kind of experience that can be the beginning of real progress in transpersonal therapy.

The Possibility of Personal Change

> *The State has adjudged me insane and I am no longer responsible for anything, so it is stupid and senseless for me to try and salvage anything out of the tangle. But since the tangle is I, I cannot let it lay as it is . . . Though I have lost every encounter, I am still not dismissed from the conflict.*

—Lara Jefferson (1948)

> *Feed and exercise a lion in a cage: you may get a fine, robust lion. In order to fulfill his destiny, we may have to turn our attention from him—to the cage.*

—Idries Shah (1972)

Do we truly have any choice in our personal drama? In transpersonal therapy the idea of free choice is often emphasized, opening up the possibility that a person can determine his or her own role or roles in life. Once a person can observe his or her personal dramas, he or she becomes more sensitive to which situations evoke which dramas. We are truly different with one person than with another at the level of personal drama, and it is to our advantage to consider which dramas we can best use, and which seem to bring unnecessary suffering.

How and when can a person rise to a level of detached awareness that will enable him to discard old dramas and decide on more fitting ones? One possible answer may be found in learning to use the "witness consciousness"; the "witness" is that part of us which observes our actions without either praise or blame. The experience of being the witness and various methods for training oneself are described in meditational systems, in the words of Gurdjieff and his followers, in the psychosynthesis literature, and elsewhere. It is difficult to find references that describe exactly how one might use this witness consciousness as a pivot point within the self to determine a new or better set of roles. There is, however, some clinical evidence that provides information on this point.

The literature of psychopathology abounds with cases describing the effects of a single traumatic incident on an individual. These descriptions agree that such effects can and do lead to a massive restructuring of behaviors, beliefs, and attitudes. Reports on the effects of religious or spiritual conversions also conclude that a single incident can produce behavioral restructuring. Less well documented, but still widespread, are incidents involving the effects of psychedelic drugs on the personality structure.

In the area of psychedelic drugs it has been found that a single, high-dose ingestion of LSD-25, for example, in a psychologically secure setting can cause extensive and relatively permanent changes in personality structure that can be measured with such crude instruments as the MMPI or the Rod and Frame test. Clinical reports (Fadiman, 1965) indicate major changes in the frequency and intensity of work habits, sexual behaviors, social concerns, and political beliefs.

Individuals often commented that at some point during their experience they felt "above their personality"; they were able to observe it as one might observe the blueprint of a complex piece of machinery. From this detached perspective, they were able to see the connections between past events and current concerns that had been unconscious until then. They also could spontaneously see the inappropriateness of these connections. One subject said, "I could see the cage I'd built, climbed into and locked. I could also see myself spending most of my life shaking the bars and bitching about my life in the cage. I had to laugh when I saw my cage was open at the top."

While in this unusual stage, many patients reported that they made a conscious decision to give up certain practices, to release emotional bonds that tied them to certain habit patterns, and simply to discontinue certain pathological attitudes and behaviors. Several years of follow-up on these subjects showed that in a number of cases the decisions made during that brief span of time had indeed been accomplished and the personality changes appeared permanent. In spite of a determined search for symptom substitution by a well-trained psychoanalyst, who was part of the clinical team, no such substitution was found.

A promising possibility may be drawn from these results, as well as from the data on religious conversions and psychopathology. It may be realistic to encourage people to pick and choose among their behavior patterns. This may be accomplished by utilizing a strategy in therapy that views the personality as a collection of personal dramas and that treats each facet or each drama as a semiautomatic performance, which can be revised or replaced if a person wills. This strategy does not lead to the therapist empathizing with the suffering of the client. In fact, from this perspective, it appears that identifying with the suffering of the client will reinforce the suffering. Not identifying with the suffering may be the first step in eliminating it from the client's repertoire.

One Self or Many Selves

> It is not appropriate to see as separate, things which cannot be distinguished.
>
> —Albert Einstein

An issue in transpersonal theory reflected in differing models of transpersonal therapy is the question of the apparent unity, or diversity, of personality. The way in which an individual therapist treats this issue may predetermine the therapeutic goals. If one believes that we are fundamentally a unity and that all separation eventually falls away with the awareness of higher consciousness, then a goal of therapy is to help the client become aware of the illusory nature of the subidentifications or partial identifications within the self. This notion is inherent in the positions of Wilber (1977) and Bentov (1977). It is a classic position within Buddhism and well-represented in Yogic thought as well.

The other position, that we are a cluster of subpersonalities, leads to different therapeutic expectations. From this point of view, it is not possible to be a single unified self; the goal is to achieve harmony among the various and independent subpersonalities. While there is a self behind the personality, the personality is best described as a collection of contrary, conflicting, overlapping, discontinuous, and diverse subsystems, any of which can dominate or regulate the other subsystems. William James (1890) takes this position, dividing the self into several layers. The outside, or bottom, layer is called the material self—that with which we identify:

> In its widest possible sense, however, a man's Self is the sum total of all that he CAN call his, not only his body and his psychic powers, but his clothes and his house, his wife and children, his ancestors and friends, his reputation and works, his lands and horses, and yacht and bank account. All these things give him the same emotions. If they wax and prosper, he feels triumphant; if they dwindle and die away, he feels cast down, not necessarily in the same degree for each thing, but in much the same way for all. (pp. 291–292)

Above the material self, James describes the social self. "A man's social self is the recognition which he gets from his mates" (James, 1890, p. 293). He suggests that we become different versions of the social self in different situations. He also suggests that a healthy decision is to pick one of these roles, the one best suited to one's life-style and circumstances, and stick to it.

Behind both the material and the social selves is what James calls the "spiritual self." The spiritual self is one's inner and subjective being. It is the active element in all consciousness:

> It is the home of interest—not the pleasant or the painful, not even pleasure or pain, as such, but that within us to which pleasure and pain, the pleasant and the painful, speak. It is the source of effort and attention, and the place from which appear to emanate the fiats of the will. (James, 1890, I, p. 298)

James remained undecided on the question of the personal soul; however, he did feel that there was something beyond individual identity. "Out of my experience . . . one fixed conclusion dogmatically emerges . . . there is a continuum of cosmic consciousness, against which our individuality builds but accidental fences, and into which our several minds plunge as into a mother-sea or reservoir." (James, cited in Murphy & Ballou, 1960, p. 324) Thus James's conclusion is that we have many selves and we have the capacity to distinguish between them. We have a manifesting or transpersonal self which transcends the lesser, and observable, material and social selves.

Since transpersonal therapy is a stance, a place from which to work, rather than a tightly defined and explicit system, transpersonal therapies differ in how they regard the self or selves. But few restrict their thinking or practices to the material or the social levels of the self.

The Use of Nonwestern Psychologies

> The important thing to realize is that the universe, through its incentive system, which we call evolution, is anxious to impart as much knowledge as possible to its sentient beings in order to allow them to move as fast as possible along the evolutionary ladder and develop their consciousness to the highest possible degree.

—I. Bentov

Terms like karma, satori, yoga, and technical practices using mantras and koans are percolating into psychological thought. Transpersonal therapy is permeated with ideas from systems which are older and more fully developed than our own, comparatively recent, European and American beginnings.

Take, for example, a term from Sufism; the term is "naf," which has as its root meaning, the impulse, or drive, to satisfy a desire. Nafs dominate or supersede reason and judgment, thus limiting our capacities. While most psychologies take a moral position with respect to drives (some impulses are detrimental, some are beneficial), the Sufi position is that *all impulses* many uncenter a person, irrespective of their external manifestation or effect. Thus, when one is undeveloped or "neurotic," nafs which are similar to the psychoanalytic descriptions of lust and aggression predominate. As these nafs are subdued, the person is faced with the next level of impulses which resemble the psychoanalytic super-ego, including self-accusation, defensiveness, excessive concern for other's evaluation of one's self, and so forth. As these are brought under control, another level of impulses threatens the balance of the self; these drive one toward gentleness, compassion, creativity, and moral action. Because the culture tends to reward and encourage these impulses, they are especially difficult to control so that one's personal evolution can continue. These impulses are still personality dominated.

For a person still more developed, he or she deals with nafs which predispose one to be liberal, grateful, trusting, and adoring. These impulses mark the transitional phase between excessive identification with personal identity and the emerging identity with the full self. As a person subdues these nafs, he or she no longer needs to perform actions for conventional reasons. The person appears to act as if the usual dichotomies are no longer limitations. "Categorizing observations or experiences into good–bad, beautiful–ugly, rich–poor, pleasure–pain disappears." (Shafii, 1974)

There are still three additional levels of nafs that are special impulses that concern spiritual teachers. They fall so far beyond the usual issues of psychotherapy as to be almost indescribable or unrecognizable in our terms of reference.

What seems to be useful about this scheme is that it offers a value-free impersonal position from which to approach the issues of health and personality development. The only problem within this framework is developing the capacity to control one's impulses so that whatever their goal or effect, they do not supersede the will or the judgment of the person.

To insist that psychotherapy ·must deal with mental illness or dysfunctional behaviors is historically recent and almost without precedence in human cultural history. If the teacher or therapist has skills, advice, support, or anything else that can be of value to the student, client, or patient, then a relationship may be established and maintained until the capacity to help, on the one side, or the capacity to be helped, on the other, is exhausted. It is not unusual for transpersonal therapists to have a sizable percentage of clients who have neither overt nor covert symptomatology but who have a continuing capacity to benefit from the therapeutic relationship.[3]

Nobody Wants to Change

Lord, make me chaste, but not yet.

—St. Augustine

If only I can get away with it this time, I promise never to steal again.

—Anonymous

People who enter therapy rarely wish to change themselves. They wish to be relieved of the suffering, anxiety, pain, failure, and uncertainty in their lives. People don't want to change their personalities. To the extent they identify with a neurosis, a facial tic, inadequate sexual performance, fears of dying, lack of meaning, phobias, and so forth, they do not see "change" as

---

[3] For those of you who scream transference neurosis or the like, rest assured that the therapists involved as well as their patients are not so naive as to ignore such issues.

exchange, but rather as loss. People don't willingly give up, shed or relinquish any part of their identity. This may not be obvious in the obscuring haze of claims and counter-claims in the mental health area, but it can easily be understood if we look at the massive failure of weight loss programs of every variety.

People who are overweight find it easy to lose weight in almost any program they adhere to. They do not find it easy to maintain the weight loss, and to identify with a lower weight. A lower weight is not just a change in weight; it is a change in identity, and as such, is stoutly resisted.

A person on a diet has voluntarily suspended his or her normal eating habits and identified with a new pattern of eating behaviors. Diets can be understood as role-playing behavior. The overweight person eats like someone else, someone whose control and utilization of food is superior to the person who goes on the diet. He or she often reports fully enjoying the diet (at first), feeling not just a reduction in calories, but an increase in feelings of pride, self-control, mastery, increased vitality, and so on.

As the diet progresses the new role leads to a new weight, new physical dimensions, the need for new clothes—a new self-image. As this new image is responded to by friends and associates, fear of change begins to affect the individual. At some crucial juncture, the fear of being changed overwhelms the determination to change and the person quickly reverts to the former weight, image, and personal identity.

Observing how often people begin or end a diet by overeating is a clue to the undercurrent of resistance inherent in the process. Personal identity is not easily transformed by diets, or by psychotherapy. What Freud called a repetition compulsion is more simply explained as a tendency to remain the same. Neither insight nor altering the contingencies of reinforcement, nor emotional catharsis, have proved to lead to lasting personality change. Changes in outward manifestations are different in quality from the basic shifts in personal orientation usually related to personality change.

The transpersonal stance accepts the resistance of the personality to change. No behavior can be lost, only temporarily extinguished; no childhood-based complex can be eradicated, only minimized in its effects. Traumatic situations are made conscious rather than left to remain unconscious, but they still exert their effects on habits and anticipations of future events.

A goal of transpersonal therapy is to stop dwelling on those portions of the personality that should be neglected and to allow the *entire personality* to exert less and less effect on the day-to-day activities of the individual. It is not that a person does not want to change; it is that the personality does not want to change. As one stops overvaluing the needs and opinions of the personality, the more inclusive and more extensive overall self can and does assume a more dominant position. The personality is shrunken in power and dominion but remains intact with all its essential strengths and weaknesses.

An example of this goal is to get patients to understand the difference between desire and craving. Desire is natural, normal, periodic, and inescapable. When you are tired, you desire sleep; when lonely, you desire companionship; when aroused, you desire activity. Craving occurs when you cannot satisfy the object of your desire and *persist* in desiring. Transpersonal therapy can teach people to regulate their desires so that they are not controlled by them. This does not lower the intensity of desires, but helps people discover the capacity to determine their own reactions to their desires. The self, as it is described in all transpersonal theories, does not desire; only the personality is capable of desiring. Therefore, any therapeutic intervention that decreases the centrality of the personality will in turn decrease the compulsive effects of desire and the debilitating effects of unfulfilled craving.

Awareness and Personality Overlap, Sometimes

> *God it is who gives. I am only a distributor.*
>
> —Mohammed
>
> *God has no other hands but mine.*
>
> —St. Teresa of Avila

Most psychotherapies assume that awareness and personality are almost simultaneous. A goal common to psychoanalysis, gestalt, and behavior modification is an increased awareness of one's self and the events, feelings, memories, and behaviors that affect one. It appears, however, that awareness can be independent of the personality. A person may respond, recall, evaluate, and carry on the business of the body without being in touch with the personality, or more accurately, without the personality being aware of the situation. Clinical reports of so-called multiple personalities are a pathological example of this phenomena. The following example, from Hilgard (1978), establishes the clear possibility that one can function, without pathology, and without the awareness of the personality:

> This research began when I stumbled on a way to get at what we call a "hidden observer." The hidden observer first appeared during a classroom demonstration of hypnotic deafness. My subject was a blind student, experienced in hypnosis; his blindness was not related to the demonstration except that it eliminated visual cues. Once hypnotized, he received the suggestion that, at the count of three, he would become completely deaf. His hearing would be restored when I placed my hand on his right shoulder.
>
> An associate and I then banged some large wooden blocks together, close to the subject's head, but he did not react to the sound. He was completely indifferent to our questions. One student asked whether some part of the subject might be aware of what was going on. After all, there was

nothing wrong with his ears. I agreed to test this and said to the subject, "Although you are hypnotically deaf, perhaps some part of you is hearing my voice and processing the information. If there is, I should like the index finger of your right hand to rise as a sign that this is the case."

The finger rose! The subject immediately said, "Please restore my hearing so you can tell me what you did. I felt my finger rise in a way that was not a spontaneous twitch." I placed my hand on his right shoulder to restore his hearing and asked him to tell me all that had happened.

He said that after I counted to produce deafness, everything had become quiet. In the silence, he started to think about a statistical problem. "I was still doing that," he said, "when suddenly I felt my finger lift; that's what I want you to explain to me."

Indicating that I would explain later, I proposed another plan, modeled after our automatic-writing experiments. I said that when I place my hands on his arm, in a manner that I demonstrated, I would be in touch with a hidden part of him that knew everything that had happened. This hidden part could give information not available to his hypnotized self. When I lifted my hand, everything would be as before, but he would not know what the hidden part had said until I gave the release signal.

Sure enough, when I placed my hand on his arm, he could report exactly how many loud sounds had been made, what questions the class had asked, and what I had said that caused his finger to rise. I brought him out of hypnosis, and he asked if he had talked as I said he would. When I said that he had, he wanted to know what he had said. I gave the signal for remembering, and he then could put it all together. (pp. 42–43)

Is it a therapeutic goal to be able to separate one's personality from sensory impressions? Can one learn to tune in and out of perceptual situations? Is it possible that the self can be experimentally isolated from the personality? Hilgard's findings will encourage researchers in consciousness to explore these issues.

FUTURE ISSUES

There are other issues surfacing within transpersonal psychology that will affect the way therapy is practiced. These include:

The Mind–Body Interface

There is a growing body of research that indicates that mental and physical symptoms are so interconnected that it is unrealistic to continue the present dichotomy between mental and physical medicine. Two underlying assumptions have emerged. First, the body is a subsystem of the mind. It is sensible to approach all symptoms from asthma to cancer as if the symptom is partially generated and maintained by mental and emotional causes. Conversely, it is also assumed that the mind is a subsystem of the body. This assumption allows one to approach all mental symptoms from delusions to phobias as if the conditions are partly generated and maintained by physical (environmental, nutritional, constitutional) causes. The resolution of these two blending streams is clearly visible in the emerging reorganization within medicine termed "holistic" or "integral" medicine. It is an issue for transpersonal therapists to determine where to place themselves on the spectrum—somewhere between "it's-all-in-the-mind" and "it's-all-in-the-body." The idea of only treating the body or only treating the mind is seen as unrealistic and without empirical justification.

The Goal of Therapy

At the beginning of this essay, it was stated that the end state of psychotherapy is the daily experience of a state known in different traditions as certainty, liberation, enlightenment, or gnosis. In psychology the term that most closely describes this level of functioning is "self-actualization," which Abraham Maslow used to describe the state of a person who is not dominated by his or her "deficiency needs." One common characteristic of self-actualized individuals is that they appear to operate with different motives and to work for different ends than most people, i.e., drives from personal power, notoriety, sexual and sensual gratification do not predominate. The expression of these drives, however, is not eliminated; these individuals merely have a less intense *need* for gratification of them.

It has been traditional (a tradition perhaps derived from Christian monasticism) to assume that people who are self-actualized or enlightened are quiet, gentle, spiritual, materially poor, sexless, dull, righteous, and whose very presence is slightly uncomfortable for the rest of us. We cannot describe the activities of the posttranspersonal therapy clients in such pious or simplistic terms. They are as likely to be at a World Series, running a corporation, enjoying a plate of oysters, or rebuilding an old car, as they are to be doing anything else. The goal of the self, unbound from the burdens and the deficiencies of the personality, seems to be to enjoy the world but not be attached to it, to be of service, but not to make a pest of oneself.

Toward a Comprehensive Psychology

It is axiomatic within the transpersonal world to recognize our need to reintroduce, study, practice, and assimilate the older and more extensively developed systems of psychology. Psychology historically has been concerned with helping individuals answer the basic questions of their existence:

> Who am I?
> Why am I here?
> Where am I going?

Transpersonal psychology is bringing together the insights of the individualistic psychologies of the West with the spiritual psychologies of the East and Middle East. The realization that our own training has been limited and that Western ideas are not the center of the psychological universe is disturbing at first. The feeling passes when one becomes aware of the amazing amount of work that has already been accomplished, but which awaits validation with the scientific and experimental tools of Western psychology, to be fully realized.

One who tastes, knows.

REFERENCES

Assagioli, R. *Psychosynthesis.* New York: Hobbs, Dorman, 1965.

Bentov, I. *Stalking the wild pendulum.* New York: Dutton, 1977.

Fadiman, J. *Behavioral change following psychedelic (LSD) therapy.* Unpublished doctoral dissertation, Stanford University, 1965.

Fadiman, J., & Frager, R. *Personality and personal growth.* New York: Harper & Row, 1976.

Grof, S. *Realms of the human unconscious.* New York: Viking, 1975.

Gurdjieff, G.I. *All and everything, The first series: Beelzebub's tales to his grandson.* New York: Dutton, 1950.

Gurdjieff, G.I. *Meetings with remarkable men.* New York: Dutton, 1968.

Hilgard, E. R. Hypnosis and consciousness. *Human Nature,* 1978, *1*(1), 42–49.

Idries Shah. *Reflections.* Baltimore: Penguin, 1972.

James, H. (Ed.). *The letters of William James* (2 vols.). Boston: Little, Brown, 1926.

James, W. *Principles of psychology.* Dover, New York: Henry Holt, 1890. Unaltered republication, 1950.

Jefferson, L. *These are my sisters.* Tulsa: Vickers, 1948.

Jung, C. G. *Memories, dreams, reflections.* (A. Jaffe, Ed. and recorder). New York: Pantheon, 1963.

Malcolm, J. The one way mirror. *The New Yorker,* May 15, 1978, pp. 39–114.

Murphy, G., & Ballou, R. (Eds.). *William James on psychical research.* New York: Viking, 1960.

Ramakrishna, *Sayings of Sri Ramakrishna.* Madras, India: Sri Ramakrishna Math, 1965.

Rosen, G. *Madness in society.* New York: Doubleday, 1969.

Shafii, M. *Developmental stages in man in sufism and psychoanalysis.* Unpublished manuscript, 1974.

Siraj-Ed-Din, A. B. *The book of certainty.* New York: Samuel Weiser, 1970.

Skinner, B. F. *Particulars of my life.* New York: Knopf, 1976.

Speeth, K., & Fadiman, J. Transpersonal psychotherapy. In R. Herink (Ed.), *Psychotherapy handbook.* New York: Jason Aronson, 1978; New York: New American Library, 1979.

Suzuki, D. T. *Zen Buddhism.* New York: Anchor, 1956.

Synthesis: The realization of the self. Redwood City: Synthesis Press, 1974.

Tart, C. (Ed.). *Altered states of consciousness.* New York: John Wiley and Sons, 1969.

Tart, C. (Ed.). *Transpersonal psychologies.* New York: Harper and Row, 1975(a).

Tart, C. *States of consciousness.* New York: Dutton, 1975(b).

Wilber, K. *The spectrum of consciousness.* Wheaton, Ill.: Quest, 1977.

Yogananda, P. *The autobiography of a Yogi.* Los Angeles: Self-Realization Fellowship, 1972.

Commentary

Being One

The Search for Transpersonal Psychology

WILLIAM J. RAY

INTRODUCTION

> *Only psychologists invent words for things that do not exist.*
>
> —C. G. Jung

> *Each man holds between his hands a silence that he wants to fill, so he fills it with his dreams.*
>
> —Merle Shain

> *Such is the nature of man, that for your first gift—he prostrates himself; for the second—kisses your hand; for the third—fawns; for the fourth—just nods his head once; for the fifth—becomes too familiar; for the sixth—insults you; and for the seventh—sues you because he was not given enough.*
>
> —Old saying

WILLIAM J. RAY • Department of Psychology, The Pennsylvania State University, University Park, Pennsylvania 16802.

EXPOSITION

"I have come to a strange land," writes the psychotherapist Allen Wheelis (1975). "I do not understand the language." "The customs are peculiar," he continues as if telling of a strange birth into a new land from which home remains distant yet always calling and reminding us of loneliness and love. The name of Wheelis's story is "The Stranger." The stranger, of course, is us, and we are all born into a strange land with only faint sensations to give direction.

INTRODUCTION

Imagine another land in which experimental psychology had not been known. Imagine too that there were no teachers and researchers of experimental psychology in the country. All that were available to the inhabitants were a few texts (Underwood no doubt) that had been brought in by travelers from other countries. Imagine too that in this country there were individuals who were interested in learning more about the world and, for lack of a better phrase, they claimed they were interested in truth. They believed that experimental psychology was one way to truth. Being as all humans are, they might have attempted to tell others. What do you do with this "experimental psychology" the elders of the community might say? How do you go about doing "experiments" others might ask. How might our would-be seekers of truth answer? Well, they might tell of famous experimental psychologists that they had heard of and the methods that had been used. For example, there was a man named Ebbinghaus, the students might say, who spent his days learning words that had absolutely no meaning at all. Is it not exciting, the students might say, that as one goes from only a few nonsense sounds like "bap," "tox," and "muk" to learning ten or more, there is a great change that takes place in learning? Why would you want to know that, the elders might say. Others might ask where have we gone wrong?

EXPOSITION

As you might imagine the students would make little headway with the elders even when they told about how other famous scientists watched rats press a bar for days at a time. Each story, however exciting to the students, seemed more and more to convince the elders that they wanted nothing to do with this "experimental psychology" that was supposed to have so much promise. Since there were no teachers to describe adequately the real reasons for why adults would spend their time learning words that meant nothing, watching hungry rats eat, and making illusions that tricked the sensory system, experimental psychology never developed in this country. Although many of the individuals of the population spent much of their time learning nonsense syllables at least for a while, the society remained much the same as it did before the introduction of "experimental psychology."

There is no doubt that some individuals might have benefited from learning "experimental psychology" and may have even come to understand why the original studies were performed in the first place. Most likely by the time that these individuals understood the meaning behind the techniques of experimentation, there remained less need for trying to explain these old techniques and more need of developing new techniques within the context of the particular culture that could convey the "old truths" of "experimental psychology."

REFERENCE TO THE INTRODUCTION

Returning to our own culture, it may seem that techniques offered by transpersonal psychologists such as meditating, spending a day watching breaths, repeating "om," or turning in a circle may have as little or as much meaning as learning nonsense syllables. The key is not in the activity but in the meaning behind the activity. In the same way that Ebbinghaus looked for words that had no associative meaning for anyone and thus were objective, Fadiman suggests to us that transpersonal psychologists seek processes that go beyond personality and thus the learned associations of a narrowed frame of reference. However, there are two requirements for these processes if they, unlike our "experimental psychology," are to serve a transformative function within our science. First, there is the requirement that there must be individuals who can and will function as "receptive-participant-observers" and who can relate their experiences of these processes of transpersonal psychology. Except possibly within the analytic traditions, there are few areas of clinical psychology today that require those who practice also to have the experience of being practiced upon, and thus to live fully the experience of the tradition. Second, even experience, whether it be of learning nonsense syllables or psychotherapy, is lacking without a teacher or guide who understands the questions being asked in the process and can relate this to the experiencer appropriately. As a matter of historical note, Ebbinghaus developed the nonsense syllable as a means of studying "higher mental processes" that previously had been considered "too subjective" for scientific study. There is, of course, as always a third requirement; this is the necessity of a context for which this work is to take place, but that is another story.

DEVELOPMENT

Lee Cronbach (1957) in his presidential address to the American Psychological Association suggested that there were two disciplines of scientific psychology. The first is that of experimental psychology. In experimental psychology, conditions of nature are modified and changed in order to observe the consequences. Because of the necessity to modify and change the conditions of nature systematically, the domain of experimental psychology becomes restricted and limited to those topics most amenable to this method. The second discipline is that of correlational psychology. By correlational, Cronbach did not mean only those studies that utilized the correlational statistic, but rather included cross cultural psychology, comparative psychology, and developmental psychology, as well as other areas. It was the task of correlational psychology to observe and discuss those experiments including man that nature had begun and was continuing. From such a tradition as this we see the emergence of Piaget's theory of development, utilization of Darwin's theory of evolution, as well as neuropsychological speculation as to the origin of consciousness. Whereas the experimental tradition emphasizes the manipulation of nature, the correlation tradition offers the observation of nature. There is, however, a third tradition that until recently has remained unobserved within both the experimental and the correlational traditions. This is the scientific study of the transformation of man. It is this tradition that transpersonal psychology is attempting to articulate and develop. In the most ideal sense, transpersonal psychology is seeking an alchemy, with consciousness and freedom as the gold.

Traditionally, it has fallen to the lot of psychotherapy to discuss the possible transformation of man, yet this tradition for the most part lacked a scientific base. What has been considered scientific about the question of transformation has been of a historical nature. The theory of evolution, or theories concerning the development of consciousness or sexuality, for example, suggest where man has been, but offer little insight into where man is going or even if man is going.

Transpersonal psychology does appear to have differentiated itself from those traditions whose goal is coping and living more comfortably within the present situation and moved toward those traditions that place psychological growth primary to pleasure and consistency. In this vein, one sees less reference to Freud and the behavioral tradition within transpersonal writings and more to Jung and the eastern traditions.

The rejection of the ideas of transpersonal psychology stems from the acceptance of a particular metatheory as to how a scientific psychology should appear. Some of the major assumptions of this metatheory are as follows:

1. Scientific psychology is rational.
2. Eastern ideas as presented in many formulations of growth and development are more religious than scientific and thus irrational and even dangerous.
3. Personal growth and development as a goal has no place in a scientific psychology.

RECAPITULATION

It now becomes the task of transpersonal psychology to question these assumptions and offer an alternative. The formulations of transpersonal psychology may appear just as crazy to the people of this time as Newton's explanation that tides on a seashore were caused by the moon must have sounded to the people of his time. In the end, the real craziness may not reside in our conceptions of concepts such as action at a distance, but rather our limited understanding of what science is all about.

If indeed transpersonal psychology can take the traditional questions of existence—who am I; why am I here; and where am I going?—and add to these a scientific formulation of development, then it is an important and even necessary movement. For all the potential of the movement, transpersonal psychology is still caught in all the paradoxes of a mind trying to experience and describe itself. It took many years for the physicists to move from understanding they were describing "out there" to realizing they were engaged in an exercise in the articulation of mind. It may take an equal number of years for transpersonal psychology to see through the East and then back home again. It may be a necessary journey. Done with awareness, it is the only journey.

CODA

At the end of the story, Allen Wheelis (1975) had the stranger say:

> Always the inner vision may be lost, and driving it away in obligation to an audience, in payment for that audience's esteem, is but one among many ways. Alone on a mountain top it may be lost, may be lost in confusion, in faintness of heart, or by fleeing from loneliness into a spurious belonging. But if I can hold on to what I know I am free to explore it

Is it science? No, but real science always begins in life.

REFERENCES

Cronbach, L. J. The two disciplines of scientific psychology. *American Psychologist*, 1957, *12*, 671–684.
Wheelis, A. *On not knowing how to live*. New York: Harper & Row, 1975.

NOTE ADDED IN PROOF

The structure of this article is taken from the Pathetique. The genius of Beethoven was that after six sections, his seventh, the recapitulation, was, unlike classical forms, pregnant with new meaning. *The return to the origin was not to start over.* I thank John Satterfield for pointing this out to me.

Chapter 3

Personal Construct Psychology

A Theory to Be Elaborated

A. W. LANDFIELD

Major theories of psychology are written by persons who are deeply committed to positions on human nature which, in their minds, stand as alternatives to other positions being espoused at the time. In reading the works of a new theorist, one may feel that the position either is not really new or is merely incomprehensible. However one may view the theory, it can be assumed that the theorist feels he has produced something new and has diligently set about the task of communicating this newness. George A. Kelly, author of *The Psychology of Personal Constructs* (1955), certainly wanted to present his colleagues with new ideas and did so with varying degrees of success—a fate experienced by most theorists. That Kelly experienced some success in communicating this newness is supported by the steady flow of manuscripts written about the theory, many of which have been contributed by persons of British, Canadian, or European background.

That an American psychologist should receive his greatest initial sup-

A. W. LANDFIELD • Department of Psychology, University of Nebraska, Lincoln, Nebraska 68588.

port from non-Americans may seem strange in the context of a comment attributed to a British author of strong Marxist convictions. He stated that Kelly was the last bastion of capitalism with its rugged individualism (Cole & Landfield, 1977, p. 350). Assuming that this comment accurately reflects the essential nature of personal construct theory, one is hard pressed to explain why American psychologists did not immediately take to the theory. Perhaps American psychologists, focusing on externally defined causes of behavior, either did not fit the tradition of rugged individualism or their rugged conceptions of science reflected a collective need to appear properly scientific. Whatever the explanation of this apparent incongruity may be, and whether or not American psychologists felt oppositional toward the Kellyan viewpoint, one thing is clear. Kelly did take a stand in opposition to what he construed as American psychology of the 1940s and 1950s. In a letter to S. I. Hayakawa, September 30, 1963, Kelly writes:

> A number of years ago . . . I was struck by the fact that every psychology textbook I read contained at least two theories of personality. The first theory was expounded, usually in the first chapter of the textbook, as an explanation of the way "science" sets about its task. But this description of scientific activities may properly be regarded as a description of the behavior of scientists—or at least an effort to describe the behavior of scientists. Hence, it is, itself, a theory of personality, limited, of course, supposedly to scientists.
>
> Having got this out of his system, the author then usually went ahead to describe the psychology of the rest of us poor mortals in terms quite unlike those he had used to describe the personality of the elite. Partly in rebellion to this, I suppose, I set about the task of developing a theory of personality in which I suppose I echoed one of the mottos of the Protestant Reformation. Instead of saying "every man his own priest," I proposed that we regard "every man his own scientist." The pathways into which this effort led me have proved, in the main, to be amusing and, I hope, more or less profitable.

REFLEXIVENESS OF THEORY

When Kelly stated that every person is his own scientist, he did not imply that the person should be construed in the role of an idealized scientist. Instead, Kelly employed science in its most human and elaborated form. In assuming that both the person and the scientist observe life events, interpret them, and anticipate in regard to them, he was not implying that the person or scientist is necessarily objective, organized, precise, and logical. Any forthright description of the scientist would include some comments about his emotionality, subjectivity, biased attitude, confusion, and illogicalness. Kelly then was employing the term scientist in its *ordinary* meaning rather than in its extraordinary context.

The analogy between "man and scientist" is of particular interest because it not only placed Kelly in the mainstream of modern science, but also raised the philosophical issue of reflexivity (Oliver & Landfield, 1962). Reflexivity of theory, which may not greatly concern the physical scientist, is an issue which the behavioral scientist can not avoid. Essentially, reflexivity points to the relationship between a theorist and his theory. If a psychologist creates a general theory that accounts for the behavior of people, it seems only reasonable and fair that the theorist should have some interest or concern about whether his theory of others also applies to himself, even to his behavior as theorist. Granted, it may be most difficult for a theorist to apply his theory about others to himself and to his own behavior as theorist. Even if one could make such an application, it might be too personal to talk about. Nevertheless, Oliver and Landfield (1962) maintain that the psychological theorist should "at least" have some concern about the reflexiveness of his theory. Kelly, in writing a psychology of behavior which encompasses both person and scientist, showed concern for the self-reflexive implications of theory.

CONSTRUCTIVE ALTERNATIVISM

In the same self-reflective way that Kelly showed concern about the relationship between theory and theorist, he also understood that a theory is more than just the particularized statements of that theory. General theories of behavior and personality reflect certain underlying assumptions about the nature of life—assumptions sometimes unacknowledged or unstated. Mindful of this philosophical issue, he began his writing by discussing what he called constructive alternativism, an assumption about the nature of the universe from which he wrote his psychology.

Kelly assumed that the universe, in part, is a creation of persons. He also assumed the existence of a reality, one that is known by interpreting it, by placing structures of meaning (constructs) on the events of one's life. He also assumed that whatever can be construed may be reconstrued. In other words, the universe is open to revision within the limits of an assumed reality. This revision of the universe, a process stretching into infinity, can, over eons of time, bring us closer in touch with the nature of our world.

Now this idea of a moving universe, which for Kelly was more than just an accumulation of facts and details, may be disquieting for laymen and even for scientists. After all, one's feeling of well-being, whether in science or everyday life, tends to become intertwined with a certainty of knowing and feeling. How many persons will experience a sense of well-being in defining life as a continuing exploration, expansion, and uncertain adventure? Yet, this may well be the truth of most of our lives. There is little comfort in a theory that questions the personal assumption that life is immediately knowable. Nonetheless, Kelly maintained that the real events of our lives are *not* free of the process of construction and reconstruction. Kelly (1970a) succinctly states his basic position in the following quotation:

> Like other theories, the Psychology of Personal Constructs is the implementation of a philosophical assumption. In this case the assumption is that whatever nature may be, or howsoever the quest for truth will turn out in the end, the events we face tody are subject to as great a variety of constructions as our wits will enable us to contrive. This is not to say that one construction is as good as any other, nor is it to deny that at some infinite point in time human vision will behold reality out to the utmost reaches of existence. But it does remind us that all our present perceptions are open to question and reconsideration, and it does broadly suggest that even the most obvious occurrences of everyday life might appear utterly transformed if we were inventive enough to construe them differently. (p. 1)

Clearly implied in the above statement are the dual themes of the mysterious nature of the human psyche and the motivational force of a quest for truth and understanding of one's life. Miller Mair (1977a) elaborates these themes in most interesting ways in his "Metaphors for Living." The following quotations from Mair capture the spirit of constructive alternativism and encourage the reader to explore more of both Kelly and Mair:

> As mentioned earlier, Kelly thought that one of the vital tasks for man was to "transcend the obvious," to break out of the "cliche" which we tend to make of our reality. So at the center of his psychology is a huge question mark concerning the nature of man: a mystery, rather than any suggestion of a pat answer or a comfortable conclusion. (p. 266)

> At any moment each man is suspended somewhere between his own birth and his own death, but also between the birth and death of the human race, the birth and death of the world, and more. If we only view him within very narrow limits of time and place we may dismiss many human struggles as trivial or neurotic which may appear in a different light if we consider a wider context and a longer journey. (p. 168)

It seems clear from the statements by Kelly and Mair that constructive alternativism is a philosophy of science, not only for psychology in particular, but also for science most generally. Kelly, in stating that life and science are matters of continuing construction and reconstruction by persons, does not support the contention of scientists who believe that a particular concept of science or branch of science is more basic or fundamental than another one. They are all constructions with useful and changing ranges of application. In taking this relativistic view of science and psychology, Kelly acknowledged that he may have sowed the seeds of his own destruction. Taking a reflexive stance in relation to his own philosophy, he stated that his position should be considered "ad interim." He also stated that the usefulness of his theory would be found in its elaboration. In this regard, several questions from the recent Nebraska Symposium (Cole & Landfield, 1977) on construct theory are enlightening. Arleen Lewis commented that one can do the most service for personal construct theory by elaborating it rather than just trying to prove it. Seymour Rosenberg commented that what were underrepresented in the discussions were Kelly's programmatic ideas for further research. He then stated, "I think the best way of keeping Kelly's contributions alive, anyone's for that matter, is by elaborating it. It is not the purist who promotes behaviorism, psychoanalysis, etc. Look what Titchener did to structuralism—we still don't know whether there was anything worthwhile there as a consequence" (Cole & Landifeld, 1977, p. 346). As to what Kelly was trying to do with his theory, participants at the symposium felt that he challenged psychologists to consider new possibilities. However, he did not want psychologists to trade one set of fixed ideas for another. Kelly's theory was designed to encourage the psychologist's continuing elaboration and exploration of ideas and his willingness to play about with the answers.

THE PERSONAL CONSTRUCT

A central unit of understanding within the theory is the personal construct. Kelly defined the personal construct as *an awareness of how two things are alike in a way that differentiates them from a third*. The person is aware or knows "along dimensions extending from precise verbal symbolization to levels of understanding which may be preverbal, difficult to express in words, identified with raw feelings, and sometimes expressible in movement, gesture and sound" (Landfield, 1977, p. 134). Although Kelly's definition of the personal construct as a dimension of awareness does not confuse the construct with verbal symbols, many constructs can be identified by words. Since much research within personal construct theory has focused on modifications of the Role Construct Repertory Test (Rep Test), a verbal task, there has been a tendency to mistakenly equate the words caught in the web of a Rep Test with the essential nature of the personal construct. At the theoretical level, the personal construct is defined as a dimension of awareness, carrying no necessary implications for exactly how such dimensions must be measured.

The issue of tacit construing was introduced by Don Bannister at the Nebraska Symposium (Cole & Landfield, 1977) when he stated that "we discuss the discussable in a verbal culture." Robert Neimeyer also contributed an interesting commentary on tacit construing:

> Because of its unobtrusiveness, it is easy to overlook the pervasiveness of
> tacit construing. Upon our first encounter with the unfamiliar object or

event, it is at first only sketchily outlined in consciousness; we may have gleaned from it only an ambiguous aura of its "style" or significance. These first tentative constructions of the new experience are tacit, and constitute the fundament of later, more articulate understandings . . . it is time we accept the challenge to broaden our methodology and expand our investigative efforts in order to plumb the full depths of human construing. (Cole & Landfield, 1977, p. 351)

Recently, Neimeyer has begun an investigation of tacit construing with materials such as crayons, clay, and cards on which one finds strange designs and textures. Nonverbal expressions are elicited about these materials and are used to anchor 13-point rating scales. An art student found the task more meaningful than the verbalizations on the usual Rep Test. Another subject felt the task allowed her to express feelings and thoughts that she did not care to verbalize.

THE REP TEST

For those readers who are unacquainted with the Rep Test and its elaborations, it is essentially a matter of asking a subject to describe combinations of acquaintances, situations, self-roles, or other events. The initial process of description involves presenting the subject with varying combinations of three events that Kelly referred to as elements. The subject is asked to differentiate and generalize among these elements by stating how two of them are similar in some important way which differentiates them from the third one. After a certain number of dimensions of personal description have been elicited, the subject is asked to rate all elements along all dimensions. Rating all elements along all dimensions allows one to create what is known as a grid. Since each element, heading a column of ratings, can be defined by the pattern of those ratings, it is possible to ascertain how much alike or different one element is from another. Since each dimension, heading a row of ratings, can be defined by the pattern of those ratings, it is also possible to ascertain how much alike or different one dimension is from another.

Now these differentiations on the Rep Test can take the form of feelings in relationship with others, perceptions of others, understandings and feelings about oneself, the identification of geographical areas, and even the appreciation of architectural forms and spaces. In other words, almost any event can be an element on a Rep Test. The very freedom with which one may employ the Rep Test for research purposes suggests that we talk about Rep Test procedures rather than Rep Tests. Furthermore, since the conventional Rep Test need not be the only way in which an investigator makes inferences about dimensions of personal meaning or understands their elaborated implications, we should not become too rooted in associating Rep Tests with the personal construct. One could carefully observe the behavior of a person in varying situations and make testable inferences about what he or she may be experiencing, i.e., the dimensions along which the person may be construing events.

For those who wish more information about Rep Tests and Rep Grids, *A Manual for Repertory Grid Technique* by Fransella and Bannister (1977), may be useful. However, it should be kept in mind that the use of a construct technique does not necessarily mean that it is being used in the best spirit of the theory. People have used grid methods without much concern for the central points of the theory that gave rise to such grids. Tests without theory tend to become lifeless objects and defeat the primary purpose of science, i.e., theory construction.

PERSONAL CONSTRUCTS AND EMOTION

In defining the personal construct as an awareness of the person, Kelly did *not* imply that a dimension of awareness can be easily verbalized. He also did *not* imply that the construct, at the level of personal awareness, was devoid of emotion. Personal constructs can be experienced as contrasts in feelings, values, or behavior. Particularly in regard to emotion, construct theory has been criticized because emotional construction has been treated too abstractly and too narrowly. Kelly, in response to this criticism, began writing about personal constructs in more emotional contexts. A hitherto unpublished manuscript (Kelly, 1977), "Confusion and the Clock," was recently distributed by the Organizing Committee of the Second International Congress on Personal Construct Theory. The following excerpts from this manuscript, which Kelly wrote after a near fatal heart attack, are most interesting when viewed from the background of these criticisms:

> But it is still Friday morning. I remember the faces of our daughter and son. There was deep concern there, but not, as far as I could see any sign of panic. My job was cut out for me; it was to survive, if I could. But, what were they to do? They could not help but be aware, even in the first hour, of the difficulties that my death would plunge them into. How well I managed to forestall those difficulties? Not very well!
>
> . . . And I thought of our first grandchild expected in a few weeks whom I might never see, and to whom I might never tell the wonderful stories that all granchildren should hear.

Although we are uncertain as to how Kelly would have elaborated the theme of emotionality, Mildred McCoy (1977) elaborated beyond Kelly's conceptions of threat, hostility, guilt, fear, and anxiety—to love, bewilderment, doubt, happiness, self confidence, and contentment. Even as McCoy defined these feelings within construct theory, she did so in most abstract ways, e.g., sadness is the "awareness of the invalidation of implications of a portion or all of the core structure." Even though this definition is abstract, one is free to experience the sadness of another person at the level of that person's construct system or at the "gut level" of experience. The abstract definition in no way denies the more personal and interpersonal experience. Construct theory does not suggest that one should instantly and constantly translate one's feelings or another's feelings into the abstract language of the investigator's theory. At certain times and for certain purposes it may be most fruitful to make this translation, but not necessarily as an interpretation to another person or as the essential way of experiencing that person. Most importantly, theory assists the theorist in ordering and reflecting upon certain experiences. It is doubtful that Kelly was intent upon dehumanizing social perception. The *professional* interpretation was intended to supplement the experiencing of human emotions rather than to supplant such personal experiencing.

THE DICHOTOMY

Readers may wonder why Kelly placed so much emphasis on *dimensions* of experience. The answer to this question, of course, is a theoretical one. It can be presumed that Kelly was aware that the major personality theorists talked about perceptual, emotional, and behavioral contrasts. Jung (cited in Jacobi, 1951) perceived opposites as a source of psychic energy. Adler (1931, 1964) observed that opposites in behavior can have the same meaning. Freud talked about man's contrasts and conflicts but did not elevate the idea of contrast to a central position in his theory, subordinating contrast and conflict to the particular contents of his theory. Even as these theorists supported the relevance of contrast in the lives of people, Kelly most clearly perceived that there would be little meaning in life without contrast. How could one experience "night" without "day"? How could one know "health" without some feeling for "sickness"? How could one experience "up" without some idea of "down"? How could one appreciate "friendship" without some experience of the alternative? Finally, could one measure without the idea of "something" in respect to "something else," e.g., higher versus lower, more versus less?

What seems so remarkable about Kelly's position on contrast is that scientists and laymen alike tend to go about their business *as if* life is just a matter of *unities*. A scientist reports a particular measurement or observation. A layman talks about this or that characteristic in another person. Then there is the occurrence of that sunset and the presence of that chair. Life is very neatly packaged as being this or that. So why worry about contrast? Certainly, the researchers of concept formation did not bother much with contrast. They defined the concept as a grouping of elements. Even Piaget, who shares certain common interests with Kelly (Salmon, 1970), did not focus on contrast. However, there has been some experimental interest in contrast as a feature of conception outside personal construct theory. Wallach (1959) stated that "attention to a contrast class would seem to be one important mechanism for making such selections, since choosing one or another contrast class tends to influence the number and kinds of properties in whose terms we define the class of interest" (p. 19).

Kelly's position on contrast as an aspect of personal construction is highlighted in his dichotomy corollary (Kelly, 1955): "A person's construction system is composed of a finite number of dichotomous constructs" (p. 59). Now this particular statement was immediately criticized by those students who were weaned on the works of Korzybski (1933) and Johnson (1946). Since the term dichotomy did not suggest "gradations" and "shades of grey," the concept of dichtomy could only point to either-or-ness, simplicity, and that which is unscientific or primitive. In spite of this "bad press" for the dichtomy, Kelly was able to communicate *his* meaning, a complex and sophisticated conception of how binary and continuous scaling can be related (Kelly, 1955, pp. 142–145).

One is struck with the paradoxical nature of the "damning" of the dichotomy. To illustrate, Korzybski named his publishing house the International Non-Aristotelian Library Publishing Company—a seemingly dichotomous, simplistic, and totally rejecting title. Whereas Korzybski could see nothing of merit in Aristotle, Kelly perceived some possibilities. Perhaps this is what creativeness is all about—perceiving possibilities in that which others dismiss as illogical, trivial, and even ridiculous.

That the modern general semanticist was more tolerant of the dichotomy seems clear in the following statement:

> The modern general semanticist, such as Weinberg (1959) or Hayakawa (1949), has assumed a more moderate position on the dichotomy. Hayakawa understands the motivating nature of the duality, perceiving that strong positions and commitments are necessary to initiate important undertakings, and that final decisions often involve dichotomies. Weinberg rewrites Aristotle's three laws. The law of identity, "A is A," becomes "A" may be assumed to remain constant for the sake of discussion." The law of the excluded middle, "Anything is either A or not-A," becomes "Anything may be classified as either A or not-A." Finally, the law of non-identity, "Something cannot be both A and not-A," becomes "Something should not be classified both as A and not-A at the same time in the same context" (pp. 82–83). Restructuring Aristotle's laws in this manner emphasizes the process of abstracting and recognizes that it is the person who does the labeling, and that anything may be understood in other ways—depending on one's purpose. Contrast and

change are both caught within these new definitions, and the similarity of
Weinberg's position to that of Kelly becomes apparent.

Kelly (1955), even as he focused on the dualities of man, did not
believe that dichotomous thinking is necessarily absolute, although a
person can use his dichotomies in this way. He also did not assume that
dichotomies are simple, although one might think, feel, and behave in
simple, dichotomous ways. Within Person Construct theory, one can
think like a Galilean or an Aristotelian yet share a feature common to all
men, that feeling, thinking, and behaving are intrinsically matters of
contrast.

Perhaps it was the extreme dialectical position of Korzybski that set
the stage for the later emergence of such reconciling positions as those of
Weinberg and Kelly. Such an hypothesis, if tenable, suggests that meaningful reconciliations of opposites occur when the dialectic is sharp and
oppositions become most clear. (Landfield, 1977, pp. 137–138)

A FUNDAMENTAL POSTULATE

Having considered the philosophy of constructive alternativism and the
general nature of the personal construct, it is time to introduce Kelly's fundamental postulate: "A person's processes are psychologically channelized
by the ways in which he anticipates events" (1955, p. 46). In these few words
Kelly is saying many things and sets the stage for a discussion of his 11
corollaries.

In this postulate, Kelly initiates his theory with the person. Rather than
introducing his psychology as the study of disembodied behavior, personality, or behavioral aggregate across people, he says his theory is about
the *person* and his *processes*. In using the term process, he means to identify
his primary subject matter, the person, as alive and kicking. Since the
person is energized, the psychologist accounts only for the directionality of
the action. Elaborating this point, one does not ask whether or not the
person is behaving in a given situation. The person always behaves in some
way. Moreover, the person behaves "constructively," i.e., by continually
construing the events of his life at some level of awareness. Even when the
person is behaving most "nonreactively," as exemplified by the catatonic
patient, he is nonetheless behaving and actively so.

In using the term *psychologically*, Kelly acknowledges the right of
other scientists to apply their particular constructs, such as those which are
physiological or sociological. He states that "A person's processes are what
they are; and psychology, physiology, or what have you, are simply systems
concocted for trying to anticipate them" (Kelly, 1955, p. 48). Implied in this
statement is the interesting idea that Kelly might have called his psychology
something else. Thus, science is most clearly seen as a creation of the
actively aware organism who makes and remakes the events of his own life.

Rephrasing the fundamental postulate, one could say that the person's ongoing feeling, valuing, and behaving (processes) are directed (channelized) by the personal constructions or dimensions of personal meaning (ways) by which he predicts (anticipates) events. This rephrasing of the postulate is helpful, but the terms event and anticipation need elaboration.

Kelly (1955) states that the person ultimately seeks to anticipate *real* events: "Anticipation is not merely carried on for its own sake, it is carried on so that future reality may be better represented." Kelly assumes a world of real events that are known through the representations or creations of man—*his* values, tools, symbols, and measurements. Moreover, one knows the usefulness of his representations of reality through the process of anticipation. In using the term anticipation, Kelly creates the motivational features of his theory: "Like the prototype of the scientist that he is, man seeks prediction" (p. 49).

Although Kelly states that the person seeks prediction, it is not for the sake of prediction. He states:

> It is his seeking to anticipate the whole world of events and thus relate himself to them that best explains his psychological processes. If he acts to preserve the system, it is because the system is an essential chart for his personal adventures, not because it is a self-contained island of meaning. (1955, p. 59)

It seems obvious from the foregoing quotations that Kelly perceives the underlying motivational force in a most personal way—as the quest for meaning, understanding, and knowledge. In this quest for personal meaning within oneself and in relation to the external world, Kelly assumes that both scientist and layman experience, observe, construct frameworks of meaning and explanation, and *anticipate* the repetitive aspects of their experience through their constructions of it. What may not be so obvious in a quick reading of Kelly is the complexity with which he views anticipation.

ANTICIPATION

Any discussion of anticipation within personal construct theory is incomplete without some mention of the construct of validation–invalidation. Validation refers to the experience of having one's predictions and anticipations supported. Although the psychologist typically speaks of his own hypotheses as being validated, an experience that influences the course of his future behavior, he often speaks nonreflexively of reinforcing his subjects. Kelly, appreciating this difference, felt that the critical experience for both investigator and his subject was better stated as validation. Validation emphasizes the idea that it is the person, whether scientist, layman, or subject, who decides about the meaning of external happenings. Thus, within personal construct theory, one refers to validational evidence in relation to personal construct systems rather than reinforcement:

> The situation for the subject then is an interpretation made within his personal construct system. The investigator hopes that his subject's interpretations of the situation will coincide with his own intentions, or conversely, that the investigator's interpretation of the understandings of his subject will validly reflect how the subject is construing the situation. (Landfield, 1977, p. 143)

When Kelly employs anticipation as the push and pull of his theory, he uses the term within different contexts of time, abstraction, awareness, precision, and personal meaning. John Hoad (Cole & Landfield, 1977) considers anticipation within the contexts of time and abstraction when he states:

> Kelly did not mean to rob the person of his life right now. Anticipations can be of the now variety: for example, "This is the best way of handling a situation right now as I project things into the future." One may speak of global versus detailed kinds of anticipations. An example of the global anticipation might be an "anticipatory conviction" about being adequate for whatever happens in the future, perhaps even one's eventual confrontation with death. Statements such as "I can ride with the punches" link longer-term, global predictions with anticipations of the "right now." (p. 352)

Expanding on Hoad's concerns about how anticipation can be misinterpreted, the reader may feel that anticipation or hypothesis is a useful tool for the scientist, but the average person does not pursue his life by constantly talking to himself about what he can and cannot specifically predict. Even though most persons are unaware of constant anticipation, this is not an argument against Kelly's position because he did not imply that anticipation must be at a high level of awareness. Kelly assumed that vital construction could be at a preverbal level or might be difficult to put into words.

Another point of confusion about the meaning of anticipation begins with the "nonexistent" scientist who uses his predictive tools in ideal ways. Writing about the person in his less idealized form, Kelly comments:

> He expects the real world to yield to his anticipations rather than to be its natural self. He is not looking for the correct way to forecast the future so much as he is looking for the future to align itself with the forecasts he has already made. (1955, p. 888)

Kelly elaborates the motivational force of anticipation in his choice corollary: "A person chooses for himself that alternative in a dichotomized construct through which he anticipates the greater possibility for extension and definition of his system" (1955, p. 64). One chooses in the direction of that which is more explicit, comprehensive, and meaningful to oneself, a seemingly straightforward and reasonable idea that tends to elude an easy construction or measurement by the objective experimenter or clinician. The problem here lies in the implicit confounding of the subject's system of meaning, value, and focus with that of the investigator. This confusion of meaning systems can be illustrated by referring to the depressed patient who "beats his head against the wall" despite the obvious pain and the alternatives of hope extended to him. How can one hold onto that which apparently is not working? Within personal construct theory, there is an explanation for this type of observer dilemma. The observer may be making the error of assuming that the constructs of the observed person are similar to his own in content or organization. Moreover, the observer may be functioning within a simplistic view that life can be neatly reduced to clear-cut pleasures and pains. Now the choice corollary implies nothing about the salience of simple pleasures and pains, and makes no assumption about the content of the choice that will be elaborated. In the context of this corollary, the depressed patient may be elaborating a most meaningful and predictable world for himself, although a most unpleasant one for the clinician whose efforts to assist him are being continually invalidated. Within personal construct theory, one may direct his life toward many anticipations other than simple pleasures and pains. A person may willingly anticipate suffering for the sake of his expanding loyalty, bravery, love, freedom, antagonism, or identity.

A final note on anticipation emphasizes Kelly's idea that the construction of change may expedite change. Restating this point, a framework for anticipating change tends to encourage change. Working from this idea, Hass (1974) postcoded the content of personal constructs elicited from two religious subgroups, one committed to the status quo and the other one open to slow or moderate change. The content postcoding procedure focused on descriptive contrasts connoting both openness and closedness to change, i.e., the dimension of change. Results of this procedure revealed that subjects in the change group whose actions supported a willingness to change also used more person descriptions suggesting the dimension of change.

THE MEANING OF PERSONAL

In his fundamental postulate, Kelly places the person at the center of his psychology. This initial emphasis on the person leads one to inquire whether Kelly is espousing a purely idiographic view. That Kelly is not assuming a completely idiographic stance becomes most clear in his 11 corollaries when he describes the person as organizing, choosing, generalizing, differentiating, dichotomizing, fragmenting, experiencing in common with and apart from others, showing empathy through social role, and suffering from anxiety, threat, guilt, fear, and hostility. All of these activities and experiences are essential ways of viewing the human being. Thus, Kelly, in defining many dimensions along which one may comprehend all persons, is taking a nomothetic or general position on human nature. Yet, he states in his individuality corollary that persons may vary in relation to these dimensions and in the particular contents of their personal construct systems. In other words, beginning from the more generalized nature of persons, he explains in varied ways how one may understand each person in a more particularized way. By offering general methods for obtaining information about the more particularized aspects of personal construction, Kelly does not impale himself on either horn of the idiographic–nomothetic dilemma. In most interesting ways, he shows how the psychologist may reconcile the need to be both more and less specific without losing either the person or his more general science.

Kelly's skill in reconciling opposing theoretical constructions within psychology can also be seen in his approach to the "phenomenological" versus the "scientifically theoretical" aspects of man. Although Kelly attended to levels of human awareness, listened carefully to statements of experience, and suggested "self-report" methodologies such as the Rep Test and Self-Characterization, he denied being "just" a phenomenologist. However, he did comment that

> it is possible to combine certain features of the neophenomenological approaches with more conventional psychology.... We have already emphasized the need to abstract behavior within the realm of the individual before making it a datum in any study of a group of individuals. (Kelly, 1955, p. 42)

As previously stated, Kelly created a psychology about the ways in which persons dimensionalize, organize, and employ their experience through anticipation. Although the theory did emphasize personal construction, his definition of the personal construct did not restrict the investigator to making inferences from self-reports. Personal constructs could be inferred from any behavior. When Kelly advised, "Ask your subject and maybe he will tell you," he was affirming the importance of enlarging the data base for understanding the human being and his experience. Kelly could listen to his psychotherapy client, focus on his statements and other behaviors, infer dimensions and organizations of personal experience, arrange them within the statements of his own general theory, and make predictions about behavior. In this process of subordinating the inferred experiences of others to his own more general framework, Kelly did not wish to do violence to the contents and feelings of personal construction. Rather, he wanted to take perspective on the person's constructions from an abstract position, a position that would allow the psychologist greater appreciation of how the person functions in both more individualized and common ways.

At a different level of discourse, the meaning of personal will now be elaborated with concrete examples, showing the usefulness of taking a more individualized approach to contrast and meaning:

Several years ago a student in his middle 20s was apprehended for behavior resembling that of the "Greater Imposter." His lack of understanding about why others should become so "up tight" over his behavior began to make sense to the clinician when this student differentiated his acquaintances by the personal language construction of "boyish mischief" versus "saintly goodness." He apparently perceived what others labeled "a serious criminal act" as just a matter of boyish mischief." His case history revealed that he was a foundling raised by contemplative priests. One may guess that these priests found comic relief in his boyish pranks, and the contrasts, "saintly goodness and boyish mischief," although not found in a dictionary of antonyms, may have represented the primary dimensionality of his ethical behavior.

That a more personalized approach to contrast is useful can also be exemplified by the client who states that the best change is to find happiness and the worst change is to commit suicide. The able clinician, not debating whether suicide is the proper antonym for happiness, and not debating whether or not his client should be understood within the client's own language system, will explore the potentiality for suicide. Taking another example, it is difficult to understand the devastating anxiety experienced by the person who objectively has departed from an ideal only slightly, but who is worried sick by the complete change in his behavior. The feelings of such a person become less perplexing to the clinician when the extremes of behavioral change are plotted within the client's frame of reference, and the psychologist remains open to the idea that the client's behavioral scales may not be equivalent to his own scales of meaning.

A most intriguing application of "personal" is highlighted by the conflict between an internally oriented and an externally oriented form of validation. A female college student made a near fatal suicidal attempt immediately following her victory in a beauty contest. She became depressed over the superficiality of the contest, which served to heighten her lack of value conviction. She stated that she had tried many philosophies only to have them questioned again and again by her boyfriend, a graduate student in philosophy. In the course of psychotherapy, she developed the idea that the most useful validation of a philosophy should be "in the living of it," rather than in the discussion of it with others. One day she stated, "I have developed a religious philosophy which I damn well am not going to share with you or anyone else. It feels good and I am relating better to people. It is a very personal matter and that is what religion ought to be."

Summarizing this section, the process of observing the contrasts of one's subject can be differentiated from two contrasting ways of understanding the other person. One may reason *only* in relation to how he personally would feel when confronted with the other person's dilemma. Again, one may reason *only* within a very specific and formal theory about how all persons feel, think, learn, and change in the same ways. To reason only in relation to one's own personal values might encourage the projection of absurd problem solutions onto the other person. To reason only in relation to a formally fixed and concrete theory might encourage one to focus on a limited number of problems and to define other problems as nonscientific.

SELF, INTEGRATION, AND SOCIAL ROLE

In this final section, three topics are considered briefly, topics that should receive special attention from those interested in elaborating the psychology of personal constructs.

Self-Conception

Kelly placed the *person* with his capacity to construe, reconstrue, and anticipate the events of his life in a position superordinate to the self. For Kelly, the self was a construction in the same way that any acquaintance or situation could be a construction. Presumably, the self or selves could take on whatever meaning and importance the person might attribute to it or them. That aspects of self could have more vital or "core" meanings seems apparent when Kelly included "the movement interpretation of threat" (1955, pp. 490–491) as an implication of his more general conception of threat. Elaborating this point, Kelly defined threat as an awareness of an imminent, comprehensive change in core structure, i.e., the person is under threat when he perceives, at some level of awareness, the possibility of a large scale change in important aspects of his system. One implication of this more general statement of threat was a hypothesis that linked imminent change and invalidation in present self-construction to difficulties in interpersonal relationships (Landfield, 1955; Willis, 1961).

A variety of studies in self-conception have been carried out within personal construct theory. A sample of these include those by Adams-Webber, 1977; Bannister and Agnew, 1977; Fransella, 1972; Isaacson and Landfield, 1965; Landfield, 1955, 1965, 1971, 1977; Landfield and Namas, 1964; Mair, 1977a,b; Radley, 1973; Ravenette, 1977; Varble and Landfield, 1969; and Willis, 1961. These studies which include a variety of subjects, e.g., children, adults, stutterers, therapists and their clients, encompass such topics as self-definition, self as metaphor, self-meaningfulness, the changing self, interpersonal threat, and the elaboration of self-role.

A most interesting self-methodology has recently been developed by Monte Page. In this approach to personal construction, the subject is first asked to list his positive, negative, and wished for characteristics. Next, he is asked to give his opposites and contrasts to these characteristics. These descriptions and their contrasts then are placed on rating sheets as pole descriptions of 13-point scales. Finally, the person is provided with 15 self-roles such as "myself as a parent," "myself as a friend," "myself as a co-worker," and he rates himself in these different roles on his self-elicited dimensions.

Kelly utilized a self-characterization measure in which he asked a subject or client to describe himself from the viewpoint of a sympathetic friend. This particular task of self-construction is a vital stage in fixed role therapy, a role-enactment procedure. Now this procedure not only shows how self may be elaborated within construct theory, but it also points up a matter of concern for those who perceive Kelly's theory as something more than a consistency formulation. Several authors (Maddi, 1976; Zurcher, 1977) have forced the theory into a consistency mold. That Kelly's interests included more than a preoccupation with behavioral consistency is indicated in a quotation from Kelly (Bonarius, 1967) in which he dispels the notion that fixed role therapy is fixed:

> Much will depend, I suspect upon whether your client now thinks he has a fixed pattern for living, or whether he realizes that his life is amenable to reconstruction and experimentation. If only the former, he may find the role of Geert less and less effectual as life moves on toward its more mature stages". (p. 516)

That Kelly did not wish to assume the search for consistency as the primary motivation of man is made amply clear in the following statements: "It is not mere certainty that man seeks; if that were so he might take delight in the ticking of the clock" (1955, p. 58). Again, he states:

> The nice thing about hypotheses is that you don't have to believe them. This, I think, is a key to the genius of the scientific method. It permits you to be inconsistent with what you know long enough to see what will happen. Children do that. What is so wonderful about the language of hypothesis is its refreshing ability to free the scientist from the entangling consistencies of adulthood. For a few precious moments he can think again like a child, and, like a child, learn from his experience rather than adhere stubbornly to his professonal identity. (1970b, p. 258)

This last sentence points to Kelly's feeling that too many psychologists are more concerned about their scientific role images than their engagement in the process of science. That children may be more creative in the process of science than adults who become rigidly consistent in their ways of living shows Kelly's larger view of the nature of science.

Kelly, without denying the significance of self-construction or consistency in the replicative theme of validation, defined the primary motivation of man as that of construing and anticipating the world about him and his relationship to it—a process which may involve daring and adventure. Kelly seemed to imply that the person seeks equilibrium to the extent that it is necessary, particularly in the contexts of threat, anxiety, guilt, and extreme self-doubt. However, in the contexts of manageable personal invalidation, play, boredom, curiosity, and courage, the person may explore the contrasts, confusions, and unknowns of his life.

In summary, one's conception of selfhood may be validated by a replicative construction of events. However, this statement does not imply that the person will necessarily avoid all experience that might either question some aspect of self or drastically elaborate it. How the person most generally defines himself, that is, degrees and areas of *confidence* in coping with change, may determine how much change the person will tolerate in himself. Thus, even as a literalistic notion of consistency hardly fits with the psychology of personal constructs, more abstract or higher order consistencies within the construct system may allow for continuing explorations of life and change.

As Kelly enlarged upon his ideas of a moving universe, he suggested that one should look for an optimal rather than a maximal stability of the personal construct system. Continual, although not necessarily extensive, change in the system would be anticipated. Also, by assuming that man chooses in the direction of an increased elaboration and definition of his system, Kelly introduced the idea of consistency in the direction of change. In this instance one would have to judge consistency at a more abstract level. Taking this more abstract approach to change helps us understand, for example, the frustration of the world traveler who is forced by circumstances beyond his control to settle permanently in a small, isolated community.

Integration

Investigators of selfhood and behavior frequently treat the person as though he were a bundle of straw, banding together the different aspects of self. Not wishing to emphasize the "bundle hypothesis" of selfhood and having a concern for the person's integrative capacities, Kelly stated his organization corollary: "Each person characteristically evolves for his convenience in anticipating events, a construction system embracing ordinal relationships between constructs" (1955, p. 56). The key word in this corollary is "ordinal." Kelly assumed that construct systems may be arranged in varying hierarchical forms, with constructs having superordinate and subordinate relations to one another.

This corollary, which focuses on hierarchical relationships among dimensions of contrast, implies that taking perspective and making decisions requires higher order construction within the personal construct system. In discussing relationships among constructs, Kelly employed many terms in addition to superordinate and subordinate. In particular, he described propositional and constellatory construction as encompassing one dimension of relatedness. Kelly defined the constellatory construct as one that fixes the other realm memberships of its elements and illustrated it by referring to typological and prejudicial ways of thinking. In contrast he defined the propositional construct as one that carries no implications regarding the other realm memberships, i.e., orthogonal, unrelated, and independent construction. Landfield (1977, p. 144) gives a fuller account of propositional and constellatory construction.

Even though Kelly stated a preference for propositional construction in which an event is seen within a complexity of independent dimensions, he clearly perceived that an overuse of propositional construction would delimit decision making. Kelly's ideas of propositional construction, together with the "check and void" Rep test grid procedure (Kelly, 1955, ch. 6), encouraged the early research on cognitive complexity, an organizational concept defined by multidimensionality in awareness (Bieri, 1955). In discussing this conception, Bannister and Mair (1968) stated that cognitive complexity became "what is now virtually a self-contained research area" (p. 70). This departure of investigative effort from its origins seems unfortunate since the complexity measurement represents only one aspect of the organization corollary. There is evidence, both theoretical and empirical, that many complexity measures do not get at the idea of construct ordination or the superordinate–subordinate relationships between constructs. This point is emphasized by Leitner, Landfield and Barr, 1975; Landfield and Barr, 1976; and Landfield, 1977. Moreover, this concern has been shared by other personal construct investigators such as Hinkle (1965) and Fransella (1972), who have worked with a procedure known as an implications grid. In this procedure, the investigator obtains information regarding how a particular construct implies another construct. To illustrate, a person may describe others along two important dimensions: friendly versus unfriendly and good teacher versus poor teacher. In this instance, good teachers invariably are considered friendly and poor teachers imply unfriendliness for this person. However, when the *if–then* question is reversed, friendliness does not necessarily imply good teaching, whereas unfriendliness does imply poor teaching. Although the implications *from* the "teacher" construct *to* the "friendly" construct are strong, the reverse relationship is not as strong. Now it can be argued that when one construct implies another strongly, but the implications are not mutual, the typical cognitive complexity measure will reveal the relationship between these two constructs as orthogonal. Nevertheless, there is a relationship between the two constructs—an ordinal one.

Social Role

Kelly's appreciation of interactive man is the focus of his sociality corollary: "To the extent that one person construes the construction system of another, he may play a role in a social process involving the other person" (1955, p. 95). This definition of social role is intriguing because it departs from the more "objective" approach to social role as behavior within a social context. In the Kellyan approach to sociality, the idea of interaction or relationship is immediately caught in the definition. Whenever a person's behavior in relation to another reflects an attempt to understand some aspect of how he thinks, feels, and values, then that person is playing a social role in relation to the other person. One might say that the best social roles involve accurate empathy. A complete disregard or disinterest in how other persons think, feel, and value would be linked to behavior that Kelly would not assign the description of social role.

Applying this definition of social role to within group interaction, Landfield (1977) asked each subject to use the personal construct scales of other group members by having each person predict (a) how the other persons would view the predictor, and (b) how the other persons would view themselves. To the extent that each person's behavior in relation to another in the group reflects that person's understanding of how the other person thinks, he would be playing a social role in relation to that person. However, if a person is to play a useful social role, Kelly states that "he need not so much construe things as the other person does as he must effectively construe the other person's outlook" (1955, p. 95). One can understand the reasoning of another person without agreeing with that person. One can also circumscribe the view of another within a larger or more abstract framework of meaning. Although commonality between two systems does not insure an effective relationship or even empathy, overlapping content of construct systems can provide a better context for communication (Landfield, 1971).

Personal construct research should move directly into contexts of social interaction, taking into consideration not only the different aspects of self and personal organization, but also the ways in which, and the extent to which, persons can anticipate, accurately and inaccurately, the construct systems of others. Studying social role processes within personal construct theory and method may highlight relationships covered over by other approaches that assume that persons symbolize, define, and contrast their personal experience in universal ways.

SUMMARY

In this chapter, the writer's view of construct theory was stated in truncated ways with a minimum of elaboration. In writing briefly about personal construct psychology, one can only hope to sketch the broad outlines of the position and to indicate a few of the directions in which psychologists are elaborating the theory at theoretical and methodological levels. Those readers who are unacquainted with the theory are advised to read George A. Kelly's (1955) two volumes; his selected papers (Maher, 1969); his summary of the theory in Bannister's *Perspectives in Personal Construct Theory* (1970); and his hitherto unpublished manuscript entitled, "The Psychology of the Unknown" (1977). More knowledgeable readers will want to look at *New Perspectives on Personal Construct Theory* (Bannister, 1977) and *The Nebraska Symposium on Motivation* (Cole & Landfield, 1977). Two volumes, one by Jack Adams-Webber on research within personal construct theory since 1965, and the other by Franz Epting on psychotherapy, are nearing completion. One may inquire about references from the Clearing House for Personal Construct Research by writing to either Dr. Epting, Department of Psychology, University of Florida, Gainesville, or Dr. Landfield, Department of Psychology, University of Nebraska, Lincoln. Complete bibliographies on research done within personal construct psychology are available.

REFERENCES

Adams-Webber, J. The golden section and the structure of self-concepts. *Perceptual and Motor Skills*, 1977, *45*, 703–706.

Adler, A. *What life should mean to you.* New York: Blue Ribbon Books, 1931.

Adler, A. *The individual psychology of Alfred Adler.* (H. L. Ansbacher and R. Ansbacher, Eds.). New York: Harper & Row, 1964.

Bannister, D. (Ed.). *Perspectives in personal construct theory.* New York: Academic, 1970.

Bannister, D. (Ed.). New perspectives in personal construct theory. New York: Academic, 1977.

Bannister, D., & Agnew, J. The child's construing of self. In J. K. Cole & A. W. Landfield (Eds.), *Nebraska Symposium on Motivation, 1976, Personal Construct Psychology.* Lincoln: University of Nebraska Press, 1977.

Bannister, D., & Mair, J. M. M. *The evaluation of personal constructs.* New York: Academic, 1968.

Bieri, J. Cognitive complexity–simplicity and predictive behavior. *Journal of Abnormal and Social Psychology*, 1955, *51*, 263–268.

Bonarius, J. C. J. De Fixed Role Therapy Van George A. Kelly. *Nederlands Tijdschrift Voor de Psychologie*, 1967, *22*, 482–520.

Cole, J. K., & Landfield, A. W. (Eds.). *The Nebraska Symposium on Motivation, 1976, Personal Construct Psychology.* Lincoln: University of Nebraska Press, 1977.

Fransella, F. *Personal change and reconstruction.* London: Academic, 1972.

Fransella, F., & Bannister, D. *A manual for repertory grid technique.* New York: Academic, 1977.

Hass, L. *Personal construct system and theological conservatism: A study of conservative Lutheran pastors.* Unpublished doctoral dissertation, University of Nebraska, 1974.

Hinkle, D. *The change of personal constructs from the viewpoint of a theory of construct implications.* Unpublished doctoral dissertation, Ohio State University, 1965.

Isaacson, G. I., & Landfield, A. W. The meaningfulness of personal and common constructs. *Journal of Individual Psychology*, 1965, *21*, 160–166.

Jacobi, J. *The psychology of C. G. Jung* (Rev. ed.). New Haven: Yale University Press, 1951.

Johnson, W. *People in quandaries: The semantics of personal adjustment*. New York: Harper, 1946.

Kelly, G. A. *The psychology of personal constructs* (Vols. I and II). New York: Norton, 1955.

Kelly, G. A. A brief introduction to personal construct theory. In D. Bannister (Ed.), *Perspectives in personal construct theory*. New York: Academic, 1970, pp. 1–29. (a)

Kelly, G. A. Behaviour as an experiment. In D. Bannister (Ed.), *Perspectives in personal construct theory*. New York: Academic, 1970, pp. 255–269. (b)

Kelly, G. A. The psychology of the unknown. In D. Bannister (Ed.), *New perspectives in personal construct theory*. New York: Academic, 1977.

Kelly, G. A. Confusion and the clock. In F. Fransella (Ed.), *Personal construct psychology 1977*. London: Academic, 1978.

Korzybski, A. *Science and sanity*. Lakeville, Conn.: International Non-Aristotelian Library Publishing Company, 1933.

Landfield, A. W. Self-predictive orientation and the movement interpretation of threat. *Journal of Abnormal and Social Psychology*, 1955, *51*, 434–438.

Landfield, A. W. Meaningfulness of ideal, self and other on client and therapist constructs. *Psychological Reports*, 1965, *16*, 605–608.

Landfield, A. W. *Personal construct systems in psychotherapy*. Chicago: Rand McNally, 1971.

Landfield, A. W. Interpretive man: The enlarged self-image. In J. K. Cole and A. W. Landfield (Eds.), *The Nebraska Symposium on Motivation, 1976, Personal Construct Psychology*. Lincoln: University of Nebraska Press, 1977, pp. 127–177.

Landfield, A. W., & Barr, M. A. *Ordination: A new measure of concept organization*. Unpublished manuscript, 1976.

Landfield, A. W., & Nawas, M. M. Psychotherapeutic improvement as a function of communication and adoption of therapists' values. *Journal of Counseling Psychology*, 1964, *11*, 336–341.

Leitner, L. M., Landfield, A. W., & Barr, M. A. *Cognitive complexity: A review and elaboration within personal construct theory*. Unpublished manuscript, 1975.

Maddi, S. R. *Personality theories: A comparative analysis*. Homewood, Ill.: Dorsey, 1976.

Maher, B. (Ed.). *Clinical psychology and personality: The selected papers of George Kelly*. New York: Wiley, 1969.

Mair, J. M. M. Metaphors for living. In J. K. Cole and A. W. Landfield (Eds.), *The Nebraska Symposium on Motivation, 1976, Personal Construct Psychology*. Lincoln: University of Nebraska Press, 1977, pp. 243–290. (a)

Mair, J. M. M. The community of self. In D. Bannister (Ed.), *New perspectives in personal construct theory*. New York: Academic, 1977, pp. 125–149. (b)

McCoy, M. A reconstruction of emotion. In D. Bannister (Ed.), *New perspectives in personal construct theory*. New York: Academic, 1977, pp. 93–124.

Oliver, D. W., & Landfield, A. W. Reflexivity: An unfaced issue in psychology. *Journal of Individual Psychology*, 1962, *18*, 114–124. (Reprinted in *ETC: A Review of General Semantics*, 1963, *20*, 187–210.)

Radley, A. R. *A study of self-elaboration through role change*. Unpublished doctoral dissertation, London University, 1973.

Ravenette, T. *Self description grids for children: Theme and variation*. Paper given at the 2nd International Congress on Personal Construct Theory, Oxford, England, July 1977.

Salmon, P. A psychology of personal growth. In D. Bannister (Ed.), *Perspectives in personal construct theory*. New York: Academic, 1970, pp. 197–221.

Varble, D., & Landfield, A. W. Validity of the self-ideal discrepancy as a criterion measure of successful psychotherapy—a replication. *Journal of Counseling Psychology*, 1969, *16*, 150–156.

Wallach, M. A. The influence of classification requirements on gradients of response. *Psychological Monographs*, 1959, *73* (No. 8).

Willis, F. *The movement interpretation of threat and level of self-acceptance.* Unpublished doctoral dissertation, University of Missouri, 1961. Also *Dissertation Abstracts*, 1961, *22*, 17–19.

Zurcher, L. A. *The mutable self.* Beverly Hills: Sage Library of Social Research, 1977.

George Kelly's Anticipation of Psychology

A Personal Tribute

WALTER MISCHEL

George Kelly was my teacher in those first graduate seminars in the mid-1950s that mattered most to me, my guide in the first exciting professional encounters with clients that opened so many vistas, and my personal friend in the too few years of his life that followed. More than anyone, he excited me most about the possibilities for psychology—a psychology that was then (as he more than anyone recognized) so barren and schizoid, insisting that its own practitioners were hypothesis-testing wisdom-seeking scientists while its "subjects" and "testees" were the reflexive victims of a unidirectional causation, "shaped" relentlessly by an external environment that would not let them reciprocate. His wisdom and extraordinary good sense in the face of neglect by a seemingly impervious academic establishment seemed impressive (sometimes heroic) from the start.

That George Kelly was a very deep, original, refreshing voice was always evident to all who knew him well. What has surprised me was not the brilliance with which he first spoke but the accuracy with which he anticipated the directions into which psychology would move two decades later.

WALTER MISCHEL • Department of Psychology, Stanford University, Stanford, California 94305.

Virtually every point of George Kelly's theorizing in the 1950s, summarized so nicely by Professor Landfield has proved to be a prophetic preface for the psychology of the 1970s—and, it seems safe to predict now—for many years to come. Long before "cognitive psychology" existed, Kelly created a truly cognitive theory of personality, a theory in which how people construe is at the core. Kelly anticipated the implications of cognition for personality theory in many crucial ways. Perhaps most important was his focus on man as a scientist who possesses a far greater freedom than psychologists previously allowed. This freedom arose from the human capacity to test hypotheses and to recategorize events in alternative ways. By reconstructing themselves more conveniently, people, Kelly insisted, do not have to be the victims of their biographies. Kelly found cognition when most psychologists had still lost their heads. Here are a few other items in random order, that merely remind us how prophetic his theorizing was:

1. His emphasis on anticipation, on the quest for meaning and understanding in the layman just as in the scientist.
2. His ideographic bent when psychologists seemed so often to equate the study of individual differences with the measurement of everybody on the same yardsticks—yardsticks that often proved to be little more than the psychologists' favorite constructs. With a twinkle in his eyes, Kelly often chided the trait psychologist for "leaving man stuck on his continuum."
3. His tolerance (indeed his relish) for inconsistency, for paradox, for change, for playing with pieces (behaviors, events) that don't seem to fit together, rather than insisting on always "adhering to the entangling consistencies of adulthood" (p. 77, this book).
4. His recognition that inconsistencies, inconveniences, seemingly hopeless traps, often could be reconstrued at higher (or different) levels of abstraction in more useful ways.
5. His deep appreciation of the interactive, social nature of man at a time when "person–environment interaction" was mostly lip service.

The core of George Kelly's psychologizing was his belief that personal constructs are the basic units and that it is personal constructs, rather than stimuli, that are crucial. To make this point in one especially animated conversation in 1965, he recalled vividly from his Navy experience during World War II how very differently he related to the same officer on different occasions depending on how, at the time, he construed that officer. He remembered that the captain seemed different to him in an informal role, chatting with his jacket off, from the way he seemed when he wore his officer's coat. "You see," Kelly said, "it is not the stimulus—the captain—but how I construed him that channelized my reactions to him."

I pounced on Kelly's example, noting that a social behavior theorist would find his story an excellent example, not of "construct control," but of "stimulus control": with his four stripes on, you see the captain one way; without his four stripes, you see him differently. To understand the construct change, I insisted, in the behavioral view, you have to include in your understanding how those four stripes came to control it and the exact conditions that now covary with it and with the relevant behaviors. Kelly's calm, kind, unperturbed response to my argument made it plain that, as usual, he could see my point of view—but was quite unmoved by it: the etiology of constructs was simply not of interest to him. Constructs were there, they channelized psychological processes, and just how they evolved or linked to "conditions" and specific action was not within his focus of concern. I think George Kelly did not want to elaborate his theory in those directions, just as he made a point of eschewing any methods or experimental studies intended to uncover "functional relations" or "controlling conditions": that was not his kind of psychology, and he wanted no part of it. As a result, in my view his theory remained exciting, provocative, but also exasperatingly incomplete. The greatest incompleteness of Kelly's thinking was that it provided a prophetic theory of construing but gave few guides for linking people's constructions either to their past or to their future performance.

I agree with Professor Landfield that Kelly's theory awaits elaboration. To have the impact it deserves, it will also need to have its methods expanded and enriched so that his always intriguing but sometimes slippery constructs can be specified. Kelly's theory is largely a theory of how we categorize, not of how those categories arise nor of how and when we act as we do in particular contexts, nor of how changes in conditions may change our constructs just as our constructs may change those conditions. That type of analysis seemed to lie outside his "range of convenience." Surely it did not seem to interest him very much. But a psychology that is purely ahistorical and relatively mute about performance is incomplete. It does not have to be, and there is reason to hope that the current moves toward a hyphenated cognitive-behavioral approach will help fill in the grand outlines that Kelly sketched years before anyone else even realized the need. George Kelly would not have wanted to "do everything"—and what he did was monumental.

Chapter 4

Psychotherapy as Coping Skills Training

MARVIN R. GOLDFRIED

Clients typically enter therapy with certain implicit, and often unverbalized, expectations of what will happen during the behavior change process. Quite often, their tacit assumption goes as follows: "I will begin by describing my problems to the therapist, who will then help me to gain some better understanding of them, may offer some advice, and perhaps assist in learning new ways to behave. Hopefully, the treatment will be successful. If it *is* successful, my problems will be resolved, I will end therapy, and will lead a relatively happy and satisfying life." To the extent that therapists feel confident in their ability to help clients with their problems, they no doubt share this view of the intervention process. It is only in very recent years, however, that therapists have begun to realize that such a view of the therapeutic endeavor is short-sighted. There is an ever-growing recognition that we need to broaden our conceptualization of therapy, adopting an orientation that goes beyond the resolution of specific problems, and instead views the intervention process as training the client in the use of more general coping skills.

MARVIN R. GOLDFRIED • Department of Psychology, State University of New York at Stony Brook, Stony Brook, New York 11794. Preparation of this chapter was supported in part by Grant MH 24327 from the National Institute of Mental Health.

If we pause for a moment and consider the complex and rapidly changing nature of contemporary society, it becomes clear that most people *continually* find themselves confronted with life problems with which they must cope (Cameron, 1978; Lazarus & Cohen, 1977; Lowenthal, Thurnher, & Chiriboga, 1975; Toffler, 1970). Few individuals—if any—will reach adulthood, achieve the goals they have set for themselves, and then live "happily ever after." The seemingly pessimistic observation made by D'Zurilla and Goldfried (1971) that "our daily lives are replete with situational problems which we must solve in order to maintain an adequate level of effective functioning" (p. 107) is a reality that therapists must continually be aware of when they design treatment programs for their clients.

The view of therapy as a vehicle for training clients in coping skills is a natural extension of the early work done in behavior therapy under the heading of "self-control." In many respects, the term "coping skills" is better suited to a description of the procedures themselves, as it does not connote any constraint of inner desires, and does imply that some sort of learning process is involved. What is learned is not so much specific solutions to given problems but rather behavioral and/or cognitive strategies that may be used in dealing with classes of problematic situations. A coping skills orientation also carries with it the very clear implication that the therapist is a teacher, supervisor, and consultant who works with clients in a collaborative effort to teach them how to function more effectively. There are a number of other more far-reaching implications of the coping skills conception of therapy, but these may best be discussed later in the chapter.

ILLUSTRATIVE COPING SKILLS

A recent book by Egan and Cowan (1979) offers a general picture of diverse life skills, together with their environmental contexts, that appear to be necessary for effective functioning throughout one's lifetime. Included among their list are skills related to physical development and functioning, intellectual development, personal functioning, value clarification, interpersonal involvement, small-group interaction, and involvement with the larger community. The task of dealing with each of these areas clearly goes far beyond the scope of this chapter. The goal instead is to illustrate the growing emphasis on coping skills training with only a few such skills, including problem solving, the use of relaxation as a coping skill, the ability to view situations more realistically, and communications skills. Following this brief description of but a few of these coping skills—which are likely to grow as the field progresses—I would like to turn to some more general issues that get to the very heart of a coping skills conception of therapy.

Problem Solving

It seems only natural to begin our discussion of training in coping skills with a description of problem solving, as it represents the most generic of all such skills. Training in problem solving is certainly not new, and has been used for years in business and industry as a means for training executives to cope more effectively with the myriad of problematic situations typically associated with their jobs. The use of such training as an intervention procedure has grown in popularity only more recently, where problem-solving skills have been construed as a way of managing one's own life. As suggested by D'Zurilla and Goldfried (1971):

> much of what we view clinically as "abnormal behavior" or "emotional disturbance" may be viewed as *ineffective* behavior and its consequences, in which the individual is unable to resolve certain situational problems in his life and his inadequate attempts to do so are having undesirable effects, such as anxiety, depression, and the creation of additional problems. (p. 107)

The various stages of effective problem solving begin with a *general orientation* that one needs to adopt before attempting to cope with certain problematic situations. Part of this orientation is an acceptance of the fact that there are going to be unavoidable situational difficulties or crises that occur in our day-to-day living, and that attempts at coping represent a natural part of living. Another aspect of this general orientation is the adoption of a set that, rather than sitting back and becoming a passive victim of circumstances, it is often possible to take active steps in trying to cope with one's difficulties. In many respects, this component of the general orientation reflects an ideological stance, which can only be fully established once an individual has had success experiences in effective problem solving. In pursuit of this generalized expectancy for self-management, another important set one needs to adopt is to "stop and think" (Dollard & Miller, 1950). This is a simple suggestion, and yet one that all too often we forget to follow. It is axiomatic that impulsive courses of action are less likely to be as effective as those that reflect careful deliberation.

In stopping to think, one moves to the next stage, that of *defining the problematic situation*. Here the focus is not on a problem that the individual "has," but rather on the situational difficulties for which an effective response is not immediately apparent. The task is to define the situation as concretely as possible, so that the goals for effective problem solving can be specified operationally. Thus, rather than stating one's mate is "inconsiderate," it is important to delineate those behaviors, within appropriate situational contexts, that are responsible for leading one to use the label "inconsiderate." In defining the situation operationally, one is also in a better position to *formulate those issues* that will be the focus of the problem-solving endeavor.

There are times when simply defining the problem and pinpointing the issues may be sufficient in suggesting appropriate courses of action. If this is not the case, however, the next stage in the problem-solving process would involve *generating alternatives*. In training an individual to generate alternative courses of action, some of the theory and research on brainstorming and creativity training become most relevant. The guidelines for this stage are twofold: One involves training the individual to withhold any judgment as to the adequacy of any potential alternative; premature consideration of whether or not a potential response is good or bad can only serve to constrain one's creativity. The second guideline is to attempt to generate a large number of possible alternatives, as the more courses of action one has at one's disposal, the greater the likelihood that an effective solution will be available for eventual selection.

The next stage involves *decision making*, which involves an attempt at predicting the possible consequences associated with each course of action. This information is then used to determine the extent to which any given alternative is likely to resolve the problematic issues formulated earlier in the problem-solving process, with as few negative consequences as possible.

In the final stage of problem solving, the individual *implements* the course of action selected, and then *verifies* the effectiveness of the alternative selected. Depending upon the extent to which the problematic situation has been resolved, the individual may discontinue the problem-solving process, consider another possible alternative, or possibly even return to an earlier phase of problem solving. This entire procedure is presented schematically in Figure 1, where a differentiation between a "strategy" and a "tactic" is also shown. This distinction basically reflects the level of abstraction inherent in any given course of action. Thus, a strategy refers to more of a general course of action, whereas a tactic deals with the specific

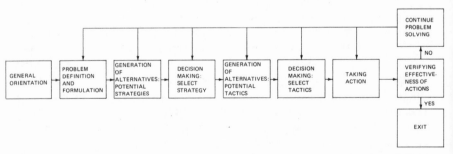

FIGURE 1. Schematic outline of the problem-solving process (from Goldfried & Davison, 1976).

behaviors associated with putting this general plan into effect. For a more detailed description of the clinical procedures involved in problem-solving training, the reader is referred to Goldfried and Davison (1976), Goldfried and Goldfried (1975), Gordon (1970), Jacobson and Margolin (1979), Robin (1978), Schneider and Robin (1975), and Shure and Spivack (1978).

In conceptualizing problem solving as representing one of the most encompassing of all coping skills, it should come as little surprise that its areas of application are indeed vast and diverse. One natural area of applicability is with *children*, as a means of assisting them in learning to function more independently. Some of the early work in this area has been carried out by Covington, Crutchfield, and Davies (1966) for training school-aged children in "life skills," and by Shaftel and Shaftel (1967) for teaching children "social values." More recently, Spivack and Shure (1974), Spivack, Platt, and Shure (1976) and Allen, Chinsky, Larcen, Lochman, and Selinger (1976) have demonstrated that training children with behavior difficulties in the use of problem-solving skills can improve their interpersonal functioning. A particularly innovative clinical procedure for use with children, called the "turtle technique," has been described by Schneider and Robin (1975). Children are told a story about a wise old turtle who is counseling a younger turtle, and describes the particularly good advantage to which they can use their protective shells. The old turtle suggests that when they run into difficult situations, including problems involving other children, they can temporarily withdraw into their shells to calm down a bit and consider the best way to respond. When used by the child in a classroom setting, this can take the form of putting one's head on the desk for a brief period of time to engage in both relaxation and problem solving.

Training in problem solving has also been applied as a method of coping with conflict situations between *children and their parents* (Gordon, 1970; Kifer, Lewis, Green, & Phillips, 1974; Robin, Kent, O'Leary, Foster, & Prinz, 1977), as a procedure for training *couples* in more effective skills for coping with their marital conflicts (Gottman, Notarius, Gonso, & Markman, 1976; Jacobson & Margolin, 1979), in training entire *families* in a method for resolving their interactional difficulties (Blechman, Olson, Schornagel, Halsdorf, & Turner, 1976; Gordon, 1970), and as a technique for increasing the effectiveness of *teachers* (Gordon, 1975) and *leaders* (Gordon, 1977).

An area that is particularly relevant to the use of problem-solving skills is that of the *maintenance* of therapeutic gains. Chaney, O'Leary, and Marlatt (1978) have used problem solving with alcoholics to assist them in coping with the problematic situations likely to result in relapse, finding that such training was indeed successful in long-term reduction of drinking. Richards and Perri (1978) were similarly successful in facilitating maintenance when problem-solving training was added to a larger treatment package for academic underachievers. Also related to the maintenance issue is the task of dealing with "reentry" difficulties, where problem solving has been used with psychiatric populations (Coché & Flick, 1975; Levendusky, 1977), and recovered heroin addicts (Copemann, 1973).

A final area of relevance involves more *situation-specific* types of problems. One example is the use of problem solving to assist individuals in coping with vocational indecisiveness (Medonca & Siess, 1976). Another example is the area of crisis intervention, typically associated with such stressful life events as divorce, separation, death of a loved one, and other life crises (McGuire & Sifneos, 1970). In these instances, the objective is not so much to train the individual in the general use of problem-solving skills, but rather by providing a therapeutic format, to assist the person to cope more effectively with a particular stressful situation.

Additional reviews of work with problem-solving training may be found in Allen *et al.* (1976), Craighead, Craighead, and Meyers (1978), and Meichenbaum (1977). No doubt we may expect to find several other areas of application discovered as clinicians and researchers continue to work in this area. It should be emphasized, however, that problem-solving skills alone are often insufficient in teaching individuals to cope with life problems. Although people can be trained to arrive at solutions that may be appropriate to problematic events, debilitating anxiety and behavioral skill deficits may undermine their ability to implement what they deemed to be the best course of action. It is for this reason that still other skills are required.

Relaxation Training

One of the more frequently used procedures for training clients to cope with anxiety is relaxation training. In the first edition of *Progressive Relaxation*, Jacobson (1929) described a procedure by which a wide variety of anxiety-related problems might be successfully treated. The procedure outlined by Jacobson for deep muscle relaxation was fairly extensive, and could involve anywhere between 50 to 200 sessions. Perhaps because of these practical considerations, and also a therapeutic zeitgeist that was not particularly receptive to such a seemingly mechanical approach to therapy, Jacobson's clinical reports of the successful use of relaxation training made little impact. It was only after Wolpe's (1958) pioneering efforts at incorporating relaxation training into a more comprehensive treatment procedure that the significance of relaxation training became more apparent.

The use of relaxation training as part of systematic desensitization was based on Wolpe's assumption that the relaxation response was inherently antagonistic to anxiety, and could therefore be most useful in deconditioning certain fears and phobias if it were contiguously paired with anxiety-arousing stimuli. In some of the early research to determine the effectiveness of systematic densensitization (e.g., Davison, 1968; Lang, Lazovik, & Reynolds, 1965; Rachman, 1965), it was found that when relaxation training was presented in itself, it was not very effective as a therapeutic technique. With increased clinical use of desensitization, and after subsequent outcome research, it became apparent that, under certain conditions, training in relaxation techniques could indeed be an effective procedure for reducing anxiety. Thus, therapists began to note that although systematic desensitization was presented to clients as a procedure for the deconditioning of specific fears, some individuals would interpret the relaxation-training aspect of the therapy as offering them a strategy for coping with stress in general (e.g., Paul & Shannon, 1966). Fortunately, these clients had not read the literature.

In the early 1970s, the literature caught up with what had been occurring clinically and several descriptions of the use of relaxation as an active coping skill appeared (Goldfried, 1971; Meichenbaum & Cameron, 1972; Suinn & Richardson, 1971). In Goldfried's (1971) reconceptualization of systematic desensitization as a vehicle for training clients in actively reducing anxiety, the emphasis was placed on the use of relaxation as a coping technique. As in the case of biofeedback, the suggestion was made to train clients to be more aware of the sensations of tension and to respond to such cues with their newly acquired relaxation skills. In order to achieve this goal, the following variations of traditional desensitization were suggested:

1. The entire desensitization procedure was described to clients within a coping framework; they were told that the procedure they were about to learn would enable them to cope with a wide variety of anxiety-provoking events. The relaxation-training portion of the technique would teach them to become better aware of the bodily cues associated with anxiety, and at the same time provide them with a skill for voluntarily relaxing away these feelings of tension.

2. Instead of using hierarchies reflecting specific themes, as one would if the desensitization process was construed as a passive deconditioning of fears, multithematic hierarchies were employed and even encouraged. Inasmuch as clients were being taught to respond to their internal cues associated with anxiety, the nature of the external event reflected in the hierarchy consequently became less important.

3. Unlike traditional desensitization, where clients are instructed to stop imagining situations when they experience anxiety, the revised procedure encouraged clients *to remain* in the imaginal situation, and to actively cope with this anxiety by relaxation. Thus, the desensitization proper was construed as a behavior rehearsal for the use of relaxation as a coping skill.

4. Following the successful coping during the consultation session, there was a greater emphasis placed on having clients apply their relaxation skills in real-life situations.

In most of the guidelines for training clients in relaxation, the lengthy procedures originally outlined by Jacobson have been abbreviated and made more manageable (Bernstein & Borkovec, 1973; Goldfried & Davison, 1976; Lazarus, 1971; Paul, 1966). Although generally following Jacobson's original guidelines, the procedures suggested by various authors vary somewhat, such as in the optimal number of muscle groups to employ, and in the most effective method of phasing out the client's reliance on external instructions. Although some writers have warned that the use of tape-recorded relaxation instructions are to be avoided (Bernstein & Borkovec, 1973), others have found it to be a most useful therapeutic aid (Goldfried & Davison, 1976). No doubt there is a fair amount of superstitious behavior that guides clinicians in their preference for a given approach. A common element across most approaches, however, involves initially training clients to alternately tense and then relax different muscle groups, and to experience the different sensations associated with both tension and relaxation. As the training progresses, they are taught to relax these muscles without initial tensing. Once they are at the point where they are capable of becoming relaxed on their own within a very short period of time, clients are then in the position to use their relaxation skills to actively cope with anxiety-provoking situations.

It is beyond the scope of this chapter to review the clinical outcome research on the effectiveness of relaxation training. The results of several studies reviewed by Goldfried (1977) suggest that relaxation may be used as an effective clinical procedure when it is presented as an active coping skill. Such a training regimen can be implemented within the context of a coping-oriented desensitization, or may be brought about by simply encouraging clients to relax when confronted with anxiety-provoking situations in real life. The use of relaxation skills has been found to be effective in the reduction of such diverse problems as speech anxiety (Gatchel, Hatch, Watson, Smith, & Gaas, 1977; Goldfried & Trier, 1974), test anxiety (Chang-Liang & Denny, 1976; Denney & Rupert, 1977; Snyder & Deffenbacher, 1977), interview anxiety (Zemore, 1975), insomnia (Davison, Tsujimoto, & Glaros, 1973; Nicassio & Bootzin, 1974), hypertension (Shoemaker & Tasto, 1975; Deabler, Fidel, Dillenkoffer, & Elder, 1973), and tension headaches (Cox, Freundlich, & Meyer, 1975). Thus, in actively using relaxation skills to cope with one's sensations of anxiety—regardless of the external situation eliciting the anxiety—one has available an effective coping skill that can generalize both over situations and time.

Cognitive Restructuring

In an attempt to offer a therapeutic approach that was completely novel and had a more "scientific" basis, the early writings in behavior therapy assiduously avoided any reference to cognitive processes. In drawing upon the research in learning, most of the procedures that were initially employed had their roots in either classical or operant conditioning. While it is clear that a fair amount of research dealing with such a cognitive variable as "mental set" date back to the early 1900s (Hilgard & Bower, 1975), most of the literature on learning that was available to the founders of behavior therapy dealt with principles of classical and operant conditioning. However, as observed by Breger and McGaugh (1965) in their critique of behavior therapy, there was a growing body of knowledge focusing on cognitive factors in learning that behavior therapists were completely ignoring. The very rapid growth of what has been called "cognitive behavior therapy" certainly indicates that the importance of such variables is now being acknowledged.

In considering the use of cognitive restructuring as a coping skill, it should be emphasized that the range of techniques falling under this generic heading are even more varied than the superstitious procedural differences associated with relaxation training. Indeed, Meichenbaum (1977) has cautioned us to be wary of a "uniformity myth" that one can inadvertently adopt when discussing the relevance and effectiveness of cognitive-restructuring procedures.

An important figure who has contributed to the growth of cognitive behavior therapy is Albert Ellis (1962). Ellis has argued—at times vigorously—that an individual's perception of a situation plays a more significant role in creating problems than does the objective nature of a situation itself. According to Ellis, such faulty labeling has its basis in certain irrational beliefs, among which are the dire need for approval and acceptance from others, and the need to perform perfectly in all things. The goal of Ellis's rational-emotive therapy is to train clients to think more logically and thereby cope with their own emotional disturbances.

Although largely neglected by behavior therapists, the work of Richard Lazarus and his associates (Lazarus, 1966; Lazarus & Cohen, 1977; Lazarus & Launier, 1978; Roskies & Lazarus, 1979) has clear relevance to the use of cognitive procedures for coping with emotional upset. In describing the interplay between cognitive processes and stress reactions, Lazarus has maintained that an individual initially engages in a "primary appraisal" of a situation, where it is labeled as being potentially threatening, challenging, or benign. The attempt at coping with stress entails a "secondary appraisal," which may involve a defensive distortion of the situation, a more

realistic assessment, or a plan for direct action. Another potential contribution that has been largely overlooked among behavior therapists is the work
of Janis (1958, 1965), who has long argued that individuals may effectively
cope with stress by cognitively preparing themselves beforehand. Although a
very strong case can be made for the possible contributions that both stress
research and cognitive behavior therapy have for each other (Roskies &
Lazarus, 1979), the psychodynamic orientation reflected in the research by
Lazarus and Janis may very well have prevented behavior therapists from
drawing upon their findings.

Among those who are more readily identified with a behavioral
orientation, a variety of different approaches for implementing cognitive
restructuring has been offered. Beck (1970, 1976) has focused on training
clients to become aware of and to modify certain illogical thought patterns,
including the tendencies to draw arbitrary inferences from events, to exag-
gerate the significance placed on any given event, to overgeneralize from a
single incident, and such "cognitive deficiencies" as the failure to attend to
or incorporate certain life experiences. Arnold Lazarus (1971) has similarly
written about maladaptive thought processes, such as tendencies to view
events dichotomously (i.e., something is either "good" or "bad") and to
assume that certain social mores are logical conclusions rather than
arbitrary conventions. Meichenbaum (1977), although acknowledging the
existence of irrational self-statements that may mediate disruptive emotions,
places greater emphasis on training the client in the use of more adaptive
coping self-statements (e.g., "Don't think about fear; just think about what
you have to do. Stay relevant.") and has integrated the use of such cognitive
skills along with coping relaxation.

Just as there are variations among clinicians and researchers in the
content of the cognitive processes that are the focus of therapy, so there are
differences in the method of training clients in using cognitive restructuring
as a coping skill. For example, it is Ellis's (1962) contention that the most
effective way of training clients to think more reasonably is by having the
therapist vigorously and repeatedly present a more reasonable perspective
on various problematic situations. Goldfried and his associates (Goldfried &
Davison, 1976; Goldfried, Decenteceo, & Weinberg, 1974; Goldfried &
Goldfried, 1975) have attempted to incorporate many of Ellis's ideas into a
social-learning framework, so as to encourage clients to take a more
systematic and active role in monitoring and reappraising their unrealistic
views in various life situations. Procedures outlined by Beck (1976) and
Meichenbaum (1977) have similarly employed social-learning principles in
training clients to use cognitive restructuring to cope with a variety of problems, including depression (Beck, 1976; Beck, Rush, Emery, & Shaw, 1979),
anxiety, anger, and pain (Novaco, 1975; Meichenbaum & Turk, 1976).
Although there are differences among these various approaches (see

Meichenbaum, 1977; Raimy, 1975), they all employ relatively structured procedures in teaching clients more appropriate ways of cognitively apprais- ing situations, and in encouraging the application of such skills in real-life situations. The current clinical effectiveness of such cognitive-restructuring procedures can be found in reviews by Beck (1976), Ellis and Grieger (1977), Goldfried (1979), and Meichenbaum (1977).

While recent work in cognitive behavior therapy has been viewed in many quarters as a most significant trend, it is important to recognize that behavior therapists have, in essence, rediscovered the wheel. If nothing else, this should offer us a lesson in the dangers of becoming too fixed within a given scientific paradigm. It should also make us wary of the possibility that the enthusiasm currently associated with the cognitive zeitgeist may cause us to go overboard and view cognitive restructuring as the sole effective ingredient in therapeutic change. Without denying the significant contribu- tions that cognitive procedures can offer, it would be a mistake to lose sight of the fact that other clinical strategies, including the encouragement of new experiences, are essential to the change process.

Our knowledge of the complex interplay between cognition and behavior is certainly far from complete. In attempting to understand the "meaning" that events have for any given individual, however, it is likely that experimental cognitive psychology can provide us with many useful concepts. Goldfried (1979) has speculated on some of these potential contributions, maintaining that the difference between individuals who "believe" or "understand" certain statements and those who "do not believe" or "cannot understand" these same statements is a function of dif- ferential past experiences that comprise the necessary referent for the utterance in question. Research by Bransford and Johnson (1972) on comprehension would suggest that therapists need to provide clients with appropriate learning experiences *prior to* their use of language or labels, which require such experiential referents for their meaning or comprehen- sion. Or, if such experiences have occurred in the client's past, but are stored in "episodic memory" (Tulving, 1972) and consequently not "being used" to gain a more accurate perception of current situations, steps may need to be taken to *retrieve and integrate* such experiences into "semantic memory" (Tulving, 1972) in such a way as to realign existing conceptual categories. One may wonder about the extent to which this latter guideline parallels what psychoanalysts have meant when they suggest that the therapist be careful in the "timing" of interpretations, offering them only when the patient appears ready to accept and "understand" certain isolated and seemingly irrelevant past events.

There is another point relevant to the concept of "meaning" that is worth noting. Although cognitive behavior therapists have suggested that "self-statements" or "internal dialogues" of individuals often serve as the mediator of emotional upset, it is not uncommon to find that clients have difficulty in reporting what they are "telling themselves" in any given situation. Nisbett and Wilson (1977) have similarly reported that research subjects are often unable to accurately provide introspective information on their cognitive processes. Instead of conceptualizing certain cognitive mediators as representing relatively coherent self-statements, it might be more appropriate to view such variables as involving affective associations, comprising the *connotative meanings* assigned to events or objects (Osgood, Suci, & Tannenbaum, 1957). Indeed, one of the major characteristics of human memory is its associative nature; associations are involved both in the meaning assigned to concepts and in the retrieval of information (Bower, 1975). Hence, a procedure suggested by Goldfried (1979) in the implementation of cognitive restructuring involves the use of an associative task, whereby clients are asked to complete such sentences as "If this other person disagrees with me, it would upset me because . . .," or "Making a mistake in front of other people would upset me because. . . ." Clinical experience with such a technique has been fruitful, in that it seems to assist clients in recognizing and subsequently reevaluating the implicit meaning they assign to given situations in their lives. The similarity to Jung's early research (Jung, 1910) on the use of word associations to determine the idiosyncratically perceived significance of certain words is striking.

Communication Skills

Just as it is reasonable to expect that problematic situations of a personal nature constitute a natural part of our lives, so it is likely that all individuals will encounter interpersonal conflicts resulting from confused communications with others. Some of the early work on interpersonal communication problems has come from family therapy, where the goal has been to alleviate an individual's problems by altering the interpersonal relationships within the family system (Haley, 1963; Jackson, 1965; Jackson, Riskin, & Satir, 1961; Satir, 1967; Watzlawick, Beavin, & Jackson, 1967). These workers have observed that in addition to the overt content of a message, there frequently exist latent messages that interfere with the communication process. These latent messages can vary in their subtlety, and typically convey *devaluation* and *attempts to control* the receiver. The effect of such communications is not only to confuse the receiver as to what is being said, but also has clear implications for the message that is sent in return. Recent research on marital conflict has demonstrated that this pattern of confused communication typically escalates into further miscommunication (Gottman, Markman, & Notarius, 1977; Margolin, 1977). In the case of distressed marital relationships, it can reach the point where negative connotations become attached to neutral or positive messages (Kahn, 1970), even though each partner may be capable of clear communication and effective problem solving with strangers (Vincent, Weiss, & Birchler, 1975).

In training an individual to develop more effective communication skills, emphasis is placed both on the ability *to send clear messages* and *to receive them accurately*. In learning to send unambiguous messages to another individual, Gordon (1970) has differentiated between "you" and "I" statements. The "you" communication not only contains an overt message, but also carries with it a devaluation of the other individual. Thus, a statement such as "You're inconsiderate and insensitive by always coming home late for dinner" suggests not only the impact that such behavior has on the sender, but also carries with it a "put down" of the other person. Such attempts at communication are often ineffective, in that they perpetuate a power struggle that can cause the receiver to view the situation as undermining his or her sense of freedom, and consequently may result in what Brehm (1966) has called "psychological reactance." In learning to be clearer in one's communication, the individual must learn to send "I" messages, where the emphasis is on communicating to the other individual *the effect* that their behavior has in a *given situation*, as well as a *suggestion* for future change. In the example given above, a more effective communication might involve: "When you come home late for dinner, I feel disappointed and frustrated. It also makes it very difficult for me to plan the meal. If you see you're going to be late, I'd appreciate it if you could somehow let me know in advance." Difficult as it might be to initially learn to emit such a deceptively simple communication, it avoids the power struggle that might otherwise lead to reactance, and at the same time provides the receiver with descriptive feedback and a request for behavior change.

In addition to learning to send clear messages, communication training entails learning to receive messages accurately. The ability to "actively listen" (Gordon, 1970) to what another person is saying, rather than thinking about one's reponse or counter-attack, is a skill essential to effective communication. In training an individual to listen actively, the person is instructed to reflect back to the sender the message he or she has heard. To follow through with our example, the receiver of the "I" message might state: "So what you're saying is that my being late makes you feel frustrated about the effort you've put into preparing dinner. And you'd like some advanced warning if it's impossible for me to make it on time." Such feedback not only assists in clarifying any miscommunication and in ensuring that the listener has accurately received the message, but also conveys the listener's understanding of and concern for what the sender is stating. Together with the communication of "I" messages, active listening can function *to define issues more clearly*, thereby setting the stage for problem solving and other attempts at negotiating behavior change within the relationship.

As in the case of learning any other coping skill, there are variations in how communication training may be implemented (Gordon, 1970; Jacobson & Margolin, 1979; Margolin & Weiss, 1975; O'Leary & Turkewitz, 1978; Satir, 1967; Weiss, Hops, & Patterson, 1973). Despite these variations, a format that is common to all approaches involves some educational phase—perhaps including self-help books (Gordon, 1970, 1975, 1977; Gottman *et al.*, 1976)—modeling, rehearsal, and eventual application in real life. As one might expect, the relevance of communication training is indeed widespread, and has been used in marital therapy (Gottman *et al.*, 1976; Jacobson & Margolin, 1979; Margolin & Weiss, 1975; O'Leary & Turkewitz, 1978; Satir, 1967; Weiss *et al.*, 1973), assertion training (Lange & Jakubowski, 1976), parent training (Gordon, 1970), leadership training (Gordon, 1977), and teacher training (Gordon, 1975). Most of the research to date demonstrating the effectiveness of communication training has been carried out within the context of marital therapy (Jacobson & Margolin, 1979; Margolin & Weiss, 1978; O'Leary & Turkewitz, 1978; Turkewitz, 1977). As implied above, however, communication training may be a necessary, but not sufficient, condition for instigating behavior change. While interpersonal conflicts stem from faulty communication, they may also involve mutually nonreinforcing behavior patterns. Consequently, it is not unusual to find communication training as constituting part of a larger intervention strategy that additionally deals with environmental and overt behavior change.

The growing recognition among behavior therapists that the area of interpersonal communications is relevant in understanding and changing human problems signifies an important, if not belated, trend. No doubt, references to such concepts as "hidden agendas," "latent meanings," and "symbolic significance" have served as conceptual barriers for behavior therapists becoming more actively involved in clinical and research work on communication training. However, if one translates such concepts into the terminology of experimental cognitive psychology and, for example, considers that interpersonal communications carry with them both *denotative* and *connotative* meanings (cf. Osgood *et al.*, 1957), the compatability with cognitive behavior therapy becomes more evident. In many distressed relationships, communication problems have been found to involve as much the connotative as the denotative meaning of the interchange. Thus, Kahn (1970) found that even when presented with direct statements of positive emotions from their spouses, husbands in distressed relationships were more likely to attribute negative connotations to such messages than were husbands in nondistressed marriages. An important area for future research would appear to be in the development and use of assessment techniques to evaluate the connotative meaning structure (i.e., "hidden agenda," "latent meaning," "symbolic significance") associated with interpersonal communications or events. Being able to plot in semantic space the personal meaning an individual attributes to various kinds of interpersonal communications (e.g., Osgood *et al.*, 1957) may provide us with information most relevant to the therapeutic change process.

ISSUES AND IMPLICATIONS

At this point, it might be profitable to step back and deal with some issues and implications that cut across all coping skills. The topics to be considered here include issues associated with the clinical implementation of any given training procedure, the relevance of perceived control, the influence of societal sex-role stereotyping on effective coping, and the scope of an appropriate setting for coping skills training.

Clinical Implementation

Given the relatively clear guidelines associated with the learning of a skill—involving the use of instructions, coaching, modeling, prompting, behavior rehearsal, feedback, and homework assignments—one would expect training clients in the use of various coping skills to be a relatively straightforward procedure. Although such guidelines certainly make for easier clinical implementation, there nonetheless are a number of possible pitfalls one might encounter. Some of the problems associated with the clinical application of behavioral procedures in general have been discussed elsewhere (Goldfried & Davison, 1976), and will not be reviewed here. Instead, this section will focus specifically on some of the considerations associated with the clinical implementation of coping skills training.

As noted at the outset of this chapter, clients frequently enter therapy with a conceptualization quite alien to a coping skills model. They often anticipate that something will be done *to* them or *for* them, and that the goal will be to alleviate certain *specific problems*. However appealing the notion may be, they rarely see the situation as providing them with the occasion for learning more general skills for dealing with their own problems. Although such expectations can often be altered by providing a more appropriate rationale for the intervention procedure, the therapist nonetheless needs to be alert to subsequent indications that the client continues to retain expectations inconsistent with a coping skills orientation. For example, in the process of training individuals in the use of relaxation as a coping skill, it is not unusual for clients to interpret the relaxation homework as a means of alleviating their anxiety, rather than providing them with practice in refining their relaxation skills. Thus, some clients report that they failed to practice relaxation at home, stating that they did not feel anxious and consequently saw no need to go through the exercise. In such instances, it is important to convey that the purpose of the homework is to *learn the skill*, and that the anxiety-reducing effects at this point should be viewed as secondary. A convenient way to help clients understand this distinction is by drawing an analogy between relaxation training and the process of learning to drive. As most people have experienced, the initial stages in learning to drive can indeed be cumbersome, as they involve deliberate and conscious efforts each step of the way. In learning to be more proficient in their driving skills, clients not only had to take lessons, but also had to engage in numerous practice sessions, where the goal was to improve their skills rather than to get anywhere in particular. The same process is involved in learning to use relaxation as a coping skill—or any other skill that may be the focus of the intervention—where the initial work carried out during the session and at home should be seen as practice sessions needed before the eventual application of these skills.

As is the case in learning most complicated skills, the change process is often gradual. Because of this gradualness, clients often find it difficult to see the progress they are making, and as a result may become discouraged. One method for helping clients to become better aware of the changes that *do* occur is to have them self-monitor their success at coping with various situations, and then to compare these coping attempts with how they responded (or might have responded) to similar situations prior to therapy. Even when they are aware that gradual change is occurring, some clients—particularly those with high standards for self-reinforcement—may be reluctant to reinforce themselves for their progress and will remain somewhat discouraged. In such instances, the therapist can ask them to include in their self-monitoring a simple one to five rating of their satisfaction with each coping attempt. In those instances where the client is less than satisfied with their performance, they can then be asked to specify precisely what they would have to do, think, or feel in that particular situation in order to have attained a rating of "five." Such a specification often helps in realigning their unrealistic standards.

Another issue relevant to the training process is the *maintenance of change* over time. As suggested earlier, a useful strategy that can be used in maintaining treatment gains involves problem-solving training. A particularly innovative approach in using problem solving to deal with relapse has been described by Marlatt and his associates in the work they have done in the treatment of alcoholics (Chaney *et al.*, 1978; Marlatt, 1978). On the basis of a cognitive-behavioral analysis of those situations that frequently led to relapse among alcoholics (negative emotional states, social pressure, etc.), Marlatt and his associates incorporated such high-risk situations into the intervention procedure itself, and used problem-solving training together with other coping skills in training alcoholics to anticipate and cope more effectively with such situations. The use of this programmed relapse strategy was found to significantly decrease both the duration and severity of relapse episodes one year after termination. Such a maintenance strategy is clearly relevant to other problem areas as well.

It should be emphasized that for individuals to *have* a coping skill in their repertoire does not ensure that they will *use* it. In addition to research findings demonstrating this phenomenon (Fremouw & Harmatz, 1975; Goldfried & Trier, 1974; Vincent *et al.*, 1975), there are numerous informal observations to indicate that this can often occur. For example, we have all observed individuals who are most proficient in helping others place upsetting situations into a more reasonable perspective, and who can do so for themselves with hindsight, but who nonetheless do not use such coping skills when they themselves are confronted with upsetting events. This is a particularly striking, if not embarrassing, phenomenon when it occurs among therapists! Although there are many reasons why an individual has difficulty in retrieving and applying a coping skill in his or her own life, one such possibility is worth emphasizing, namely, the availability of a signal or cue for coping. In the use of various coping skills, the appropriate signal entails a perceived sense of emotional upset. In order to have such a state of arousal function as a cue, however, the individual must *be aware* that it exists at the time. All too often, we assume that our clients are adept at appropriately labeling their states of arousal, despite the ample evidence that cognitive, physiological, and behavioral components of emotionality are often poorly correlated (Lang, 1978). The question for the therapist then becomes how to assist clients most effectively to get "in touch" with their feelings. One approach has been suggested by Birbaumer (in press), who recommends the use of biofeedback as an aid in training individuals to become more aware of sympathetic arousal and in the appropriate labeling of such physiological states. Numerous other procedures have been attempted clinically, most of which are associated with a humanistic orientation (e.g., Gendlin, 1973; Perls, 1969; Rogers, 1951; Schutz, 1967). It is clear that behavioral interventions, particularly when viewed within a coping skills model, need to place greater emphasis on the individual's affective states. In adding the emotional component to a cognitive-behavioral orientation, the possibilities for rapprochement with other therapeutic approaches become more evident.

Perceived Control: A Double-Edged Sword

Intrinsic to a coping skills conception of human functioning is that individuals are not only capable of dealing effectively with various problematic situations, but are also aware of their abilities to do so. Rotter

(1966) has maintained that an individual's perceived locus of control may be viewed along a dimension, depending on whether or not one expects that reinforcers are determined by internal or external variables. According to Rotter:

> When a reinforcement is perceived by the subject as following some action of his own but not being entirely contingent upon his action, then, in our culture, it is typically perceived as the result of luck, chance, fate, as under the control of powerful others, or as unpredictable because of the great complexity of the forces surrounding him. When the event is interpreted in this way by an individual, we have labeled this a belief in *external control*. If the person perceives that the event is contingent upon his own behavior or his own relatively permanent characteristics, we have termed this a belief in *internal control*. (p. 1)

Brehm (1966) has suggested that perceived control can function as an important source of motivation, in that individuals tend to resist the influence of others if they believe that such influences undermine their perceived freedom of choice. As suggested earlier in this chapter, psychological reactance can result from an interpersonal communication that carries with it the demand that one person do another's bidding.

Although Rotter originally proposed the locus of control variable as constituting a generalized expectancy, one can certainly question whether or not such an expectancy does indeed generalize to all life situations typically confronting individuals. A basic question for investigation would be the extent to which perceived locus of control differs from one class of situation to another, depending on the individual's available coping skills for dealing with each set of events. As noted by Ajzen and Fishbein (1977), greater attitude-behavior consistency may be obtained when a given attitude and behavior are relatively situation-specific. Bandura (1977) has similarly maintained that the perception of self-efficacy may be assessed within the context of specific problematic situations.

In a review of the research literature dealing with situation-specific expectancies, Phares (1976) concludes that "subjects learn more, perform better, and are rendered less anxious when aversive stimuli are under their own control or else are predictable" (p. 33). For example, studies have indicated that the aversiveness of stimuli can be undermined by individuals' belief that they have control over such stimuli (Geer, Davison, & Gatchel, 1970; Glass, Singer, Leonard, Krantz, Cohen, & Cummings, 1972), and that this perceived control has its positive effects even if attempts at dealing with the situation were never implemented (Glass, Singer, & Friedman, 1969). Outcome research on clinically related issues has similarly indicated that when a "coping" emphasis is added to the intervention procedures, their therapeutic impact is enhanced (e.g., Davison *et al.*, 1973; Denney & Rupert, 1977; Goldfried & Trier, 1974; May, 1975). Lazarus and Launier

(1978) have suggested that the effectiveness of perceived control in coping with aversive stimuli may be understood in terms of the very definition of psychological stress itself. According to their conceptualization, stress reactions occur in situations that strain an individual's coping resources. Thus, when individuals expect that they can successfully cope with a given event, there will be an undermining of their perception of the situation as being stressful.

Most discussions of perceived control have presented it as a favorable characteristic. To the extent that individuals do not believe that they are able to control the forces in their lives and, over a period of time have reached a state of "learned helplessness" (Seligman, 1975), they are typically found to be psychologically depressed. Thus, the assumption is frequently made that the more perceived control individuals have, the better off they will be. Certainly, this has been implied throughout this chapter. However, the fact of the matter is that we are often confronted with difficult life situations over which we have *little or no control*, or where we come upon problematic situations for which there *are* no good solutions. It is when individuals continue to approach such events with a sense of perceived control that we may observe its detrimental effects. For example, Glass (1977) has maintained that the Type A individual—who is continually "on the go" and approaches tasks with a sense of urgency—has a strong need to control the environment, continually making active attempts at coping. The difficulty arises when such efforts persist even in the face of uncontrollable situations. Glass reports data indicating that "although individuals are capable of adjusting to threats to their sense of environmental control, such adjustments have aftereffects which render them less able to cope with subsequent demands and less resistant to later stress and strain" (p. 173). The Type A individual's persistent attempts at coping lead to emotional and physical exhaustion, and eventually to a behavioral picture that very much resembles learned helplessness. This unrealistic sense of perceived control and its behavioral concomitants takes its toll psychophysiologically, such as in the higher incidence of coronary disease.

It is both appropriate and helpful to view the concept of perceived control as comprising a continuum, where the end points are maladaptive. At the one extreme, we have depressed individuals who do not perceive themselves as having much ability to control anything in their lives; at the other extreme there are the Type A individuals, who believe that they are capable of coping with everything. *It is noteworthy that the extremes on the perceived control dimension parallel sex-role stereotypes in our culture* (Tavris & Offir, 1977). It is also of interest to note that there exists a differential incidence of depressive and Type A behavior patterns among women and men in our society (Chesler, 1972; Glass, 1977). Some of these societal influences on coping and perceived control are considered next.

Societal Influences on Coping: Sex-Role Stereotyping

To deal with the issue of training in coping skills as a way of alleviating human problems, without also considering the role that society plays in either fostering or limiting individuals' coping attempts, is clearly shortsighted. This is hardly a new insight, and has been dealt with at length by others (e.g., Rappaport, 1977; Sanford, 1966). Among the issues that need to be considered is the extent to which our society perpetuates certain tasks, or constrains one's coping skills in ways that would tax any "reasonable" person's attempts at coping. One example is the very strong emphasis placed on the work ethic in our society. Thus, Argyris (1966) reports that the overwhelming majority of complaints reported by top and middle management concern the overload problem, which they find increasingly difficult to deal with. What is particularly striking is that the president of one such company, although acknowledging that this indeed was the case, also reported that this was to be expected and was part of the job! Consequently, in considering the role that society plays in limiting our ability to cope, it is important to recognize those factors we consider self-evident, as they are often invisible.

As a result of the feminist movement, we are becoming increasingly aware of the ways that societal sex-role definitions may limit coping attempts on the part of both women and men (Bem, 1979; Chesler, 1972; Farrell, 1974; Fasteau, 1974; Tavris & Offir, 1977). As reported by Broverman, Broverman, Clarkson, Rosenkrantz, and Vogel (1970), clinicians consider healthy women in our society to be less independent, adventurous, aggressive, and competitive than men. This finding complements the observation by Parsons and Bales (1955) that the male role is primarily instrumental in nature—directed toward getting the job done—whereas the female role is characterized by greater expressiveness and is associated with more consideration for the welfare of others. Although men and women may each be trained to function effectively within a particular domain, the complex nature of our society is now such that we are confronted by tasks requiring both sets of skills (Bem, 1979).

The numerous ways that sex-role stereotyping constrains effective coping among women have been amply documented (Chesler, 1972), and have led to the increased use of assertion training and other programs for women to expand their available coping skills. Only very recently have there been attempts to question how the male sex-role stereotype limits men's effective coping (David & Brannon, 1976; Farrell, 1974; Fasteau, 1974; Pleck & Sawyer, 1974). For example, Fasteau (1974) describes the stereotypic male role as follows:

> The male machine is a special kind of being, different from women, children, and men who don't measure up. He is functional, designed

mainly for work. He is programmed to tackle jobs, override obstacles, attack problems, overcome difficulties, and always seize the offensive. He will take on any task that can be presented to him in a competitive frame-work, and his most important positive reinforcement is victory. He has armor plating which is virtually impregnable. His circuits are never scrambled or overrun by irrelevant personal signals. He dominates and outperforms his fellows, although without excessive flashing of lights or clashing of gears. His relationship with other male machines is one of respect but not intimacy; it is difficult for him to connect his internal cir-cuits with those of others. In fact, his internal circuitry is something of a mystery to him and is maintained primarily by humans of the opposite sex. (p. 1)

Compare the above description with the coronary-prone Type A person— typically male—who is overly competitive, aggressive, continually rushed, and generally achievement-oriented (Glass, 1977).

The effect of sex-role stereotypes on judged adequacy of coping is clearly illustrated when members of each sex display opposite sex-role behaviors. For example, Deaux and Taynor (1973) found that females were not rated as highly as males when they functioned well in a hypothetical interview situation, while males were rated as far more inferior than the females when the interview did not go well. Similarly, men who are success-ful in various occupations are typically rated more highly than women in comparable positions, but are judged to be more of a failure when they do not achieve a certain level of competence occupationally (Feather & Simon, 1975). And finally, research on the self-disclosure of personal upset in objec-tively disturbing situations has found it to be far more acceptable for women than for men (Derlega & Chaikin, 1976).

In adopting a behavioral orientation to evaluate successful and unsuc-cessful coping, the functional nature of such an approach defines the ade-quacy of coping attempts in terms of their consequences. As a result of this functional orientation, behavior therapy faces the potential danger of encouraging what is likely to be reinforced by the individual's environment, thereby maintaining a societal status quo that, in itself, may at times be harmful in its effects. Winett and Winkler (1972) raised this issue in con-junction with the use of behavioral procedures in the classroom. Davison (1976) addressed himself to this problem when he suggested that the use of behavior therapy procedures for modifying homosexual behavior may only encourage a societal view that homosexuality is maladaptive. This general issue is also well illustrated with the increased popularity of assertion training for women. Although assertion training had been available to behavior therapists for a number of years, it was only as a function of the feminist movement that its particular relevance for female clients was noted. In many of the early descriptions of assertion training, behavior therapists emphasized the importance of fostering behavior patterns that were "appropriate" to the client's particular situation. This, in essence, reflects the behavior therapist's functional stance, where the effective behavior pattern to be encouraged is that which is likely to be reinforced by one's environment. That the environment might unwittingly be reinforcing a maladaptive behavior pattern among women was never an issue that logically followed from the behavioral viewpoint. On the other side of the ledger, it should be emphasized that behavior therapists may be in a particularly good position to respond to, and to incorporate societal changes into their definition of effective coping, as they are not locked into a particular theoretical conceptualization of competence or normality. What is ultimately needed, however, are data on the "larger picture," involving an evaluation of the long-term as well as short-term effects of various behavior patterns associated with male and female sex-roles.

There are, in fact, some longitudinal findings to indicate that there exist long-term positive consequences for nonstereotypic sex-role behavior patterns. For example, Maccoby (1966) found masculine characteristics in girls and feminine traits in boys to be associated with greater intellectual development. Mussen (1962) reported that although traditionally masculine boys functioned most effectively during their adolescence, they displayed poorer adjustment as they reached adulthood. And Kagan and Moss (1962) noted that young girls who remained "tomboys" the longest were likely to be achievement oriented as an adult. In some of the pioneering research on psychological androgyny in adulthood, Bem (1979) has demonstrated that "masculine" men have difficulty in coping with situations requiring nurturance, while "feminine" women lack the ability to deal with situations requiring independence.

The need for a more comprehensive repertoire of coping skills is clear in light of the rapidly changing nature of our society, where acceptable role behaviors are in a continual state of reevaluation, and where role requirements change over the course of one's lifetime (e.g., Levinson, 1978). Bem (1979) has argued that a move toward greater psychological androgeny would provide us with the ability to cope more effectively with the different types of situations in which we are likely to find ourselves. As a step in this direction, more women are developing a wider range of coping skills, such as increased assertiveness, thereby offering them a greater sense of perceived control over their lives. The need for a comparable broadening of coping skills among men is only just beginning to be recognized (David & Brannon, 1976; Farrell, 1974; Fasteau, 1974; Pleck & Sawyer, 1974). For men to move toward the direction of psychological androgeny, they need to develop the ability to deal with situations requiring interpersonal intimacy, emotional expressiveness, and appropriate dependency. For those with an unrealistically high sense of perceived control, something akin to "passivity training" might be in order, where the goal would be to teach such individuals to deal differently with situations in which one's active coping attempts might be inappropriate or ineffective. This clearly expands our concept of coping skills, so that instead of always consisting of active steps in *doing something* to handle a situation, it also includes a passive acceptance of what is there, and the ability to experience any associated discomfort.

The Scope of and Setting for Coping Skills Training

One may legitimately raise the question at this point regarding the scope of coping skills. At the outset of this chapter, a coping skill was described as any class of cognitive or overt behavior patterns that would deal effectively with problematic situations. Egan and Cowan (1979) have called these "life skills," which encompass such diverse areas as physical well-being, values, interpersonal functioning, intellectual development, small group interaction, and involvement with the larger community. It is clear, however, that the specific cognitive processes and behavior patterns associated with each of these several areas is in need of further specification. One of the limitations of a behavioral approach is that it does not adequately specify the content of effective coping. While much has been written about how different behavior patterns are learned, the classes of variables likely to be maintaining a behavior pattern at any given time, and the procedures for behavior change, all of this is discussed in the context of "the behaviors of interest." Unfortunately, behavior therapists have no good guidelines for deciding upon those aspects of functioning that are legitimately "of interest." The content of many behavioral concepts tend to be based on pragmatic, rather than theoretical, philosophical, or even empirical grounds. Thus, we have an interest in assessing and studying phobias and unassertive behavior primarily because we have therapeutic procedures that are geared toward the modification of such behaviors.

It is becoming increasingly apparent that for the technology of behavior therapy to truly make an impact on the alleviation of human problems, we need clearer guidelines on the scope of such problems, and more information on those skills required for effective coping. Two complementary research strategies that address themselves to this need are the epidemiological or social ecology approach suggested by Lazarus and his associates (Lazarus & Cohen, 1977; Lazarus & Launier, 1978) and the task analysis paradigm employed by Schwartz and Gottman (1976). Lazarus's epidemiological strategy involves an analysis of stress and coping within the naturalistic setting, evaluating both the short- and long-term effects of various coping attempts made by individuals in dealing with stressful life events. The task analysis approach of Schwartz and Gottman works within a laboratory context, and studies the specific cognitive, behavioral, and physiological variables that differentiate individuals who are effective in coping with certain types of situations (e.g., interpersonal assertion tasks), from those who are less effective. The complementary nature of both research strategies is reflected in the fact that the first is capable of delineating the full range of stressful life events and eventual consequences of various coping strategies—that is, the situations and behaviors or cognitions "of interest"—while the second provides a more detailed analysis of the specific behavioral and cognitive components that differentiate successful from unsuccessful coping within each area.

As various coping skills become more specifiable and the means for their acquisition more straightforward, the question should arise as to whether psychotherapy is the best setting in which to promote the learning of these skills. With the rapid growth of self-help organizations and books, it is already becoming increasingly evident that much of what has traditionally been carried out within the therapeutic consultation session is now being offered directly to the population at large. In many respects, this trend is most consistent with a coping skills view of therapy, where the goal is to *train*, not treat, clients. As suggested by Miller (1969) in his presidential address to the American Psychological Association, the time may have come when mental health professionals need to take what they know about training individuals in more effective coping and "give it away" to everyone. This seemingly radical suggestion is consistent with the recommendation of President Carter's Commission on Mental Health that a national effort be made to encourage such "natural support systems" as the family, neighborhood, religious organization, and self-help group in facilitating more effective functioning among its members.

To the extent that our knowledge of those situational tasks that tax individuals' coping attempts uncovers problematic events that are persistent and predictable, it makes sense to engage in primary prevention and train people fairly early in life in the use of relevant skills for coping with such difficulties. Successful attempts have already been made in teaching elementary school children in the use of problem-solving skills, either within the context of a preventive intervention (Allen et al., 1976), or as a more basic educational program in "life skills" (Covington et al., 1966). Unfortunately, such efforts are far too isolated and infrequent to make the needed impact. When one thinks of all the difficult situations with which individuals must cope throughout their lifetime, it seem strange that our society does little in routinely training people in the use of coping skills. Viewed within this broader perspective, one must seriously question the very strong emphasis our educational system places on teaching people to cope with intellectual and achievement-oriented tasks at the expense of any preparation for the multitude of personal situations that we are likely to confront (cf. Sanford, 1966). At the very least, the "happily ever after" myth needs to be challenged, as it no doubt results in much unexpected and unpredicta-ble stress. Being "prepared" in advance for stressful situations itself may render them somewhat less debilitating (Janis, 1958), and certainly makes the need for training in coping skills more apparent.

SUMMARY AND CONCLUSIONS

This chapter has presented a conceptualization of therapy as training in coping skills, whereby clients are provided with various coping strategies to be used in dealing with different types of problematic life situations. The conceptualization was illustrated with but a few possible coping skills, including training in problem solving, in the use of relaxation for coping with anxiety, in the ability to reevaluate situations more realistically, and in communication skills. In discussing these skills within the context of experi-mental cognitive psychology, some of the points of similarity between a behavioral approach and intervention approaches associated with other orientations have been noted. The chapter has also discussed some guidelines for the clinical implementation of coping skills. While the con-cept of perceived control was described as an essential ingredient in the use of coping skills, it was noted how the perceived control continuum may be maladaptive at both extremes. The observation was also made on the ways that sex-role stereotypes tend to place limits on the range of coping skills available to men and women in our society. The need for a comprehensive social ecology approach for outlining life tasks and varying coping attempts was discussed as a much-needed research strategy, to be used in conjunction with a more detailed task analysis of each coping skill. The chapter has con-cluded by pointing to some of the ultimate implication that a coping skills conception of therapy has for training individuals in effective coping, employing social systems outside of the therapeutic context.

Acknowledgments

The author would like to thank Donald Meichenbaum, Ethel Roskies, and Lonnie Snowden for their most helpful comments on an earlier version of this paper.

REFERENCES

Ajzen, I., & Fishbein, M. Attitude-behavior relations: A theoretical analysis and review of empirical research. *Psychological Bulletin*, 1977, *84*, 888–918.
Allen, G. J., Chinsky, J. M., Larcen, S. W., Lochman, J. E., & Selinger, H. V. *Community psychology and the schools*. Hillsdale, N.J.: Lawrence Erlbaum, 1976.

Argyris, C. Interpersonal barriers to decision making. *Harvard Business Review*, 1966. *44*(2), 84–97.

Bandura, A. Self-efficacy: Toward a unifying theory of behavior change. *Psychological Review*, 1977, *84*, 191–215.

Beck, A. T. Cognitive therapy: Nature and relation to behavior therapy. *Behavior Therapy*, 1970, *1*, 184–200.

Beck, A. T. *Cognitive therapy and the emotional disorders.* New York: International Universities Press, 1976.

Beck, A. T., Rush, A. J., Emery, G., & Shaw, B. F. *Cognitive therapy of depression.* New York: Guilford, 1979.

Bem, S. L. Beyond androgyny: Some presumptuous prescriptions for a liberated sexual identity. In J. Sherman & F. Denmark (Eds.), *Psychology of women: Future directions of research.* New York: Psychological Dimensions, 1979.

Bernstein, D. A., & Borkovec, T. D. *Progressive relaxation training: A manual for the helping professions.* Champaign, Ill.: Research, 1973.

Birbaumer, N. Biofeedback training: A critical review of its clinical applications and some possible future directions. *European Journal of Behavioural Analysis and Modification*, in press.

Blechman, E. A., Olson, D. H. L., Schornagel, C. Y., Halsdorf, M., & Turner, A. The family contract game: Technique and case study. *Journal of Consulting and Clinical Psychology*, 1976, *44*, 449–455.

Bower, G. H. Cognitive psychology: An introduction. In W. K. Estes (Ed.), *Handbook of learning and cognitive processes. Vol. I: Introduction to concepts and issues.* Hillsdale, N.J.: Lawrence Erlbaum, 1975.

Bransford, J. D., & Johnson, M. K. Contextual prerequisites for understanding: Some investigations of comprehension and recall. *Journal of Verbal Learning and Verbal Behavior*, 1972, *11*, 717–726.

Breger, L., & McGaugh, J. L. Critique and reformation of "learning theory" approaches to psychotherapy and neurosis. *Psychological Bulletin*, 1965, *63*, 338–358.

Brehm, J. W. *A theory of psychological reactance.* New York: Academic, 1966.

Broverman, I. K., Broverman, D. M., Clarkson, F. E., Rosenkrantz, P. S., & Vogel, S. R. Sex-role stereotypes and clinical judgments of mental health. *Journal of Consulting Psychology*, 1970, *34*, 1–7.

Cameron, R. The clinical implementation of behavior change techniques: A cognitively oriented conceptualization of therapeutic "compliance" and "resistance." In J. P. Foreyt & D. P. Rathjen (Eds.), *Cognitive-behavior therapy: Research and application.* New York: Plenum, 1978.

Chaney, E. F., O'Leary, M. R., & Marlatt, G. A. Skill training with alcoholics. *Journal of Consulting and Clinical Psychology*, 1978, *46*, 1092–1104.

Chang-Liang, R., & Denny, D. R. Applied relaxation as training in self-control. *Journal of Counseling Psychology*, 1976, *23*, 183–189.

Chesler, P. *Women and madness.* Garden City, New York: Doubleday, 1972.

Coché, E., & Flick, A. Problem solving training groups for hospitalized psychiatric patients. *Journal of Psychology*, 1975, *91*, 19–29.

Copemann, C. D. *Aversive counterconditioning and social training: A learning theory approach to drug rehabilitation.* Unpublished doctoral dissertation, State University of New York at Stony Brook, 1973.

Covington, M. V., Crutchfield, R. S., & Davies, L. B. *The productive thinking program.* Berkeley, Calif.: Brazelton, 1966.

Cox, D. J., Freundlich, A., & Meyer, R. G. Differential effectiveness of electromyograph feedback, verbal relaxation instructions, and medication placebo with tension headaches. *Journal of Consulting and Clinical Psychology*, 1975, *43*, 892–898.

Craighead, W. E., Craighead, L. W., & Meyers, A. W. New directions in behavior modification with children. In M. Hersen, R. M. Eisler, & P. M. Miller (Eds.), *Progress in behavior modification* (Vol. 6). New York: Academic, 1978.

David, D. S., & Brannon, R. (Eds.). *The forty-nine percent majority: The male sex role*. Reading, Mass.: Addison-Wesley, 1976.

Davison, G. C. Systematic desensitization as a counterconditioning process. *Journal of Abnormal Psychology*, 1968, *73*, 91–99.

Davison, G. C. Homosexuality: The ethical challenge. *Journal of Consulting and Clinical Psychology*, 1976, *44*, 157–162.

Davison, G. C., Tsujimoto, R. N., & Glaros, A. G. Attribution and the maintenance of behavior change in falling asleep. *Journal of Abnormal Psychology*, 1973, *82*, 124–133.

Deabler, H., Fidel, E., Dillenkoffer, R., & Elder, S. T. The use of relaxation and hypnosis in lowering high blood pressure. *American Journal of Clinical Hypnosis*, 1973, *16*, 75–83.

Deaux, K., & Taynor, J. Evaluation of male and female ability: Bias works two ways. *Psychological Reports*, 1973, *32*, 261–262.

Denney, D. R., & Rupert, P. A. Desensitization and self-control in the treatment of test anxiety. *Journal of Counseling psychology*, 1977, *4*, 272–280.

Derlega, V. J., & Chaikin, A. L. Norms affecting self-disclosure in men and women. *Journal of Consulting and Clinical Psychology*, 1976, *44*, 376–380.

Dollard, J., & Miller, N. E. *Personality and psychotherapy*. New York: McGraw-Hill, 1950.

D'Zurilla, T. J., & Goldfried, M. R. Problem solving and behavior modification. *Journal of Abnormal Psychology*, 1971, *78*, 107–126.

Egan, G., & Cowan, M. A. *People in systems: A model for development in the human-service professions and education*. Monterey, Calif.: Brooks/Cole, 1979.

Ellis, A. *Reason and emotion in psychotherapy*. New York: Lyle Stuart, 1962.

Ellis, A., & Grieger, R. (Eds.). *Handbook of rational-emotive therapy*. New York: Springer, 1977.

Farrell, W. T. *The liberated man*. New York: Random, 1974.

Fasteau, M. F. *The male machine*. New York: McGraw-Hill, 1974.

Feather, N. T., & Simon, J. G. Reactions of male and female success and failure in sex-linked occupations: Impressions of personality, causal attributions, and perceived likelihood of different consequences. *Journal of Personality and Social Psychology*, 1975, *31*, 20–31.

Fremouw, W. J., & Harmatz, M. G. A helper model for behavioral treatment of speech anxiety. *Journal of Counsulting and Clinical Psychology*, 1975, *43*, 652–660.

Gatchel, R. J., Hatch, J. P., Watson, P. J., Smith, D., & Gaas, E. Comparative effectiveness of voluntary heart rate control and muscular relaxation as active coping skills for reducing speech anxiety. *Journal of Consulting and Clinical Psychology*, 1977, *45*, 1093–1100.

Geer, J. H., Davison, G. C., & Gatchel, R. J. Reduction of stress in humans through non-veridical perceived control of aversive stimulation. *Journal of Personality and Social Psychology*, 1970, *16*, 731–738.

Gendlin, E. T. Experiential psychotherapy. In R. Corsini (Ed.), *Current psychotherapics*. Itasca, Ill.: Peacock, 1973.

Glass, D. C. *Behavior patterns, stress, and coronary disease*. Hillsdale, N.J.: Lawrence Erlbaum, 1977.

Glass, D. C., Singer, J. E., & Friedman, L. N. Psychic cost of adaptation to an environmental stressor. *Journal of Personality and Social Psychology*, 1969, *12*, 200–210.

Glass, D. C., Singer, J. E., Leonard, H. S., Krantz, D., Cohen, S., & Cummings, H. Perceived control of aversive stimulation and actual arousal as determinants of emotion. *Journal of Personality and Social Psychology*, 1972, *21*, 41–51.

Goldfried, M. R. Systematic desensitization as training in self-control. *Journal of Consulting and Clinical Psychology*, 1971, *37*, 228–234.

Goldfried, M. R. The use of relaxation and cognitive relabeling as coping skills. In R. B.

Stuart (Ed.), *Behavioral self-management: Strategies, techniques, and outcomes.* New York: Brunner/Mazel, 1977.

Goldfried, M. R. Anxiety reduction through cognitive-behavioral intervention. In P. C. Kendall & S. D. Hollon (Eds.), *Cognitive-behavioral interventions: Theory, research, and procedures.* New York: Academic, 1979.

Goldfried, M. R., & Davison, G. C. *Clinical behavior therapy.* New York: Holt, Rinehart, and Winston, 1976.

Goldfried, M. R., & Goldfried, A. P. Cognitive change methods. In F. H. Kanfer & A. P. Goldstein (Eds.), *Helping people change.* New York: Pergamon, 1975.

Goldfried, M. R., & Trier, C. S. Effectiveness of relaxation as an active coping skill. *Journal of Abnormal Psychology,* 1974, *83,* 348–355.

Goldfried, M. R., Decenteceo, E. T., & Weinberg, L. Systematic rational restructuring as a self-control technique. *Behavior Therapy,* 1974, *5,* 247–254.

Gordon, T. *PET: Parent effectiveness training.* New York: Wyden, 1970.

Gordon, T. *T.E.T.: Teacher effectiveness training.* New York: Wyden, 1975.

Gordon, T. *L.E.T.: Leader effectiveness training.* New York: Wyden, 1977.

Gottman, J. M., Markman, H., & Notarius, C. The topography of marital conflict: A sequential analysis of verbal and nonverbal behavior. *Journal of Marriage and the Family,* 1977, *39,* 461–477.

Gottman, J., Notarius, C., Gonso, J., & Markman, H. *A couple's guide to communication.* Champaign, Ill.: Research, 1976.

Haley, J. Marriage therapy. *Archives of General Psychiatry,* 1963, *8,* 213–234.

Hilgard, E. R., & Bower, G. H. *Theories of learning* (4th ed.). Englewood Cliffs, N.J.: Prentice-Hall, 1975.

Jackson, D. D. Family rules: Marital quid pro quo. *Archives of General Psychiatry,* 1965, *12,* 589–594.

Jackson, D. D., Riskin, J., & Satir, V. A method for analysis of a family interview. *Archives of General Psychiatry,* 1961, *5,* 321–337.

Jacobson, E. *Progressive relaxation.* Chicago: University of Chicago Press, 1929.

Jacobson, N. S., & Margolin, G. *Marital therapy: Treatment strategies based on social learning and behavior exchange principles.* New York: Brunner/Mazel, 1979.

Janis, I. *Psychological stress.* New York: Wiley, 1958.

Janis, I. Psychodynamic aspects of stress tolerance. In S. Klausner (Ed.), *The quest for self-control.* New York: Free Press, 1965.

Jung, C. G. The association method. *American Journal of Psychology,* 1910, *21,* 219–269.

Kagan, J., & Moss, H. *Birth to maturity.* New York: Wiley, 1962.

Kahn, M. Non-verbal communication and marital satisfaction. *Family Process,* 1970, *9,* 449–456.

Kifer, R. E., Lewis, M. A., Green, D. R., & Phillips, E. L. Training predelinquent youths and their parents to negotiate conflict situations. *Journal of Applied Behavioral Analysis,* 1974, *7,* 357–364.

Lang, P. J. The psychophysiology of anxiety. In H. Akiskel (Ed.), *Psychiatric diagnosis: Explorations of biological criteria.* New York: Spectrum, 1978.

Lang, P. J., Lazovik, A. D., & Reynolds, D. J. Desensitization, suggestibility, and pseudotherapy. *Journal of Abnormal Psychology,* 1965, *70,* 395–402.

Lange, A. J., & Jakubowski, P. *Responsible assertive behavior: Cognitive/behavioral procedures for trainers.* Champaign, Ill.: Research, 1976.

Lazarus, A. A. *Behavior therapy and beyond.* New York: McGraw-Hill, 1971.

Lazarus, R. S. *Psychological stress and the coping process.* New York: McGraw-Hill, 1966.

Lazarus, R. S., & Cohen, J. B. Environmental stress. In I. Altman & J. F. Wohlwill (Eds.), *Human behavior and the environment: Current theory and research.* New York: Plenum, 1977.

Lazarus, R. S., & Launier, R. Stress-related transactions between person and environment. In L. A. Pervin & M. Lewis (Eds.), *Perspectives in interactional psychology*. New York: Plenum, 1978.

Levendusky, P. *Contract milieu: Self-control alternative to the token economy*. Paper presented at the Association for the Advancement of Behavior Therapy, Atlanta, December 1977.

Levinson, D. J. *The seasons of a man's life*. New York: Knopf, 1978.

Lowenthal, M. F., Thurnher, M., & Chiriboga, D. *Four stages of life*. San Francisco: Jossey-Bass, 1975.

Maccoby, E. E. Sex differences in intellectual functioning. In E. E. Maccoby (Ed.), *The development of sex differences*. Stanford, Calif.: Stanford University Press, 1966.

Margolin, G. *A sequential analysis of dyadic communication*. Paper presented at the Association for the Advancement of Behavior Therapy, Atlanta, December 1977.

Margolin, G., & Weiss, R. L. Contracts, cognition, and change: A behavioral approach to marriage therapy. *The Counseling Psychologist*, 1975, *5*, 15–25.

Margolin, G., & Weiss, R. L. *A comparative evaluation of therapeutic components associated with behavioral marital treatments*. Unpublished manuscript, University of California, Santa Barbara, 1978.

Marlatt, G. A. Craving for alcohol, loss of control, and relapse: A cognitive-behavioral analysis. In P. E. Nathan, G. A. Marlatt & T. Løberg (Eds.), *Alcoholism: New directions in behavioral research and treatment*. New York: Plenum, 1978.

May, R. L. *The treatment of test anxiety by cognitive modification: An examination of treatment components*. Unpublished doctoral dissertation, University of Kansas, 1975.

McGuire, M. & Sifneos, P. Problem solving in psychotherapy. *Psychiatric Quarterly*, 1970, *44*, 667–673.

Meichenbaum, D. H. *Cognitive behavior modification: An integrative approach*. New York: Plenum, 1977.

Meichenbaum, D., & Cameron, R. *Stress inoculation: A skills training approach to anxiety management*. Unpublished manuscript, University of Waterloo, Ont., 1972.

Meichenbaum, D. & Turk, D. The cognitive-behavioral management of anxiety, anger and pain. In P. Davidson (Ed.), *The behavioral management of anxiety, depression and pain*. New York: Brunner/Mazel, 1976.

Mendonca, J., & Siess, T. Counseling for indecisiveness: Problem-solving and anxiety-management training. *Journal of Counseling Psychology*, 1976, *23*, 339–347.

Miller, G. A. Psychology as a means of promoting human welfare. *American Psychologist*, 1969, *24*, 1063–1975.

Mussen, P. H. Long-term consequents of masculinity of interests in adolescence. *Journal of Consulting Psychology*, 1962, *26*, 435–440.

Nicassio, P., & Bootzin, R. A comparison of progressive relaxation and autogenic training as treatments for insomnia. *Journal of Abnormal Psychology*, 1974, *83*, 253–260.

Nisbett, R. E., & Wilson, T. D. Telling more than we can know: Verbal reports on mental processes. *Psychological Review*, 1977, *84*, 231–259.

Novaco, R. *Anger control: The development and evaluation of an experimental treatment*. Lexington, Mass.: Lexington Books, 1975.

O'Leary, K. D., & Turkewitz, H. Marital therapy from a behavioral perspective. In T. J. Paolino, Jr. & B. S. McCrady (Eds.), *Marriage and marital therapy: Psychoanalytic, behavioral, and systems theory perspectives*. New York: Brunner/Mazel, 1978.

Osgood, C. E., Suci, G. J., & Tannenbaum, P. H. *The measurement of meaning*. Urbana, Ill.: University of Illinois Press, 1957.

Parsons, T., & Bales, R. F. *Family, socialization and interaction process*. New York: Free Press, 1955.

Paul, G. L. *Insight vs. desensitization in psychotherapy.* Stanford, Calif.: Stanford University Press, 1966.

Paul, G. L., & Shannon, D. T. Treatment of anxiety through systematic desensitization. *Journal of Abnormal Psychology,* 1966, *71,* 124–135.

Perls, F. *Gestalt therapy verbatim.* Lafayette, Calif.: Real People Press, 1969.

Phares, E. J. *Locus of control in personality.* Morristown, N.J.: General Learning Press, 1976.

Pleck, J. H., & Sawyer, J. (Eds.). *Men and masculinity.* Englewood Cliffs, N.J.: Prentice-Hall, 1974.

Rachman, S. Studies in desensitization—I: The separate effects of relaxation and desensitization. *Behaviour Research and Therapy,* 1965, *3,* 245–251.

Raimy, V. *Misunderstandings of the self.* San Francisco: Jossey-Bass, 1975.

Rappaport, J. *Community psychology: Values, research, and action.* New York: Holt, Rinehart, and Winston, 1977.

Richards, C. S., & Perri, M. G. Do self-control treatments last? An evaluation of behavioral problem solving and faded counselor contact as treatment maintenance strategies. *Journal of Counseling Psychology,* 1978, *25,* 376–383.

Robin. A. L. *The parent-adolescent problem solving communication program.* Unpublished manuscript, University of Maryland, Baltimore County, 1978.

Robin, A. L., Kent, R., O'Leary, K. D., Foster, S., & Printz, R. An approach to teaching parents and adolescents problem-solving communication skills: A preliminary report. *Behavior Therapy,* 1977, *8,* 639–643.

Rogers, C. R. *Client-centered therapy.* Boston: Houghton Mifflin, 1951.

Roskies, E., & Lazarus, R. S. Coping theory and the teaching of coping skills. In P. Davidson (Ed.), *Behavioral medicine: Changing life styles.* New York: Brunner/Mazel, 1979.

Rotter, J. B. Generalized expectancies for internal versus external control of reinforcement. *Psychological Monographs: General and Applied,* 1966, *80,* (1, Whole no. 609).

Sanford, N. *Self and society,* New York: Atherton, 1966.

Satir, V. *Conjoint family therapy: A guide to theory and technique* (Rev. ed.). Palo Alto: Science and Behavior, 1967.

Schneider, M., & Robin, A. L. *The turtle technique: A method for the self-control of impulsive behavior.* Unpublished manuscript, State University of New York at Stony Brook, 1975.

Schutz, W. C. *Joy.* New York: Grove, 1967.

Schwartz, R., & Gottman, J. Toward a task analysis of assertive behavior. *Journal of Consulting and Clinical Psychology,* 1976, *44,* 910–920.

Seligman, M. E. P. *Helplessness.* San Francisco: Freeman, 1975.

Shaftel, F. R., & Shaftel, G. *Role-playing for social values: Decision-making in the social studies.* Englewood Cliffs, N.J.: Prentice-Hall, 1967.

Shoemaker, J., & Tasto, D. Effects of muscle relaxation on blood pressure of essential hypertensives. *Behaviour Research and Therapy,* 1975, *13,* 29–43.

Shure, M. B., & Spivack, G. *Problem-solving techniques in childrearing.* San Francisco: Jossey-Bass, 1978.

Snyder, A. L., & Deffenbacher, J. L. Comparison of relaxation as self-control and systematic desensitization in the treatment of test anxiety. *Journal of Consulting and Clinical Psychology,* 1977, *45,* 1202–1203.

Spivack, G., & Shure, M. B. *Social adjustment of young children.* San Francisco: Jossey-Bass, 1974.

Spivack, G., Platt, J. J., & Shure, M. B. *The problem-solving approach to adjustment.* San Francisco: Jossey-Bass, 1976.

Suinn, R. M., & Richardson, F. Anxiety management training: A nonspecific behavior therapy program for anxiety control. *Behavior Therapy,* 1971, *2,* 498–510.

Tavris, C., & Offir, C. *The longest war: Sex differences in perspective.* New York: Harcourt, Brace, Jovanovich, 1977.

Toffler, A. *Future Shock*. New York: Random, 1970.

Tulving, E. Episodic and semantic memory. In E. Tulving & W. Donaldson (Eds.), *Organization of memory*. New York: Academic, 1972.

Turkewitz, H. *A comparative outcome study of behavioral marital therapy and communication therapy*. Unpublished doctoral dissertation, State University of New York at Stony Brook, 1977.

Vincent, J. P., Weiss, R. L., & Birchler, G. R. A behavioral analysis of problem solving in distressed and nondistressed married and stranger dyads. *Behavior Therapy*, 1975, *6*, 475–487.

Watzlawick, P., Beavin, J. H., & Jackson, D. D. *Pragmatics of human communication: A study of interactional patterns, pathologies, and paradoxes*. New York: Norton, 1967.

Weiss, R. L., Hops, H., & Patterson, G. R. A framework for conceptualizing marital conflict, a technology for altering it, some data for evaluating it. In F. W. Clark & L. A. Hamerlynck (Eds.), *Critical issues in research and practice: Proceedings of the fourth Banff International Conference on behavior modification*. Champaign, Ill.: Research, 1973.

Winnet, R. A., & Winkler, R. C. Current behavior modification in the classroom: Be still, be quiet, be docile. *Journal of Applied Behavior Analysis*, 1972, *5*, 499–504.

Wolpe, J. *Psychotherapy by reciprocal inhibition*. Stanford, Calif.: Stanford University Press, 1958.

Zemore, R. Systematic desensitization as a method of teaching a general anxiety-reducing skill. *Journal of Consulting and Clinical Psychology*, 1975, *43*, 157–161.

Cognitive Behavior Therapy as Psychodynamics Revisited

RICHARD S. LAZARUS

For some time it has been apparent that the cognitive behavior therapy movement was to be the basis of rapprochement between psychodynamic and behavior therapy. Goldfried's most welcome paper, on which I am to comment here, leaves no doubt about this, although the trend is also clear in the writings of many others who claim a cognitive behavior therapy identity. I, for one, am happy with this, since I have never believed in the theoretical or practical soundness of the traditional "either/or" mentality characteristic of so-called scientific psychology. I am also pleased that Goldfried, and I hope others as well, are coming to the conclusion that I am not one of the "bad guys" merely because of a stereotypical link with psychoanalysis or psychodynamics which, among arch behaviorists, seem to be dirty words. It can be fun to play good guys and bad guys, but it is the kind of fun that belongs better in "Star Wars" than in sophisticated clinical thought that tries to deal with that most complex and stubbornly difficult-to-comprehend species, *homo sapiens*. Anyway, let it be said at the outset that I agree with the general thrust of Goldfried's conceptualization of psychotherapy as cop-

RICHARD S. LAZARUS • Department of Psychology, University of California, Berkeley, California 94720.

ing skills training, and with the idea that a client's thoughts are functional keys to emotion and how life is managed.

Nevertheless, rather than contributing to a love fest, I want first to express some friendly irony, and then critically examine some of Goldfried's arguments. As to the irony, the "discovery" that people say things to themselves which shape their feelings and reactions brings to mind a joke I was told as a child: "When is a door not a door?" The answer was: "When it is ajar." I cannot escape the feeling that, similarly, the answer to the question "When is it okay to be psychodynamic?" is: "When the word 'psychodynamic' is changed to 'cognitive.'"

I surely do not wish to denigrate the importance of the forward step in speaking of "connotative meanings" in a client's self-statements, or of referring to the "latent" as distinguished from the "overt" content of the client's message. When one considers that the intellectual mentors of behavior therapy have included Pavlov, Watson, Skinner, and Eysenck, it is electrifying to find Goldfried taking cognitively oriented therapists to task for allowing dynamic concepts such as "hidden agendas" and "symbolic significance" to act as barriers to the advancement of theory. I like the message. Still, as one who has seen some value in the psychodynamic position and having been among those who used such terms for a long time, I must also feel a bit ambivalent, too. Why has it suddenly become okay again, even "in," to think in such terms? I suppose the answer is that progress often starts with backward steps before one returns to the point of origin.

How, after all, is "connotative meaning" as spoken by Goldfried different from the "hidden agendas" of the psychodynamicist? The great Freudian germ of truth was, after all, that people are inept in coping and in distress because they carry around with them childhood agendas that get in the way of their adult good sense. I can agree that the psychoanalytic focus is too heavily based in the past and within the person (see also Wachtel, 1978), and that it was a corrective step to realize that maladjustment and distress depend equally on the external environment. But, as in all pendulum swings, we seldom stop in the middle. The swinging regress is the behaviorist claim that it is solely environmental rewards and punishments that get us into trouble, and that intrapsychic events are irrelevant, or worse, scientific abominations. We should all be glad that such a simplistic extreme seems finally to be breaking down, and that we can still make good use of some of the psychodynamic concepts—though perhaps disguised in a new jargon—without compromising recent gains.

Nevertheless, I see difficulties in the way Goldfried and other cognitive behavior therapists conceptualize mediating cognitive processes. Among the most serious is the natural tendency most clinicians have of taking pathology as the starting point for understanding. Elsewhere, for example, Goldfried (Goldfried & Goldfried, 1975), has drawn on Ellis's (1962) valuable concept that adaptational and emotional difficulties are the result of faulty premises or beliefs about oneself and the world. Since my own trademark is a cognitive approach to stress, emotion, and coping, this is a very attractive idea to me, and I have long seen clear parallels between my conceptualization and that of Ellis. We seem to agree that the way a person appraises an encounter with the environment shapes the quality and intensity of the emotional response and the choice of coping strategy. Such appraisals, in turn, result from beliefs or assumptions about oneself and the world, as well as from values and commitments. From this standpoint, it makes sense to view therapy as a way of getting the client to "rationally restructure" problem situations in order to get faulty coping and troubling emotions to disappear.

The trouble arises from the corollary assumption that only accurate perceptions of reality (or assumptions about life) can be adaptationally effective and desirable. First of all, reality is itself not easily defined (Watzlawick, 1977). Second, by taking pathology as the point of departure, one rules out as useless all the things people do and think that simply make them feel good or produce positively toned emotions, even when one has to bend reality a bit to maintain certain illusions. Poets have long argued that life is intolerable without illusion, as Eugene O'Neill did in *The Iceman Cometh*, but mental health workers seem monogamously wedded to reality testing as the main hallmark of psychological well-being. As I shall claim below, there is good reason to think that this value is overstated, and leaves out much of what the normal, adequately, or even optimally functioning person does (Lazarus, 1978, 1979). Since research on cognitive appraisal and coping among such persons has not been performed, we cannot say for sure whether or not my claim is sound, but the Goldfried–Ellis position does not allow us to even consider it.

Consider first the question of stressful cognitive appraisals. Under roughly comparable circumstances, often ambiguous as to outcome, some people construe a stressful encounter as a threat, that is, as impending harm, while others see the same set of circumstances as a challenge. There is every reason to believe that those who can put a good light on things have better morale, function better socially and at work, and perhaps even have better somatic health (cf. Lazarus, Cohen, Folkman, Kanner, & Schaefer, in press; Lazarus, Kanner, & Folkman, in press). The rationale behind rational-emotive psychotherapy pays no attention to the powerful role played in ordinary living by positively toned emotional states. The pathology-centered treatment of emotions is parallel to the ecclesiastic tradition of the Middle Ages, emphasizing as it did the negative and focusing on the primitive, irrational character of emotion. Ironically, this is also the manner in which psychoanalysis has dealt with the subject (cf. Socarides, 1977).

Pathology as the point of departure also leads to difficulties in one's theory of coping. In a very high proportion of damaging life encounters there is little or nothing that can be done by the person to change the actual situation. Examples include terminal illness, incapacitation, aging, bereavement, social inequity, the concentration camp (Benner, Roskies, & Lazarus, 1979), and a host of other intractable or nearly intractable human conditions. This is not to say one cannot cope with these conditions, but rather that the most suitable form of coping in many instances includes tolerating, minimizing, accepting, avoiding, denying, or detaching. Such intrapsychic coping processes are pathological only when, in specific instances, they prevent essential adaptive actions, for example, getting medical help for a suspicious lump (Katz, Weiner, Gallagher, & Hellman, 1970) or when experiencing a heart attack (Hackett & Cassem, 1975).

This point can be made more systematic by noting that there are at least two functions of coping (Lazarus, 1978). One function is to act instrumentally to change a bad situation for the better, say, by changing oneself or confronting the external social conditions. Direct actions are particularly important in situations of anticipatory coping, when one can still mitigate or prevent harm by preparing for an upcoming confrontation. The second function of coping is to regulate the distressing emotion itself which arises from a harm or threat appraisal. The regulation is accomplished by cognitive or intrapsychic processes. Elsewhere (cf. Lazarus & Launier, 1978) this has been referred to as palliation. Such a process does not change the situation but helps the person feel better and, by so doing, may even facilitate functioning.

Only direct action forms of coping, predicated on achieving a correct assessment of reality instead of an irrational one, are emphasized by Goldfried and Ellis and, in fact, by the behaviorist tradition. I maintain that this leaves a serious gap, though one that is probably correctable by some suitable additions to the theory. Although people often can be helped by getting them to see the hard realities and the illusory and irrational nature of their assumptions about living, we often also need the luxury of some illusions, and therapy in some instances might better revolve around helping the person to think more positively about his or her plight rather than fixating on the painful truth. So much of life is ambiguous that there is much room for variation in appraisal. One's cup can be half full rather than half empty and, in fact, perhaps we should not think of this as a matter of illusion at all.

Moreover, when we actually study well-functioning persons, we find that they use a considerable share of palliative coping, including avoidance, detachment, denial (e.g., Becker, 1973), tranquilizers, alcohol, intermixed freely with the instrumental or problem-solving modes of coping so venerated in our culture and by mental health professionals. This is, of course, readily subject to empirical test, and some of my own current research is designed to find out how adequately functioning persons, those not seen in therapy, actually handle stressful encounters.

Despite these reservations, and my sense that cognitive behavior therapists have been guilty of euphemisms that disguise their movement toward psychodynamic concepts and away from an extreme behaviorism, I am sanguine about where things now seem headed. For one thing, the practical concerns of therapists such as Goldfried provide one of the best arenas for describing patterns of coping and how effective they are, both action oriented and intrapsychic or cognitive, as well as for evaluating cognitively focused interventions. Empirical research on coping is in its infancy, and the cognitive behavior therapy movement has been among the boldest in translating abstract ideas into concrete strategies of coping, both direct action modes (e.g., assertiveness training) and cognitive or intrapsychic ones (e.g., rehearsal, tactics for thinking a problem through). This work, expanded to take in well-functioning people, offers a solid prospect for increasing our understanding of the coping process and the kinds of intervention that could be helpful in treatment, prevention, and education.

REFERENCES

Becker, E. *The denial of death*. New York: Free Press, 1973.

Benner, P., Roskies, E., & Lazarus, R. S. Stress and coping under extreme conditions. In J. E. Dimsdale (Ed.), *The Holocaust: A multidisciplinary study*. Washington, D.C.: Hemisphere, 1979.

Ellis, A. *Reason and emotion in psychotherapy*. New York: Lyle Stuart, 1962.

Goldfried, M. R., & Goldfried, A. P. Cognitive change methods. In F. H. Kanfer & A. P. Goldstein (Eds.), *Helping people change*. New York: Pergamon, 1975, pp. 89–116.

Hackett, T. P., & Cassem, H. Psychological management of the myocardial infarction patient. *Journal of Human Stress*, 1975, *1*, 25–38.

Katz, J. L., Weiner, H., Gallagher, T. G., & Hellman, L. Stress, distress, and ego defenses. *Archives of General Psychiatry*, 1970, *23*, 131–142.

Lazarus, R. S. *The stress and coping paradigm*. Paper presented at conference on The Critical Evaluation of Behavioral Paradigms for Psychiatric Science, Salishan Lodge, Gleneden Beach, Oregon, November 3–6, 1978 (Department of Psychiatry and Behavioral Sciences, University of Washington, Seattle).

Lazarus, R. S. *The costs and benefits of denial*. Paper presented at conference, on Effectiveness and Cost of Denial, Haifa University, Israel, June 10–15, 1979.

Lazarus, R. S., & Launier, R. Stress-related transactions between person and environment. In L. A. Pervin & M. Lewis (Eds.), *Perspectives in interactional psychology*. New York: Plenum, 1978, pp. 287–327.

Lazarus, R. S., Cohen, J. B., Folkman, S., Kanner, A., & Schaefer, C. Psychological stress and adaptation: Some unresolved issues. In H. Selye (ed.), *Guide to stress research*. New York: Van Nostrand, in press.

Lazarus, R. S., Kanner, A., & Folkman, S. Emotions: A cognitive-phenomenological analysis. In R. Plutchik & H. Kellerman (Eds.), *Theories of emotion*. New York: Academic, in press.

Socarides, C. W. (Ed.). *The world of emotions*. New York: International Universities Press, 1977.

Wachtel, P. L. Internal and external determinants of behavior in psychodynamic theories. In L. A. Pervin & M. Lewis (Eds.), *Perspectives in interactional psychology*. New York: Plenum, 1978, pp. 263–286.

Watzlawick, P. *How real is real?* New York: Vintage, 1977.

Principles of Cognitive Therapy

RICHARD C. BEDROSIAN and AARON T. BECK

INTRODUCTION

The major purpose of this chapter is to address a number of practical and strategic issues involved in the conduct of cognitive therapy. Despite the fact that there has been a surge of interest in cognitive therapy in recent years (Mahoney, 1977), the idea that emotional suffering is related to cognition is by no means new. Victor Raimy (1975) has described in considerable detail the diverse historical threads that have been associated with the development of cognitive therapy.

The following exhortation by Marcus Aurelius epitomizes the radical cognitivist position: "If thou are pained by any external thing, it is not this thing that disturbs thee, but thine own judgment about it. And it is in thy power to wipe out this judgment now." The philosophical roots of cognitive therapy can also be traced to more recent figures in Western intellectual history. Immanuel Kant (1798) considered the substitution of "private sense" for "common sense" to be basic to the development of all mental disorders.

RICHARD C. BEDROSIAN and AARON T. BECK • Department of Psychiatry, The University of Pennsylvania, Philadelphia, Pennsylvania 19104.

According to Kant, judgments made on the basis of "common sense" are modified by feedback from others: judgments that arise from "private sense," on the other hand, remain idiosyncratic and are not tested in the external world. Two centuries later, Alfred Adler (1936b) drew a similar distinction between "private intelligence" and "common sense."

Throughout the relatively brief history of psychotherapy, many writers (Adler, for example) have proposed, in one form or another, that effective psychological treatment requires the elimination or modification of faulty ideas. As Adler (1936a) described it, the primary task of the patient in psychotherapy is to realign his or her private viewpoint with a more commonsense view of the world.

Harry Stack Sullivan (1953), one of the early proponents of a more active, interpersonally oriented form of treatment, considered the correction of "parataxic distortions," (namely, the patient's misperceptions of situations) to be crucial to the outcome of psychotherapy. George Kelly (1955) developed a system of psychotherapy based upon his cognitive theory of personality. In his fixed-role therapy, Kelly worked directly to change the disordered "personal constructs" or schemata, which he assumed constituted the core of the patient's disorder.

DEFINITION OF COGNITIVE THERAPY

Cognitive therapy is a set of treatment techniques that aim to relieve symptoms of psychological distress through the direct modification of the dysfunctional ideation that accompanies them. The therapy is based upon a broad theory of psychopathology, which details the intricate reciprocal interaction among cognitions, emotions, behavior, and environment (Beck, 1967/1972). Cognitive therapy is compared and contrasted below with a number of other treatment approaches.

Cognitive Therapy and Psychoanalysis

Orthodox psychoanalysts and psychodynamically oriented practitioners have shown an unwillingness to accept patients' reports of their inner experiences at face value. According to psychodynamic theory, the patient's conscious experience functions as a "screen," behind which the more significant unconscious meanings reside. In contrast, the cognitive therapist uses a phenomenological approach, since he or she utilizes the patient's conscious experience of a particular situation as basic data for the development of a treatment plan. The cognitive therapist's conceptualizations are based on configurations present in the patient's phenomenal field, without reference to defense mechanisms or unconscious conflicts. In cognitive therapy, the patient's automatic thoughts are revealed through focused questioning by the therapist and careful introspection by the patient: These techniques differ sharply from the method of free association, which is employed to uncover unconscious material in psychoanalysis. Unlike psychoanalysis, cognitive therapy does not demand an extensive review of the patient's early developmental history, nor does it strive for the recovery of repressed memories. The cognitive therapist may well discuss prior developmental problems or conflicts with significant others, if they are relevant to the patient's current difficulties, but the basic model of treatment does not demand that such issues surface in every case.

Unlike the psychoanalyst, the cognitive therapist does not attempt to stimulate the patient's fantasies by assuming a blank, impassive demeanor: instead treatment is approached as a collaborative venture. The cognitive therapist employs techniques that are explicit, "above board," and readily comprehensible to the patient. Thus a treatment method that is essentially manipulative, for example, "paradoxical intention" (Newton, 1968), is eschewed if its rationale is not clear to the patient or if it cannot be applied with the informed consent of the patient. The cognitive therapist tries to maintain a genuine stance at all times during treatment, except for clearly defined instances of role playing.

Cognitive Therapy and Behavior Therapy

In both behavior therapy and cognitive therapy, the treatment hour is overtly structured, and the therapist assumes an active role. The goals of both forms of therapy are circumscribed, unlike the open-ended goals of the evocative therapies (Frank, 1961). Along with the behavior therapist, the cognitive therapist generally maintains a here-and-now focus in treatment. Both schools of therapy endorse the belief that a patient can correct a maladaptive reaction pattern without insight into the precise origin of the symptom.

Despite the considerable similarity between cognitive therapy and traditional behavior therapy, there are some definite theoretical and practical differences between the two approaches. Although both modalities focus on specific symptoms and behavior problems, cognitive therapy also concentrates explicitly on the ideation associated with the symptoms. The traditional behavior therapist has preferred to focus on the patient's overt actions, which can be verified by independent observations. Unlike the behavior therapist, the cognitive therapist seeks not only to produce symptom reduction, but to modify attitudes, beliefs, and expectations as well. When he or she utilizes introspective data, the cognitive therapist goes beyond merely describing another link in the stimulus–response chain, however. According to the cognitive theory, thinking processes constitute a quasi-autonomous system, which can function independently of the environment at times. The cognitive therapist is not limited to the use of a strict conditioning model to understand mental processes.

Cognitive therapy has assimilated a number of diverse treatment techniques, such as Meichenbaum's (1977) self-instructional methods. Other interventions are employed which are clearly behavioral. Without the cognitive theory, however, cognitive treatment would be simply a formless potpourri of therapeutic techniques.

Cognitive Therapy and Rational-Emotive Therapy

Although the cognitive therapist assumes an active role during the therapy, he or she attempts to work within the patient's frame of reference at all times. Unlike more didactic approaches such as rational-emotive therapy, which assumes that psychological problems stem from a "universal" set of irrational ideas, cognitive therapy seeks to elicit and modify the patient's *specific, idiosyncratic* cognitive distortions. The underlying model of cognitive therapy assumes that changes in the patient's thinking come about as a result of *experiential* learning, not through authoritative statements by the therapist. Consequently, there is a greater emphasis upon behavior experiments and other forms of real-life learning in cognitive therapy than in rational-emotive therapy and other approaches. As Ellis (1977) has pointed out in his review of *Cognitive Therapy and the Emotional Disorders*, cognitive therapy is more "behavioristic" than rational-emotive therapy. Finally, although cognitive therapy is similar to rational-emotive therapy in terms of theoretical assumptions, the model underlying cognitive therapy is more detailed and has been subject to greater experimentation, particularly in the area of depression (Beck, 1967/1972, 1976).

MEANINGS AND EMOTIONS IN PSYCHOPATHOLOGY

While both psychoanalysts and orthodox behaviorists tend to distrust patients' descriptions of their psychological processes, the cognitive therapist accepts individuals' interpretations of events as basic, "rock-bottom" data. In order to understand emotional reactions to an event, a distinction must be made between the dictionary or "public" meaning of an occurrence, and its personal or private meaning. The public meaning of an event is formal and objective, devoid of any personal significance or connotation. If a boy is teased by his friends, the objective meaning of the event is simply that they are harassing him. On the other hand, the personal significance for the boy who is teased is more complex, for example, "I'm a weakling," or "They hate me." Private meanings are frequently unrealistic, since most individuals lack opportunities to check their authenticity.

The idea that the personal meaning of an event determines the emotional response constitutes the core of the cognitive model of emotions and emotional disorders. Individuals may need to concentrate on their thoughts and images at the time of a particular event in order to describe its personal meaning (see subsequent section, "Identifying Dysfunctional Thoughts and Their Relationships to Symptoms"). When a person attaches an unrealistic meaning to an event, he or she may experience an excessive or inappropriate emotional response as a consequence. A woman lying in bed who believes that every noise is a prowler will feel excessive anxiety.

Note that in the very act of self-observation, patients begin to adopt a position of greater distance and objectivity vis-à-vis their thoughts. During the course of cognitive therapy, through the therapist's approach, the self-monitoring tasks, and the homework assignments, three key epistemological principles are conveyed to the patient: (1) perceptions or interpretations of reality are not identical to reality itself; (2) interpretations of reality are dependent upon cognitive processes, which are themselves inherently fallible; (3) beliefs are hypotheses which are subject to disconfirmation and modification. We assume that the best way for a patient to adopt such an epistemological framework is through accumulated learning experiences, rather than through a purely didactic effort on the part of the therapist.

According to the cognitive model, if we know the meaning a person attaches to a certain situation, then we should be able to predict his or her emotional reaction. An individual will find particular relevance in the objects and events which touch upon his or her *personal domain*. Central to the domain is the individual's self-concept, his or her physical attributes and personal attributes, his or her goals and values. Clustered about the self-concept are the animate and inanimate objects in which the person has an investment; for example, family, friends, and material possessions. Other elements of a person's domain vary in degree of abstraction: from his or her school or ethnic group to the more tangible ideals of justice or morality. The concept of personal domain helps to explain how a person can become elated if a member of his or her ethnic group is honored, or conversely, how an individual can feel outraged if a fellow group member is persecuted.

An outline of the kinds of ideational content associated with the various neurotic disorders is presented in Table I. The depressed patient perceives the loss of something essential for happiness, and anticipates continued negative outcomes in the future: consequently, he or she experiences sadness, disappointment, and apathy. On the other hand, the manic patient overvalues his or her experiences and becomes elated as a result. An anxious patient anticipates unavoidable danger to his or her domain and feels anxiety or panic. The phobic individual also anticipates physical or psychological harm, but in definable situations that can be avoided. Paranoid individuals believe that others are deliberately abusing

TABLE I. Ideational Content of Neurotic Disorders[a]

Neurotic disorder	Idiosyncratic ideational content
Depression	Devaluation of domain
Hypomania	Inflated evaluation of domain
Anxiety neurosis	Danger to domain
Phobia	Danger connected with specific, avoidable situations
Paranoid state	Unjustified intrusion on domain
Hysteria	Concept of motor or sensory abnormality
Obsession	Warning or doubting
Compulsion	Self-command to perform specific act to ward off danger

[a] Beck (1976), p. 84.

them and experience anger over the supposed injustices to which they have been subjected. The thoughts of an obsessional person also focus on risk or danger, but differ from those of the anxiety neurotic in that they are concerned with an action the patient believes he or she should have taken, or one he or she should not have taken. Compulsions, such as excessive hand washing, are attempts to relieve obsessions through actions which the patient believes will ward off danger.

COMMON TYPES OF COGNITIVE DISTORTIONS

While the range of cognitive distortions is potentially infinite, certain types of errors in thinking seem to occur with regularity in clinical practice. The following classifications are not meant to be exhaustive or all-inclusive, but are offered simply to assist the therapist in structuring his or her observations:

1. *Selective abstraction*: involves focusing on a detail out of context, such that the significance of the total situation is missed (Beck, 1976). For example, a college professor lecturing to a large class might selectively attend to a member of the audience who had fallen asleep, while ignoring the many students who appeared alert and interested. Selective abstraction represents a form of stimulus set. The individual is predisposed to perceive specific situational factors relevant to his or her idiosyncratic sensitivities, such as failure, danger, or rejection, and to be relatively impervious to other stimuli.

2. *Arbitrary inference*: refers to conclusions that are made on the basis of inadequate or improper information. Basically, arbitrary inference

represents a response set. The depressed individual, for example, is prone to interpret almost any kind of event in terms of his or her performed conclusions. The anxious patient indiscriminately interprets his or her perceptions of stimuli in terms of personal danger.

3. *Overgeneralizations*: are blanket judgments or predictions based upon a single incident. Our college professor might say to himself, "I've always bored people with my lectures," or "I'm a dull person." Overgeneralizing is also a manifestation of a response set. The individual has a preexisting global belief that is triggered by a particular type of event. He or she then interprets the specific event in terms of broad, overgeneralized concepts.

4. *Personalization*: in its most extreme form, is exemplified by the paranoid individual's ideas of reference and persecutory delusions. Less dramatic forms of self-reference occur in neurotic patients, who tend to overestimate the extent to which particular events are related to them. Thus, a graduate student who encountered a winter storm on his way to a qualifying exam assumed that the treacherous weather conditions were somehow directed at him personally (Schuyler, 1973).

5. *Polarized thinking*: involves sorting information into one of two dichotomous categories, good or bad, success or failure, acceptance or rejection, and so forth. Beck (1976) discussed the case of a young man for whom anything short of complete acceptance from others signified rejection and led to subsequent feelings of sadness. Similarly, some individuals who lack self-control in eating and drinking conceptualize their problem behaviors in terms of total abstinence versus unrestrained consumption, while they fail to consider a more moderate level of food or alcohol intake as a viable goal.

6. *Magnification and exaggeration*: another manifestation of the tendency to make extreme judgments, refers to an overemphasis upon the most unpleasant, negative consequences that can arise in any situation. Thus, an anxiety-prone man planning to take an automobile trip may dwell on the possibility of being killed in an accident. Frequently, the feared consequences are relatively rare occurrences such as airplane crashes and rare diseases.

7. *Assuming excessive responsibility*: illustrated dramatically by the bizarre ideation of some psychotic individuals who believe they are to blame for floods, earthquakes, and other natural disasters. Patients with less bizarre ideation may nonetheless attribute negative events to their supposed personal deficiencies. A research scientist blamed himself for the fact that a subordinate had falsified a substantial body of data, although he had been absolved of responsibility for the incident by his superior.

8. *Incorrect assessments regarding danger versus safety*: relate to both physical harm and psychosocial harm. Included in the category of "physical

risks" are a number of situations associated with common phobias: being attacked by animals or other people, falling from high places, suffocating, and so on. Psychosocial harm refers to negative feelings such as humiliation and sadness, which occur as a result of insults, criticisms, or rejection. A person who overestimates the risk involved in situations, such as the woman who feared suffocation in a wide variety of conditions, is likely to be excessively anxious and to lead an overly constricted or isolated life. On the other hand, a person who habitually underestimates danger or risks, may be prone to have accidents or may repeatedly encounter difficulties with others.

9. *Dysfunctional attitudes about pleasure versus pain*: reflect the beliefs some individuals hold regarding the prerequisites for true happiness or success. We have treated a number of graduate students, for example, who were convinced that their future happiness and self-worth were contingent upon the attainment of a particular degree. The lives of people who are dominated by pleasure–pain rules may have a grim, overdriven quality. Moreover, the setting of unrealistic goals as a basis for happiness or self-respect can lead to feelings of depression, since failure to meet the goals can provoke a loss of self-esteem and a sense of hopelessness. Examples of some of the attitudes that render people vulnerable to depression (Beck, 1976) are listed below:

   a. It's wonderful to be popular, famous, wealthy; it's terrible to be unpopular, mediocre.
   b. If I make a mistake, it means that I'm inept.
   c. My value as a person depends on what others think of me.
   d. I can't live without love. If my spouse (sweetheart, parent, child) doesn't love me, I'm worthless.
   e. If I don't take advantage of every opportunity to advance myself, I will regret it later.

10. *"Tyranny of the shoulds;" automatic self-injunctions*: similar to pleasure–pain rules in that they represent unrealistically high standards for human conduct (Horney, 1950). Samples from the common "shoulds" listed by Beck (1976) include:

   a. I should be the utmost of generosity, consideration, dignity, courage, unselfishness.
   b. I should be the perfect lover, friend, parent, teacher, student, spouse.
   c. I should never feel hurt; I should always be happy and serene.
   d. I should know, understand, and foresee everything.
   e. I should never be tired or get sick.

THE THERAPEUTIC COLLABORATION

The most effective format for psychotherapy involves therapist and patient in a collaborative venture. By regarding the patient as a collaborator, the therapist conveys respect and gains valuable assistance. On the other hand, the presentation of therapy in a mysterious light induces dependency by implying that the patient lacks the ability to completely understand and participate in therapy. Demystifying the treatment process helps to define the patient as a more competent person, who is fully capable of initiating and maintaining the steps necessary for self-improvement.

At the outset, the therapist should present a thorough rationale for the use of cognitive therapy, geared to the particular patient's level of sophistication. In this regard, the assignment of reading material such as *Coping with Depression* (Beck & Greenberg, 1974) and a few chapters from relevant books (Beck, 1976; Ellis, 1975) for home reading can be quite helpful. As indicated by Heitler (1976), the use of pretherapy preparation strategies has consistently increased the effectiveness of various forms of psychological treatment. In our view, the more the patient knows about what will occur in therapy and the nature of his or her role in the process, the greater the therapeutic response.

Although the Rogerian facilitative conditions of warmth, empathy, and positive regard for the patient are not necessarily seen now as *sufficient* for positive outcome in psychotherapy (Bergin & Suinn, 1975), the cognitive therapist who has failed to acquire these skills will encounter difficulties in treating the more problematic patients. Similarly, the therapist's own confidence in the efficacy of what he or she has to offer can influence the outcome of therapy (Frank, 1974). Optimally, the cognitive therapist should have a wide repertoire of interpersonal behaviors from which he or she can draw therapeutic interventions. It is likely that the active therapist gradually acquires a broad spectrum of interpersonal skills as a result of interactions with a variety of patients.

By actively soliciting information from the patient regarding the content of treatment, the therapist can help minimize the patient's passivity and dependency. This type of approach can be implemented by such relatively simple strategies as beginning the session with the question, "What problems should we put on our list of things to discuss today?"

Cognitive therapy can be conceptualized as regarding the patient and the therapist as "personal scientists" (Kelly, 1955). The therapist's behavior itself should resonate with such a view. That is, the patient should be helped to understand that therapy is a trial-and-error approach, that failure of an intervention can help to facilitate the treatment process, and that the feedback provides a basis for the therapist to modify his or her approach. In negotiating with the patient and in adjusting his or her approach according to the demands of the particular situation, the therapist acts as a powerful role model.

Resistance

As Mahoney (1974) has pointed out, the topic of resistance or "counter-control" has been relatively untouched in the behavior therapy literature. Nonetheless, the cognitive therapist needs to be sensitive to and actively solicit evidence of disagreement, noncompliance, and other uncooperative behaviors on the part of the patient. Inquiring near the end of the session, "Was there anything I said today that irritated you?" conveys the message that the patient's negative reactions are valuable data and should be freely discussed. There is some experimental evidence that forewarning patients about potentially inconvenient or troublesome aspects of homework and other therapeutic assignments can increase adherence (Bedrosian, 1977). Material elicited from the patient regarding his or her negative reactions toward therapy and the therapist provides indispensable information that enables the therapist: (1) to modify the actual treatment approach, and (2) to identify and modify important dysfunctional cognitions. Therapists, whether neophytes or experienced, tend to be thwarted by patient's repeated qualifications or skepticism, expressed in phrases such as "Yes, but . . ." These "obstacles" should be dealt with in the same ways as any other problems: investigate and evaluate the relevant cognitions.

An interesting vignette concerning the use of negative reactions as "grist for the therapeutic mill," comes from the case of a severely depressed, suicidal young woman. In the middle of an interview, the therapist sniffled to clear his sinuses. The patient, who had been focusing her gaze elsewhere, asked, "Why are you laughing at me?" The therapist explained to the woman that he had been clearing his nasal passages, and then demonstrated for her how the sound had been produced. The patient thus became aware that she had *automatically* assumed that the sound had been a snicker directed at her. The incident forcefully illustrated the way in which she constantly scanned her interpersonal field for cues indicating rejection from others, and distorted information in the process.

The vignette described above also underlines another crucial element in cognitive therapy, *experiential learning*. A didactic approach frequently fails to produce long-term improvements in functioning, since it excludes the patient as a participant observer and as an active problem solver, and thus inhibits "deutero-learning," the acquisition of more generalized modes of self-management. In contrast, knowledge acquired by the patient as a result of behavioral experiments, active discovery, and enlightening experiences, has a much more immediate, forceful impact. Moreover, the therapist's credibility will suffer eventually unless the patient can confirm the principles conveyed during treatment through his or her own experience. For example, the therapist can assure the client that feelings stem from thinking, but this assertion will remain in the realm of the hypothetical until it can be demonstrated in "real life" that when the patient experiences hopeless, self-critical thoughts he or she feels sad.

Neither the therapist nor the patient should expect major changes in cognitive processing of data to occur after one or two treatment sessions. Particular dysfunctional themes will appear repeatedly, and may necessitate the repetitive use of specific interventions. Similarly, people with serious difficulties will suffer setbacks in the course of recovery, as they fluctuate in their degree of belief in dysfunctional cognitions. Once again, the therapist should display an adaptive, rational attitude for the patient, by maintaining his or her optimism, and by demonstrating how the identification of recurring areas of vulnerability is of prime therapeutic value.

THE THERAPEUTIC PROCESS

By formulating an overall strategy for a given case, the cognitive therapist provides a sense of continuity in the treatment for himself or herself as well as for the patient. While the therapist usually enters each session with a set of objectives (for example, to elicit cognitions regarding self-efficacy, teach coping skills for anxiety, and so on), the patient should be an active participant in the setting of an agenda for the therapy hour. The use of a relatively well-structured approach within the interview underscores for the patient the notion that therapy involves the progressive pinpointing and solution of specific problems, as opposed to unsystematic self-exploration. Even when a structured approach is employed, however, the therapist must be especially flexible and sensitive to the changing needs of the patient. Moreover, since most therapeutic techniques overlap one another, often more than one problem can be attacked simultaneously. For example, suppose an anxiety-prone patient is asked to monitor his or her automatic thoughts during an anxiety attack. Simply by assigning the task, the therapist has begun to evaluate the validity of the dysfunctional thoughts. Likewise, by assuming the role of chronicler of his or her cognitions, the patient is likely to adopt a position of greater distance and objectivity vis-à-vis the anxiety.

The major task confronting the therapeutic "team" during the first interview is the development of a specific formulation of the patient's problems. Essentially, the therapist needs to help the patient verbalize his or her chief complaints in a way that sets the stage for subsequent interventions. Thus, global statements such as "I can't handle my problems" will need to be operationalized, translated into more concrete terms; for example, "I'm so anxious that the only time I leave the house is to buy food." As global problems are broken down into potentially manageable components, patients often begin to experience relief from discomfort and an increase in optimism.

As the patient reviews his or her major complaints, the therapist may be able to identify many diverse problems that arise from similar factors. The process of "problem reduction" is exemplified by the following case example. A woman had severely restricted her lifestyle due to a fear of elevators, tunnels, hills, closed spaces, riding in an open car, riding in an airplane, swimming, walking fast or running, strong winds, and hot muggy days. Treatment of each phobia separately through the use of systematic desensitization might have been a lengthy, expensive process. Careful assessment revealed a common element in all of her symptoms, namely, an overwhelming fear of suffocation. By focusing on this "common denominator" of the fears, the therapist and patient were able to neutralize all her phobias fairly rapidly.

The concept of problem reduction also applies to specific disorders such as depression, which consists of a particular configuration of symptoms. The therapist can gear his or her interventions toward certain key components of the disorder, such as inertia, hopelessness, or low self-esteem while improvements in mood, appetite, and sleeping pattern will accompany positive changes in other areas of functioning.

BEHAVIORAL INTERVENTIONS IN THE EARLY
STAGES OF TREATMENT

For many patients, it may be desirable to focus on behavioral interventions during the early stages of treatment. This emphasis is particularly applicable to severely depressed patients who experience apathy, anhedonia, and immobility. Such individuals will need to alter their patterns of withdrawal and immobility before they can fully apply themselves to the task of changing their cognitions. Cognitive and behavioral techniques should be seen as complementary, however, since the use of the latter may provide the therapist with the first entry point into the patient's belief system. To illustrate, let us consider the case of a depressive middle-aged man who complains of feeling so distressed that he is unable to leave the house alone. Clearly, the removal of such an incapacitating symptom will be one of the first goals of treatment. In addition to conducting a thorough *behavioral* analysis (Kanfer & Saslow, 1965) of the problem (failure to leave the house alone), the therapist should also attempt to delineate the *cognitive* elements of the complaint by asking the following sorts of questions:

1. When you begin to consider the prospect of going out, what thoughts occur to you?
2. Suppose you actually decided to leave the house, then shaved, showered, dressed, and so forth. Imagine you're standing at the door, ready to open it. What thoughts are running through your head now?
3. What do you predict might happen to you if you were to leave the house alone?

Although the number of behavioral techniques available to the cognitive therapist is, of course, quite large, the following methods have proven to be useful, expecially with depressed and anxious patients:

1. *Activity Scheduling.* Disorganized obsessive or apathetic patients find it beneficial to plan their daily activities in some detail, with the therapist's assistance.

2. *Mastery and Pleasure Monitoring.* Patients are asked to record their activities, noting those that provide them with a sense of either mastery or pleasure, or both. One goal served by this technique is to increase the patient's sense of control over his or her life, while directly attacking his or her sense of anhedonia. If the patient insists, "Nothing brings me enjoyment anymore," he or she can be asked to rate the actual pleasure derived from such activities (for example, on a five-point scale). The patient is unlikely to give identical "pleasure" ratings to all his or her activities. The therapist can then seize upon any variation observed in the patient as evidence for the notion that at the very least, some activities are *less unpleasant* than others. For anxious or phobic patients, mastery experiences may involve approaching more closely the feared situations.

3. *Graded Task Assignments.* By performing successive approximations to a desired behavior the patient can slowly work his or her way to a desired goal. Thus, a severely depressed individual who has ceased to prepare his or her own food may work toward the goal of preparing a full-course meal, by starting with boiling an egg, or even heating a pan of water. A similar approach can also aid the patient who suffers from symptoms of anxiety. For example, a woman with a fear of driving began a series of graded assignments by driving her car to the end of her street and then back. She gradually extended the round trip until she could drive in heavy traffic. At the same time, she noted her vivid visual images of getting into severe accidents.

4. *Behavior Rehearsal.* Through the use of role playing and imagery, the patient can be prepared for potentially stressful life events. For example, a teacher felt anxious about confronting his supervisor upon returning to work, after a bout of anxiety and depression had necessitated a lengthy leave of absence. He and the therapist role played a number of potential interactions with the supervisor, including those which the patient feared

most. When the patient played the supervisor, the therapist was able to display for him the appropriate assertive behavior. The patient was subsequently able to utilize the strategies he developed in therapy during his interview with the supervisor, who, perhaps not surprisingly, turned out to be less threatening than he had imagined.

5. *Behavior Experiments*. Contrary to current misconceptualizations regarding cognitive therapy (for example, Ledwidge, 1978), the cognitive therapist does not simply attempt to get the patient to "change his or her mind." Indeed, if persuasion or reassurance were sufficient to change cognitive distortions and dysfunctional assumptions, few patients would enter treatment, since most of them have already received these quasi-therapeutic interventions from the significant others in their lives. By designing "real world" experiments, the patient and therapist can work together to test the validity and utility of dysfunctional cognitions by assuming the roles of coinvestigators. A young man who worked the counter in a busy newsstand was convinced that since he had become depressed, women were no longer attracted to him. The therapist explained to him that before work could begin on his heterosexual behavior, it was necessary to determine whether, in fact, women had ceased to find him appealing. He was asked to record on a daily basis, the number of women who reacted to him in a flirtatious manner. As it turned out, far more women flirted with him each day than he had predicted. In fact, he had even received an outright proposition during the week of record keeping!

The importance of obtaining a solid "data base" before attempting specific interventions is illustrated by the following case. A woman who at one time had suffered from paranoid delusions continued to anticipate rejection and disapproval from others after her psychotic symptoms had remitted. Her anticipation of rejection rested on the assumption that she knew what others were thinking. Therefore, she was asked to conduct a behavioral experiment during the therapy hour, to determine the accuracy of her "ESP." She tried repeatedly to guess the therapist's thoughts, which he had written down on a file card, and was incorrect in every instance. She replicated the experiment with her husband each night for the following week, again with total inaccuracy. Thereafter, she worked at reminding herself about her failure at "mind reading," whenever she automatically predicted rejection or disapproval from others. Further, the experiment also underlined the need for the patient and her husband to improve the clarity of their communications, a point of view which the therapist had been promulgating unsuccessfully for some time.

Behavior experiments are quite useful in the treatment of individuals suffering from symptoms of anxiety. For example, a woman in her mid-twenties began experiencing panic attacks in stores, the laundromat, and other public places. Her anxiety was associated with the conviction that something terrible was about to happen to her. She began to curtail her trips out of the house due to her anxiety attacks. Along with her husband, the therapist escorted her to the entrances of various stores. As she conducted her business successfully in one store after another, without the anticipated consequences occurring, her anxiety began to diminish, and she experienced greater confidence in her ability to go out shopping alone.

IDENTIFYING DYSFUNCTIONAL THOUGHTS AND THEIR RELATIONSHIPS TO SYMPTOMS

One of the prime goals of cognitive therapy is the identification and modification of maladaptive thoughts associated with the patient's symptoms. As described elsewhere (Beck, 1976), "the term 'maladaptive thoughts' is applied to ideation that interferes with the ability to cope with life experiences, unnecessarily disrupts internal harmony, and produces inappropriate or excessive emotional reactions that are painful" (p. 235). It should be emphasized, however, that the therapist and the patient need to arrive at some agreement concerning what kinds of thoughts are interfering with the patient's well-being and attainment of life goals; otherwise a collaborative effort cannot be sustained. In order to achieve a consensual definition of the cognitive distortions that require modification, the therapist and patient must work as coinvestigators of the patient's thought processes.

Frequently, patients report being aware only of situations or activating stimuli and their emotional reactions to them, without being able to identify the intervening ideation. Such individuals are unaware of the role of thinking in determining their emotional reactions and their behavior. Nonetheless, clinical experience indicates that people can become keen observers of their own thought processes as they learn to pinpoint themes of which they were previously unaware. For example, an otherwise self-disciplined young woman complained that she engaged in extensive eating binges for no apparent reason. Initially she believed that her bouts of overeating not only were beyond her control, but also reflected mysterious inner forces that took possession of her will. She was asked to keep a detailed record of her thoughts during the binges, as well as during the periods in which she felt tempted to overeat. Her record keeping began to reveal that her excessive food consumption was consistently preceded by thoughts concerning her imagined inferiority to others, which in turn led to anxiety, self-revulsion, and subsequently to overeating. She was eventually able to control the rumination about her inferiority, and thereby aborted the eating binges.

As suggested previously, reporting on one's thought processes is a skill that can be taught during the therapy session. Consequently, the cognitive therapist needs to develop a repertoire of methods for eliciting automatic thoughts within the interview situation. One technique involves asking the patient to reexperience the troublesome situation, and to reveal the dysfunctional thoughts associated with the incident. Sometimes the patient will find it hard to visualize an incident that occurred outside the session, however. Problem situations that involve interpersonal interactions can be recreated in the interview through the use of role playing. For example, a young woman who experienced tension during social encounters, was asked to initiate a casual social conversation with the therapist, geared toward discovering where he grew up, how many siblings he had, and so forth. During the conversation, she reported thinking, "He's going to think I'm boring" and "I'm not going to know what to say next."

Much like a good stage manager, the cognitive therapist should be able to use appropriate materials and props. Thus, an unemployed college graduate who reported that he was too anxious to even read through the "want ads," was handed a newspaper to peruse during the therapy hour. After he revealed a veritable barrage of anxiety-inducing thoughts, (I won't ever find a job; I'm a nothing, a failure. I'll never find a place for myself in the world, etc.), he and the therapist were able to formulate and test methods for terminating the dysfunctional ideation during the remainder of the hour. The young man was able to concentrate on the task at hand by continuously reminding himself that job hunting is a learning experience and that his vocational difficulties had no bearing on his worth as a person. In a later session, a similar procedure was used, which involved the patient's use of the therapist's phone to call prospective employers for inteviews.

The majority of our patients who record their dysfunctional thoughts between sessions typically use the "Triple Column" technique (for a more detailed discussion of this and other cognitive techniques, see Beck, Rush, Shaw, & Emery, 1978). The Triple Column method requires that the patient:

1. Briefly describe an upsetting situation.
2. Identify the emotions associated with it.
3. List the corresponding automatic thoughts.
4. Provide rational responses to the dysfunctional ideation.

The unemployed young man discussed above made the following recording:

1. Sitting around in kitchen, watching television.
2. Depressed, sad, angry, and tired.
3. I will never find a job; I will never have a career. I have no friends or lovers. I can't snap out of my depression. I may never be happy.
4. I've just begun looking for a job. It takes time. I don't have to find a career immediately. I will make friends as I become more outgoing.

People have liked me before. As I learn to solve my problems, I may find some contentment.

Initially, of course, patients are simply asked to focus on recording their unpleasant dysfunctional thoughts, feelings, and the situations in which the feelings and ideation emerge. The use of rational responses, which will be discussed in greater detail below, generally occurs at a later stage in treatment.

For some individuals, dysfunctional thinking may be accompanied by vivid imagery. One woman reported visualizing her family looking sad and downcast whenever she thought about her inability to find success in a profession. Subsequent questioning revealed that she assumed that her family considered her to be a complete failure.

TECHNIQUES FOR CHANGING NEGATIVE COGNITIONS

Distancing and Hypothesis Testing

The majority of patients entering treatment do not question the validity of their hypotheses or conclusions; instead they equate their inferences with reality. As mentioned above, self-monitoring enables people to begin to adopt a more objective view of their thought processes. The process of enabling a person to reevaluate ingrained beliefs and judgments is referred to as "distancing." The therapist's role involves making the patient's standards and assumptions *explicit* (rather than devaluing them or pursuing a more didactic course of action) so that rational decisions can be made regarding their accuracy or utility. Global judgments such as, "I'm a failure," generally reflect selective abstraction, overgeneralization, or one of the other patterns of cognitive distortions. As the basis for such judgments becomes more explicit, the patient can be assisted in evaluating the adequacy of his or her beliefs. Likewise, behavioral experiments, similar to the ones already discussed, can be formulated and conducted.

A middle-aged scientist and executive repeatedly expressed the belief that he was a failure in his job. Rather than accept this assertion at face value, the therapist pressed for more specific details. What was expected of him in his current position? What portions of the job was he failing to carry out? Were there parts of work at which he felt successful? What kinds of feedback had he received from his colleagues and superiors? Would he be retained in his position despite an unsatisfactory performance? For how long? As it turned out, the man had climbed steadily through the ranks of a highly competitive organization for over fifteen years, and had been rated consistently high by his superiors. When the components of his job were broken down and analyzed separately, there were few areas in which he could discern a concrete basis for his negative evaluation. There were however, a number of job-related situations that were not actually threatening and in which the anxiety was inappropriate; these areas, then, became the focus of treatment.

As long as the therapist assumes the role of an investigator, rather than an authority who dispenses pat reassurances, he or she is likely to discover that a portion of the patient's thinking does, indeed, have a basis in reality, as in the example of the preceding paragraph. Nonetheless, objective reality seldom matches the dire assessments of our patients. The actual problem, "experiencing anxiety in job-related situations" is a manageable, eminently treatable problem; the global overgeneralization "I am a total failure" is refractory until reduced into a cognitive-behavioral problem.

The following case illustrates how the "distancing" process enabled a patient to discriminate between realistic, legitimate concerns about her marriage and those worries that were based upon distorted thinking.

A young woman, who was unemployed, complained of feeling inferior to her husband, a successful professional, and his colleagues. She often expressed the belief that her husband would leave her in favor of one of his female co-workers, with whom it was assumed he would have more in common. The patient was rather vague as to whether there were other reasons why her husband would prefer such a woman to her. Consequently, she agreed that it would be useful, first of all, to determine whether she and her husband shared common interests and values. To her surprise, she compiled a lengthy list of shared attitudes that seemed to touch upon every important area of life. The therapist then suggested that since the list reflected only her point of view, she might take the experiment one step further by asking her husband to compile, independently, a list of his own. Upon comparison, the two lists showed a remarkable degree of similarity. Thus, the outcome of the experiment failed to support her belief that she and her husband had little in common. As she "distanced" herself from her more global, catastrophe-oriented cognitions regarding her husband, the patient was able to shift her attention to some more concrete problems that did exist in the marriage, such as her spouse's inability to express his opinions and preferences to her.

Decentering: Altering the Personalization of Events

Decentering refers to the process of prying the patient loose from the belief that he or she is the focal point of all events. A case study by Schuyler (1973) illustrates how a graduate student was able to modify his habitual tendency to personalize situations. Although he experienced a great deal of anxiety prior to examinations, the patient interpreted his failure on an oral exam for an advanced degree as evidence that fate had singled him out for hardship and suffering. On his way to take the oral examination a second time, the patient slipped and fell on a patch of snowy ground, and became quite anxious in the process. Identifying the relevant thought, "The snow has been put there so that I would fall," he recalled discussions with his therapist about his propensity to personalize external events. As he looked around him, he noticed that automobiles were skidding and that other people were also losing their footing on the icy pavement. The realization that the snow was not directed at him as a personal hardship was followed by the disappearance of his anxiety.

Many individuals in treatment who experience anxiety in public places and social situations report thinking that everyone is watching them, or that others are acutely aware of their tension or shyness. One general strategy for the therapist to take in such cases is to work with the patient to establish *concrete criteria* to determine when he or she is (and is not) the focus of attention, and what behaviors or attributes are being attended to by others. Note that participation in this task itself requires a shift in focus on the part of the patient, since he or she is required to adopt the perspective of another person. Typically, socially anxious individuals are so preoccupied with their own internal reactions that they actually notice very little about others' reactions to them, although paradoxically, they attribute keen powers of observation and utter objectivity to those around them. As patients become aware of how infrequently *they* attend closely to others and how limited their own observations are, they come to realize that the attentional processes of most people are similarly constrained, and increased relaxation in social situations becomes possible.

Dysfunctional cognitions such as, "No one has this kind of problem but me," or "Others have't experienced tension or discomfort in similar situations," are often reflective of a tremendous naiveté about the inevitable stresses associated with normal living. Such assumptions can be discounted if the patient can obtain data about the lives of others, through direct contact with people in the natural environment, through group therapy (Shaw & Hollon, 1978), through information given by the therapist, and through bibliotherapy. For example, a young unemployed man in his early twenties was living in his parents' home, where he experienced constant friction with his father. He perceived friction as indicative of his and his family's psychopathology, and expressed despair of ever resolving the conflicts with his father. The therapist, on the other hand, tried to reinterpret the conflict as a natural, predictable stress associated with the family life cycle, a stress which was capable of resolution. Sensing the strong similarities between his own background and that of the patient, the therapist gave the young man a copy of a paper he had written concerning the way in which he had come to terms with his own father. When the young man's preoccupation with his status in his family or origin was diminished, he was able to focus more closely on completing the next appropriate developmental task, achieving financial and attitudinal independence. As his competency in the outside world increased, his family interactions were no longer so strained and labile.

Changing the Attribution of Responsibility

Depressed patients seem especially prone to attribute adverse occurrences, even those beyond their control, to their own personal deficiencies. "Reattribution" techniques (Beck *et al.*, 1978) are useful to individuals who engage in unrealistic self-blame. The goal of such techniques is to delineate the many factors contributing to a negative experience, rather than simply absolving the patient of all responsibility. Reviewing the relevant data, the therapist and patient attempt to assign responsibility in a logical fashion. A more objective mode of attributing responsibility reduces depressogenic self-criticisms, permits more realistic problem solving, and allows the patient to realistically determine what, if anything, he or she can do to prevent the occurrence of similar events in the future.

The technique of reattribution is illustrated by the following case. A lawyer worried about an upcoming case he was to try in court, and believed that he would be totally responsible for an unfavorable verdict. The therapist and the patient identified in detail each factor involved in a case decision by jury (jury composition, length of trial, opposition presentation, etc.). Using a "pie" diagram, the lawyer estimated the relative degree of influence exerted by each factor upon the outcome of the trial. Similarly, he was asked to assess the degree of influence *he* had over each factors. Using this method, the patient concluded that he only contributed 35% to the results of the trial, and of that amount, a much smaller proportion reflected the actual quality of his preparation.

Decatastrophizing: "What If" Techniques

In predicting the worst possible consequences for themselves, anxiety-prone individuals seldom utilize all the data available to them. Moreover, the fact that the dire imaginal consequences fail to occur is usually not taken into account when subsequent predictions are made. Thus, when confronted with a patient who is prone to catastrophize, the cognitive therapist seeks to increase the range and specificity of information taken into account by the individual, and to broaden the time perspective he or she characteristically employs.

For example, a medical student with a fear of speaking in front of his classmates and appearing foolish, expressed the belief that he could never live such an experience down (Beck, 1976). Rather than accept the patient's fears at face value, the therapist began questioning him about precisely what might happen if the young man's *worst* fears came true and he did appear ridiculous before his peers. Would his career be ruined? Would his family disown him? Would he feel badly? For how long? And then what? During the course of the questioning the student realized that he was endowing the public-speaking situation with a disproportionate degree of significance. Note that the therapist did not attempt to dissuade the young man from his prediction that the talk itself would not go well; to have done so would have unnecessarily risked damaging his future credibility in the patient's eyes. On the other hand, through his style of questioning, the therapist conveyed his belief that the patient's discomfort and embarrassment, however intense, would be time-limited and therefore tolerable. The student's subsequent presentation to the class was poorly organized (perhaps due to his anxiety), and although he felt disheartened for a few days afterwards, he did not perceive the affair as a catastrophe. Prior to the next talk, he experienced much less anticipatory anxiety, and reported feeling more comfortable during the actual presentation as well, apparently because he perceived the consequences of poor performance as less threatening than previously.

In questioning about the basis of a patient's fears, the therapist should avoid appearing smug or sarcastic. An attitude that combines curiosity but minimizes threat, is indicated when making inquiries into sensitive areas. Rather than remind patients that their expectations have been inaccurate, the therapist should encourage them to write down their predictions for evaluation at a later date. In this way, a recorded body of indisputable data that fail to support the patient's catastrophic predictions can be accumulated. As one negative consequence after another fails to materialize, the patient's belief in the certainty of impending disaster begins to weaken.

Acquiring and Practicing Rational Responses for Dysfunctional Thoughts

After learning to recognize their maladaptive ideation, patients can begin to produce more adaptive, rational thoughts during bouts of anxiety, hopelessness, or self-criticism. Some examples of dysfunctional cognitions (DC) and the associated rational responses (RR) are listed in Table II.

The ability to think of rational responses during an actual stressful situation represents the end point of a learning process that begins with the patient's identification of his or her maladaptive thoughts, as described earlier. Needless to say, few patients can produce rational responses during the early stages of treatment. Further, most individuals show a high degree of belief in the dysfunctional thoughts at the time they enter treatment. The behavior experiments, the encountering of mastery experiences, and other

TABLE II. Examples of Dysfunctional Cognitions (DC) and the
Corresponding Rational Responses (RR)

DC:	How could I accept that invitation? What can I say to them? I hope I don't look anxious or depressed. Will I be able to keep myself from shaking or stuttering?	RR:	I've known these people for years. By concentrating on these worries, I just bring some of the symptoms on. My best bet is to play things by ear. Even if I'm nervous, people won't necessarily notice it.
DC:	I'm not a competent teacher. In fact, I'm not too bright.	RR:	Others whom I respect think I'm competent and reasonably intelligent. Putting myself down doesn't accomplish anything and only makes me feel bad.
DC:	I will look foolish to others.	RR:	I *may* look foolish on occasion. No one is perfect. I can *accept myself* for my inept behavior no matter how others feel about me.

therapeutic interventions all help to chip away at the conviction with which the patient's dysfunctional beliefs are held.

Initially, rational responses need to be jointly formulated by therapist and patient and rehearsed during the therapy session. Most likely the dysfunctional thoughts the patient has recorded during the previous week will be used as the targets. The therapist can prepare the patient for the assignment in the following way:

"Now that you have begun to recognize some of the ideas which upset you, we can work on actually changing those troublesome thoughts. One method which works for many people is to learn to answer their automatic thoughts, in a way we'll discuss shortly, by using rational responses. For now, I just want to teach you to think of the rational responses here in the session, and at home on your own, in connection with some thoughts that you've already recorded. At first, you may not be able to think of the rational responses at the times when you're actually experiencing stress. But that's to be expected, since you've had much more experience with producing the upsetting thoughts. Gradually, though, you'll be able to think of the rational responses in difficult situations, probably by beginning with those which are less stressful for you. Eventually, the rational responses can become as automatic as your negative thoughts are now. It just takes time and practice. Also, for the time being you won't fully believe in the rational responses."

By emphasizing that the development of rational responses is a slow, incremental process the therapist avoids giving the patient unrealistic expectations, and prevents the method from being seen in a magical or mechanistic light. Further, the patient is forewarned that initially the rational responses may not be easily produced or readily believed.

It is not uncommon in our experience for an entire session to be spent on rehearsing and writing down responses to each thought on the patient's daily log. The therapist takes the lead, initially, in demonstrating responses, then gradually withdraws his or her prompting as the patient becomes more proficient. Role playing can also be used to teach the patient the response technique. One way to introduce the role playing is to say, "Suppose I was a friend or relative of yours and I made the following statements to you. How would you answer me?" In general, role playing engages the patient's interest into what might have been an overly serious intellectual enterprise.

After practicing in the therapy session, the patient's first task is to produce rational responses to thoughts that have already been recorded on the daily log. If he or she can think of the responses during an actual stressful situation, so much the better, but this would be unrealistic as an initial goal. An analogy to a motor skill, such as basketball, may be helpful to present to the patient: A child practicing in the school yard may be able to dribble behind his back and execute all sorts of trick shots, but will freeze at first when he gets into a real game. As his skills become more automatic through repetition, he finds that he can perform the more difficult skills in his repertoire during the stress of an actual game.

Identifying and Modifying Pervasive, Dysfunctional Assumptions

As treatment proceeds, it is likely that the same or similar themes will surface again and again in the patient's thinking. As the therapist becomes aware of such themes, he or she should begin to share his or her observations with the patient. Frequently the patient is already well aware of the underlying assumptions. In other instances, the therapist's observations will be rejected out of hand by the patient. It is wise for the therapist to stay within the patient's "latitude of acceptance" (Beck, 1976) and avoid becoming embroiled with the patient in a debate over the validity of various observations and inferences.

We assume that insight, *per se*, is not sufficient for psychological change. Therefore, even when pervasive cognitive patterns have been detected, the patient will need to engage repetitively in behavioral experiments, rational responding, and other techniques which facilitate the restructuring of his or her belief system.

"DEUTERO-LEARNING"—TEACHING THE PATIENT
TO APPLY THE COGNITIVE TECHNIQUES TO NEW
AREAS OF CONCERN

Perhaps the most gratifying therapeutic outcome occurs when the patient not only experiences relief of his or her symptoms, but also understands the therapeutic methods well enough to apply them to novel problems. As pointed out elsewhere (Beck, 1976), the sense of mastery derived from solving one problem can inspire the patient to tackle other long-avoided difficulties. Each success experience weakens the patient's belief that he or she is impaired or unable to function adequately.

A young man in his early twenties sought help at our clinic for chronic symptoms of depression and anxiety. At the beginning of treatment, he was withdrawn and anxious in interpersonal situations, idle and apathetic most of the time, in sum, barely able to function as an adult. Initial changes in mood occurred through the use of behavioral tasks, which reinvolved him in meaningful activities. Then he learned to control his anxiety attacks, which had occurred as often as once a day. The next major area of concern involved job hunting, finding leads, interviewing, and so forth. As it became clear that he was on his way to obtaining a worthwhile job, the patient expressed a desire to focus on another problem, impotency. By this time, his confidence in his problem-solving ability was quite high, and he had become proficient at warding off dysfunctional cognitions. He was able to resolve the problem with impotency rapidly, and halted negative thoughts about his masculinity and sexual prowess in the process. Finally, the patient decided to tackle what he described as his "last bastion," his repetitive cycle of overeating and self-induced vomiting. He and the therapist were able to approach the problem of overeating with what had become an established format for them. In the course of the treatment, the young man resolved several additional problems on his own, such as conflicts with his family, without the explicit intervention of the therapist.

One way in which the therapist can foster deutero-learning by the patient is to make sure that he or she can verbalize the steps that were involved in solving a particular problem. As new problems are brought up, the therapist can ask, "Do you think there's anything we employed in solving Problem X that can be applied to this new area?"

In one sense, mild relapses during the course of treatment can be highly favorable, since they allow the patient to solidify his or her grasp of the coping skills acquired in therapy. When setbacks occur, they can be relabeled by the therapist as fortuitous opportunities for the consolidation of prior learning.

TERMINATION: HOW FAR SHOULD THERAPY GO?

An entire volume could be devoted to the controversy over what constitutes a positive outcome in psychotherapy. In our clinical work we strive for symptom reduction and improved psychosocial adjustment, as opposed to vague abstractions such as "self-actualization." Our view is that it is not necessary to help a patient solve all his or her problems, nor is it mandatory that all dysfunctional beliefs be modified. The notion that psychotherapy can somehow lead people to a conflict-free existence may well be a dysfunctional idea itself.

Like any other practitioner, the cognitive therapist should prepare the patient for termination. Cognitions concerning the patient's view of the end of treatment can be handled in a similar manner as other beliefs. Similarly, the therapist and patient can anticipate some problems that might crop up in the future, devising strategies for dealing with them. If the patient has already weathered a few setbacks, this fact can be emphasized as a favorable prognostic sign. It goes without saying that different styles of termination will be required for different patients; certainly some will need to leave treatment gradually, as they demonstrate to themselves that they can function adequately during the ever-widening intervals between appointments.

Thus, gradually tapering the frequency of the sessions and then providing booster sessions at gradually lengthening intervals (2 months, 3 months, 6 months) can provide the opportunity to review progress and fortify some of the technical procedures that undergo slippage with time. Such follow-up visits also motivate the patient to continue to work on his or her problems. In this way, cognitive therapy can achieve its ultimate goal: to promote a continuing process of learning that will prepare the patient to deal successfully with problems in successive phases of his or her life and to attain his or her own reasonable goals.

REFERENCES

Adler, A. The neurotic's picture of the world. *International Journal of Individual Psychology*, 1936, *2*, 3–10. (a)

Adler, A. Trick and neurosis. *International Journal of Individual Psychology*, 1936, *2*, 3–13. (b)

Beck, A. T. *Depression: Clinical, experimental and theoretical aspects.* New York: Harper & Row, 1967. Republished as *Depression: Causes and treatment.* Philadelphia: University of Pennsljvlania Press, 1972.

Beck, A. T. *Cognitive therapy and the emotional disorders.* New York: International Universities Press, 1976.

Beck, A. T., & Greenberg, R. L. *Coping with depression.* New York: Institute for Rational Living, 1974.

Beck, A. T., Rush, A. J., Shaw, B. F., & Emery, G. *Cognitive therapy of depression: A treatment manual.* Philadelphia: Center for Cognitive Therapy, 1978.

Bedrosian, R. C. Strategies of task presentation and self-monitoring behavior (Doctoral dissertation, Miami University, 1977). *Dissertation Abstracts International,* 1978, *38*, 9B, 4439.

Bergin, A. E., & Suinn, R. M. Individual psychotherapy and behavior therapy. In M. R. Rosenzweig & L. W. Porter (Eds.), *Annual Review of Psychology,* 1975, *26*, 509–556.

Ellis, A. *How to live with a "neurotic" at home and at work.* New York: Crown, 1975.

Ellis, A. Review of *Cognitive therapy and the emotional disorders* by A. T. Beck. *Behavior Therapy,* 1977, *8*, 295–296.

Frank, J. D. *Persuasion and healing.* Baltimore: Johns Hopkins Press, 1961.

Frank, J. D. Therapeutic components of psychotherapy. *Journal of Nervous and Mental Disease,* 1974, *159*, 325–342.

Heitler, J. B. Preparatory techniques in initiating expressive psychotherapy with lower-class, unsophisticated clients. *Psychological Bulletin,* 1976, *81*, 339–352.

Horney, K. *Neurosis and human growth: The struggle toward self-realization.* New York: Norton, 1950.

Kanfer, F., & Saslow, G. Behavioral analysis: An alternative to diagnostic classification. *Archives of General Psychiatry,* 1965, *12*, 529–538.

Kant, I. (*The classification of mental disorders.*) Konigsberg, Germany: Nicolovius, 1798.

Kelly, G. *The psychology of personal constructs.* New York: Norton, 1955.

Ledwidge, B. Cognitive behavior modification: A step in the wrong direction? *Psychological Bulletin,* 1978, *85*, 353–375.

Mahoney, M. J. *Cognition and behavior modification.* Cambridge, Mass.: Ballinger, 1974.

Mahoney, M. J. Reflections on the cognitive learning trend in psychotherapy. *American Psychologist,* 1977, *32*, 5–13.

Meichenbaum, D. *Cognitive-behavior modification: An integrative approach.* New York: Plenum, 1977.

Newton, J. Considerations for the psychotherapeutic technique of symptom scheduling. *Psychotherapy: Theory, Research and Practice,* 1968, *5*, 95–103.

Raimy, V. *Misunderstandings of the self.* San Francisco: Jossey-Bass, 1975.

Schuyler, D. Cognitive therapy: Some theoretical origins and therapeutic implications. *International Mental Health Research Newsletter,* 1973, *15*, 12–16.

Shaw, B. F., & Hollon, S. *Cognitive therapy in a group format with depressed outpatients.* Unpublished manuscript, University of Western Ontario, 1978.

Sullivan, H. S. *The interpersonal theory of psychiatry.* New York: Norton, 1953.

A Manual for
a Cognitive Therapy

VICTOR RAIMY

While discussing standards for evaluating systems of psychotherapy in his 1976 book, *Cognitive Therapy and the Emotional Disorders*, Beck wrote that "the system of psychotherapeutic procedures should be well defined and clearly and explicitly described." In the present chapter, Beck and Bedrosian have done just that. In a relatively brief compass they have brought together in a highly organized fashion the basic principles and techniques necessary for understanding and practicing Beck's particular approach to cognitive therapy. Although most everything relating to therapeutic procedures found in this chapter can also be found in Beck's 1976 book, the present format makes his system far more accessible to those who seriously wish to employ or evaluate his approach to treatment.

The value of such a manual as this should not be underestimated. It not only provides novice and experienced therapists with highly specific and concrete descriptions of therapy procedures, but it also greatly facilitates opportunities for research on the approach. Some years ago B. F. Skinner (1957) pointed out that the "engineering" aspects of a theory or model are equally important with the development of the theory itself. Bedrosian and Beck have thus provided both clinician and researcher with a lucid,

VICTOR RAIMY • 6770 Hawaii Kai Drive, Honolulu, Hawaii 96825.

specific, and concrete blueprint for practicing and evaluating one of the most recent arrivals on the therapeutic scene.

Although the utilization of cognitive principles in psychotherapy is often thought to be a strictly modern invention (except perhaps for Adler), the fundamental proposition that psychological disturbances are due primarily to faulty thinking has been a central or peripheral consideration ever since the hypnotists of the last century anchored their treatments in attempts to "expunge faulty ideas from the mind." Unfortunately, most of the older therapists obscured the role of cognition in their treatments by the directional sets imposed by other principles that they honored more highly, and by the lack of systematic attention to the cognitive hypotheses they themselves employed. For cognition has been accorded only a very minor role in human behavior until recently. One might even conjecture that Pascal's 17th century observation that, "Man is a reed, the weakest in nature, but he is a thinking reed" had been perversely corrupted to mean that thinking, not man, is the weakest reed in nature.

As Bedrosian and Beck point out in their introduction, however, those who placed their faith, as did Pascal, in the power of the thought have flourished through the years, albeit somewhat obscurely as far as the mainstream of psychotherapy was concerned. Alfred Adler, Albert Ellis (1962), and George Kelly (1955), to mention only a few, were clearly engaged in some form of cognitive therapy. Even the Freudians often concentrate on cognitive modification in treatment.

The advent of very recent cognitive approaches brings with it something that the pre-1950 cognitive therapies lacked—systematic attention to the developing of cognitive tools that could be tied directly to the cognitive principles undergirding the approach. Although, as I have pointed out elsewhere (Raimy, 1975), the noncognitive therapies have contributed a vast number of techniques for uncovering and modifying distorted cognitions, the systematic explication of these techniques as cognitive has but rarely been attempted. Bedrosian and Beck, however, are now rapidly making up for such neglect. Their identification in Chapter 5 of this book of ten "Common Types of Cognitive Distortions" (pp. 132–134) as well as their six "Techniques for Changing Negative Cognitions" (pp. 143–149), while certainly not exhaustive of either realm, is an excellent foundation not only for explaining how a cognitive therapist thinks, but also in providing a useful vocabulary for studying what happens in a cognitive approach.

Not all proponents of cognitive therapy remain as consistently cognitive as do Bedrosian and Beck. That marvelous self-contradiction, "cognitive behaviorism," still attracts the fancy of those loath to give up conditioning as a first principle in the acquisition and dissolution of psychological disturbance. Bedrosian and Beck, however, have incorporated "behavioral techniques" and "behavioral experiments" into their procedures primarily as cognitive aids.

Critics of any cognitive approach to therapy often voice two primary objections to the cognitive assumptions. They often question whether the therapist can readily distinguish between what Beck refers to as dysfunctional thoughts and the more realistic thoughts that produce adaptive behavior. Also questioned is the assumption that the patient's interpretation of events must be accepted as "basic 'rock-bottom' data."

Other cognitive therapists, as well as Bedrosian and Beck, rarely question their ability to discriminate between their patients' rational and irrational thoughts. Instead, the typical attitude seems to be that while not infallible in making such discriminations, most of the time they are right. If mistakes are made, they believe they can be rectified with the help of the patient. One explanation for the cognitive therapist's apparently naive assumption lies in the fact that therapists, much like everyone else, spend most of their lives, personally as well as professionally, distinguishing fact from reality in others as well as themselves. As William McDougall (1923) phrased it in another context, these skills "become delicately responsive in an extraordinary degree, as well as very strong through much exercise." The issue is, however, one that can be subjected to objective research.

Research would be far more difficult if not impossible on the other assumption that the patient's interpretations are basic to the understanding of his behavior. The veracity of the patient's report could obviously be studied, but the "basic data" for any psychological model depends upon the axioms of that model. Thus if one holds as axiomatic the primacy of unconscious drives in the display of behavior, the phenomenological assumptions of the cognitive therapist make little sense.

Since Beck dealt more thoroughly with this second assumption in his 1976 book (Chapter 2), the justification is presented only scantily in the present chapter. In view of the known complexity of human thinking, readers may well question the statement that the patient's interpretations are rock-bottom data. They are, of course, correct. One of the reasons why therapy is often prolonged is that the patient's cognitions, even when reported accurately, are often contradictory, resulting in the confusion that is often the hallmark of mental disturbance. Harry Stack Sullivan (1953) pointed out a quarter of a century ago that paratactic distortions acquired in early childhood often persist unchanged into adulthood. Of greatest interest, however, is Sullivan's insistence that more accurate but contradictory conceptions of the distorted experience were also learned during development, yet the patient frequently behaved in accord with the faulty belief. Sullivan's observation that a paratactic distortion often exists side by side with a more correct belief can be verified by any therapist who takes the time to examine his patient's thinking in this respect. Thus, even though the cognitive therapist assumes that the patient's revealed beliefs are basic data, the basic data are often presented in a highly complex fashion.

Even though there are now considerable data attesting to the effectiveness of cognitive therapy (Ellis & Grieger, 1977; Meichenbaum, 1977; Rush, Beck, Kovacs, & Hollon, 1977), there is still much for cognitive therapists to do before they can rest content. We still need to know how effective cognitive therapy is in comparison with other approaches. There is also the most basic question that few if any therapies have attempted to answer—what is the essence of cognitive therapy which distinguishes it from other therapies? What irreducible principles define the realm of this approach? My own guess is that there can be a multitude of cognitive approaches varying greatly in the manner in which they are applied. Despite the strength of a conviction, distorted or otherwise, beliefs can be modified under many different circumstances.

REFERENCES

Beck, A. T. *Cognitive therapy and the emotional disorders*. New York: International Universities Press, 1976.

Ellis, A. *Reason and emotion in psychotherapy*. New York: Lyle Stuart, 1962.

Ellis, A., & Grieger, R. *Handbook of rational-emotive therapy*. New York: Springer, 1977.

Kelly, G. A. *The psychology of personal constructs* (Vols. I & II). New York: Norton, 1955.

McDougall, W. *An introduction to social psychology*. New York: Scribner, 1923.

Meichenbaum, D. H. *Cognitive behavior modification: An integrative approach*. New York: Plenum, 1977.

Raimy, V. *Misunderstandings of the self: Cognitive psychotherapy and the misconception hypothesis*. San Francisco: Jossey-Bass, 1975.

Rush, A. J., Beck, A. T., Kovacs, M., & Hollon, S. Comparative efficacy of cognitive therapy and pharmacotherapy in the treatment of depressed patients. *Cognitive Therapy and Research*, 1977, *1*, 17–38.

Skinner, B. F. *Verbal behavior*. New York: Appleton-Century-Crofts, 1957.

Sullivan, H. S. *The psychiatric interview*. New York: Norton, 1953.

Chapter 6

Psychotherapy and the Structure of Personal Revolutions

MICHAEL J. MAHONEY

It is perhaps not uncommon to feel uncomfortable about discussing something when one is sorely aware of the incompleteness of one's understanding. At the same time, there is more than a kernel of truth in the notion that one's ignorance—or at least one's awareness of it—may be an important element in furthering theoretical developments. New insights may lead to better understanding, and they also tend to reveal new challenges and whole panoramas of unexplored issues. In preparing this chapter, I have struggled with a variety of questions and dilemmas that relate to my own limited understanding. Should I remain conservatively close to the data and focus on assertions of which I am confident, or should I freely expand on some emerging and more speculative conjectures? For better or for worse, the editor of this volume influenced my decision by requesting "think pieces" and encouraging contributors to ramble freely in their thoughts and impressions of therapeutic process and procedure. At his insistence, I shall therefore offer some speculations about several issues. In accord with the request to emphasize conceptual over empirical issues, I have attempted to free my remarks as much as possible from the bondage of extant data. This has led

MICHAEL J. MAHONEY • Department of Psychology, The Pennsylvania State University, University Park, Pennsylvania 16802.

me, at several places, to offer conjectures that I would usually reserve for the kinds of informal communication that are often associated with elevated blood alcohol. Likewise, as is already apparent, I have taken the liberty of employing personal pronouns somewhat liberally—perhaps to communicate that my remarks are personal conjectures rather than adamant pronouncements.

Before I proceed to my remarks, I would like to preface them with a few comments that may place them in perspective. When I began my psychological education, I started from a familiar point—psychoanalysis. My interest and enthusiasm for dynamic approaches was short-lived, however, and I was soon swept up in operant psychology. My respect for the empirical and applied commitments of behavior modifiers has been enduring, and it was further reinforced when I moved into a social-learning framework. The role of cognitive processes in human adjustment and distress became my primary interest, and for the past several years I have been wearing the uniform of a "cognitive behavior modifier" or "cognitive therapist." Beliefs have a way of changing, however, and this chapter represents my first formal discussion of any real concerns about the conceptual adequacy of current cognitive social-learning approaches. In the pages that follow, I shall briefly sketch some of those concerns and outline some of the issues that are in the forefront of my own shifting attention. For their impact on my beliefs—both past and present—I am indebted to a number of colleagues. The publication of their names would be superfluous to most of them, but I would like to at least express my gratitude in print. I have valued their stimulation and I am grateful for their continuing support of my attempts to remain flexible and uncommitted in my intellectual undertakings. The struggle to avoid strong theoretical investments is, I believe, a very difficult one. However, while the life of an intellectual gypsy may not afford the comforts of a conceptual home, it does offer a richness of experience and an appreciation of movement that are at least partially compensatory.

CONCERNS ABOUT CURRENT COGNITIVE THERAPIES

I chose to focus first on concerns about current cognitive and cognitive-behavioral therapies for at least two reasons: (1) they are the therapies with which I have been most closely associated, and (2) they are, I believe, on the cutting edge of current empirical developments and refinements in psychotherapy. I have, in fact, defended these therapies against several recent attacks and continue to view them as some of the most promising and research-worthy candidates among contemporary contenders. My remarks are thus intended to be constructively self-critical and intellectually honest. While enjoying the excitement and apparent promise of cognitive approaches to psychotherapy, I have become increasingly aware of what I consider shortcomings in their conceptualization and treatment of human distress. Since the efficacy of these procedures has been examined elsewhere (Mahoney & Arnkoff, 1978; Meichenbaum, 1977), I shall restrict my comments to theoretical issues and their procedural ramifications.

Theoretical Issues

I continue to endorse what is perhaps the first premise of most contemporary cognitive therapies—namely, that human adjustment and maladjustment are often a reflection of underlying cognitive processes. Although studies bearing on this assumption warrant continuing refinement, the extant data offer considerable corroboration. I am more concerned with other aspects of the theoretical substrate that appears to underly cognitive approaches. For the sake of exposition, I shall list them before briefly elaborating each concern. It is my opinion that, at the present time, cognitive and cognitive-behavioral therapies:

1. Tend to overlook, disregard, and sometimes openly attack the potential importance of unconscious processes.
2. Tend to view feelings narrowly, as phenomenal artifacts that are to be controlled rather than experienced.
3. Are poorly integrated with *current* theories of cognition.
4. Place an excessive emphasis on the isomorphism between words and beliefs.
5. Place an excessive emphasis on the role of rationality in adaptation.
6. Implicitly endorse a judgmental distinction between therapist and client.
7. Are developing a potentially dangerous orthodoxy and defensiveness.

These are complicated issues, to be sure, and each warrants at least brief elaboration.

Unconscious Processes. There are many possible reasons why the cognitive therapist might be biased against unconscious processes—the most striking of which may be their association with an ideological competitor (psychoanalysis). That such a bias exists is evident from the fact that many of the most eminent cognitive-behavioral theorists today are quite reticent about the importance of unconscious processes. This silence is intriguing in that a recent survey suggests that many of these same people report an appreciation of the possible significance of these processes (Mahoney,

1978a). Unconscious factors are nevertheless rarely explored in contemporary cognitive-behavioral writing. Beck's (1976) "automatic thoughts" have come closest to an acknowledgment of unconscious cognition, and yet it is clear from his writing that this concession is not meant to imply an extensive network or system of unconscious beliefs.

For reasons that will be elaborated in a moment, I would argue that the existence of such a network is not only possible but very probable, and that the practical implications are both challenging and inescapable. I am not here advocating a psychoanalytic formulation of that network and I think it is important to remember that unconscious processes were postulated long before Freud (Ellenberger, 1970). I believe it is reasonable, however, to assert that many of the idiosyncratic acquired rules that direct a person's behavior are rarely "accessible" to them. This is obviously a bold, if not blasphemous, assertion by someone who alleges to have been trained as a behavior modifier. Before sharing some of my reasons for tendering it, however, I think it may be worth relating that my current receptiveness to possible unconscious processes did not evolve either rapidly or painlessly. Those who have endured an orthodox behavioral bootcamp can probably relate to the negative terms that are there associated with discussions of the "unconscious"—viz., Freud, mentalism, lack of scientific rigor, and so on. It was therefore with great trepidation that I first explored the cogency of such assumptions as:

1. Unconscious processes are unscientific.
2. The espousal of unconscious processes necessarily implies an endorsement of *all* of Freud's (or anyone else's) assertions.
3. Unconscious processes are unimportant considerations in understanding or treating human distress.

The first assumption was easy to reject. This was also the case with the second, but I was impressed with my own former (unconscious?) failure to challenge it.

The third assumption is perhaps the most important because it bears an empirical implication—viz., either (a) unconscious processes have been shown to be unimportant, or (b) they have not been shown to be important. These are, of course, different implications. The former denotes a blanket rejection based on exhaustive research with all possible unconscious processes. This is obviously inaccurate. The second implication is at least more conservative in that it only argues that the extant data on extant notions of the unconscious have failed to suggest its importance. To evaluate the validity of this assertion one must, of course, ask such questions as "How extensive is the extant research?" "How rigorous is that research?" and "What tentative conclusions seem to be warranted?" It would be impossible to survey the relevant literature in a volume (let alone a chapter) and I shall make no pretense to being familiar with the intricacies of such an expansive domain. What I have sampled has left me with the impression that methodological rigor has often been lacking and that the more rigorous inquiries have only rarely demonstrated clinically significant promise. I would hasten to add, however, that the vast majority of these studies have emanated from analytic and neoanalytic theorizing. The indictment of the latter, if it is warranted, does not logically entail a blanket rejection of all unconscious processes.

I have purposely postponed discussing the definition of the term "unconscious," partly to demonstrate the very point I am making. Whether you, the reader, are amenable, adverse, or equivocal to the possible importance of this topic, your reading of the last few pages will have almost certainly involved cognitive and perceptual processes of which you were unaware. At the most superficial level, you were probably unaware of your eye movements, page turning, and continued life support functions (respiration, digestion, etc.). Less apparent, perhaps, were some of your tacit assumptions about what you were reading—e.g., that I was using the term "unconscious" in a traditional (or nontraditional) manner, that its *meaning* was the same each time it was used, and that I was referring to Sigmund Freud rather than Anna. A critic might readily argue that these are trivial matters that can be made "conscious" by a simple shift of attention. It is, after all, a trite point to say that a person is only partially aware of the vast number of sensations that could be attended to in a given instant. Our limited attentional mechanisms force us to focus selectively on a small subset of the experiential options. We must be careful, however, not to presume that all unconscious processes are potentially conscious.

But now we are back to terminology. What is meant by the terms "conscious" and "unconscious"? This distinction is a familiar one to those who believe in it and a foreign one to those who do not. Neither spends much time trying to spell out a definition. For the sake of discussion, however, we can adopt the somewhat restrictive definition employed during the lengthy debate on the role of "awareness" in learning (cf. Bandura, 1969; Grings, 1973). That is, we can equate consciousness with the person's ability to verbalize something. This definition is problematic for several reasons that are perhaps far afield from the point being made here. It is clear that people often *demonstrate* an awareness that they cannot verbally *communicate* (e.g., in recognition memory and the tip-of-the tongue state). This may be one of the reasons that such skills as shoelace-tying are so hard to teach unless demonstration is added to verbal instruction. The inadequacy of words as an index of awareness is perhaps unnecessary to defend (Polanyi, 1966). More challenging is the assertion that some of the information retained by our nervous systems is very primitive and partially inaccessible via language. This possibility is suggested by several lines of theory and evidence.

First, humans have been "thinking" much longer than they have been verbalizing. The development of language and a shared symbol system was, to be sure, a significant one and there can be little doubt that some of our thought patterns are as much the slave as the master of language. It is important to recognize, however, that human memory and nonverbal "reasoning" were apparent long before the emergence of words. Likewise—and perhaps more importantly—it is very unlikely that language development marked the end of more primitive thinking modes. As much as we sometimes might like to, we cannot forget that we are animals whose brains show the clear vestiges of very slow evolution (Jaynes, 1977; Jerison, 1973; MacLean, 1973). The higher cortical functions are a relatively recent development and still account for an unknown proportion of our memory and thinking. Mental images (visual and otherwise) may be more primitive in their processing—a possibility that is consistent with the notable persistence of some forms of visual (versus verbal) memory and the evolutionary priority of vision over audition. The extent and possible significance of nonverbal fantasy is also increasingly apparent (Klinger, 1971; Singer, 1974), and it is clear that mental images can convey propositional information (Lang, 1977).

A second argument for the consideration of unconscious processes comes from continuing research on hemispheric specialization (cf. Davidson, 1978; Galin, 1974; Ornstein, 1972; Schwartz, Davidson, & Maer, 1975). Even though the average person does not walk around with the divided consciousness of a split-brain patient, it seems increasingly apparent that an intact corpus callosum is hardly a guarantee of symmetrical consciousness. It is now widely agreed that the left hemisphere is more "verbal" and logical than the right. More recent and controversial are conjectures that the right hemisphere may play a differential role in at least some categories of affect and in nonverbal fantasy. Is the right hemisphere more primitive or less conscious? A confident affirmation of that question could have far-reaching practical implications. It would, for example, encourage further explorations of therapies that take into account the primary hemispheric involvement (e.g., Davidson, 1978; Tucker, Shearer, & Murray, 1977). Although somewhat simplistic, it would also suggest that a focal issue in consciousness involves the left hemisphere's ongoing attempts to "understand" and verbalize the activities and memories of the right hemisphere.

A third argument for the possible importance of unconscious processes stems from the fact that a significant portion of human learning is conveyed nonverbally. Bandura (1977) has aptly noted that there are four primary sources of learning: (1) direct associative experience, (2) vicarious experience, (3) symbolic instruction, and (4) symbolic logic. Note that only two of these invoke symbolic communication. The preverbal child obviously learns to adapt without being able to verbalize the contingencies. Nonverbal experiences—especially affective ones—continue throughout the lifespan and are probably retained in a memory form that is only partially accessible via linguistic searches. We may try to describe the intensity of an adolescent romance, but words are seldom adequate. Visual mementos, fantasies, and an associated song usually elicit much more of the original affect than a simple verbal inquiry.

A fourth argument hinges on the widely acknowledged phenomenon of decreased awareness during extensive use of a skill. In many forms of cognitive and motoric skill acquisition, the person may begin in a state of constant vigilance and self-instruction. The novice driver is a case in point. After refinement and extensive practice, a relatively complex skill can become so automatic that the person can carry on other cognitive activities while performing. Some skills become so automatic that they are very difficult to describe verbally (e.g., shoelace-tying). The point here is that our brains seem to be capable of developing a cognitive shorthand that allows us to execute a well-practiced skill with little or no awareness. Beck (1976) has hypothesized that this same trend toward automaticity is evident in many clients whose maladaptive thinking patterns have become habitual and automatic. It is not far from here to the conjecture that many of the thought patterns and reasoning skills developed in childhood may become relatively automatic and difficult to identify. This may be one of the reasons for the apparent promise of strategies that force the client to reconstruct and appraise habitual thought patterns.

It is important to note here that the battle over the role of awareness in learning has little to do with the assertion that at least some of our functional memory has poor verbal accessibility. I continue to agree with Bandura's (1969) assertion that awareness (i.e., the ability to verbalize contingencies) is a facilitative, but not essential, factor in learning. There is a substantial difference between learning and retention, however. The points being made here are that (a) we probably learn much more than we can verbalize; (b) unless we practice verbalizing them, many of our motor and cognitive skills tend to become progressively less accessible to language; and (c) stored information does not have to be communicable to exert an influence on our thoughts, feelings, or actions.

A fifth and, for this chapter, final defense of unconscious processes comes from clinical and phenomenological reports (e.g., Hilgard, 1977). The hard-nosed experimentalist has often been skeptical of such phenomena as hypnosis and other altered states of consciousness (Tart, 1969). The reasons for that skepticism are perhaps less relevant here than its wisdom.

It is very difficult to account for many of these phenomena without recourse to a discussion of different cognitive systems or mechanisms that are associated with different kinds of awareness and control. The empirical bankruptcy of such notions as repression and perceptual defense are perhaps all too apparent (Dixon, 1971; Holmes, 1974). There are possible explanations for the impotence of these pioneering concepts (Sackeim & Gur, 1978) and, in any case, they do not automatically invalidate a host of other phenomena. If unconscious factors are indeed an empirical illusion, we must at least be impressed with their tenacious clutch on the imagination of psychologists. Their intuitive importance is aptly summarized by William James in his own phenomenological explorations:

> Our normal waking consciousness, rational consciousness as we call it, is but one special type of consciousness, whilst all about it, parted from it by the filmiest of screens, there lie potential forms of consciousness entirely different. . . . No account of the universe in its totality can be final which leaves these other forms of consciousness quite disregarded. (1901/1958, p. 298)

Since this section is already quite lengthy, I shall conclude it with one brief comment. Unconscious processes may or may not be important in human distress and adaptation. It is my personal conjecture at this point in time that they are probably more important than has been acknowledged by cognitive-behavioral theorists. There are, of course, good reasons for being cautious in this domain if only because of the inferential complexities entailed. It may be the case that the inferential risks involved in unconscious conjectures could be more than compensated for by their empirical returns. The apparent reluctance of workers in this area to remain open to this possibility may itself be costly. As has been amply demonstrated in the annals of science, researchers tend to find what they are looking for—and to overlook what they don't expect (Mahoney, 1976). We have just witnessed two decades of operant research in which cognitive factors were excluded from study on the *a priori* grounds that they were unimportant. The operant researcher seldom "saw" any cognitive influence partly because he or she seldom looked for it. I would like to think that cognitive researchers will not repeat this scenario in the appraisal of unconscious processes.

Feelings. Although feelings serve as the common "entry point" for almost all forms of therapy, they occupy very different roles depending on the ideological perspective of the therapist. In most contemporary cognitive approaches, feelings are viewed as the products (or by-products) of thoughts. As such, they are to be controlled by the appropriate modification of the latter. In addition, there is a clear bias against "evocative" therapies, the concept of catharsis, and the idea that feelings are somehow "stored" or retained by the person. This latter bias may also stem from the generalized avoidance of anything remotely associated with psychodynamic formulations. It is interesting to note that the cognitive therapist seems comfortable with the "storage" of information, but is reluctant to extend the storage metaphor to feelings.

Several important questions come to mind in exploring this issue. For example, how is one to discount the widely reported subjective enjoyment when a person is encouraged to express or experience a formerly inhibited emotion? There are, of course, conceptual alternatives to the hydraulic reservoir model employed in psychoanalysis, and it might be worthwhile to explore briefly the potential importance of affect and some kinds of affective expression in psychotherapy.

First, reports of subjective relief after affective expression seem to cluster around "negative" affect (e.g., anger and anxiety). One might postulate then that such expressions may help to establish or affirm an empathic and accepting relationship between therapist and client. Likewise, if the individual is afraid to experience or express some category of affect, one might expect that disinhibitory exercises would result in sensations of relief. This might be the case in instances where, for example, the individual is afraid to be angry or anxious. Many persons who fear "losing control" may be communicating a fear of the affective expressions involved. For the individual who tacitly assumes that negative feelings are personal flaws, any signs of dysphoria may themselves be alarming. In these cases it may be more therapeutic initially to encourage the client to experience these feelings (rather than avert or control them). Just as the snake phobic may benefit from graduated exposure to a serpent, the feeling phobic may be aided by a similar exposure to his or her feelings.

A third possibility is that there may be an emotional parallel to the Zeigarnik effect. This conjecture suggests that the "unfinished business" referred to by the gestalt therapist may have to do with the completion (or closure) of a previously interrupted sequence. If the sequence involved a strong affect element and this was originally denied expression, it is *possible* that its expression might be subjectively satisfying or otherwise therapeutic. It would, in fact, be consistent with the apparent impact of evocative techniques in the treatment of severe grief reactions (e.g., Gauthier & Marshall, 1977). This conjecture is not far afield from Freud's notions of repetition compulsion and abreaction. I would not, however, endorse the idea of diffusely stored feelings that accumulate and "spill over" into symptomatic expressions. More tenable is the notion that "catharsis" is not the discharge of amorphous energy but rather the expression of previously inhibited affect associated with a given belief or memory. Since autonomic nervous system (ANS) arousal can interfere with central nervous system (CNS) processing, it is possible that such expressions may actually facilitate belief change if they reduce the arousal and its CNS interference.

It is worth noting here that many contemporary models of human behavior imply that our experience can be neatly divided into three realms—thought, feeling, and action. These are, after all, congruent with the major anatomical divisions of the nervous system. While I would endorse the importance of integrating our psychological models with physiological knowledge, I question whether the above-mentioned tripartite can be defended on a neurological basis. Survival-relevant memories are not likely to be "purely cognitive" and it is virtually impossible to separate the three realms in any pragmatic analysis. The cognitive therapist can no more work exclusively on a cognition than the evocative or behavior therapist can work exclusively on a feeling or behavior, respectively. Whatever else a propositional memory may be, it is probably a complicated entity that must be activated en masse—i.e., with informational, affective, and behavioral implications. Interestingly, orthodox specialists believe that producing change in their pet element will effect changes in the other two and rare is the counselor who addresses all three in a balanced fashion.

A fourth argument for the possible importance of feelings in therapy has to do with the primitive and relatively dominating role of affect in human experience. Our negative feelings are partly signals of (as well as reactions to) perceived threats or challenges in our life. Given two beliefs of equal subjective credibility, I would predict that the one with stronger sympathetic correlates will usually dominate. This is, of course, quite reasonable from an evolutionary and survival perspective since the vigilant and apprehensive organism is probably more likely to survive (albeit timorously) than the more complacent one. This may also explain why extreme autonomic arousal tends to override intellectual processes. As most therapists would probably acknowledge, it is usually futile to try to rationalize with a hysterical client. Until the autonomic arousal is brought within an acceptable range, very little cognitive processing is possible. Likewise, a single traumatizing experience can sometimes override thousands of nontraumatic exposures and produce a painful parallel to the gambler's fallacy—i.e., that past trials notwithstanding, it is the *next* trial that will bring trauma.

Finally, there is the possibility that at least some human learning is state dependent.[1] By this I mean that the anxious client may be most receptive to change when he or she is anxious and the depressed client may learn to deal with depression more effectively if the depression is present. This does not negate the earlier point of CNS override when ANS arousal is excessive, but it suggests that a moderate degree of relevant dysphoria may actually facilitate the acquisition of insight and appropriate coping skills. This conjecture, if valid, would raise serious questions about the wisdom of

---

[1] I am indebted to Diane B. Arnkoff, Aaron T. Beck, and Michael Gelder for conversations that contributed to these conjectures.

striving to avoid even mild dysphoria during therapy. It would also rein-troduce the earlier issue of amorphous versus specific affect. Generating a particular emotional state may be helpful in the sense that it affords practice of coping skills that could be useful during a naturalistic experience of that emotion. This is, in fact, the fundamental assumption underlying the current "coping skills therapies" (Mahoney & Arnkoff, 1978). More intri-guing, however, is the possibility that some of the cognitive elements associated with dysphoria (negative affect) are most easily identified (and perhaps altered) when the person is experiencing that dysphoria. The entire constellation may have to be reintegrated in order to deal with any of its components. This would again challenge the conventional practice of avoid-ing dysphoria during cognitive-behavioral therapy.

More important than any specific conjectures on the nature of affective processes in psychotherapy, however, is the general prejudice against them that is now apparent in cognitive quarters. Almost all therapists "attend to" client's feelings and, indeed, use them as guideposts and progress markers during counseling. More at issue is the presumed nature and treatment of emotional experiences. At this point in time there is a strong and perva-sive assumption among cognitive-behavioral therapists that feelings are phenomena to be controlled (rather than expressed). The empirical warrant for this assumption is, I think, just as sparse as that of its near opposite (viz., that the expression of feelings is *sufficient* for the success of therapy). With some conceptual flexibility we might be better prepared to examine empirically those persons and situations in which affective expression (versus control) might facilitate therapeutic changes.

Current Cognitive Theories. Since this point is more extensively dis-cussed in Arnkoff's chapter in this volume, a very brief statement will perhaps suffice. Where they lay claim to any theoretical model at all, cogni-tive therapists tend to adopt a sensory information-processing perspective. This approach is evident in my own earlier writing (Mahoney, 1974) and in Bower's recent attempt to integrate cognitive theory and therapy (Bower, 1978). The inadequacies of such models are outlined by Weimer (1977) in his comparison of sensory and motor theories of cognition. The latter are illustrated in the works of Gibson (1966), Hayek (1952), Turvey (1974), and others (cf. Weimer, 1977; Weimer & Palermo, 1974). Motor theories basically argue that the brain is more constructive than tradtional sensory models have asserted. Rather than being a relatively passive repository of sensations and associations, it is an actively creative organ that constructs (rather than copies) a map of the world:

> What the motor metatheory asserts is that there is no sharp separation between sensory and motor components of the nervous system which can be made on functional grounds and that the mental or cognitive realm is intrinsically motoric, like all the nervous system. The mind is intrinsically

> a motor system, and the sensory order by which we are acquainted with
> external objects as well as ourselves . . . is a product of what are, correctly
> interpreted, constructive motor skills. (Weimer, 1977, p. 272)

Although this model does not equate "motor" with "behavior," it is
noteworthy that the latter can play a significant role in the brain's construction of reality. This is, of course, congruent with the emphasis on the power
of behavioral performance in cognitive-behavioral therapies (Mahoney,
1977).

Although they clearly warrant more extensive scrutiny, it looks as
though contemporary motor theories may be superior to their sensory com-
petitors in terms of (a) their compatability with modern knowledge in
neuroanatomy and physiology, (b) their ability to handle the concepts of
consciousness and choice, (c) their compatability with an open (versus
closed) cybernetic system, and (d) their ability to encompass the concept of
"feedforward" as well as feedback. Feedforward deals with the organism's
active role as cocreator of the stimulation to which it is responsive. Cognitive-behavioral therapists might therefore benefit from an exploration of
these conceptual alternatives to closed-loop computer models. The latter
have served an important heuristic function, but their limitations are now
more apparent than their assets.

Word-Belief Isomorphism. As is extensively reflected in their therapeutic procedures, cognitive therapists tend to place considerable confidence
in the ability of words to convey beliefs. In their defense, it might be pointed
out that one must work with what is available and words are clearly the
most practical form of interpersonal communication. On the other hand, I
have been repeatedly impressed by the ability of some therapists to identify
maladaptive client beliefs via less verbal assessments (e.g., fantasy, dream
report, and projectivelike exercises). It is easy to lapse into the habit of
literal listening and to assume that a person's introspective self-reports are
to be seen as undisputed reflections of their "inner life." It was thus with
some delight that I came across the following advice from George Kelly,
one of the pioneers of cognitive therapy:

> Often a beginning therapist finds it helpful to close his cerebral dictionary
> and listen primarily to the subcortical sounds and themes that run
> through his client's talk. Stop wondering what the words literally mean.
> Try to recall, instead, what it is they sound like. Disregard content for the
> moment; attend to theme. Remember that a client can abruptly change
> content—thus throwing a literal-minded therapist completely off the
> scent—but he rarely changes the theme so easily. Or think of these vocal
> sounds, not as words, but as preverbal outcries, impulsive sound gestures,
> stylized oral grimaces, or hopelessly mumbled questions. (1958, cited in
> Maher, 1969, p. 229)

One need not return to Freud's symptom–symbol assumption to appreciate
that a person's deep structure rules may be reflected as much in their non-

verbal behavior as in their attempts at self-description. Words are crude and inadequate labels for some of the neural processes we refer to as "thought." They are the imperfect reflection of processes that they, in turn, influence, and we can never hope to observe that process in the richness of its complexity.

Rationality. The term "rationality" has been extensively misused by some cognitive therapists, many of whom simultaneously consecrate it as the key to personal adjustment. As discussed by Bartley (1962), traditional views of rationality have been consistently self-contradictory in the sense of being unable to meet their own criteria. His "comprehensively critical rationalism" is unique in eschewing this embarrassment, but it is hardly a philosophy that lends itself to the authoritarian claims of prior rationalists. In its technical usage, "rationality" refers to a system of criteria or rules for making warranted inferences. Logic is one such set of rules. In the cognitive therapies, however, the term "rationality" has come to imply a naively simplistic form of "good reasoning." It is presumed that there is a "right" way to think—i.e., one which is rational and therefore "good." Wrong ("irrational") thinking patterns are said to lead to distress. Remedial training in rational thinking is the strategy of choice, and it is encouraged by what might be called the "poof myth"—viz., when a person is led to recognize the irrationality of his or her beliefs, this insight will itself cause the beliefs to vanish. In at least some individuals, this insight may fuel an already raging fire of self-denigration and self-preoccupation. Thus, Watts (1951) notes that:

> There is, indeed, a viewpoint from which this "rationalization" of life is not rational . . . seeing that it is unreasonable to worry does not stop worrying; rather, you worry the more at being unreasonable. (pp. 69–70)

He goes on to argue that the brain, and specifically the cortex, is often given disproportionate power over our everyday experience of reality. Although undeniably important in our survival, the cognitive processes of memory recall, planning, and rational evaluation may seduce us into concentrating on the symbolic constructions of past and future rather than the experiential reality of the present. In this analysis, rationality is adaptive only to the point that it maximizes (rather than supplants) our contact with reality. I am in particular agreement with this line of thinking in situations where the need to be rid of a problem is more distressing than the problem itself. This is, of course, a "higher order" cognitive pattern in the sense that the presumed culprits are not the beliefs that contribute to the problem so much as the beliefs that demand that it not be a problem.

Although I would hardly question the importance of human thought patterns in adjustment and maladjustment, the key role of rationality may require a much closer examination than it has been thus far accorded. Several contemporary theorists seem to concur that:

1. Irrational thought patterns cause psychological distress.
2. Rational thinking is more adaptive.
3. Rationality is (therefore) adaptive.

The empirical warrant for each of these assumptions is far from overwhelming. Although there is accumulating evidence that certain thought patterns may be associated with some kinds of psychological distress, it is not yet clear that the "rationality" of those patterns is of prime importance. A critic could easily cite data to the effect that ostensibly irrational thinking is often quite "adaptive" (e.g., in faith healing and some religious beliefs). Likewise, one could argue that rationality (in the nonpopular sense) may sometimes lead to (rather than reduce) distress. Philosophical inquiries into some of the mysteries of the human situation often lead, quite logically, to feelings of existential dysphoria. The point of all this is not to say that rationality is irrelevant, but only to suggest that our current conceptions of it are naive and that its role in adjustment has yet to be adequately evaluated. We need to draw a distinction between the *rationality* and *realism* of a belief and to explore the role of each in personal distress. The term "rationality" is here used to refer to the logical warrant for an inference whereas "realism" refers to its accurate description of the world.

A related issue here has to do with the processes of belief change. As noted above, many contemporary workers seem to assume that an insight into one's irrationality is sufficient for its elimination. An implicit notion has been that certain beliefs can be literally purged from one's system and that they can be "replaced" by more adaptive ones. This is probably a naive formulation at best and—although we are far from understanding the physiological changes that accompany belief change—I think we should remain open to the possibility that beliefs are never eradicated.[2] Although the evidence on memory permanence is still very controversial, it may be unwise to reject it out of hand (Penfield, 1975). Even if some memories are impermanent, though, it is possible that belief change is less a matter of extraction than distraction. That is, we may be modifying the prepotency of a belief rather than its literal existence in our nervous system. Belief-changing experiences may serve to reduce the strength or frequency with which a belief is activated, partly by strengthening an incompatible belief that serves to inhibit its competitor. Under circumstances that are as yet poorly understood, the old belief may be reactivated (in which case we observe clinical relapse). It might be heuristic—if only for the sake of brainstorming—to think of belief change in terms of internal *attentional* shifts. The belief that dictates momentary action and affect may be that which "commands" more tacit attention because of its strength, autonomic components, or the lack of

---

[2] I am again indebted to Diane B. Arnkoff, Aaron T. Beck, and Michael Gelder for conversations that contributed to these conjectures.

a competitor. Is it possible, then, that the literature on selective attention may have relevance for our understanding and refinement of belief change? This remains to be seen, but it is interesting that the concept of attention is itself gaining increased attention as an important factor in the regulation of arousal (e.g., Borkovec & O'Brien, 1977; Sarason, 1975).

Combining the above conjectures with the earlier ones on affect, one can ask whether belief change might be sometimes facilitated by procedures that supplement standard "rational reevaluation" strategies. Exploration of the sources of a belief could include nonverbal fantasies and the tracing of its roots to earlier (perhaps childhood) experience. This tracing might activate or facilitate the expression of associated affect. The rational (logical) evaluation of a belief may be a less significant component of change than the behavioral experiment that tests the reality (rather than rationality) of the belief. This would not necessarily imply that the rational analysis is a useless component since it may still function as a facilitator of the experimental performance. When a belief is rejected (as either irrational or unrealistic), this may occur either suddenly or gradually. The affective component is often more slow to change than the cognitive component—a phenomenon that is sometimes illustrated in the felt discrepancy between "head and heart." One final conjecture is that the proposal of a counter-belief may facilitate affective change more effectively than the simple rejection of the former belief. The reasons for this will be explored in a moment, but they relate primarily to the notion of competition among beliefs. Needless to say, all of the foregoing assertions are conjectural and warrant empirical scrutiny.

Judgmental Distinction. Since Diane Arnkoff and I are just now collecting data on this issue, I shall be brief and impressionistic on the implicit dichotomy between therapist and client in the cognitive therapies. Despite exciting research on the potential value of a fallible "coping" model over one which is perfect and masterful, it is my impression that many modern cognitive therapists continue to function out of a disease model. This is an irony which they share with behavior therapists who criticize such a model on the one hand and yet, on the other hand, manage to communicate that the people with problems are clients and the people with solutions are therapists. Despite their explicit endorsement of an educational model of intervention, many cognitive and behavior therapists seem to dichotomize the roles of teacher and learner. The implication seems to be that the teacher "knows it all" and that the therapist experiences no problems.

It is, in my opinion, very rare to find a person who does not occasionally experience at least modest amounts of distress. In an intervention model where the therapist is portrayed as a paragon of adjustment, the portrayal may not only be inaccurate but also stress producing (for both the therapist and client). The client may perceive an unrealistic discrepancy between his adjustment and that of his therapist, and the latter may suffer under the burden of a superhuman image. The stigma associated with experiencing personal problems is, I think, apparent in the reluctance of many graduate students to reveal these dilemmas to their advisers and the tendency of behavior therapists to seek private counseling from their nonbehavioral colleagues (Lazarus, 1971; Mahoney, 1978b). This same stigma is, I fear, all too apparent in the cognitive therapies as well.

Orthodoxy and Defensiveness. My concern here is with the zealous enthusiasm that has infiltrated cognitive quarters in the last few years. Enthusiasm is a necessary and valuable component in research, of course, but it can be dangerous when it is channeled into selective patterns of "confirmation," dogmatism, and defensiveness. This kind of channeling tends to encourage orthodoxy and isolationism, which, in turn, take their scientific toll. The beginnings of such developments are, I think, already apparent in some cognitive quarters. Ellis (1977), for example, has made the rather immodest claim that rational-emotive therapy (RET) has empirical support that is "immense—indeed almost awesome." This same spirit is discernible in other writers, and the seeds of elite isolationism seem to be sprouting. Thus, in the survey I mentioned earlier (Mahoney, 1978a) it was found that cognitive theorists were much less inclined to read both cognitive and behavioral literatures than were the eminent behaviorists surveyed. In a positive sense, this may reflect the fact that cognitive theorists have achieved an increasing sense of independence and confidence in their emerging paradigm. They may, in Kuhn's (1962) analysis, be on their way toward "normal science" activity.

On the other hand, this enthusiasm and orthodoxy may be excessive, premature, and potentially harmful. The storm and strife of paradigm revolution may make normal science a welcome arrival, but we should keep in mind that some of the most exciting insights occur during the perceptual semieclecticism that comes only during the transition from one paradigm to another. Once we trade our old bifocals for a new set, we have settled into a new way of contructing reality and we have given up the momentary glimpses of a variety of possible constructions that may have come in between. It is perhaps an individual matter, but I would prefer to proceed slowly with cautious optimism rather than rapidly with wild enthusiasm.

Procedural Issues

The foregoing theoretical issues are partially reflected in the procedures employed by contemporary cognitive therapies—and often in the procedures that they ignore or criticize. For the sake of exposition, I shall again list my concerns. At the present time, I believe that the cognitive and cognitive-behavioral therapies:

1. Tend to be unduly restrictive in their approach to the assessment of cognitive processes.
2. Are poorly suited to persons or problems that might be better served by an approach that includes the expression of feelings.
3. Are often mechanically focused on the surface structure content of thought rather than its deep-structural themes.
4. Are unduly restrictive in their use of intervention strategies.

Since some of these concerns may be clarified in the next section of the chapter, I will only briefly elaborate here.

There are, to be sure, innovations in the assessment of cognition that appear to be promising, but few of these go beyond the naive inadequacy of introspective self-report. Asking a person about the content of his or her thought may be helpful insofar as the person is honest and accurate in their reporting. However, I would argue that these sporadic samples of the stream of consciousness are sorely inadequate. The stream is wide and variable, and its contents may offer only a crude reflection of the deeper generative themes that direct experience. No single assessment mode is likely to be adequate, but a multimodal convergence may prove helpful. In this regard I believe the cognitive therapist might do well to consider supplementing self-reported thoughts with such assessment techniques as (a) an ongoing experiential diary, (b) dream reports, (c) projective fantasies, and (d) memory recall of personally significant experiences. The accurate identification of a person's most fundamental beliefs is, at best, an awesomely complex task, but I believe it can be better approximated through a wider range of cognitive assessment strategies than is presently employed. The use of nonverbal techniques may be particularly important in such assessment.

Although the role of affect in therapy remains poorly understood, there are few glimmers of insight or even interest emanating from current cognitive therapies. Likewise, it is not clear that the *control* of feelings should be the ultimate goal of intervention. Whatever else they may be, emotions are an integral part of human experience and it is probably naive to think that the higher parts of our brain should (or could) ever attain total control over the autonomic nervous system. Such a hierarchical goal is incompatible with the reciprocity of the ANS and the CNS, not to mention the holistic nature of our overall functioning. Instead of teaching our clients that feelings are things to be averted, regulated, or otherwise controlled, perhaps we should be suggesting that feelings are a unique part of what it is to be human. In such a conceptualization, emotions are not only reactions and signals, but also processes in their own right. The person may want to learn various skills that could influence both the experience and the expression of feelings, but this is hardly a therapeutic imperative. Choice then becomes a more relevant issue than control, and the person is correspondingly more free to experiment with a range of activity–passivity in affective experience.

My third and fourth concerns again relate to an excessive emphasis on surface structure content and reliance on a few cognitive change strategies. Since my elaboration of these concerns would preview some of my remarks in the next section, I shall simply move on to it.

SOME KUHNIAN CONJECTURES

Thus far in this chapter I have used my concerns about current cognitive-behavioral therapies as a vehicle for discussing issues that are in the forefront of my own theoretical attention. I should perhaps reiterate that I believe these therapies also represent some of the most promising recent developments in therapeutic refinements. My concerns can therefore be viewed as those of a cautious advocate rather than a caustic adversary. Whatever it is that we accomplish in therapy, I believe it is mediated by cognitive changes. Prevailing conceptions of therapeutic process and the necessary or facilitative conditions for improvement are, in my opinion, sorely inadequate. Once we have agreed that counseling is primarily an educational experience that involves alteration of relevant thought patterns, the theoretical consensus quickly diminishes. Thereafter, conjectures on the nature of therapy and its facilitative ingredients are so abundant as to be almost staggering. There is perhaps no other domain in the behavioral sciences which can claim such a multitude of models for the same phenomenon.

This theoretical surfeit is itself exacerbated by frequent confusions about the difference between a therapy and the procedures it dictates. Very few therapies can be isolated on the basis of unique procedures; most counselors draw from a common pool of techniques. More differentiating, perhaps, is the total schema and rationale into which these specific procedures are woven. Whether the efforts of psychotherapy researchers would be better spent on holistic evaluation of therapies or piecemeal evaluation of techniques is a question that will probably continue to fuel controversies for some time to come. The procedure of role reversal, for example, may have very different effects when it is removed from the context in which it would be used in gestalt therapy. On the other side of the coin, it is much easier to evaluate operationally specified techniques rather than such elusive phenomena as a multifaceted therapy. The latter is pragmatically more relevant to everyday practice but considerably more elusive in terms of methodological standardization.

I have no pat resolution for this dilemma, nor can I offer an integrative model that would condense our vast theoretical diversity into a succinct crystal of consensus. What I would like to share, however, is a conjecture that bears on both of these issues. I have long been impressed by some of the parallels between Thomas Kuhn's (1962) analysis of scientific revolutions and my own impressions of clinical change. In *The Structure of Scientific Revolutions*, Kuhn depicts how scientists' beliefs are challenged and changed during the course of ideological revolution. During "normal science," the core assumptions about an area of inquiry are taken for granted and the problems that exist are often viewed as peripheral nuisances. This is, I think, strikingly similar to the psychotherapy client who is satisfied with his or her fundamental beliefs (about self, life, work, etc.) but who would like some assistance in dealing with a relatively restricted problem (e.g., a specific phobia or minor skill deficit).

According to Kuhn, what leads to ideological revolution among scientists is the development of crises that threaten the core assumptions of the prevailing paradigm. These usually take the form of anomalous experiences (data) that contradict the predictions or assumptions of the paradigm. The cogency of its theoretical foundations are then placed in doubt and the period of crisis is marked by extensive emotionality, desperate attempts to salvage the system, and sometimes a retreat to blind faith in earlier assumptions. Interestingly, these assumptions are seldom realized (let alone evaluated) except during a phase of crisis—suggesting that they usually operate at a tacit level. The outcome of that evaluation is usually (1) continuing crisis, (2) reentrenchment, or (3) resolution through major changes in the core assumptions (revolution). Kuhn points out that revolution occurs only when an alternate paradigm is available, and that it is often accompanied by feelings of renewed confidence and an altered perception of the entire domain in question.

The clinical parallels to some of Kuhn's ideas are intriguing. Persons with minor or restricted problems, for example, seem to be comfortable with their core assumptions about reality; they are requesting peripheral adjustments in their system (e.g., coping skills). The psychotic individual is a good example of someone who has "revolted" against an old paradigm and whose core assumptions are at variance with those of society. The chronically anxious or depressed client may or may not exhibit signs of paradigm crisis. If their core beliefs are being challenged, paradigm crisis may be experienced. This might be the case in an instance where someone is facing the invalidity of the assumption that wealth brings happiness. The successful executive may experience the dysphoria of crisis when he or she realizes that many years of effort have been invested in a mythical contingency. For other individuals, the dysphoria may stem from their firm belief in the basic tenets of a maladaptive personal paradigm (e.g., one which assumes that they are helpless or inadequate). The core beliefs in a personal paradigm may be predominantly tacit and are perhaps best reflected in recurrent themes of behavior and affect. Since the cognitive foundations of one's place in (and relationship to) the world are probably developed in childhood, it would not be surprising if they were nonverbal and unrealistic. The inferential errors described by Beck (1970) are perhaps rooted in early childhood when superstitions and overgeneralizations abound. Such cognitive myths may become strongly ingrained through selective attention to their confirmation (Jones, 1976). Since they often involve very fundamental issues of existence—such as one's personal worth, worldly dangers, and one's warrant for hope—it would not be surprising if core beliefs were associated with strong feelings (e.g., of despair, anxiety, and so on). These beliefs, which form the foundational core of a person's ongoing experience, may be extremely difficult to verbalize, let alone modify. This is not to say that they are immutable, but only that they may be so tacit and pervasive that their identification and alteration probably requires powerful and perhaps extensive therapeutic experiences, many of which may need to be nonverbal. This latter conjecture suggests that techniques involving imagery or fantasy and motoric performance may be particularly promising in the alteration of core beliefs.

When a personal revolution does occur, one would expect it to be both painful and profound. There should be at least preliminary resistance to giving up old beliefs and perhaps a desperate attempt to salvage some of them. The absence of an alternative paradigm (belief system) would be expected to deter revolution. Thus, two of the primary functions of the therapist may be to (1) assist the client in perceiving or developing an alternate paradigm, and (2) guide the client through experiences that challenge the old paradigm. In one sense, then, the therapist may often be striving to induce (rather than reduce) crisis by orchestrating experiences that are anomalous with (and destructive of) a maladaptive personal paradigm. The goal may often be revolution rather than resolution. If it does occur, the revolution is probably pervasive—affecting many domains of everyday experience—and it might even involve *perceptual* changes as the person begins to construct reality from a different perspective. The phenomenology of a successful personal revolution is aptly portrayed by Walsh (1976) in his retrospective account of the changes he experienced during 20 months of therapy:

> One of the most wondrous discoveries of all was the slowly dawning awareness of a formerly subliminal, continuously changing stream of inner experience (p. 100). . . . As I spent more time tuning into my experience, my perceptual sensitivity increased (p. 101). . . . There were several changes in affect, in particular a reduction in anxiety and worrying and a concomitant increase in positive emotions (p. 103). . . . My self-image also began to alter (p. 104). . . . One unexpected but greatly appreciated change was an increase in energy (p. 105). . . . The catalytic nature of the therapy experience interacted with everything else in my life. . . . This voyage of discovery was the most incredible I've ever known. (p. 111)

Although there are points where the analogy falters, it is my impression that many of Kuhn's observations are relevant to our understanding of psychotherapy process. The initial pain, perceptual shifts, and eventual relief associated with successful personal revolutions are quite understandable if the individual's cognitive foundations are undergoing major upheaval. Likewise, it should not be surprising that more peripheral problems would require less extensive effort and are associated with more specific changes in adaptation. It is much easier to help an individual refine their coping skills than it is to guide them through a personality overhaul.

Some of the implications of the foregoing analogy can be translated into a number of emerging hypotheses:

1. A therapy is more likely to be effective when the person or problem demands peripheral (as opposed to core) changes in the person's adaptation paradigm; this implies that specific adjustment problems (e.g., phobias) should generally be more responsive to treatment than pervasive disorders (e.g., generalized anxiety, chronic depression, existential dilemmas, negative self-concept, the psychoses).
2. Although they are more difficult to achieve, core cognitive changes are probably facilitated by:
   a. Early intervention (e.g., in children)
   b. Use of nonverbal techniques (due to the nonverbal storage of some core assumptions)
   c. The perceived availability of an alternate belief system
   d. Awareness (or "insight") with regard to the core beliefs to be changed
   e. The performance of any behavior that is:
      i. Prohibited by prior assumptions about the self or world
      ii. Consistent with emerging assumptions about the self or world
      iii. Salient in its contradiction of (i) and corroboration of (ii)
      iv. Attributed to internal (personal) causes
3. A peripheral change is less likely to be enduring to the extent that it violates (and fails to successfully challenge) a core assumption.
4. Core belief changes, when they occur, will be associated with more pervasive and enduring shifts in affect, action, and thought.

Many of these assertions are illustrated, I believe, in the strategic moves of the effective therapist. Almost irrespective of ideological label, such a therapist often exhibits a strategic pattern that is consistent with much of the foregoing analysis. When peripheral changes are requested by the client and the performances or experiences do not (in the therapist's opinion) reflect a need for extensive personality restructuring, appropriate skills training exercises are usually offered (or the client is referred to a therapist who specializes in such training). When fundamental beliefs about the world or self are involved, however, it is not uncommon for the therapist to begin by establishing rapport, trust, and a communication of caring. Entering the client's "assumptive world" (Frank, 1961), the therapist does not initially attack the person's beliefs but rather encourages them to clarify some of the pervasive themes in their thinking (rules, scripts, etc.). When the latter are verbalized, the client is encouraged to explore their source as well as their predictions. In a sense, then, the therapist has climbed into the client's "normal science" framework and offers support and assistance in examining that structure and its alternatives. Acting more like a guide than a guru, the therapist often suggests "experiments" that may challenge fundamental beliefs by confronting the person with new or unexpected experiences (Kelly, 1955). Meanwhile, the client is being encouraged to construct an alternate belief system to which he or she may shift when the old one finally collapses.

Whether these Kuhnian conjectures are either valid or heuristic is clearly open to dispute. On the one hand, I can foresee limitations to the analogy and some problems in its evaluation. On the other hand, I have found it personally intriguing in terms of its potential ability to encompass much of what we call "psychotherapy" under a single schema. In counseling for relatively minor (peripheral) problems, our strategies are perhaps more uniform and straightforward. When the presenting problem is viewed as a reflection of fundamental misperceptions of the self or world, however, we use a wide variety of techniques to accomplish essentially the same thing—that is, a personal revolution. This point is cogently made by Raimy (1975) in his analysis of the strategic parallels among diverse therapies. If these analyses are correct, the differences among our therapeutic weapons and battle plans may be much less extensive than is commonly assumed.

CONCLUSION

I began this chapter with a discussion of some of my concerns about current cognitive-behavioral therapies. This allowed me to share some emerging conjectures on such issues as the potential importance of unconscious processes, the role of affect in therapy, and the role of rationality in adaptation. While I would still endorse many of the assumptions of the various cognitive therapies, I question whether their current theories and procedures are as yet adequate to our understanding of human adaptation. Whether the conjectures I have shared here will facilitate such understanding is, of course, a matter that requires empirical scrutiny.

Bringing some of these concerns into a broader context, the last part of the chapter focused on the diversity of theoretical perspectives through which psychotherapy is viewed. Drawing on Kuhn's analysis of the structure of scientific revolutions, I sketched some parallel conjectures about the possible structure of personal revolutions. While such an analogy may not promise either to unite or integrate our diverse therapeutic efforts, it may offer an overall schema in which we can take our respective places.

REFERENCES

Bandura, A. *Principles of behavior modification.* New York: Holt, Rinehart, & Winston, 1969.

Bandura, A. *Social learning theory.* Englewood Cliffs, N.J.: Prentice-Hall, 1977.

Bartley, W. W. *The retreat to commitment.* New York: Knopf, 1962.

Beck, A. T. Cognitive therapy: Nature and relation to behavior therapy. *Behavior Therapy,* 1970, *1*, 184–200.

Beck, A. T. *Cognitive therapy and the emotional disorders.* New York: International Universities Press, 1976.

Borkovec, T. D., & O'Brien, G. T. Relation of autonomic perception and its manipulation to the maintenance and reduction of fear. *Journal of Abnormal Psychology,* 1977, *86*, 163–171.

Bower, G. H. Contacts of cognitive psychology with social learning theory. *Cognitive Therapy and Research,* 1978, *2*, 123–146.

Davidson, R. J. Specificity and patterning in biobehavioral systems: Implications for behavior change. *American Psychologist,* 1978, *33*, 430–436.

Dixon, N. F. *Subliminal perception: The nature of a controversy.* New York: McGraw-Hill, 1971.

Ellenberger, H. F. *The discovery of the unconscious.* New York: Basic Books, 1970.

Ellis, A. Rational-emotive therapy: Research data that supports the clinical and personality hypotheses of RET and other modes of cognitive-behavior therapy. *The Counseling Psychologist,* 1977, *7*, 2–42.

Frank, J. D. *Persuasion and healing.* Baltimore: Johns Hopkins Press, 1961.

Galin, D. Implications for psychiatry of left and right cerebral specialization. *Archives of General Psychiatry,* 1974, *31*, 572–583.

Gauthier, J., & Marshall, W. L. Grief: A cognitive-behavioral analysis. *Cognitive Therapy and Research,* 1971, *1*, 39–44.

Gibson, J. J. *The senses considered as perceptual systems.* Boston: Houghton Mifflin, 1966.

Grings, W. W. The role of consciousness and cognition in autonomic behavior change. In F. J. McGuigan & R. A. Schoonover (Eds.), *The psychophysiology of thinking.* New York: Academic, 1973.

James, W. *The varieties of religious experience.* New York: New American Library, 1958. (Originally published, 1901.)

Jaynes, J. *The origin of consciousness in the breakdown of the bicameral mind.* Boston: Houghton Mifflin, 1977.

Jerison, H. J. *Evolution of the brain and intelligence.* New York: Wiley, 1973.

Hayek, F. A. *The sensory order.* Chicago: University of Chicago Press, 1952.

Hilgard, E. R. *Divided consciousness: Multiple controls in human thought and action.* New York: Wiley, 1977.

Holmes, D. S. Investigations of repression: Differential recall of material experimentally or naturally associated with ego threat. *Psychological Bulletin,* 1974, *81*, 632–653.

Jones, R. A. *Self-fulfilling prophecies*. Hillsdale, N.J.: Lawrence Erlbaum, 1976.

Kelly, G. A. *The psychology of personal constructs*. New York: Norton, 1955.

Klinger, E. *Structure and functions of fantasy*. New York: Wiley, 1971.

Kuhn, T. S. *The structure of scientific revolutions*. Chicago: University of Chicago Press, 1962.

Lang, P. J. Imagery in therapy: An information processing analysis of fear. *Behavior Therapy*, 1977, *8*, 862–886.

Lazarus, A. A. Where do behavior therapists take their troubles? *Psychological Reports*, 1971, *28*, 349–350.

MacLean, P. D. *The triune concept of the brain and behavior*. Toronto: University of Toronto Press, 1973.

Maher, B. *Clinical psychology and personality: The selected papers of George Kelly*. New York: Wiley, 1969.

Mahoney, M. J. *Cognition and behavior modification*. Cambridge, Mass.: Ballinger, 1974.

Mahoney, M. J. *Scientist as subject: The psychological imperative*. Cambridge, Mass: Ballinger, 1976.

Mahoney, M. J. Reflections on the cognitive-learning trend in psychotherapy. *American Psychologist*, 1977, *32*, 5–13.

Mahoney, M. J. Cognitive and non-cognitive views in behavior modification. In P. O. Sjoden & S. Bates (Eds.), *Trends in behavior therapy*. New York: Academic, 1978. (a)

Mahoney, M. J. Therapist liberation. *Behavior Therapy*, 1978, *9*, 676–677. (b)

Mahoney, M. J., & Arnkoff, D. B. Cognitive and self-control therapies. In S. L. Garfield & A. E. Bergin (Eds.), *Handbook of psychotherapy and behavior change* (2nd ed.). New York: Wiley, 1978.

Meichenbaum, D. *Cognitive-behavior modification: An integrative approach*. New York: Plenum, 1977.

Ornstein, R. E. *The psychology of consciousness*. San Francisco: Freeman, 1972.

Penfield, W. *The mystery of the mind*. Princeton, N.J.: Princeton University Press, 1975.

Polanyi, M. *The tacit dimension*. Garden City, N.Y.: Doubleday, 1966.

Raimy, V. *Misunderstandings of the self*. San Francisco: Jossey-Bass, 1975.

Sackeim, H. A., & Gur, R. C. Self-deception, self-confrontation, and consciousness. In G. E. Schwartz & D. Shapiro (Eds.), *Consciousness and self-regulation* (Vol. 2.). New York: Plenum, 1978, pp. 139–197.

Sarason, I. G. Anxiety and self-preoccupation. In I. G. Sarason & C. D. Spielberger (Eds.), *Stress and anxiety* (Vol. 2). New York: Wiley, 1975, pp. 27–44.

Schwartz, G. E., Davidson, R. J., & Maer, F. Right hemisphere lateralization for emotion in the human brain: Interactions with cognition. *Science*, 1975, *190*, 286–288.

Singer, J. L. *Imagery and daydream methods in psychotherapy and behavior modification*. New York: Academic, 1974.

Tart, C. T. (Ed.). *Altered states of consciousness*. New York: Wiley, 1969.

Tucker, D. M., Shearer, S. L., & Murray, J. D. Hemispheric specialization and cognitive behavior therapy. *Cognitive Therapy and Research*, 1977, *1*, 263–274.

Turvey, M. T. Constructive theory, perceptual systems, and tacit knowledge. In W. B. Weimer & D. S. Palermo (Eds.), *Cognition and the symbolic processes*. Hillsdale, N.J.: Lawrence Erlbaum, 1974, pp. 165–180.

Walsh, R. N. Reflections on psychotherapy. *Journal of Transpersonal Psychology*, 1976, *8*, 100–111.

Watts, A. W. *The wisdom of insecurity*. New York: Random, 1951.

Weimer, W. B. A conceptual framework for cognition psychology: Motor theories of the mind. In R. Shaw & J. D. Bransford (Eds.), *Acting, perceiving, and knowing: Toward an ecological psychology*. Hillsdale, N.J.: Lawrence Erlbaum, 1977, pp. 267–311.

Weimer, W. B., & Palermo, D. S. (Eds.). *Cognition and the symbolic processes*. Hillsdale, N.J.: Lawrence Erlbaum, 1974.

"De-Controlling" Cognition and Cognitive Control

Toward a Reconciliation of Cognitive and Dynamic Therapies

KENNETH S. BOWERS

Mahoney has made the job of the critical reviewer a difficult one. On one hand, he has been his own harshest critic, and on the other hand, he has introduced so many different themes that it would be both difficult and inappropriate to attempt a review of them. Consequently, I shall be highly selective in my comments, and take the opportunity to extend a few of his observations in order to draw out some of their important implications.

First of all, I am rather taken with the fact that Mahoney has been led by an appreciation of a Kuhnian analysis of scientific revolutions into an explicit recognition that some changes to be produced by therapy are more profound and strike more at the core of a person's functioning than others. Implicit in the concept of "core" changes is the notion that some surface signs and symptoms of distress are simply manifestations of underlying (and often unconscious) conflicts or assumptions that have developed over a long period of time. This notion of core problems and changes therein is a far cry from a more behavioristic view that overt symptoms *are* the problem to be changed by skills training or by some altered environmental contingencies. To be sure, symptoms are often problematic in and of themselves, and the

KENNETH S. BOWERS • Department of Psychology, University of Waterloo, Waterloo, Ontario, Canada N2L 3G1.

patient-client can often benefit considerably from a successful therapeutic assault on his or her overt symptomatology. Moreover, the successful elimination of symptomatic behavior may well lead to a significant alteration of the internal psychological organization that had previously supported the overt symptomatology (Wachtel, 1977). However, therapeutic failures that occur in a skills-training or behavioristic mode of intervention may result from the fact that *sub rosa* conflicts and beliefs can be highly peremptory, and relatively resistant to therapeutic efforts that focus on the overt behavior or readily accessible cognitions of the patient-client. In these cases, uncovering or abreactive forms of therapy may be more beneficial. Let me give just one example of what I mean.

I once saw a patient who had been involved in various therapies for about two years in an attempt to eliminate a persistent hair-pulling syndrome. When I saw the young woman, she was 17 years old and completely bald. By use of a hypnotic dream technique, I discovered that she had seen her older brother the last time when the latter was in the hospital just prior to (unsuccessful) brain surgery. Part of the preparation for such surgery obviously involves having one's head shaved. My patient reexperienced this last visit with her (bald-headed) brother in a highly cathartic session. Afterwards, when the patient was alerted, she had no apparent memory for the abreactive experience, stating simply that, "I must have been upset because I have tears on my cheeks."

She did not again mention the incident of seeing her bald-headed brother until the next (and final) session, and did so only in the context of how psychologically unprepared she had been for her brother's death. Later in this final session, she again became upset when I asked if she had ever felt somehow responsible for the death of her brother. She reluctantly acknowledged having had this idea, and then vehemently denied that her brother's death was (literally) causing her to pull her hair. When I agreed, she became especially emotional, adding, "you're the first doctor ever to say that." Finally, as she began to calm down somewhat, I said, "Sue, do you need to pull your hair any more?" Sue: "No." Therapist: "Well, why don't you just stop." Sue: "Okay." The patient never again pulled her hair. The entire treatment took four, one-hour sessions. Whether or not rational appeals or direct attempts to extinguish the hair-pulling behavior would have been equally successful is of course, a moot point. On the face of it, the ability of the patient to abreact this last visit to her brother was an important condition for her relatively quick progress; whether it was a necessary condition is impossible to say.

I have emphasized the abreactive nature of this (abbreviated) case study rather than the recovery of lost memory, because, as I subsequently learned from the referring agency, *the patient had long known and talked about this last visit to her brother,* though not once did she mention it to me before the cathartic session conducted under hypnosis, and only once afterward. It seems to me that this case is a good illustration of the complex way that cognition and affect can interact in effecting therapeutic benefits: Memory of the traumatic incident was therapeutically insufficient, and conscious recall of the abreactive experience was (apparently) unnecessary for the cessation of the hair-pulling behavior. Such complexities notwithstanding, this case and others like it (e.g., Watkins, 1971) seem to me ample grounds for taking seriously Mahoney's caveat that the typical "practice of avoiding dysphoria during cognitive-behavioral therapy [must be challenged]."

Presumably, the basis for such a practice is that "there is a strong and pervasive assumption among cognitive-behavioral therapists that feelings are phenomena to be controlled (rather than expressed)." Though the concept of control is psychologically complex and multidimensional, there *is* an important sense in which control implies inhibiting affective displays. Thus, many television commentators were clearly "fighting for control" over their emotions when reporting on the J.F. Kennedy assassination. And I think Mahoney is probably correct in his implication that most cognitive-behavior therapists, though perhaps accepting of such displays, are unconvinced of their therapeutic value. Instead, the emphasis is on *doing* something to alter the cognitions, behavior, or circumstances that have led to the dysphoric state of affairs.

I have a lot of sympathy for this position, but at the same time, I find that such "doings" can be very hard to engender in at least some patient-clients who have not yet been able to experience the affective dimensions of their problems, and who have instead converted affect into some symptom complex the affective roots of which are obscure, at least to the patient. In other words, "getting in touch with one's emotions" may not be sufficient for therapeutic progress, but it may be for some persons a necessary first step—one that enables them to profit from the various therapeutic techniques that cognitive-behaviorists have developed. Basically, my argument is that it may sometimes be necessary to lose control in one way (i.e., to experience and display the emotional aspects of a problem) in order to gain control in another way (i.e., to solve the problematic aspects of one's life and circumstances).

There is a related issue that I can only raise here without the elaboration it deserves. The cognitive-behaviorist's emphasis on cognitive control—of *doing* something to change one's thoughts, behavior, or circumstances—seems excessively organized around rational and willful efforts to produce significant change. There is, in contrast, a rich therapeutic tradition that argues that such willful attempts by the patient can sometimes be quite counterproductive, and indeed can often constitute a form of psychological resistance to significant therapeutic change. Janet, Freud, and Morton

Prince, each in their own way, all realized that it was often beneficial to circumvent the patient's willful, active efforts to control the contents of thought, and instead, to engender a psychological state of passive receptiveness (Deikman, 1971) in order to discover what thoughts, fantasies, or affects emerge. Like night dreams, such cognitive "emergents" often have surprise value, precisely because they, like dreams, are not the end product of willfully directed thought. Insofar as such unwilled emergents may help to define the patient's problem domain, the subsequent application of more active cognitive strategies can be more aptly targeted and sharply focused. Again, we have here an example of how giving up control in one sense may subsequently help to establish better control in another way.

In conclusion, it is perhaps worth emphasizing that giving up (certain kinds) of control and of experiencing the sometimes surprising and emotional consequences, implies a domain of *sub rosa* concerns that the patient-client does not ordinarily perceive, notice, or experience. Whether or not we should refer to these (typically) unnoticed concerns as "unconscious" is perhaps less critical than realizing their potential importance both in defining the patient's problems, and in suggesting certain therapeutic strategies. If cognitive-behavior therapists can begin to take such "decontrolling" experiences seriously, and more dynamic therapists can begin to see the value of problem-solving strategies in effecting significant change (e.g., Wachtel, 1977), then perhaps we can hope for the resolution of a long-standing ideological conflict that is at least reconciling if not revolutionary.

Acknowledgment

I would like to thank Dr. Donald Meichenbaum for his comments on an earlier draft of this paper.

REFERENCES

Deikman, A. J. Bimodal consciousness. *Archives of General Psychiatry*, 1971, *25*, 481–489.
Wachtel, P. L. *Psychoanalysis and behavior therapy: Toward an integration*. New York: Basic Books, 1977.
Watkins, J. G. The affect bridge: A hypno-analytic technique. *International Journal of Clinical and Experimental Hypnosis*, 1971, *19*, 21–27.

Chapter 7

Cognitive Behavior and Its Roles in Psychotherapy

An Integrative Account[1]

JOSEPH WOLPE

During this century, on the impetus of the contributions of Pavlov, Thorndike, Watson, Hull, and Skinner, the behaviorist movement took shape. What distinguished it from all previous approaches to psychology was that the behaviorist movement treated the data of the field under the same rules that applied to the physical sciences (Pratt, 1939). Even the most complex and subtle forms of human experience were seen as functions of the physical organism. An impressive accumulation of knowledge of the lawful relations of learning and performance resulted.

However, there have always been psychologists who have rejected the behaviorist viewpoint (e.g., Masserman, 1946; Wolberg, 1970; Zilboorg, 1941) on the ground that it fails to take account of mental life. They regard cognition as belonging to an order of activity that transcends biology. They believe that in mental life, although still subject to the influences of bio-

---

[1] This chapter is a slightly modified version of *Cognition and Causation in Human Behavior and its Therapy*, which appeared in the *American Psychologist*, 1978, *33*, 437–446.

JOSEPH WOLPE • Department of Psychiatry, Temple University, Eastern Pennsylvania Psychiatric Institute, Philadelphia, Pennsylvania 19129.

logical causality, a person is in some respects a free agent. This belief can be refuted if it can be shown that cognitive behavior is a biological function that belongs like any other behavior to the lawful universe of science. The examination of this and related matters, undertaken in this chapter, provides this demonstration.

The need for this kind of examination has recently been accentuated by the *volte face* of Albert Bandura (1974), a leading psychologist who has made conspicuous contributions to behavior theory and therapy. In his *Principles of Behavior Modification* (1969), Bandura had stated:

> All behavior is inevitably controlled, and the operation of psychological laws cannot be suspended by romantic conceptions of human behavior, any more than indignant rejection of the law of gravity as antihumanistic can stop people from falling. . . . The process of behavior change involves substituting new controlling conditions for those that have regulated a person's behavior. (p. 85)

In 1974 he repudiated this position, and aligned himself with the critics of behaviorism in holding that it embodies an erroneously "mechanisitic" view of human behavior. He declared (1974, p. 859) that "the fabled reflexive conditioning in humans is largely a myth," and contended that an adequate account of human learning must recognize that "contrary to the mechanistic metaphors, outcomes [i.e., reinforcing events] change human behavior through the intervening influence of thought."

To the extent that our perception of things and situations in the world around us is a prime determinant of our actions, "thought" has indeed a central role in human behavior. The way we react to situations varies according to how we perceive them. This is quite obvious and was originally taken for granted by Skinner (1953) (whom Bandura seems mainly to have in mind in his references to "radical behaviorists"). But Bandura goes a long way beyond this when he claims that the intervening influence of thought is required to effect human behavior change.

I shall present grounds for the proposition that thought obeys the same "mechanistic" laws as other behavior. There is no need for the invocation of an entity or a realm of activity independent of the mechanism-controlled organism. If there were, Locke (1971) would have been right when he called my use of cognitions in behavior therapy nonbehavioristic. Not only the moment-to-moment content of thought (specific cognitions), but its very faculty is, as will be seen later in this chapter, comprehensible in behavioristic terms. The additions and revisions of behavior theory and therapy (Beck, 1976; Ellis, 1962; Mahoney, 1977; Meichenbaum, 1975) that are in various ways connected with the idea of an independent realm of activity will be shown to be unjustified.

COGNITIONS (AND EMOTIONS, TOO) ARE
CAUSES OF BEHAVIOR

Skinner's *Science and Human Behavior* (1953) provided a remarkably comprehensive overview of the forces and functions that control the development of human behavior. It would be easy to derive from it an extensive schema for behavior analysis for clinical purposes, because *inter alia* it takes cognitive events into account in a wide-ranging and systematic way. However, Skinner has recently (1971, 1975, 1976) adopted a much more restrictive view of cognitive events, denying their usefulness as data. For example, he has stated (1976) that "mental life is an inference, a construction, rather than something directly observed." It is, of course, desirable to try as far as possible to adhere to data that are public and capable of independent verification; but as Ryle (1949, see pp. 11ff) has shown, to a great extent mental life *is* public. In any case, it is impossible realistically to dispense with mental events in human behavior (even though these are often in large measure private). What I am writing now, and what Skinner wrote last year could not have been written without mental activity—his and mine. Those mental, and largely private, events were indispensable antecedents and accompaniments to the writing. They were a necessary part of the concatenation of factors that caused our pens to set forth our arguments on paper.

An individual's knowledge of the world consists entirely of private events. His first response to an object is his perception of it, and that is a private event. What he perceives determines his subsequent behavior. The responses set off by the perception depend on previous conditioning in the presence of similar objects.

Images evoked in the absence of objects (for example, the architectural image evoked by the word "Parthenon") are conditioned perceptions—in line with what Skinner called "conditioned seeing" (1953, p. 266). If actual perceptions can be causal antecedents of overt behavior, it is only to be expected that conditioned perceptions can also be.

In addition to perceptual and motor behavior, there is, of course, autonomic behavior, some of which is correlated with the feelings aroused in us that we call our "emotions." Everyday experience seems to demonstrate abundantly the influence of emotions on other behavior. We make approaches to people who excite us pleasantly when we perceive them, and often even when we merely imagine them, in contrast to our responses to those who excite us unpleasantly. It has repeatedly been demonstrated that the presence of an autonomic component in a stimulus complex can result in a response quite different from that which occurs without it. For example, Adam (1967, p. 106 ff) found that the elimination of visceral afferent impulses markedly alters conditioned motor responses. Although Skinner (1953, p. 167, 1971, 1975) has always disputed the role of emotions in behavioral causation, his objection has really been to the invocation of vague "inner states." He has not been blind to the causal relevance of emotional events in well-defined contexts. For example, he describes (1953, p. 70) how a pigeon that has failed to receive reinforcement engages in emotional behavior and "will turn again to the key when the emotional response has subsided."

LEARNING AND REINFORCEMENT

Bandura correctly states that behaviorists nowadays discuss learning predominantly in Skinnerian terms; i.e., with reference to external reinforcers—an account that certainly very often fits the facts. The events that follow a stimulus–response sequence are often decisive with regard to whether or not, and to what extent, functional bonding is established, so that the likelihood of the stimulus being followed by the response is increased (or decreased). This has been abundantly shown with respect to a great many motor habits and some autonomic habits (Kimmel, 1967; Miller & DiCara, 1968; Pavlov, 1927; Skinner, 1953). Conditioning of words, images, and ideas can also be facilitated by external rewards (Pavlov, 1955; Razran, 1971). External reinforcers are of many kinds—eating food and receiving tokens or praise are among the more commonplace.

However, there are a host of instances in which learning occurs in the absence of any evident external source of reinforcement. I do not need an external reinforcement to learn from a dictionary that a podium is a high table used for lecturing, or that the German word for "sky" is "Himmel." The mere presentation of these pairs of symbols in juxtaposition may result in the one consistently evoking the other. However, there are internal sources of reinforcement that may be operating in such instances (see below).

The requirements of operant conditioning theory are also often not fulfilled in unlearning. The unlearning of a response is supposed to be related to the response being followed by consequences that have negative effects—usually nonreinforcement and sometimes punishment (Skinner, 1953, pp. 69–72). The facts surrounding many instances of unlearning are not in accord with this. The extinction manifest in verbal forgetting is not the result of unreinforced evocations of the verbal response, but of the excitation of other verbal responses that compete with that response (e.g., McGeogh, McKinney, & Peters, 1937). The process involved here is evidently reciprocal inhibition (Osgood, 1946, 1948). In behavior therapy, the elimination of undesirable behavior is very often achieved *without* the unreinforced elicitation of that behavior. For example, a woman's habitual shoplifting of 18 years' duration was revealed by behavior analysis to be based upon anxiety at surrendering things, and the motor habit of shoplifting was lastingly eliminated *by overcoming that anxiety response habit* by systematic desensitization (Wolpe, 1973, p. 240). The elicitation of shoplifting behavior in no way entered the treatment. Shoplifting ceased because the emotional behavior that was its necessary antecedent was eliminated, evidently due to the building up of conditioned inhibition on the basis of reciprocal inhibition (Wolpe, 1958, 1976a). The point being stressed here is that the operant conditioning paradigm is irrelevant to many instances of learning and unlearning.

It seems to be a reasonable assumption that learning is always the same physiological process in the same nervous system, no matter what is connected to what. A quarter of a century ago, I showed how a simple neurological model[2] facilitates and unifies the conceptualization of many instances and aspects of learning (Wolpe, 1949, 1950, 1952a,b,c, 1953, 1958, pp. 6–31). The model is based on the assumption that learning depends upon the development of conductivity (synaptic function) between neurons whose endings are in apposition—an assumption for which impressive evidence exists (Culler, 1938; Olds, 1975; Olds, Disterhoft, Segal, Kornblith, & Hirsh, 1972; Woody & Engel, 1972). The processes involved in the development of synaptic function are just beginning to be defined (Huttunen, 1973; Olds, 1975; Young, 1973, 1975; and later in this chapter). We may legitimately use what is known as a framework for suggesting what *might* be happening at synapses during learning that accords with observations at the behavioral level. We may take advantage of a realistic model without assuming that it represents ultimate reality.

As noted above, external reinforcement is positively correlated with much (but not all) learning. It is relevant to ask how external reinforcement might influence events at the synapse. As Hull (1943) observed, a common feature of external reinforcements is that they all reduce "drive"—states of central neural excitation, which are manifested by bodily activity and due to states of bodily need (such as food or water deprivation) or strong external stimulation (such as noxious stimulation). Reduction of central neural excitation (manifested, for example, by reduced motor activity) results from the reduction of the need or from the removal of the external stimulation. It seems that this somehow produces a "cementing" effect at active synaptic points: both real consummatory behaviors and brain rewards are correlated

---

[2] In recent years, there has been a widespread indisposition to consider learning as a function of the nervous system, though no behaviorist doubts that that is what it is. The nervous system is not a totally black box. It has long been known (e.g., Dale, 1937; Lloyd, 1946) that stimulus–response sequences depend on the particular functional connections that have been formed between neurons. For a recent review, see Eccles (1975).

with a cessation of firing in "a special kind of drive neuron" (Olds, 1975, pp. 386–387).

Given that there is only one learning process and that external rein- forcement is a source of drive reduction in much learning *but not all*, we must inquire if there are other possible sources of drive reduction when learning occurs in the absence of external reinforcement. The answer is in the affirmative. *Every* response, even if it is only a perceptual response, must be correlated with some measure of central neural excitation, the cessation of which, as noted above, is drive reduction. Although of lower magnitude, this is an event of the same class as a drive reduction occasioned by the allaying of a need such as hunger. The strength of cognitive learning is naturally enhanced if concomitant arousals are reduced by the particular perception. For example, a greater measure of reinforcement will occur when the perception allays curiosity (Berlyne, 1960). Learning may simi- larly be expected to be enhanced to the extent that there are arousals sec- ondary to the perceived stimuli—such as the aesthetic pleasure that the word "sky" might evoke (Berlyne, 1971). (The feeling is, of course, the sub- jective correlate of the neural excitations that are at the actual locus of learning.) These low-level reinforcements are the apparent basis of the fact that we are continuously learning, registering the sequences of our experience, throughout our waking lives. In the mere fact of experience, there is drive, and inevitable drive reduction, and, therefore, inevitable reinforce- ment.

While drive reduction at the behavioral level is perhaps the commonest correlate of reinforcement, drive increment may be one, too—as in the experiments showing that raising the level of stimulation is reinforcing (for example, the addition of light by Hurwitz, 1956 or sweetness by Sheffield & Rob, 1950) and in those showing that hypothalamic stimulation is reinforc- ing (Olds, 1962, 1975). It is thus credible that in the formation of cognitive habits, reinforcement can be provided either by the cognition-arousing exci- tations, or by the reduction of these excitations—or both. Presumably, according to circumstances, either can lead to cessation of firing in Olds's (1975, p. 386) "special kind of drive neurons".

COGNITION IN RELATION TO OTHER RESPONSES

All three behavioral modalities—motor, autonomic, and cognitive— participate in most human behavior, in parallel and in sequence. For ex- ample, if an attractive woman acquaintance enters the visual field of a man sitting in a cafe, his first response is to perceive her. Then, emotionally aroused, he begins to move toward her, while imagining ways of extending the association. It will be argued that every bit of this behavior, including the cognitive, has its form determined by its antecedents—in contrast to the traditional view that cognitive behavior has some degree of autonomy from the causal stream.

We all have an *impression* of freedom that makes us susceptible to the idea that cognitive behavior belongs to a domain that is distinct from the physiological and does not obey the same rules. Ryle (1949) referred to this presumed domain as the "Ghost in the Machine." He showed its separation from the body to be due to the mistake of regarding different aspects of the same phenomenon as different entities. The dogma of the Ghost in the Machine maintains "that there occur physical processes and mental processes; that there are mechanical causes of corporeal movements and mental causes of corporeal movements (p. 22)." Obviously, this poses the insoluble problem of explaining how a nonmaterial event can have effects on nerve tissue. No such problem exists when the physical and the mental are both seen as functions of the nervous system.

The following paragraphs from Ryle's book crystallize some of the key points of his brilliant analysis of the relationship between the physical and the mental:

> When a person talks sense aloud, ties knots, feints or sculpts, the actions which we witness are themselves the things which he is intelligently doing. He is bodily active and he is mentally active, but he is not being synchronously active in two different "places", or with two different "engines". There is the one kind of activity, but it is one susceptible of and requiring more than one kind of explanatory description. (Ryle, 1949, p. 50)

If we take the example of talking aloud, the need for more than one kind of explanatory description is plain. There may be no physical or physiological difference between one man gabbling and another talking sense, but the logical differences are enormous. It is not sounds, but the sequences of meaning that matter:

> I discover that there are other minds in understanding what other people say and do. In making sense of what you say, in appreciating your jokes, in unmasking your chess-stratagems, in following your arguments and in hearing you pick holes in my arguments, I am not inferring to the workings of your mind, I am following them. Of course, I am not merely hearing the noises that you make, or merely seeing the movements that you perform. I am understanding what I hear and see. But this understanding is not inferring to occult causes. It is appreciating how the operations are conducted. (pp. 60–61)

> Certainly there are some things which I can find out about you only, or best, through being told of them by you. The oculist has to ask his client what letters he sees with his right and left eyes and how clearly he sees them. . . . But the sequence of your sensations and imaginings is not the sole field in which your wits and character are shown; perhaps only

for lunatics is it more than a small corner of that field. I find out most of
what I want to know about your capacities, interests, likes, dislikes,
methods and convictions by observing how you conduct your overt
doings, of which by far the most important are your sayings and writings.
It is a subsidiary question how you conduct your imaginings, including
your imagined monologues. (p. 61)

James G. Taylor (1962) used Ryle's analysis of the relationship
between physical and mental events as a springboard for his epoch-making
studies that showed how visual perception develops through the conditioning
of motor responses to intercompensating integrations of proprioceptive
inputs and visual inputs. Taylor made ingenious use of data from his own
experiments and earlier ones by Stratton (1897) and Ivo Kohler (1951) on
the long-term effects on visual perception of the constant wearing of prismatic lenses that distort the visual field—for example, transposing left and
right. (Such a prism also has the effect that when the head is turned, the
world sweeps by in the direction of the movement of the head but at twice
the speed.) A very significant finding is that after a time *the perceptual field
corrects itself while the subject is still wearing the prism* (Taylor, 1962, p.
188). This happens only after he has learned to make correct movements
toward seen objects on the basis of proprioceptive and tactile cues. After
using manual exploration again and again to locate objects by trial and
error, the subject becomes increasingly skillful at finding and manipulating
them; a few days later the *perceived* field right itself to conform with the
spatial reality. *Without* the prism, at this point, the visual field is found to
be reversed, but is in turn corrected in time through behavior. These findings beautifully demonstrate that visual perception is not "photographic,"
but a function of a learning mechanism that adjusts the effects of visual
stimulation in accordance with the reinforcement of motor responses.

On the basis of his observations, Taylor formulated an account of the
evolution of visual perception in the young child. In the couse of the child's
interactions with the physical world, certain of his responses to visual
stimuli are reinforced, mainly by proprioceptive feedback. Such condition-
ings, in relation to multitudinous combinations of physical and proprioceptive stimuli, are the basis of *visual constancy*—our remarkable ability to
perceive an object, e.g., a kettle or a face, as *the same*, despite the different
visual stimuli the object delivers from every angle and every distance.
However, for our present purpose, the important implication of Taylor's
experiments is that they showed unequivocally that *perception is a kind of
behavior, an active responding of the nervous system, and not a passive
registration prior to behavior.*

The foregoing considerations provide a fundamental answer to what
Ullmann (1970) called the "challenge to behaviorists to deal with the
activities that are labeled cognitions." They undermine the arguments of the

cognitivist critics of behaviorism who impugn it as too "mechanistic" for the complexities of human consciousness. The same lawfulness that applies to other behavior applies to cognitive behavior. This makes it easy to see the error of Bandura's contention (1974, p. 860) that change in human behavior occurs "through the intervening influence of thought." Thoughts are responses, whether they are perceptions or imaginings. Like other responses, thoughts are evoked when the relevant neural excitations occur. They are a subset of learnable responses, and inasmuch as they have stimulus aspects, may be conditioned to other thoughts and to responses in other categories. They are not part of a separate *mechanism* of learning that only human beings possess.

In the same vein, it is interesting to note that the critics' own formulations, closely examined, do not really arrive at independence from the causal stream. Thus, we have Bandura saying of human learning (1974, p. 859): "So-called conditioned reactions are largely self-activated on the basis of learned expectations rather than automatically evoked." If an expectation is learned, it will be evoked *when and only when* the stimulus conditions to which it is the learned response occur. Its evocation will be automatic, and it will in turn automatically evoke *its* learned consequents. Bandura goes on to say (p. 867): "People may be considered partially free insofar as they can influence future conditions by managing their own behavior." But when people influence future conditions, the ways in which they do so are determined by their make-up, which is shaped by their biology and their previous conditioning, and by the totality of stimuli, internal and external, perceived and imaginal, that act upon them at the material time. They are never able to act like gods detached from causality. If a person makes a decision that alters the course of events, we always need to ask, "What were the causes of the decision?," and the answer can never be "Nothing." Freedom is only possible in the way proposed by John Locke (1690) and reiterated in modern analyses (e.g., Ayer, 1973)—that a person is free to the extent that his actions are in accord with his desires.

COGNITION IN RELATION TO BEHAVIOR THERAPY

In the field of psychotherapy, the belief that cognition is a happening detached from behavior has been a source of confusion for generations. And now, *mirabile dictu*, this belief and its progeny of confusions have begun to infiltrate behavior therapy—the psychotherapy of behaviorism! (See, for example, Beck, 1976; Goldfried & Goldfried, 1975; Mahoney, 1977.)

Mahoney (1977) applauds "the recent appearance of efforts to integrate cognitive and behavioristic approaches to psychotherapy." From what has emerged in our consideration of cognition, this is very much like talking of integrating hematology with medicine, or the study of nitrogen with the study of gases. The "integration" that Mahoney advocates has always existed in the practice of behavior therapy (Wolpe, 1958), as I shall outline below. In fact, of course, the idea of "integration" makes sense only on the assumption that cognition is something other than behavior.

The cognitivists have persuaded themselves that behavior therapists have bypassed cognition.[3] For example, Beck (1976) asserts that behavior therapists do not recognize cognition and "detour around thoughts." Such an assertion could only be made by a person who is not very familiar with the manner in which behavior therapy of the neuroses is actually conducted. We may note, before going on to that topic, that in a general way cognition is *unavoidable* in behavior therapy, as it is in any form of psychotherapy, and, indeed, in almost all human activities. Inevitably, the patient perceives the therapist, thinks "Here is a man who may help me," notices the furniture and the decor of the office, perceives the therapist's gestures and his words, and responds to what he perceives in emotions and in words. If behavior therapists have not made a point of such things, it is because to do so is as redundant as to mention, when recording that a patient received an intravenous injection, that a syringe was used. The indispensability of cognition in human interactions makes nonsense of the cognitivist's "discovery" that behavior therapy has omitted cognition.

Cognition in Behavior Therapy Practice

Behavior therapists have deliberately influenced their patients' thinking ever since formal behavior therapy of the neuroses came into existence (Wolpe, 1954, 1958). It has been a matter of routine to make statements that prepare the patient for procedures based on conditioning principles (Wolpe, 1958, pp. 111–112, 116–117), and to convey the permissive, non-moralizing attitude characteristic of the behavioristic approach. A typical introductory statement is the following:

> Because it is through learning that you have acquired your unfortunate reactions, the procedures that we will undertake to change them will be an implementation of principles of learning. We will procure an unlearning of the undesirable actions, and wherever necessary, a learning of new habits. We will work together to bring about a relearning within you.

Having thus set the stage, the behavior therapist goes on to *behavior analysis*—the gathering of information from which he may deduce the stimulus–response relations involved in the patient's unadaptive habits (Wolpe, 1973, pp. 22–52). This means that he takes a history of each of the

---

[3] This is a facet of the widely prevalent myth that behavior therapy is simplistic and deals with isolated sets of behavior.

patient's complaints in order to determine the controlling stimulus patterns. He responds to the patient's disclosures with remarks and questions that stimulate further disclosures. This give-and-take continues with the background history of early family relations, education, and love life.

The history taking is, in a sense, the beginning of therapy, though it precedes therapeutic *procedures*. The patient's complaints are dissected and displayed. In describing his experiences, the patient evokes associated thoughts and associated emotions. If weak anxiety responses are elicited during pleasant emotional responses to the therapist, some inadvertent deconditioning of unadaptive anxiety responses may take place (Wolpe, 1958, p. 193). The final phase of the initial behavior analysis consists of the administration of questionnaires that supply further stimulus–response information (Wolpe, 1973, p. 28). Almost everything, so far, is predominantly in the cognitive department.

Behavior analysis is a logical offshoot of a conditioned response view of neurosis, and was, therefore, naturally an intrinsic part of behavior therapy from the beginning (Wolpe, 1958). Without it the therapist cannot tell where to direct his habit-changing efforts. Unadaptive emotional habits call for emotional solutions; unadaptive cognitive habits (misconceptions, wrong associations) for cognitive solutions.

Although behavior analyses show that the central requirement in the treatment of most neuroses is the overcoming of persistent unadaptive anxiety response habits (Wolpe, 1958, 1973), misconceptions are common, and in a minority of cases are the main basis of neurotic anxiety. For example, a person may fear elevators because he wrongly believes that he would suffocate if the elevator got stuck, and another's life is severely constricted because he wrongly believes that his recurrent chest pains have a cardiac origin. The appropriate treatment of such cases is to correct the wrong belief, i.e., the wrong habit of thought. Some very severe multisymptomatic neuroses are based on misconceptions. In a 35-year-old woman (Wolpe, 1973, pp. 57–79), 10 years of suffering marked by great irritability, almost constant depression, and frequent tantrums were found to be based on the belief instilled by her psychiatrists that she was biologically incapable of normal sexual function. When, in the course of her first three sessions, she was made to realize the error of this idea, she improved dramatically, and went on to a complete recovery that has now lasted for seven years.

As previously stated, such cases are a minority. It is much more common to have to deal with anxiety that is triggered by situations that the patient *knows* to be harmless—though it should be noted that a number of neuroses have *both* misconceptual bases and unadaptive conditioned anxiety bases. Deconditioning of anxiety response habits is usually accomplished by applying the experimentally based paradigm of reciprocal inhibition

(Wolpe, 1952d, 1958, 1976a). Numerous anxiety-inhibiting responses are in clinical use, of which the commonest are active muscle relaxation, and assertive and sexual responses. In addition, deliberate use can sometimes be made of the anxiety-inhibiting power of the emotional responses that the psychotherapeutic situation as such elicits in many patients and that are the basis of a great deal of inadvertent deconditioning of anxiety in all psychotherapies (Wolpe, 1973, p. 268).

Besides the correcting of misconceptions, there are several other behavior therapy techniques whose primary target is change in cognitive habits—for example, Taylor's (1955) thought-stopping technique and some of Cautela's (1967) and Homme's (1965) covert conditioning procedures. Since these were developed on conditioning principles, Mahoney (1977) is quite mistaken as seeing them as beginning "to challenge the long-standing dichotomy between radical behavioristic approaches and the traditional insight therapies."

What Mahoney calls "the cognitive revolution" has added nothing of visible value to the practice of behavior therapy. As noted earlier, some of its basic procedures are routine to behavior therapists. As to the rest, there is to date not a single study that shows that the addition of nonbehavioristic practices improves on the impressive and lasting outcomes that behavior therapy achieves in neurotic cases (Wolpe, 1958, 1973). Any comparative study, to be satisfactory, would have to allow for the inadvertent therapeutic effects that all psychotherapies share, and to separate cognitively based anxiety from directly conditioned anxiety. Even behavior therapy research has often fallen short in respect of the latter requirement (Wolpe, 1977), though seldom in the former.

Is All Psychotherapeutic Change Cognitive Change?

Ellis (1962, 1974) takes the position that neurotic problems are *all* due to wrong ways of thinking, and that thought correction is the essence of what is needed to overcome them—a position shared by Meichenbaum (1975), Beck (1976), and Raimy (1976). He devotes the bulk of his therapeutic efforts to "combating irrational beliefs." We have seen that this is appropriate for those neurotic fears that are based on misconceptions, but Ellis claims that all of them are so based. In practice, though, he often seems to project on to the patient the irrational beliefs he supposes the patient ought to have (see, for example, Ellis, 1962, pp. 126–128). The view that the psychotherapeutic task is exclusively a matter of cognitive correction seems mistaken, both because it is contrary to established facts about autonomic responses, and because it is not supported by clinical data.

Some facts about autonomic responses that are in conflict with cognitive exclusivism in psychotherapy are the following:

1. Since, as we have seen, cognitive responses are a subset of behavioral responses, cognition-directed treatment procedures must be a subset of behavioral procedures—and not the other way around, as claimed by Beck (1976, p. 320).

2. When a situation that is encountered in reality evokes anxiety, *imagining* it usually also evokes anxiety (e.g. Wade, Malloy, & Proctor, 1977), though the subject can scarcely be *believing* that the image is dangerous. The supposition that the anxiety is a conditioned response that is arousable by both real and imaginary images fits the facts entirely comfortably.

3. An extensive literature shows that for a conditioned response to be weakened, its evocation must always in some way be involved in the operations that weaken it (Hinde, 1966; McGeogh, 1932; Pavlov, 1927). Cognitive events can change autonomic habits only if they have autonomic effects. False feedback experiments at one time seemed to suggest that systematic desensitization might diminish anxiety on the basis of cognitive change (Valins and Ray, 1967). Better controlled experiments subsequently revealed that information is followed by decrements of anxiety *only* when it is veridical—i.e., when it actually reduces anxiety responding (Gaupp, Stern, & Galbraith, 1972; Kent, Wilson, & Nelson, 1972; Rosen, Rosen, & Reid, 1972; Sushinsky & Bootzin, 1970).

The following *clinical* facts are contrary to the cognitivist position:

1. Most neurotic patients are afraid of situations that they clearly know are not objectively dangerous, and this is usually the case, contrary to Beck's (1976) contention, even *while* they are anxious.

2. The stimulus to a neurotic anxiety response may be such that it is inconceivable how it could be regarded as a threat, for example, fear of the sight of a test-tube full of blood.

3. A patient who is continuously anxious may be found to have a specific persistent fear, e.g., of going insane. Strong reassurance may convince him to the contrary, yet, his anxiety may not materially diminish. A few inhalations of a carbon dioxide–oxygen mixture (Wolpe, 1973, p. 157, 183) may lastingly remove that anxiety (e.g., Latimer, 1977; Steketee & Roy, 1979). This can scarcely be explained as a matter of cognitive correction.

4. A clinical experiment that unintentionally provided some data contradicting the "pure cognitive theory" was reported by Seitz (1953). In treating 25 patients with psychocutaneous excoriation syndromes, he encouraged them to express, during his interviews with them, their hostile feelings toward other people, while explicitly discouraging "acting out"

their aggressions in their life situations. Of the 25, 11 disobeyed him, *and in these 11 alone, the skin cleared up.* As we so often also find in teaching assertive behavior, emotional change does not follow understanding, but requires outward behavior on the basis of that understanding.

CONCLUSION

Delightful as it is to regard ourselves as partially free agents, and not entirely under the domination of the causal sequences that relentlessly channel the course of events for everything else in nature, this freedom is, alas, only an illusion. We always do what we must do. Our thinking is behavior and as unfree as any other behavior. Our perceptual responses keep us constantly in touch with the world around us. Learning connects the sequences of our experience. We have an almost limitless capacity for adaptive learning, and for the learning of skills and dispositions. All the learning takes place automatically. If we are conditioned to patterns of behavior that are unadaptive, only the learning process can replace them with adaptive patterns. Emotional reconditioning, or cognitive correction, or both, may be required.

Acknowledgments

I gratefully acknowledge the substantively helpful comments of Steven C. Fischer, Louis Gershman, Laura W. Phillips, Leo J. Reyna, and David Wolpe.

REFERENCES

Adam, G. *Interoception and behaviour.* Budapest: Akadémiai Kiadó, 1967.
Ayer, A. J. *The central questions of philosophy.* London: Weidenfeld & Nicholson, 1973.
Bandura, A. *Principles of behavior modification.* New York: Holt, Rinehart & Winston, 1969.
Bandura, A. Behavior theory and the models of man. *American Psychologist,* 1974, *29,* 859–869.
Beck, A. T. *Cognitive therapy and the emotional disorders.* New York: International Universities Press, 1976.
Berlyne, D. E. *Conflict, arousal and curiosity.* New York: McGraw-Hill, 1960.
Berlyne, D. E. *Aesthetics and psychobiology.* New York: Appleton-Century-Crofts, 1971.
Cautela, J. R. Covert sensitization. *Psychological Reports,* 1967, *20,* 459–468.
Culler, E. Observations on direct cortical stimulation in the dog. *Psychological Bulletin,* 1938, *35,* 687–688.
Dale, H. Transmission of nervous effects by acetylcholine. *Harvey Lecture,* 1937, *32,* 229–245.
Eccles, J. C. Under the spell of synapse. In F. G. Worden, J. P. Swazey, & G. Adelman (Eds.), *The neurosciences: Paths of discovery.* Cambridge, Mass.: Colonial, 1975.
Ellis, A. *Reason and emotion in psychotherapy.* New York: Lyle Stuart, 1962.

Ellis, A. *Humanistic psychotherapy: The rational-emotive approach.* New York: Julian Press and McGraw-Hill, 1974.

Gaupp, L. A., Stern, R. M., & Galbraith, G. G. False heart-rate feedback and reciprocal inhibition by aversion relief in the treatment of snake avoidance behavior. *Behavior Therapy*, 1972, *3*, 7–20.

Goldfried, R. R., & Goldfried, A. P. Cognitive change methods. In F. H. Kanfer & A. P. Goldstein (Eds.), *Helping people change.* New York: Pergamon, 1975.

Hinde, R. A. *Animal behaviour.* New York: McGraw-Hill, 1966.

Homme, L. E. Perspectives in psychology—XXIV control of coverts, the operants of the mind. *Psychological Record*, 1965, *15*, 501–511.

Hull, C. L. *Principles of behavior.* New York: Appleton-Century, 1943.

Hurwitz, H. B. M. Conditioned responses in rats reinforced by light. *British Journal of Animal Behavior*, 1956, *4*, 31.

Huttunen, M. O. General model for the molecular events in synapses during learning. *Perspectives in Biology and Medicine*, 1973, *17*, 103–108.

Kent, R. N., Wilson, G. T., & Nelson, R. Effects of false heart-rate feedback on avoidance behavior: An investigation of "cognitive desensitization." *Behavior Therapy*, 1972, *3*, 1–6.

Kimmel, H. D. Instrumental conditioning of autonomically mediated behavior. *Psychological Bulletin*, 1967, *67*, 337–345.

Kohler, I. Über Aufbau und Wandlungen der Wahrnehmungswelt. *Oesterreichische Akademie der Wissenschaften: Proceedings 227*, 1951, Vol. *I* (monograph).

Latimer, P. Carbon dioxide as a reciprocal inhibitor in the treatment of neurosis. *Journal of Behavior Therapy and Experimental Psychiatry*, 1977, *8*, 83–85.

Lloyd, D. P. C. Facilitation and inhibition of spinal motoneurons. *Journal of Neurophysiology*, 1946, *9*, 421–438.

Locke, E. A. Is "behavior therapy" behavioristic? *Psychological Bulletin*, 1971, *76*, 318–327.

Locke, J. *An essay concerning human understanding.* Book II, Chapter XII, 1690.

Mahoney, M. J. Reflections on the cognitive-learning trend in psychotherapy. *American Psychologist*, 1977, *32*, 5–13.

Masserman, J. H. *Principles of dynamic psychiatry.* Philadelphia: Saunders, 1946.

McGeogh, J. A. Forgetting and the law of disuse. *Psychological Review*, 1932, *39*, 352–370.

McGeogh, J. A., McKinney, F., & Peters, H. Studies in retroactive inhibition. IX. Retroactive inhibition, reproductive inhibition and reminiscence. *Journal of Experimental Psychology*, 1937, *20*, 131–141.

Meichenbaum, D. H. Self-instructional methods. In F. H. Kanfer & A. P. Goldstein (Eds.), *Helping people change.* New York: Pergamon, 1975.

Miller, N. E., & DiCara, L. V. Instrumental learning of vasomotor responses by rats: Learning to respond differentially in the two ears. *Science*, 1968, *159*, 1485.

Olds, J. Hypothalamic substrates of reward. *Physiological Reviews*, 1962, *42*, 554–604.

Olds, J. Mapping the mind onto the brain. In F. G. Worden, J. P. Swazey, & G. Adelman (Eds.), *The neurosciences: Paths of discovery.* Cambridge, Mass.: Colonial, 1975.

Olds, J., Disterhoft, J. F., Segal, M., Kornblith, C. L., & Hirsh, R. Learning centers of rat brain mapped by measuring latencies of conditioned unit responses. *Journal of Neurophysiology*, 1972, *35*, 202–219.

Osgood, C. E. Meaningful similarity and interference in learning. *Journal of Experimental Psychology*, 1946, *36*, 227–301.

Osgood, C. E. An investigation into the causes of retroactive inhibition. *Journal of Experimental Psychology*, 1948, *38*, 132–147.

Pavlov, I. P. *Conditioned reflexes.* (G. V. Anrep, trans.). New York: Liveright, 1927.

Pavlov, I. P. *Selected works.* Moscow: Foreign Languages Publishing House, 1955.

Pratt, C. C. *The logic of modern psychology*. New York: Macmillan, 1939.

Raimy, V. Changing misconceptions as the therapeutic task. In A. Burton (Ed.), *What makes behavior change possible?* New York: Brunner/Mazel, 1976.

Razran, G. *Mind in evolution*. Boston: Houghton Mifflin, 1971.

Rosen, G. M., Rosen, E., & Reid, J. R. Cognitive desensitization and avoidance behavior. *Journal of Abnormal Psychology*, 1972, *80*, 176–182.

Ryle, G. *The concept of mind*. London: Hutchinson, 1949.

Seitz, P. F. D. Dynamically oriented brief psychotherapy: Psychocutaneous excoriation syndrome. *Psychosomatic Medicine*, 1953, *15*, 200–242.

Sheffield, F. D., & Roby, T. B. Reward value of a non-nutritive sweet taste. *Journal of Comparative and Physiological Psychology*, 1950, *43*, 471–481.

Skinner, B. F. *Science and human behavior*. New York: Macmillan, 1953.

Skinner, B. F. *Beyond freedom and dignity*. New York: Knopf, 1971.

Skinner, B. F. The steep and thorny way to a science of behavior. *American Psychologist*, 1975, *30*, 42–49.

Skinner, B. F. *Reflections on behaviorism and society*. Englewood Cliffs, N.J.: Prentice-Hall, 1978.

Steketee, G., & Roy, G. Carbon dioxide/oxygen in the deconditioning of anxiety reactions, submitted for publication, 1979.

Stratton, G. M. Vision without inversion of the retinal image. *Psychological Review*, 1897, *4*, 341–360; 463–481.

Sushinsky, L. W., & Bootzin, R. R. Cognitive desensitization as a model of systematic desensitization. *Behaviour Research and Therapy*, 1970, *8*, 29–33.

Taylor, J. G. Personal Communication, 1955.

Taylor, J. G. *The behavior basis of perception*. New Haven: Yale University Press, 1962.

Ullmann, L. P. On cognitions and behavior therapy. *Behavior Therapy*, 1970, *1*, 201–204.

Valins, S., & Ray, A. A. Effects of cognitive desensitization on avoidance behavior. *Journal of Personality and Social Psychology*, 1967, *7*, 345–350.

Wade, T. C., Malloy, T. E., & Proctor, S. Imaginal correlates of self-reported fear and avoidance behavior. *Behaviour Research and Therapy*, 1977, *15*, 17–22.

Wolberg, L. R. The psychodynamic–behavioral polemic. *International Journal of Psychiatry*, 1970, *9*, 155–162.

Wolpe, J. An interpretation of the effects of combinations of stimuli (patterns) based on current neurophysiology. *Psychological Review*, 1949, *56*, 277–283.

Wolpe, J. Need-reduction, drive-reduction, and reinforcement: A neurophysiological view. *Psychological Review*, 1950, *57*, 19–26.

Wolpe, J. The formation of negative habits: A neurophysiological view. *Psychological Review*, 1952, *59*, 290–299. (a)

Wolpe, J. The neurophysiology of learning and delayed reward learning. *Psychological Review*, 1952, *59*, 192–199. (b)

Wolpe, J. Primary stimulus generalization: A neurophysiological view. *Psychological Review*, 1952, *59*, 8–11. (c)

Wolpe, J. Experimental neurosis as learned behavior. *British Journal of Psychology*, 1952, *43*, 243–268. (d)

Wolpe, J. Theory construction for Blodgett's latent learning. *Psychological Review*, 1953, *60*, 340.

Wolpe, J. Reciprocal inhibition as the main basis of psychotherapeutic effects. *Archives of Neurological Psychiatry*, 1954, *72*, 205–226.

Wolpe, J. *Psychotherapy by reciprocal inhibition*. Stanford, Calif.: Stanford University Press, 1958.

Wolpe, J. *The practice of behavior therapy* (2nd ed.). New York: Pergamon, 1973.

Wolpe, J. *Theme and variations: A behavior therapy casebook.* New York: Pergamon, 1976. (a)

Wolpe, J. Behavior therapy and its malcontents. II. Multimodal electicism, cognitive exclusivism and "exposure" empiricism. *Journal of Behavior Therapy and Experimental Psychiatry,* 1976, 7, 109–116. (b)

Wolpe, J. Inadequate behavior analysis: The Achille's heel of outcome research in behavior therapy. *Journal of Behavior Therapy and Experimental Psychiatry,* 1977, 7, 1–3.

Woody, C. D., & Engel, J., Jr. Changes in unit activity and thresholds to electrical microstimulation at coronal-pericruciate cortex of cat with classical conditioning of different facial movements. *Journal of Neurophysiology,* 1972, 35, 230.

Young, J. Z. Memory as a selective process. *Australian Academy of Science Report: Symposium on Biological Memory,* 1973, pp. 25–45.

Young, J. Z. Sources of discovery in neuroscience. In F. G. Worden, J. P. Swazey, & G. Adelman (Eds.), *The neurosciences: Paths of discovery.* Cambridge, Mass.: Colonial, 1975.

Zilboorg, G. (In collaboration with G. W. Henry). *A history of medical psychology.* New York: Norton, 1941.

And Now for Something Completely Different

Cognition and Little *r*

GERALD C. DAVISON

Wolpe has not minced words in his critique of cognitive trends in contemporary behavior therapy. My response to him will be similarly blunt. Differences of opinion are, to my mind, the essence of our scientific enterprise, and Wolpe provides a good opportunity to examine important theoretical developments by the unambiguous way he sets forth his case.

Basically, Wolpe's essay is composed of a series of blanket, unsupported—and often unsupportable—assertions, declared emphatically as if they are demonstrated facts, and when resting at all on data, relying on published reports that ignore or are inconsistent with prevailing theories and data.

Offered here is a sampling of assertions stated as fact: "The responses set off by the perception (of an object) depend on previous conditioning in the presence of similar objects." "Images evoked in the absence of objects . . . are conditioned perceptions." "Shoplifting [behavior, in a woman treated by Wolpe] ceased because the emotional behavior that was its necessary antecedent was eliminated, evidently due to the building up of

GERALD C. DAVISON • Department of Psychology, University of Southern California, Los Angeles, California 90007. Preparation of this paper was facilitated by NIMH Research Grant #MH 2432706.

conditioned inhibition on the basis of reciprocal inhibition." "*Every* response, even if it is only a perceptual response, must be correlated with some measure of central neural excitation, the cessation of which . . . is drive reduction. Although of lower magnitude, this is an event of the same class of a drive reduction occasioned by the allaying of a need such as hunger. The strength of cognitive learning is naturally enhanced if concomitant arousals are reduced by the particular perception." "These findings [that a subject can adjust to distortions from prismatic glasses via interactions with the physical environment] beautifully demonstrate that visual perception is . . . a function of a learning mechanism that adjusts the effects of visual stimulation in accordance with the *reinforcement* of motor responses (italics added)." "Thoughts are responses . . . and . . . may be conditioned to other thoughts and to responses in other categories." "If weak anxiety responses are elicited during pleasant emotional responses to the therapist, some inadvertent deconditioning of unadaptive anxiety responses may take place" "What Mahoney calls the 'cognitive revolution' has added nothing of visible value to the practice of behavior therapy." "There is to date not a single study that shows that the addition of nonbehavioristic practices improves on the impressive and lasting outcomes that behavior therapy achieves in neurotic cases."

It would take a separate reply to critique all of these unverified statements on which Wolpe bases his argument that workers who speak of cognition in terms different from his are misguided. I must restrict myself instead to an examination of what I deem his main contentions.

An initial misunderstanding—and a most unfortunate one since it seems to underlie his concern about cognitive trends in behavior theory and behavior therapy—is that to embrace a cognitive viewpoint is to forsake determinism. Wolpe's nemesis is Bandura (1974), whose thinking has evolved from a relatively straightforward mechanism in the early and mid-1960s to recent statements that human thought processes play a role in behavior. Bandura does not claim novelty in taking the view that human cognition influences what we do at the autonomic and motoric levels. Anyone even vaguely familiar with the "new look" perception literature of the 1940s, for example (cf. Bruner, 1951; Blake & Ramsey, 1951), will recall that psychologists long ago forsook the passive organism view of humankind and infrahumankind as well. Data are plentiful that the organism is an active, *constructive* creature in mediating between inputs (stimuli) and outputs (responses). To be sure, investigators differ on how to *conceptualize* these inner workings, but even a passing familiarity with both the history of experimental psychology and of contemporary developments in cognitive psychology shows that what we choose to call "thought" or "cognition" must be included in any account of behavior—especially complex human behavior (cf. Bower, 1978; Neisser, 1967). Indeed, this constructive aspect of human thinking is widely recognized to be a useful aid in understanding the very nature of scientific inquiry (cf. Kuhn, 1962). And to embrace such cognitive viewpoints does not necessarily blackball a scientist from the determinist club, a fact that, at some points in his paper, Wolpe himself appears to acknowledge.

So, what's all the fuss about? To the degree that behavior therapists are beginning *formally* to acknowledge the cognitive processes of themselves and of their clients, we are doing no more than beginning to catch up with that body of experimental psychology on which our applied science purports to rest.

Wolpe feels that these developments are not new in behavior therapy. He attempts to persuade us by quoting from some of his earlier work, suggestive of the fact that he was aware of the utility of using scientific metaphors like attitudes, misconceptions, and the like, in the context of his *S–R* Hullian connectionism. As someone who diligently studied Wolpe's pioneering papers of the 1950s, and especially his classic 1958 book, may I be allowed to observe that his *formal* acknowledgment that people think and that we should find some way to talk about this, *is* new. This is not to say that Wolpe was ever nonmediational—how could one claim this when one soberly considers the *procedure* of systematic desensitization (in which the only overt behavior worthy of note is the raising of an index finger when the anxiety-inhibition process is failing)? Wolpe has always been mediational, never radically behavioristic, *but* his mediators have always been of a stimulus–response variety, reflected currently in his use of the phrases "cognitive behavior" and "perceptual behavior" rather than simply cognition or perception, and seen also in his efforts to explain perception in conditioning terms. Whatever one thinks of these particular efforts, germane to our present discussion is whether such *s–r* mediational accounts of complex human behavior represent what some term the cognitive revolution in behavior therapy. I suggest Wolpe is talking about quite a different "cognitive" framework from what I believe cognitive behavior therapy[1] can be.

In the 1960s—with Wolpe very much in the forefront—behavior therapy vehemently downplayed the role of cognition (even of the *s–r* variety) in therapeutic behavior change. Wolpe, for instance, emphasized the importance of autonomic learning, building his version of behavior therapy upon reciprocal inhibition at the neural autonomic level. (And his present effort still reflects his continuing commitment to reciprocal inhibition.) And for their part, applied behavior analysts were stressing—and continue in this vein—the automatic nature of instrumental learning, with

---

[1] As an aside, may I observe that this new phrase, "cognitive behavior therapy," threatens to be as unfortunate as its predecessor "behavior therapy." The latter has continually forced the mediationalists among us to insist that we do not ignore the inner life of our clients and that "behavior" can refer to unobservables (the little *r*'s); and the former suggests a confluence of cognitive psychology and behaviorism—something many psychologists find amusing, if not obfuscating.

contingencies operating directly on overt behavior, cognitive (or any other mediational) processes playing *no* role at all in learning or relearning. So to assert that there is nothing new under the sun is not defensible.

But to urge caution in populating the black box with a host of strange-sounding cognitive metaphors would be, I trust, something Wolpe and I could agree on. Further, to urge caution by reminding ourselves that the data are far from in, that we must remain tentative in what we say we know—this too is something I trust there is general agreement on.

The crucial metatheoretical point that Wolpe is missing—or at least not showing that he appreciates—is that "stimulus," "response," "cognition," and all the rest are *explanatory fictions*. They are words referring to concepts that we *make up* to explain what we call data.

Let me elaborate. There is an important distinction to be drawn between *S–R* mediational theories (cf. Mowrer, 1939; Staats & Staats, 1963) and cognitive theories. Mowrer's major contribution was metatheoretical in that, stated simply, he proposed that we could fruitfully construe mental and emotional life as functionally equivalent to overt behavior. Thereby, one could bring to bear on these "little *r*'s" the knowledge we had amassed on the big *R*'s. This paradigmatic statement lies at the root of much contemporary behavior therapy, even when unacknowledged, and the importance of this metatheoretical contribution is not to be underestimated.

This is different from the cognitive revolution in behavior therapy, though it is only recently being recognized (cf. Davison & Neale, 1978; Goldfried, 1979). Recent proposals are that we adopt a truly cognitive view of maladaptive behavior and its alteration; that we take seriously what cognitive psychology has to offer; and that we attempt to integrate cognitive theories into behavior therapy (see Landau, 1978, for an example of this in the area of semantic memory and phobia, as well as for a clear exposition of what a cognitive point of view would mean for behavior therapy). This trend is entirely different from what Wolpe says has always been a part of behavior therapy.[2] There are constructs and there are constructs. Media-

---

[2] En passant, nearly all published work relating cognition and behavior therapy is *s–r* mediational as well, and not truly cognitive in the sense I am using the word here. For example, Meichenbaum's (1977) innovative research rests explictly on the assumption that thoughts are nothing but those little *r*'s that are our legacy from Mowrer, Miller, and others. It is true that colleagues like Meichenbaum and Wolpe talk of the importance of our perception of the world for how we behave in it, but when one seriously considers what this "perception" really entails, one finds, I suggest, merely a passing acknowledgment of the fact that humans (and animals) code inputs before they emit outputs. One has at best something like a "coding response," which itself is in need of the scrutiny that perception and problem solving have enjoyed for years among cognitive psychologists. The focus of therapy in the *s–r* mediational framework is on increasing or decreasing the frequency or strength of these "coding *r*'s" rather than on a study of how people actually encode information. Both viewpoints will turn out to be important, I suspect; suffice it to say at this time that they are *different* viewpoints.

tional theories can include many different kinds of mediators. A "little *r*" theory is not a cognitive theory in the sense that a contemporary cognitive theory is. For the latter, reinforcement schedules are, at best, of peripheral interest. What truly defines a cognitive viewpoint is the *structuring* of experience (or what is popularly referred to nowadays as information processing). Humankind imposes a structure on life, and it is this that behavior therapists are being urged to attend to. This is what the cognitive revolution in behavior therapy is all about, and it is not what Wolpe asserts to us has existed over the past 20 years.

In his desire to preserve his quasi-neurological reciprocal inhibition model of psychotherapy, Wolpe is ignoring some of the complexities that others have been dealing with explicitly. The clearest example of this, to my mind, is his continued insistence that assertion is but one of several parasympathetic responses that can be counterposed to the sympathetic response of anxiety. Wolpe is overlooking the intricate societal and value issues surrounding a serious consideration of assertion *per se*. What, for example, is assertion? How is it to be contrasted with aggression? And under what conditions is a given topographic response an assertive one or an aggressive one? Does one's gender have anything to do with it, or do the circumstances of one's life, e.g., being in the military versus being in academic life? Given that one decides to encourage a client to be more assertive, what *form* should the assertive repertoire take for different individuals? And, perhaps most directly, after talking about assertive behavior for 30 years, since Salter (1949), has anyone even attempted to demonstrate that an assertive response is parasympathetic, or that it is incompatible with anxiety, however anxiety is measured?

To me it is no accident that the subtle questions have been raised in recent years by behavioral workers who unabashedly take a cognitive perspective on behavior therapy (e.g., Goldfried & Davison, 1976; Lange & Jakubowski, 1976; Lazarus, 1971). For a careful consideration of such questions *requires* that one go beyond observables and that one invoke mediators that go far beyond little *r*'s. Anthropologists, sociologists, and political scientists—whose work we ignore at our own risk (cf. Davison, 1978)—routinely employ cognitive metaphors as they attempt to grapple with the complexities of human existence. As behavior therapy continues becoming more and more sophisticated, we will, I believe, have to forsake the strictures of both a radical and a mediational behaviorism.

Science thrives on controversy, on disagreement. There are sociopolitical forces that influence the concepts that are allowable, fashionable, in a given period of time (cf. Davison & Neale, 1978). For better or for worse (and clearly I think for better) behavior therapy is looking within the organism for variables that will account for available data and lead to interesting, useful hypotheses for future study. If we take seriously our relationships with experimental psychology, it is unwise to ignore contemporary experimental psychology, which is very heavily cognitive in nature. And it is unnecessary and counterproductive to insist that behavior therapists all along have incorporated cognitive factors into their metatheory, theorizing, and practices. Behavior therapy as we enter the 1980s is very different from what it was in the 1950s, when pioneers like Wolpe were staking out new areas of theorizing and application at a time most of us were concerned about our acne problems. Wolpe's contributions, along with those of others, changed the nature of psychotherapy irrevocably. The viewpoints and theories they put forward have served us well. Like all good theories they gave rise to research, much of which suggests that the initial abstractions are not as useful as theories and viewpoints that have more recently been proposed. When behavior therapists claimed to be relying on learning principles, they were many years behind those S–R experimentalists whose work they said they were using. In the past 10 years or so, we have been "going cognitive" and have continued this tradition of being years behind what experimentalists have been concerned with. *But* we do seem to have lost our cognitive virginity, and *that is* important, and *that* is something Wolpe's paper does not evidence an appreciation for. It is far too early to know how fruitful our cognitive trends will be, but that is hardly a reason to derogate those who wish to explore in this direction, and certainly too early to announce that such attempts are doomed to failure.

REFERENCES

Bandura, A. Behavior theory and the models of man. *American Psychologist*, 1974, *29*, 859–869.

Blake, R. R., & Ramsey, G. V. (Eds.). *Perception: An approach to personality*. New York: Ronald Press, 1951.

Bower, G. H. Contacts of cognitive psychology with social learning theory. *Cognitive Therapy and Research*, 1978, *2*, 123–147.

Bruner, J. S. Personality dynamics and the process of perceiving. In R. R. Blake & G. V. Ramsey (Eds.), *Perception: An approach to personality*. New York: Ronald Press, 1951, pp. 121–147.

Davison, G. C. Not can but ought: The treatment of homosexuality. *Journal of Consulting and Clinical Psychology*, 1978, *46*, 170–172.

Davison, G. C., & Neale, J. M. *Abnormal psychology: An experimental clinical approach* (2nd ed.). New York: Wiley, 1978.

Goldfried, M. R. Anxiety reduction through cognitive-behavioral intervention. In P. C. Kendall & S. D. Hollon (Eds.), *Cognitive-behavioral interventions: Theory, research, and procedures*. New York: Academic, 1979.

Goldfried, M. R., & Davison, G. C. *Clinical behavior therapy*. New York: Holt, Rinehart & Winston, 1976.

Kuhn, T. S. *The structure of scientific revolutions*. Chicago: University of Chicago Press, 1962.

Landau, R. J. *The use of semantic structures in the assessment of fear*. Unpublished manuscript, State University of New York at Stony Brook, 1978.

Lange, A. J., & Jakubowski, P. *Responsible assertive behavior*. Champaign, Ill.: Research, 1976.

Lazarus, A. A. *Behavior therapy and beyond*. New York: McGraw-Hill, 1971.

Meichenbaum, D. H. *Cognitive behavior modification: An integrative approach*. New York: Plenum, 1977.

Mowrer, O. H. A stimulus–response analysis of anxiety and its role as a reinforcing agent. *Psychological Review*, 1939, *46*, 553–565.

Neisser, U. *Cognitive psychology*. New York: Appleton-Century-Crofts, 1967.

Salter, A. *Conditioned reflex therapy*. New York: Farrar, Straus, 1949.

Staats, A. W., & Staats, C. K. *Complex human behavior*. New York: Holt, Rinehart & Winston, 1963.

Imaginal Processes

Therapeutic Applications and Theoretical Models

MERRILL P. ANDERSON

The past twenty years have seen a proliferation of therapeutic approaches and techniques that rely on the cognitive capacities subsumed under the terms imagery, imagining, fantasy, and mental rehearsal. While a variety of imagery and fantasy techniques have been used in psychodynamic therapies from Freud and Jung to some contemporary European therapeutic approaches (Singer, 1974), the recent rise of interest in the United States has been largely in the area of behavioral and cognitive-behavioral techniques. Since Wolpe's introduction of systematic desensitization (1958), behaviorally oriented clinicians have shown an increased willingness to rely on the imaginal capacities of their clients and an increased creativity in designing ways to put those capacities to use. This renewed interest of clinicians in imaginal processes has been paralleled in psychology as a whole by the resurrection of imagery and other cognitive processes as legitimate topics of empirical investigation (Holt, 1964; Segal, 1971; Sheehan, 1972).

Although imagery-based therapy techniques are receiving increasing

MERRILL P. ANDERSON • Division of Social Sciences, University of Minnesota, Morris, Minnesota 56267. This chapter was completed while the author was supported by Alcohol, Drug Abuse, and Mental Health Administration National Research Award No. 1-F32-MH07473-01 from the National Institute of Mental Health.

attention from therapists and researchers, there is considerable conceptual confusion and imprecision about the nature of their use of imagery. Different techniques suggest different theoretical interpretations of the processes by which they lead to change, and of the means by which imaginal thinking contributes to those processes. There is, in short, little agreement about the most useful way of thinking about imaginal processes and the therapeutic roles they play. This chapter argues that there is a need for clinical scientists and practitioners to move toward resolving some of the conceptual ambiguity surrounding their use of these processes.

IMAGERY IN BEHAVIORAL AND COGNITIVE-BEHAVIORAL THERAPIES

Systematic Desensitization

Systematic desensitization was the first of the contemporary behavior therapy procedures to rely on the client's imaginal abilities. The success and popularity of desensitization may well have set the precedent for the use of imagery in subsequent behavioral and cognitive-behavioral procedures. Indeed, as shall be discussed later, some of the more recent techniques are essentially variants of this basic procedure.

Desensitization was designed as a treatment for phobias. As outlined by Wolpe (1973), the procedure consists of the following steps. First, the client and therapist construct a hierarchy of anxiety-arousing situations related to the problem area. Second, the client is trained in the use of an anxiety-competing response. Typically, this is a progressive relaxation procedure (Jacobson, 1938) consisting of alternate tensing and relaxing of muscle groups supplemented by deep breathing. Third, while the client is relaxed, the therapist tells him to visualize the least anxiety-arousing scene from the hierarchy. If the client indicates that he experiences any anxiety while imagining the scene, the therapist has him terminate the scene and concentrate on relaxing. After relaxation has replaced anxiety, the therapist tells the client to imagine the scene again. This process continues until the client reports that he can imagine the particular scene without experiencing any anxiety. They then progress to the next scene on the hierarchy, and repeat the process. They continue in this fashion until the client is able to imagine the most anxiety-arousing scene without experiencing any anxiety.

Wolpe (1958) conceptualizes the mechanism of change in desensitization as a process of reciprocal inhibition, the blocking of anxiety responses to anxiety-arousing stimuli by the elicitation of an incompatible or inhibitory response. As a result of the inhibition of the anxiety response, the conditioned link between the stimulus and the response is thought to be weakened, and the connection between the stimulus and the new, incompatible response strengthened. With the conditioned anxiety reaction now supplanted by a new, more positive or neutral conditioned emotional reaction, the client is free to develop more adaptive approach behaviors.

The basic effectiveness of desensitization for reducing anxiety to the imagined scenes and for facilitating approach behavior to *in vivo* situations appears to be fairly well established (Bandura, 1969), although the extent to which this has been conclusively demonstrated has recently been questioned (Kazdin & Wilcoxon, 1976). There is still controversy, however, about the processes through which desensitization achieves its effects. While Wolpe (1978) still adheres to a conditioning model, other theorists have placed more emphasis on the mediating role of cognitive and social variables than on conditioned physiological arousal as an explanation (Bandura, 1969; Jacobs & Wolpin, 1971; Mahoney, 1974; Wilkins, 1971).

In desensitization, cognitive representations (images) are used instead of the actual anxiety-arousing stimuli. The procedure works as well or better with actual stimuli (Bandura, 1969), but this often proves difficult to arrange, especially in clinical situations. The theoretical rationale for using imagery, aside from the practical advantages of flexibility and ease, is the assumption that cognitive representations of situations can become conditioned stimuli that are capable of eliciting the same autonomic arousal patterns as exposure to *in vivo* anxiety-arousing situations (Wolpe, 1973).

In order to arrive at a better understanding of the imaginal component of desensitization, it is helpful to examine the instructions that are typically given to a client during scene presentations (Wolpe, 1973). The client is told to visualize the specific scene as clearly as possible, and to imagine the scene as though he were actually in it, rather than observing it from afar. The therapist gives a brief description of the scene, waits until the client indicates that the image has been clearly formed, and then allows the client five to seven seconds to maintain the scene before terminating it. The therapist's description of the scene includes only the most basic details necessary to define the scene. In addition to using imagined hierarchy scenes, Wolpe occasionally supplements the relaxation procedure with calm, tranquil scenes (e.g., laying on a river bank watching a leaf floating down river).

Wolpe (1973) states that the most common problem encountered with the imagery component of the procedure is an inability on the part of the client to generate scenes that have a sufficient sense of reality. He suggests three techniques for overcoming this type of obstacle. The therapist can describe the scene in more detail, he can ask the client to describe his own image, or he can hypnotize the client. Wolpe notes that this problem is more likely to occur when presenting the more anxiety-arousing scenes from the hierarchy.

An early variant of the basic desensitization procedure was the technique of "emotive imagery" reported by Lazarus and Abramovitz (1962). They found it difficult to use relaxation while desensitizing phobic children.

As an alternative they developed an imaginary story that involved the child's favorite heroes from television, movies, and comic books. Imagining the story was supposed to evoke comfortable, calm, and relaxed feelings in the child. While the child was imagining his heroes, the therapist would inject the hierarchy scenes into the story. Because the hierarchy items were presented in the context of stronger, positive feelings, they would, presumably, fail to elicit an anxiety reaction.

Several observations about the use of imagery in desensitization may be offered. First, and fundamentally, the function of imagined scenes in Wolpe's model is the evocation of autonomic states, both positive and negative. Imagined scenes are assumed to elicit affective reactions that are equivalent, at least in their essential pattern if not in strength, to reactions to *in vivo* situations. There is ample evidence that imaginal activity can indeed stimulate physiological arousal (Barber & Hahn, 1964; Grossberg & Wilson, 1968; Mathews, 1971). However, as mentioned earlier, there is considerable disagreement about whether or not the treatment effects attributable to desensitization are mediated by peripheral conditioning.

A second observation that can be made about the use of imagery in desensitization is that vividness of clarity of the imagined scene should be related to the effectiveness of the treatment. Wolpe (1973) emphasizes the importance of obtaining clear, realistic imagery, and Lazarus (1964), his collaborator at the time, states that successful treatment requires that the patient be able to "picture the imagined scenes sufficiently clearly, vividly, and realistically for them to evoke anxiety at the outset" (p. 66). The reciprocal inhibition model would therefore seem to imply that the more vivid the imagined scene, the more successful it would be in arousing the appropriate emotional responses, and hence the more complete and successful the conditioning process would be. Imagery is so central to the entire procedure that clarity or vividness would still seem to be an important variable even if one does not subscribe to this model. If a person is unable to form the assigned images, it is difficult to understand how he is receiving the benefits of the treatment, whatever the actual mechanisms of change.

The data relating imagery vividness to therapeutic outcome in desensitization have been sparse, but those extant have not been very supportive of the foregoing assumption (Davis, McLemore, & London, 1970; McLemore, 1972). The major difficulty in this line of research may relate to the absence of satisfactory methods for assessing imagery vividness (McLemore, 1976). This, in turn, is related to disagreement about the most useful way of conceptualizing imagery vividness, imagery ability, and even imagery itself (Lang, 1977; McLemore, 1976; Richardson, 1977; Sheehan, 1972). The types of measures used most often include rating scales of imagery vividness, spatial ability tests, memory tests, and questionnaires (Richardson, 1977). A number of studies have examined the relationships among potential measures of imagery ability, but clear recommendations about which is the most valid and useful measure for examining the relationship between imagery ability and treatment outcome have not emerged (Anderson, 1975; Danaher & Thoresen, 1972; Hiscock, 1978; McLemore, 1976; Rehm, 1973; Rimm & Bottrell, 1969).

In summary, systematic desensitization has been an influential treatment procedure that has spawned or influenced some of the techniques to be discussed in following sections. While a substantial amount of work remains to be done on identifying the processes through which imagining contributes to the effectiveness of the technique, desensitization has opened the door to further empirical investigations on the role of imagery processes in behavior change.

Implosion and Flooding Procedures

These two approaches to eliminating phobic arousal invoke a rationale and method that is almost opposite of that used in desensitization. In both implosion (Stampfl & Levis, 1967) and flooding (Rachman, 1968) an attempt is made to elicit high levels of anxiety by having the client repeatedly imagine intense, exaggerated scenes about the phobic situation. This contrasts with the emphasis on graduated exposure in desensitization, where the goal is to minimize the amount of anxiety elicited during scene presentation.

Implosion and flooding are usually differentiated on the basis of the type of content clients are instructed to imagine. The distinguishing feature of implosive imagery seems to be that much of the content of the imagery themes is based on psychoanalytic assumptions about the nature of the conflicts underlying the phobia (Rimm & Masters, 1974). Conflict areas that are often depicted in the imagery include orality, anality, sexuality, guilt, rejection, aggression, and loss of impulse control. This is in keeping with the original description by Stampfl and Levis (1967) of the procedure as a "learning-theory-based psychodynamic-behavioral therapy." Flooding, on the other hand, consists of imagining a variety of intense and frightening situations involving the phobic object, but without the emphasis on psychodynamic elaborations. The imagery in flooding may be exaggerated and improbable, but it remains relatively close to the phobic area. The theoretical rationale for both techniques is substantially the same. Prolonged exposure to intensely fear-provoking stimuli without the experience of actual aversive consequences is thought to lead to extinction of the fear response because of nonreinforcement (Stampfl & Levis, 1967).

The imagery procedure of the two techniques proceeds in the following manner (Rimm & Masters, 1974; Watson & Marks, 1971). After determining the nature and extent of the phobic reaction, the therapist initiates the imagery. He describes the scene in vivid, multisensory detail, including both behaviors, environmental events, and the client's feeling reactions to the imaginary situation. Typically, there is a progression within the scene from the least to the most frightening events, but this is not always the case. The "least" frightening scenes in these procedures are still designed to elicit high levels of anxiety. While he is imagining the scene, the client is watched closely by the therapist for signs of anxiety (facial expressions, muscle tension) and may even be questioned about his reactions. As soon as the therapist is convinced that his client is not experiencing anxiety in response to a scene, he will shift to a new scene in order to maintain the client's anxiety at a high level. With implosion, the therapist's description of the imaginary material is often embellished with theatrical accompaniments (e.g., therapist growling, clapping his hands, touching the client, or using the sound of a fan to simulate a buzz saw), while with flooding, the therapist presents the descriptions in a monotonous manner. With both procedures, the scenes are presented continuously until the client reports no further affective arousal.

Several points can be made about the use of imagery in these procedures, and in comparison with its use in desensitization. First, the function of the imagery, according to the original models, is to elicit emotional arousal. The maladaptive emotional reaction is the target of the treatment, and this reaction must be elicited for extinction to occur. Second, the basic themes and the details of the scene are determined by the therapist rather than the client. A third point is Lang's (1977) observation about the relative emphasis on response versus stimulus elements in these procedures (as contrasted with desensitization). A substantial portion of the therapist's descriptions in flooding and implosion focuses on the client's own affective reactions to the imagined events. In desensitization, the therapist primarily describes the basic stimulus elements of the scene. Fourth, and particularly with implosion, the content of the imaginary scenes crosses the line from the frightening-but-realistic category to the frightening-but-unrealistic category. Bandura (1969) speculates that this crossover may suggest new fears to the client and hence provide a basis for later maladaptive arousal. Fifth, the vividness of the imagery in implosion may be affected by the therapist's theatrical accompaniments. Although the intent is clearly to enhance the imagery, it also could be distracting and lead to lower involvement.

Although there have been case reports of therapeutic successes with these procedures (Boulougouris & Marks, 1969), reviewers of the evidence from controlled comparative studies suggest that their efficacy has not been established (Bandura, 1969; Morganstern, 1973). The theoretical model of the therapeutic process involved has also been questioned (Borkovec, 1972; Watson & Marks, 1971), and Morganstern (1973) has suggested that cognitive expectancy factors may be an important factor in the positive results occasionally reported. There have not been any investigations of the relationship between imagery variables (vividness, ability) and treatment effectiveness. Because of the equivocal evidence, the risk of increasing the patient's fears, and the availability of alternative treatments, both Bandura (1969) and Singer (1974) suggest caution and restraint in using these procedures.

Covert Conditioning Techniques

Joseph Cautela has developed a collection of imagery-based techniques that are assumed to function according to operant-conditioning principles. Covert sensitization, covert reinforcement, and covert modeling, the three most widely used of his techniques, are discussed in this section. The remaining techniques—covert extinction (Cautela, 1971a), covert negative reinforcement (Cautela, 1970a), and covert response cost (Cautela, 1977)— are substantially the same in their general approach and in their use of imagery.

Cautela's approach is based on what he calls the homogeneity assumption and the interaction assumption (Cautela, 1977). The homogeneity assumption asserts that the same functional relationships that hold for overt behavior and environmental events also hold for covert behavior and covertly presented stimuli. Covert in this usage refers to imagery. Just as an overt behavior can be reinforced or punished by its consequences, a covert behavior can be reinforced or punished by covertly presented consequences. According to the interaction hypothesis, overt and covert responses and stimuli can functionally interact with each other. This means that overt behavior can be elicited or caused by covert stimuli, and, conversely, covert behavior can be elicited or caused by overt stimuli. Mahoney (1974) recognizes a third, implicit assumption in this approach, which he terms the automaticity assumption. This is the assumption that conditioning occurs automatically when two events are placed in temporal contiguity, regardless of whether the response actually produced the consequence or not. In other words, it is sufficient for a pleasant event or thought to follow an overt or covert behavior for it to have a reinforcing effect on that behavior or thought, regardless of any perceived or real causal relationship between the two.

The validity of these assumptions and the adequacy of Cautela's conceptualization of the procedures as conditioning techniques have been seriously questioned by other reviewers of his work (Kazdin, 1977; Mahoney, 1974; Singer, 1974). As Kazdin (1977) notes, however, this is not equivalent to saying that the techniques themselves are worthless. Rather, the mechanisms through which they contribute to behavior change may be different than those posited by Cautela. The procedures of the three most frequently used and investigated of these techniques are summarized in the following sections.

Covert Sensitization. Covert sensitization (Cautela, 1967, 1977) is an imaginally based aversion, or punishment, procedure designed for use with problematic approach behaviors (e.g., overeating, smoking, deviant sexual behaviors, and alcohol or drug abuse). In essence, it consists of making a highly aversive imaginal consequence follow imaginal enactment of the maladaptive approach behavior. After initial assessment, the therapist presents the client with a conditioning rationale for the development of problem and for the therapeutic procedure. Included in the rationale are instructions about how the client is to imagine the described scenes. The same basic rationale and imagery instructions are given in all of the techniques. The client is urged to involve all of his senses in the imaginary scene, and to imagine the scene as though he were experiencing it, rather than as though he were observing it. This is followed by a practice scene, after which the client is questioned about the clarity and emotionality of the scene. The therapist then asks the client to imagine a sequence of events leading up to the initiation of the problem behavior, along with the beginnings of the behavior itself (e.g., reaching for food or cigarettes). At the point of initiation of the problem behavior, the therapist vividly describes an extremely unpleasant, noxious, and disgusting scene, usually involving nausea and vomit. After having developed the unpleasant imagery, the client is told to switch to a more pleasant, relieving scene. On the first trial with each scene, the therapist describes it to the client, and on subsequent trials the client is expected to imagine the sequence on his own. After each trial the therapist checks the clarity and arousal capacity of the scene. A variety of different scenes may be used for different aspects of the approach behavior (with the noxious imagery remaining the same for each). Finally, presentation of the aversive imagery is usually interspersed with "self-control" scenes in which the client imagines himself successfully resisting the temptation to engage in the maladaptive approach behavior.

As mentioned above, covert sensitization has been used for a variety of problematic approach behaviors. Mahoney (1974) concludes his review of the empirical literature on the technique with the statement that it has been most consistently successful as a treatment for sexual deviations, has been less consistently successful with obesity, and has not been consistently successful at all with drinking and smoking.

Covert Reinforcement. Covert reinforcement is based on the operant procedure of positive reinforcement and is designed for use in developing approach behaviors to feared situations (Cautela, 1970b, 1977). After giving the client the conditioning rationale and basic imagery instructions mentioned earlier, the therapist helps the client develop a few pleasant scenes that will serve as reinforcers in the procedure. The therapist then describes a scene in which the client engages in the desired approach behavior, and at appropriate points along the way, is cued to imagine one of the pleasant scenes by saying the word "reinforcement." The reinforcing scene often does not have any relationship to the desired behavior sequence. As with covert sensitization, the therapist describes the scene on the initial trial, and the patient then practices it on his own. Mahoney's (1974) review of the literature on covert reinforcement suggests that its effectiveness had not been very convincingly demonstrated at that point in time, a conclusion that has been maintained in a more recent review (Mahoney & Arnkoff, 1978).

Covert Modeling. Covert modeling (Cautela, 1971b) is a technique based on Bandura's work on behavior change through exposure to the behavior of others (Bandura, 1971). Bandura conceives of the modeling process as a largely cognitive enterprise, with a heavy emphasis on attentional, encoding, and cognitive rehearsal processes rather than on conditioning processes. Nevertheless, Cautela suggests that modeling behavior can be thought of "as an operant learned in infancy and then reinforced on an intermittent schedule" (Cautela, 1977, p. 61). Apparently, this is meant to ensure the operant basis for the covert version of the process. Cautela does not, however, make clear the differential implications of this conceptualization for his covert-modeling technique.

After the usual behavior analysis, rationales, and instructions are given, the covert-modeling procedure proceeds in the following manner. Initially, the therapist describes a scene depicting another person (other than the client) engaging in the problem behavior. After the client can imagine the sequence with the other person satisfactorily, he may be asked to imagine observing himself engaging in the behavior, and finally, he may imagine himself involved in performing the behavior. This last stage appears to be identical to the content of the imaginings in covert reinforcement, but without the use of reinforcing scenes. Cautela (1977) has likened this progression in the identity and perspective of the model to an operant-shaping procedure.

Covert modeling has received more empirical corroboration than the other covert-conditioning techniques. This is largely the result of a series of investigations by Alan Kazdin. His studies have repeatedly demonstrated the effectiveness of the procedure in overcoming snake phobias (Kazdin, 1973, 1974a,b) and in developing assertive behavior (Kazdin, 1975). More specifically, his research has suggested the following guidelines about the content of the imagined scenes: a coping model is more effective than a mastery model (Kazdin, 1973), multiple models are more effective than single models (Kazdin, 1975), models with similar characteristics to the client are more effective than dissimilar ones (Kazdin, 1974a), imagining oneself as a model is no more effective than imagining another person

(Kazdin, 1974b), and the addition of covert reinforcement to covert modeling enhances the effectiveness of the latter (Kazdin, 1975). Kazdin has also
investigated some imagery process variables. Some of the studies mentioned
above included subject ratings of the clarity of their imagery but none of
them showed any relationship between clarity and outcome (Kazdin,
1974a,b, 1975). In one study, subjects were asked to narrate their scenes.
Analysis of the coded descriptions showed that subjects who elaborated
their scenes beyond the assigned content tended to show greater improvement in developing assertive behavior (Kazdin, 1975).

Observations and Summary. From this brief overview of Cautela's
techniques, several observations seem warranted. First, the imagery in these
techniques is more dynamic and of longer duration than the imagery in
desensitization, which requires visualizing defined, almost static scenes for a
few seconds. Second, the imagery content is more realistic (with the exception of covert sensitization) than it is in implosion and flooding, and hence
may be more informative about new patterns of behavior. Third, the
images in covert sensitization and covert reinforcement are supposed to function as punishers and reinforcers, and as such, should elicit appropriate
negative and positive emotional reactions. That it is clearly intended to do
so is indicated by the therapist's questioning of the client about the emotive
capacities of the imagery after each scene presentation. Emotional arousal
is therefore an intended function of imagery in these two techniques. As
mentioned above, the conditioning basis of these techniques has been
seriously questioned (Mahoney, 1974). A fourth observation, then, is the
suggestion that the imaginal activity in these techniques may contribute to
change by providing clients a chance to rehearse new response information
(Kazdin, 1977; Mahoney, 1974). Perhaps the repeated imaginal rehearsals
serve to consolidate the essential information about the new behavior
sequence and facilitate its recall. Similar speculations about the therapeutic
value of imaginal rehearsal are discussed later in this chapter in the sections
on Bandura and Paivio.

Cautela's collection of procedures represents an important step in the
development of imagery-based therapeutic techniques. While his procedures
have received only modest empirical support and have been questioned on
theoretical grounds, they have served a heuristic function and have stimulated both research and clinical innovation. It should also be noted that
Cautela was one of the first theorists to endorse the value of imagery-based
techniques as a means of improving patients' self-control (in the sense that
patients could learn techniques and practice them on their own). Finally,
covert modeling may turn out to be the imagery procedure with the widest
generality in that it can be used not only to overcome maladaptive behavior
patterns, but also as a means of refining currently adaptive behavior.

Anxiety Management Training

Anxiety management training (AMT) was developed as a variant of desensitization (Suinn & Richardson, 1971), and is similar to a procedure developed by Sipprelle (1967). AMT was designed to serve as a self-control technique for use by clients in coping with a wide range of maladaptive anxiety responses and tensions. It was contrasted with desensitization which, with its fear specific hierarchy, was seen as having limited usefulness as a general coping strategy. Two versions of the procedure have been developed. The original procedure employed a conditioning rationale and begins with the client learning how to generate high levels of anxiety by imagining a variety of frightening scenes (Suinn & Richardson, 1971). Clients are especially urged to become aware of the physiological cues for the onset of the anxious feelings while they are imagining. This is followed by training in both muscle relaxation and in imagining pleasant and success scenes that will later be used as competing responses. The key feature of the technique is a training session in which the client is instructed to generate anxious arousal by imagining different scenes, to attend to the incipient anxiety cues, and then to switch to either relaxation, pleasant scene, or success scene when the cues are noted. According to the conditioning explanation of the therapeutic process, the anxiety cues function as conditioned stimuli for the relaxation and positive feelings brought about by the imagery. As a result of the training, these competing responses should be automatically elicited by any future anxiety cues, regardless of their source.

The revised AMT program drops the conditioning explanation but preserves the original intent of the technique as a general coping skill (Richardson, 1976). A substantial portion of the revised procedure is devoted to discussions about the role of irrational beliefs, self-statements, and imagery in generating maladaptive arousal. These discussions are followed by exercises designed to aid clients in developing personalized, rational, calming perspectives. Much of this discussion is based on the ideas of Ellis (Ellis & Harper, 1975) and Meichenbaum (1977). Along with these discussions, clients are trained in relaxation and in positive imagery methods. After these stages have been completed, clients are told to generate high levels of anxiety by recreating imaginally some of their maladaptive beliefs and fears. When arousal is at a peak, clients are told to use their relaxation and positive imagery skills along with their rational perspectives to reduce the arousal. Following this session, clients prepare a list of their most troublesome anxiety-arousing situations and practice "coping imagery." They imaginally rehearse being in each situation, experiencing the beginnings of anxious arousal, and then coping with the arousal via the various techniques developed earlier.

The purposes of the imagery component in these techniques is relatively straightforward. First, in both the original and revised procedures, imaginary scenes are used to elicit emotional arousal, both positive and negative. This is the same function imagery serves in desensitization, implosion and flooding, and in some of Cautela's techniques. Second, in the revised version, the coping imagery procedure can be thought of as having a relatively direct rehearsal function. Coping skills are reviewed and consolidated by applying them imaginally to a number of situations. This is similar to the function ascribed to the imaginal activity in covert modeling in the previous section. Third, the imagery component in the revised procedure includes the rehearsal of cognitive behaviors (beliefs and self-statements) as well as situational and overt behavioral factors. This rehearsal is a feature that has not been explicitly included in the previous techniques, but which AMT has in common with several of the procedures discussed in the following sections.

Meichenbaum's Self-Instructional Techniques

A frequent element in much of Donald Meichenbaum's work has been the role of self-talk, or private monologues, in generating, maintaining, and coping with anxiety. The distinguishing feature of his use of imagery has been the deliberate inclusion of such self-talk in the imaginary activity. The two procedures discussed in this section are coping imagery and stress inoculation training. The reader is referred to Meichenbaum's recent book (1977) for a more complete description of these and related procedures.

Coping Imagery. This procedure is basically an extension of desensitization. The therapist begins by exploring the client's problem, giving special attention to helping the client identify the anxiety-generating thoughts that are typically involved in his maladaptive arousal. The therapist introduces the notion that these thoughts are the most immediate source of the client's arousal and that one way to cope with the anxiety is to develop a set of thoughts, or self-instructions, that will both counteract the arousal and lead to more adaptive behaviors. The client is then trained in a relaxation procedure (a more abbreviated procedure than that used in desensitization) and, in conjunction with the therapist, constructs a hierarchy of anxiety-arousing scenes. From this point the procedure is similar to desensitization in that the client progresses through imaginal presentations of the hierarchy scenes until he is able to handle all of the material. The initial scenes are presented in the standard desensitization format, with the client terminating any scene as soon as it arouses anxiety. Meichenbaum refers to this step as "mastery imagery." In subsequent scene presentations, however, some important changes from the traditional procedure are introduced. If a client experiences any anxiety while imagining a scene, he is told to allow himself to experience some of the feelings and then to visualize himself coping with the anxiety by using the relaxation technique and the self-instructions he developed earlier. After practicing several scenes in this manner, a second coping imagery variation is introduced. In this version, the therapist induces anxiety by including it in his description of the scenes (rather than waiting for the client to indicate that a scene has made him anxious), and then has the client imagine coping with it in the prescribed manner. This technique is essentially identical with anxiety management training, and is suggestive of Meichenbaum's later technique of stress inoculation training. Coping imagery was found to be more effective in reducing test anxiety than systematic desensitization (Meichenbaum, 1972).

Meichenbaum (1977) makes several observations about the use of imagery in procedures such as this. He views the whole desensitization procedure and his variant of it as a form of covert modeling. By taking this position, he embraces a conception of the therapeutic process that emphasizes the active cognitive learning of new responses through imaginal rehearsal and other means, rather than the passive counterconditioning of one response by another. In this view, the imagery component of the procedure serves a rehearsal function. In an earlier article (Steffy, Meichenbaum, & Best, 1970), Meichenbaum and his colleagues suggested that imaginal rehearsal contributes to change in three ways: (1) it fosters quicker recognition of the initial signs of anxiety and tension; (2) it allows a wider range of situations to be included in the therapy session (thereby influencing generalization of treatment effects); and (3) it leads to more emotional arousal. In short, imaginal rehearsal, as used in his techniques, is thought of as contributing to change by *generating affective arousal*, by improving the client's *perception* of both internal and external anxiety cues, and by improving his *memory* for the new coping procedures. These functions of imagery are similar to the functions ascribed to imagery in the procedures discussed earlier, regardless of the theoretical processes presumed to be operating. In later sections of this chapter it will become apparent that theorists in other areas of psychology also point to the close relationships between imagery, perception, memory, and emotional arousal.

Stress Inoculation Training. Stress inoculation training is Meichenbaum's later and more elaborate procedure (Meichenbaum, 1977; Meichenbaum & Turk, 1975). It is similar to anxiety management training in that it has at its core the deliberate arousal of anxiety or stress followed by practice in using a variety of cognitive coping procedures. Meichenbaum divides the procedure into three phases: education, rehearsal, and application. In the education phase, the therapist is concerned with introducing and converting (noncoercively) the client to the therapist's orientation—namely, that it is what a person says to himself in anxiety-producing situations that differentiates anxious from nonanxious individuals. Imaginary activity is involved in the latter two phases of the treatment. In the rehearsal phase it is used in two different ways. First, it is used as a way of identifying a client's typical anxiety-producing thoughts and images. The therapist may have the client imaginally recreate a previous anxiety situation with instructions to pay particular attention to the thoughts and images that seem to accompany the situation. Second, the client is encouraged to imaginally rehearse the use of more adaptive self-instructions in stress situations. In addition to the self-instructional training, the client also receives training in a variety of other coping techniques in this phase, thus allowing him a choice of strategies when he is actually faced with an anxiety-producing situation. The application phase of the procedure consists of exposing the client to a real laboratory stressor such as electric shock, cold water pain, or ischemic pain. In this phase of the training program, imagery rehearsal of coping techniques is used immediately before exposure to the stressor.

In addition to the use of coping self-instructions and imagery rehearsal, Meichenbaum and Turk (1975) recommend using imagery distraction techniques to enhance pain tolerance. The three distractive techniques they recommend are: imaginative inattention (fantasize a distracting, perhaps incompatible scene), imaginative transformation of pain (minimize or relabel the pain sensations), and imaginative transformation of context (construct a story around the pain). It is instructive to note that these distractive techniques are at a different level of thought than self-instructions. Self-instructions are *meta* to other cognitive activities. They are designed to tell a person what to think about, or what kind of cognitive activity to engage in. The imagery distraction techniques on the other hand, are alternate cognitive activities that one could self-instruct oneself to engage in. Turk (1976) found the stress inoculation procedure highly effective in improving tolerance of ischemic pain when compared to a pseudotraining group.

In addition to the three functions of imagery identified in the coping imagery procedure, stress inoculation training introduces two additional functions. First, imaginal recreation of past experiences can be used to help improve a client's recall of relevant anxiety producing thoughts and images. This recall use of imagery has, of course, a long history in psychology, dating back to Freud's early techniques of using imagery as a means of reaching early childhood memories. The second function of imagery introduced by these procedures is that of imaginal distraction (although Turk and Meichenbaum are by no means the only investigators to have used imagery for this purpose). There is an important difference between imaginal distraction and imaginal rehearsal of behavior patterns. With distraction, the imaginary activity is the new, alternate behavior that is being developed. With most of the other techniques, imagery is used as a *means* of developing the new behavior pattern by either generating arousal, or by rehearsing behavior and thought sequences, or by aiding in recall.

Systematic Rational Restructuring

This technique was developed by Marvin Goldfried, and is a combination of desensitization and Ellis's rational-emotive therapy (Goldfried, 1977; Goldfried & Goldfried, 1975; Goldfried, Decenteo, & Weinberg, 1974). It is very similar in concept to Meichenbaum's coping imagery procedure, though the two techniques were developed independently. Part of that similarity is in their use of imagery, and, as a result, the present discussion of Goldfried's technique will be brief.

Clients are presented the basic rational-emotive rationale that their feelings are primarily determined by their thoughts. They are given an overview of Ellis's list of irrational assumptions, followed by an analysis of their own problems in terms of these beliefs, and by the development of a set of more rational cognitions to substitute for the irrational ones. To train clients in the use of the more rational perspectives, a hierarchy of anxiety-related situations is developed, and they work their way through it in the same manner as in the coping imagery procedure.

The procedure differs from Meichenbaum's procedure primarily in the type of cognitions that are rehearsed, with systematic rational restructuring focusing on the role of irrational beliefs, and Meichenbaum's procedure focusing on specific self-instructions. Although there is a clear distinction between these two types of cognitions, there is no empirical evidence that the distinction is a functionally significant one. The conceptual distinction is between more general beliefs or cognitive structures and more specific statements or thoughts that would presumably derive from the more abstract structures (Meichenbaum, 1977).

With respect to the use of imagery, Goldfried and Goldfried (1975) state that they use imaginal presentations primarily for practical reasons, i.e., it is inconvenient or impossible to recreate every situation *in vivo*. They also point out that imaginal presentation allows the therapist to exert greater control over the procedure by limiting the client's exposure to the anxiety-provoking situation. Beyond these reasons, the functions that imagery serves in this procedure appear to be identical to those identified in Meichenbaum's coping imagery procedure.

IMAGERY IN PSYCHODYNAMIC THERAPIES

Psychoanalysis

As Singer (1974) noted in his thorough review of the uses of imagery in psychotherapy, classical psychoanalytic therapy does not focus on, or encourage the development of, imagery and imagination as such. Imagery material is used only to the extent that the analysand brings his dreams, fantasies, and daydreams into the analytic session. In psychoanalytic theory, images and words are the two types of symbols used in thought. Images are typical of the more primitive, primary process mode of thought, which is characterized by its irrationality and close relationship to instinctual tensions and energies. Words are the preferred medium of the secondary process mode of thought, which is characterized by its rationality and reality orientation. Images are formed in response to instinctual needs or tensions and in the irrational manner of the primary process, afford some measure of satisfaction for those needs or tensions. Hence, the occurrence of imagery is always indicative of an unfulfilled instinctual need or wish.

The principal way in which people become aware of this type of thought is through their dreams. Dream images are not, however, considered direct expressions of the instinctual wish; they are, instead, always seen as having a defensive purpose. The actual, or manifest, content of the image is assumed to mask the instinctual wish, or latent content, that is being expressed through the dream. If the instinctual wish were expressed directly, it might cause the ego to be overwhelmed with anxiety; therefore it has to be disguised or distorted in a defensive manner. In therapeutic work the dream image is not developed for its own sake, but is taken as a starting point for a series of verbal associations by the patient accompanied by interpretive comments from the analyst. As a result of this procedure, the defensive disguise is circumvented, the unconscious wish or conflict is discovered, the emotion attached to it is expressed, and the patient learns to express the wish or conflict in words. In summary, psychoanalysts use the patient's reports of imagery in dreams, daydreams, and fantasies as a starting point in their effort to uncover and identify the important emotional themes, patterns, and conflicts of the patient.

Imagery in the Work of Carl Jung

In contrast to Freud, Jung considered the imagery contained in dreams, fantasies, and daydreams as the primary data for therapeutic work. A key to understanding Jung's view of the function of dreams is the idea of compensation, or complementarity. Jung thought of dreams as statements from the unconscious portion of the psyche about the actual subjective state of the dreamer. Typically, these statements reflect imbalances in the psyche for which the person must compensate in some manner if he is to avoid problems and realize his individuality more fully. In contrast to Freud, Jung did not think of dream images as a defensive screen. Instead, he viewed them as the symbolic language of the unconscious, which, unfortunately, most modern people have not learned to understand. In order to aid the dreamer in understanding his own dream symbolism, Jung emphasized the actual dream content and had the person become actively involved in the images. This method is known as *active imagination* and may include a variety of activities such as recreating or redreaming the dream and describing the images in detail, drawing or painting the images, or writing an account of the dream. According to Jungian theory, the person will arrive at an understanding of the message from his unconscious after this exploration and expansion of the dream imagery. Once the message is clear, the therapist then helps the patient apply the new insight to his current life situation. In a basic sense, the function fulfilled by dreams in Jungian therapy is the same as in psychoanalysis, in spite of clear differences in theory and technique. In both procedures, the dream is used as a means of identifying the important emotional themes, patterns, and conflicts of the dreamer.

European Daydream Methods

As noted by Singer (1974), the imagery-based approaches of Desoille, Leuner, and Fretigny and Virel share several common elements. All involve relaxation by the client, followed by a theme suggested by the therapist around which the patient constructs a fantasy or daydream. At appropriate points in the patient's description, the therapist may intervene with questions and with suggestions about ways of coping with the imagery situations that arise. Each of these approaches has a set of initial symbolic scenes that are presumed to reflect the most common areas of emotional conflict. Interpretation of the fantasy content is generally based on Freudian and Jungian ideas about symbolism.

Compared to the Freudian and Jungian uses of dream imagery, these techniques represent a movement away from reliance upon the spontaneous imagery productions of the patients and toward a more directed type of imaginary activity. The imaginary activity is still used by the therapist as a means of identifying important emotional themes and of eliciting affective reactions. With contemporary daydream techniques, however, the imaginary activity is seen as more intrinsically therapeutic than was the case with Freud and Jung. Among these techniques, the emphasis placed on discussion of the fantasy differs, with one of the techniques, Desoille, apparently relying almost exclusively on the daydream activity itself as the curative factor, and the other two using it as a basis for further discussion and interpretation.

IMAGERY IN DAYDREAMS, FANTASY, AND OBSERVATIONAL LEARNING

Jerome Singer: Imagery, Daydreams, and Psychotherapy

Jerome Singer has been concerned with the naturalistic occurrence and function of imagery and fantasy processes, as well as with the therapeutic uses to which these capacities have been adapted (Singer, 1974, 1975). The following discussion reviews his ideas about the naturalistic role of imagery processes, and about the therapeutic contributions these processes can make.

Naturalistic Daydreaming and Fantasy Processes. Singer (1974) begins with the idea that the brain is continuously active. It is always processing information. He cites evidence from sleep and dream research to support his conclusion that the brain is active even during sleep states. According to Singer, the information that is available for processing at a given moment comes from two sources. The first source is the sensory organs, which provide information about both the external environment and the person's bodily state (hunger, pressure, movement); the second source is the fund of centrally stored information. The key distinction between the two is that the second source involves manipulating or processing stored information rather than new sensory information. Singer maintains that information from both sources is usually being processed almost simultaneously, even though people generally have learned to "gate out" their awareness of the internal processing in favor of their processing of external sensory information. Situational factors often influence which source of information a person is most aware of processing. When there is a reduction in sensory stimulation (e.g., sensory deprivation experiments, boring or repetitive tasks), one is more likely to be aware of the processing of stored information. Conversely, in an emergency situation, a person is more likely to be involved in the processing of sensory information. In his own research, Singer has attempted to differentiate between people on the basis of their relative disposition toward internal versus external processing (Antrobus, Coleman, & Singer, 1967; Singer, 1966, 1974), and on the basis of the typical content of their internal processing (Singer & Antrobus, 1972).

Singer (1974) takes the position that the centrally stored information is encoded in both verbal and imaginal forms. Because of its abstract nature and greater generalizability, the verbally coded information is presumed to be especially useful in logical thinking, problem solving, and communication. The imagery code is particularly suited to rapid parallel processing as opposed to the more sequential processing required by verbally encoded material. The term *parallel processing* suggests that a visual image can be quickly scanned for information in an analogous way to the manner in which an optic array can be visually scanned. In addition, the imagery format involves information at a sensory level, and as a result, is connected more closely with the affect system.

Singer believes that the continuous processing of centrally stored information serves valuable functions in the regulation of behavior. To begin with, he notes that most of the information that is processed is connected with the unfinished issues or business facing an individual and with which he experiences some degree of emotional involvement. The continuous processing of information related to these issues is seen as being of aid in assimilating the information about these topics into an individual's cognitive structures or schemata.

In addition to the task of simply assimilating and organizing information, Singer speculates that a major function of this internal processing is to aid in the anticipation of, and in the planning and rehearsal for, future circumstances. A related benefit of the ongoing internal processing may be improvement in the problem-solving process. Because of the more fluid and flexible nature of the internal processing, ideas and images often coalesce into new and different patterns. This forming and reforming of patterns may often be the source of creative insights.

Imagery and Behavior Change. In his 1974 book, Singer surveys a broad spectrum of imagery-based therapeutic systems and techniques, along with a sampling of research on imagery and related processes in other areas of psychology. One of his expressed objectives in doing so was to glean from the many different techniques and research areas some practical implications and suggestions for the use of imagery in therapy. A summary of his major conclusions is presented below.

The first conclusion is that a patient's spontaneous imagery productions—dreams, daydreams, and fantasies—are especially useful as a means of identifying important emotional themes and issues. Spontaneous imagery productions can also be used as a reflection of the ways in which the patient orients himself cognitively to his world. That is, the stylistic features of the imagery productions yield clues about the patients' generalized expectancies, anticipatory schema, and assumptions about his world. The special advantages of spontaneous imagery productions for these purposes seem to be that they provide a way of circumventing whatever self-deceptions the patient uses in normal discourse; that they reflect a different, perhaps broader, kind of sensitivity and awareness than that found in more conscious, intentional, task-oriented thinking; and that they have a close connection with the affect system.

A second and related point about the use of imagery in therapy is that it serves as a means of generating emotional reactions. Singer (1974) maintains that the concrete, sensory nature of imaginal material endows it with special ability to create a context for emotional reactions. In therapeutic work this characteristic has far-reaching implications. Through the medium of the patient's imagery ability, the therapist and patient are able to bring previous and potential circumstances and their associated emotional reactions into the therapy setting where they can be identified, experienced, and perhaps, overcome.

Singer also asserts that a major contribution of imagery and daydream techniques to therapeutic change is the opportunity they offer for planning, anticipation, and rehearsal of behavioral strategies for problem-related areas. Through imagination a person can anticipate contingencies and explore ways of coping with them. Singer believes that all of the imagery therapies lead to these kinds of effects, though perhaps the newer behavioral therapies are more explicit in their cultivation of imagery for these purposes.

Singer's final point, and one that in some ways encompasses the other three, is that imagery therapies can be thought of as a means of training the patient in the use and control of his own imaginal capacities. As a result of exposure to an imagery-based therapeutic procedure, the patient becomes more sensitive to his ongoing internal processing. He learns about the ways in which he tends to be adversely affected by it, and about ways of controlling and using the content for more adaptive purposes. The result of this improved control over imagery processing may be enhanced self-awareness and self-confidence on the part of the patient.

Eric Klinger: Imagery and Fantasy

Eric Klinger's book *The Structure and Functions of Fantasy* (1971) offers a unified theory of the structure and function of fantasy processes along with a thorough review of fantasy and fantasy-related topics. While he does not explicitly address therapeutic uses of fantasy and imagery, Klinger's theory contains provocative ideas about the nature of fantasy, which have implications for the therapeutic use of imagery-based procedures. The following review of his theory attempts to focus selectively on those points that are most relevant to therapeutic uses of imagery.

The Theory in Brief. Consistent with Singer's position, Klinger asserts that fantasy represents, along with dreaming, the baseline or background cognitive activity that is always occurring, especially when a person is not engaged in more intentional cognitive activity. He defines fantasy as verbal reports of mental activities that are not intentionally focused on problem solving (reasoning) or on scanning the environment (perception), that are not evaluated by the person with respect to their practical utility, and that have a quality of effortlessness or lack of intentionality. Fantasy can easily occur concurrently with other responses as long as they do not require intentional directed thought. Klinger prefers to distinguish imagery and fantasy. He argues that while fantasy has a substantial imaginal component, other processes also contribute to the experience of fantasy (e.g., unconscious processes, affective arousal), and that fantasy is, consequently, more complex than a simple series of images.

The bulk of Klinger's theory is concerned with factors influencing the structure and content of fantasy. Klinger begins with the argument that imagery, thought, and perception can be thought of as efferent responses or behaviors, and as such should be subject to the same contingencies as motor behavior. He follows this with an analogy between the structure of fantasy segments and the concept of response integration. With respect to motor behavior, an integrated response refers to an overlearned sequence of responses that flows smoothly, almost automatically, and that requires less effort and attention than an unintegrated act. It can be thought of as a generalized plan or schema that is flexible and sensitive to feedback. The response sequence may contain imaginal, perceptual, and motor components. The more smoothly the sequence operates, the less one is aware of the separate components. This is especially true of the imaginal component, which is thought of as serving an anticipatory function. When feedback indicates a state of affairs within the anticipated range, perception confirms the anticipatory image and merges with it.

Klinger cites a number of parallels between fantasy segments and integrated motor response sequences that justify his analogy between the two. The principle characteristics of fantasy that lead to the analogy are that fantasy content segments seem to occur smoothly and automatically, and are organized within content segments. In addition, they can occur concurrently with other integrated behavior as long as more directed thought is not required. The difference between fantasy sequences and integrated response sequences is that fantasy does not involve perceptual feedback. Because feedback is critical in guiding the unfolding of an integrated response sequence, this difference has implications for some of the structural aspects of fantasy, especially the sequencing of segments. Klinger takes the position that the sequencing of fantasy segments can be considered a respondent process in the sense that each segment is elicited by the previous one. He hypothesizes that affective reactions aroused by one fantasy segment may both disrupt the current segment and elicit the next one.

Moving from the structure to the content of fantasy, Klinger maintains that the content of fantasy segments is highly correlated with a person's "current concerns." These are defined as areas in which a person is working toward a goal or incentive, and in which his progress has either been interrupted or the attainment of the goal is still uncertain. The critical point is that the person is still in a state of involvement with the goal, and this involvement or orientation toward the goal potentiates fantasy segments relevant to the goal. Klinger makes it clear that current concerns do not directly determine fantasy content; they are only probabilistically associated with them. In Klinger's view, the processing of fantasy segments may serve adaptive functions with respect to these current concerns. First, the relatively free-wheeling recycling of response elements typical of fantasy may serve to keep a person in a state of readiness or vigilance with respect to the different incentives with which he is involved. Second, in the processing of fantasy segments, information about the goal and about relevant behavior sequences may be reorganized in ways that suggest new plans or approaches for achieving goals.

Therapeutic Implications. It should be reiterated that Klinger's theory explicitly addresses nonvolitional, undirected thinking. As such, his theory has some clear implications for the therapies that make use of more spontaneous forms of imagery. The most important of these is that Klinger's analysis supports the previously noted use of spontaneous imagery and fantasy as a means of identifying the current concerns, or important emotional themes and patterns, of an individual. It is not surprising that this should be the case since the original impetus for Klinger's book was his frustration with the inadequacy of existing theory about personality assessment via projective techniques, especially the Thematic Apperception Test (TAT).

Even though Klinger is not directly concerned with explaining the nature of deliberate, intentional, imaginal rehearsal of responses, his theory suggests some ways in which this type of rehearsal may contribute to change. As mentioned earlier, Klinger thinks of integrated response sequences as consisting of imaginal, motor, and perceptual components, with the imaginal component being characterized as anticipatory, or as a state of readiness to perceive feedback of a certain configuration. By imaginally rehearsing a new response sequence, one may be developing, learning, and practicing that component of the full, integrated sequence. As a result of the deliberate practice, the new response sequence becomes more integrated and can be executed more smoothly and quickly in actual situations. Another result of engaging in deliberate imaginal rehearsal may be that the new, more adaptive routine assumes the status of a new fantasy segment that will, henceforth, be elicited on a regular basis by associated affective cues. Over time, as this fantasy segment is evoked in a variety of situations, and its elements are organized and reorganized, it may become progressively more integrated and personalized, and consequently more readily available for use in a variety of situations.

Albert Bandura: Imagery in Observational Learning

Albert Bandura's theory of observational learning (Bandura, 1977b) has led to the development of therapeutic techniques that rely on exposing clients to behavioral models who demonstrate the behaviors that are to be learned (Bandura, 1971). Bandura's explanation of the mechanisms through which observational learning occurs draws heavily, and increasingly, on cognitive and mediational concepts (Bandura, 1977a,b, 1978). The following summary of his theoretical position emphasizes the role he assigns to imagery and imaginal rehearsal processes.

Bandura recognizes four stages of observational learning. A person who is exposed to a model must (1) attend to the model's behavior, (2) retain the response information in memory for learning to occur, (3) possess the requisite skills in the component motor processes of the modeled

behavior, and (4) have adequate incentive to exercise that skill for performance to occur. Imagery processes are involved in the retention stage of
this model. Bandura states that information about that modeled behavior
must be centrally stored so that it may be recalled at a future time and used
as a guide to reproduce the behavior.

Retention is influenced by the manner in which the information is
encoded for storage. Following the ideas of some cognitive psychologists
(e.g., Paivio, 1971b), Bandura recognizes two types of memory codes: verbal
and imaginal. He emphasizes the usefulness of verbally based codes
somewhat more than that of imaginal codes (Bandura, 1977b), because he
maintains that verbally based codes are more concise, and hence hold more
information than imaginal codes. He acknowledges, however, that in actual
practice the two codes are usually used in tandem, and that this arrangement probably leads to the most effective retention. Once response information has been adequately encoded, the rehearsal of either the actual behavior
or the coded information about the behavior enhances retention and subsequent recall. Because it is often inconvenient to engage in overt behavioral
rehearsal, symbolic or mental rehearsal of the behavior itself or of the
memory code, can serve an important function.

Bandura and his colleagues have conducted a series of studies that
point to some important parameters of encoding and rehearsal processes.
Gerst (1971) found that imaginal codes and concise verbal labels were both
more effective than verbal descriptions of modeled behavior in enhancing
subsequent recall. Postexperimental interviews suggested that imaginal
codes were rehearsed more frequently than other codes. Bandura and Jeffery (1973) investigated the influence of different symbolic codes and
rehearsal practices on recall of modeled behavior. Immediate coding and
rehearsal of coded information was associated with more accurate recall
than was delayed coding and rehearsal. Bandura, Jeffery, and Bachicha
(1974) found that the meaningfulness and retrievability of the code were
associated with improved reproduction of modeled behaviors. In addition,
meaningful codes were found to require fewer rehearsals than meaningless
codes. These investigators speculated that the most successful codes are not
direct copies of modeled behaviors, but, rather, are higher order, more
abstract codes constructed from features and properties of the modeled
behavior. Such codes would presumably have more generality than direct
copies. Jeffery (1976) found that immediate covert rehearsal followed by
motoric rehearsal was more effective than either form of rehearsal alone in
leading to recall of response information. Jeffery infers that covert rehearsal
serves an organizational function in that it allows time for the development
of an adequate code and it also serves to strengthen the memory trace.

Therapeutic Implications. Bandura's work has clear relevance for
those imagery-based therapies that involve the covert rehearsal of behavior

sequences. The principle implication is that imaginal rehearsal may contribute to therapeutic change by virtue of its effects on memory for response and consequence information. Information that is more effectively coded and stored can be more easily retrieved for use as a guide to reproduce the behavior in appropriate circumstances. Recent theorizing by Bandura (1977a) on the role of self-efficacy expectations in mediating behavior change has further implications for the use of imaginal rehearsal techniques. Bandura suggests that imaginal rehearsal by itself is not as effective as overt behavioral rehearsal in changing efficacy expectations. Imaginal rehearsal may, however, be an important component process that leads to improvements in efficacy expectations which then facilitate the person's eventual overt rehearsal of the behavior. Actual behavior rehearsal then provides stronger, more veridical feedback regarding the accuracy of self-efficacy expectations.

IMAGERY IN COGNITIVE PSYCHOLOGY

The discussion thus far has centered on therapeutic uses of imaginal processes and on theoretical models of the nature and function of these processes in therapy related phenomena. The focus of the remaining portion of the chapter shifts to a survey of the conceptions of imagery offered by investigators in the area of cognitive psychology. Typically, these theorists are concerned with explaining (or explaining away) the role of imagery in such cognitive functions as memory, language, learning, and perception.

Paivio and the Dual-Coding Hypothesis

Allan Paivio is recognized as one of the more influential recent theorists in cognitive psychology because of his pioneering work on the empirical study of imagery (Paivio, 1971a). His careful empirical investigations and theorizing on the role of imagery processes in language, learning, and memory have done much to reintroduce and gain acceptance for imagery as a theoretically important topic.

In his investigations, Paivio (1971a, 1972) operationally defines and manipulates imagery in one or more of three different ways. First, imagery is defined according to the image-arousing properties of various stimulus materials. In general, concrete (sensory) stimuli are considered more likely to elicit imagery than abstract stimuli. Pictures are, of course, the most concrete stimulus materials (next to objects), but words also can be rated for their imagery-arousing values on a dimension of concreteness–abstractness (e.g., *apple* versus *information*) (see Paivio, Yuille, & Madigan, 1968). A second research strategem has been to investigate various experimental instructions about the use of imagery as opposed to alternate mediational strategies for learning and memorizing. A third approach involves the assessment of individual differences in imagery ability and the prediction of task performance on this basis.

Paivio's basic assumption is that information or knowledge is stored in one of two basic coding systems: imaginal or verbal. The imagery system is assumed to be specialized for representing concrete, sensory information, and the verbal system is specialized for representing more abstract and conceptual information. According to Paivio (1971b, 1972), the form in which information is represented in each system differs, and these differences have implications for how the information stored in each is processed. Information in the imagery system is stored as spatial units, which are subject to parallel processing. This means that the spatial representation can be rapidly scanned for information, much as one would visually scan an external layout. The verbal system consists of information stored in linguistic units, or implicit auditory representations, which can be processed in a sequential manner, similar to what one does while reading prose passages.

Having made these distinctions, Paivio (1971b, 1972) speculates that in actual practice, the cognitive system uses both codes in an interactive manner. His dual-code hypothesis suggests that the superior memory and learning results obtained with concrete materials and imagery instructions are due to an increased probability that both coding systems are used in processing such information. It is assumed that with more abstract materials there is a greater likelihood that the processing relies relatively more on the verbal coding system. In Paivio's analysis, the redundancy in the coding of the concrete material allows for more associative connections to be made. This effect, combined with the greater speed of the parallel processing, accounts for the mnemonic advantages associated with imagery mediation.

While a majority of Paivio's research has been on the effects of imagery manipulations on memory for lists of words or for pairs of words, he has extended that work (Paivio, 1971a) to an examination of imagery and memory for connected discourse (phrases, sentences, and paragraphs). Paivio reasons that highly concrete passages are more likely to elicit coding in both imaginal and verbal codes, and that this leads to superior recall for the thematic content of the passage. This reasoning was supported in a study by Yuille and Paivio (1969), in which recall for highly concrete, thematically organized passages was superior to recall for more abstract, randomly organized passages. In discussing this study, Paivio (1971a) interprets the findings in the following manner:

> These findings are consistent with the idea that thematic presentation in the case of highly concrete passages permits the subject to generate a visual image of the setting of the story together with some of the salient

elements in it, and from such an organized, thematic image to reconstruct the verbal content. This is conceptually related to the effect of stimulus imagery in paired-associate learning in that the image in the present case also provided an effective means of retrieving associated information that had previously been presented in the connected passage (or as we assumed). (pp. 22–23)

This view has important implications for the processes through which imagery-based therapy techniques may contribute to change. It suggests that the imagined scenes used in the therapy techniques may function as mnemonic devices that both organize relevant response information and facilitate its retrieval. In techniques such as self-instructional training that include verbally expressed thought sequences in the imaginal scene, the imaginal components may function as stimuli to which the more adaptive thoughts are attached and which aid in their retrieval. In short, Paivio's position suggests that imagery rehearsal of behavior may lead to improved memory for the new response pattern.

Additional implications of Paivio's research for the therapeutic use of imagery include the following. First, describing a scene as concretely as possible may be a way of increasing the probability of a client's actually experiencing imagery. A perusal of transcripts of scene descriptions used in different techniques (Goldfried & Davison, 1976; Rimm & Masters, 1974) shows that most of them are relatively concrete in their descriptions. This is especially true of implosion, flooding, and covert sensitization, all of which require vivid imagery to elicit theoretically important physiological reactions. As a result of the concreteness of these descriptions, the aversive imagery may be more easily and permanently remembered. Depending on one's evaluation of these treatments, this may be either a desirable or an undesirable outcome. Even in the techniques that emphasize the development of new behavior patterns and in which physiological arousal is less an issue, concretely detailed descriptions of the scenes may facilitate the occurrence of imagery. A second and related implication is the idea of training clients who report weak imagery in the use of concrete descriptions as a way of enhancing their experience of imagery. A third implication is that the quality of a client's imagery may be assessed by evaluating the concreteness of his description of his own imaginings.

Imagery versus Propositions: A Debate

A central question in contemporary cognitive psychology centers around the question of the form in which knowledge is stored and represented. The key issue is whether or not knowledge is stored in quasi-sensory formats such as Paivio's imaginal and verbal codes, or in a more abstract, common format. The former position uses the concept of imagery as an explanatory construct in describing processes of learning, memory, and language. The latter position rejects the usefulness of imagery as an explanatory construct and opts for the concept of propositional representation of information (Anderson & Bower, 1973; Pylyshyn, 1973). In an influential theoretical article, Pylyshyn (1973) stated the case against imagery representation of knowledge and argued for a more abstract form of representation. The basic idea is that the knowledge is not stored in sensory specific formats but is stored, instead, in deeper, more abstract structures that contain information about meanings, relations, concepts, and properties, and which are thought of as having a propositional format. Propositions are described as data structures that contain assertions about relations between concepts and properties of objects. A simple proposition may consist of a relationship between two concepts or properties. For example, the statement, "The ball is round" consists of the concept *ball*, the property *round*, and the relationship *is*. Simple propositions can be linked in network fashion to encompass all of the concepts and relations in a given bit of knowledge.

While the concept of propositional networks is similar to that of semantic networks, the proponents of the position (Kieras, 1978; Pylyshyn, 1973) explicitly state that the propositional representation itself should not be thought of as semantic in nature. A sentence is not represented as a network of implicit verbal stimuli, but rather as a network of the meanings represented by the words. Stated another way, knowledge of a photograph is not stored as a spatial-picture, but as information *about* the various objects and relations in the picture. When this knowledge or information is processed, as in a recall situation, a person may "hear" covertly spoken words, or "see" covert images, but these are experiences associated with the processing function and should not be equated with the form in which the information is stored.

A critical point in Pylyshyn's (1973) argument against the mental imagery position is its implication that the end product of the original perceptual processing (the mental representation) is in essentially the same form as the original input. This representation must then be reperceived and reprocessed through quasi-perceptual channels in order to be used as meaningful information at a later point in time. Pylyshyn considers this hypothetical process to be an inadequate account on several grounds, and makes the argument for a propositional form of representation that contains perceptually interpreted information *about* the original stimulus. This propositional representation is thought of as more like a description of the original stimulus scene than like a picture of it. He continues:

> A description is propositional; it contains a finite amount of information, it may contain abstract as well as concrete aspects and, especially relevant to the present discussion, it contains terms (symbols for objects,

attributes, and relations) which are the results of—not inputs to—perceptual processes. (Pylyshyn, 1973, p. 11)

A picture or image is not stored, but the conscious experience of imagery
may be, essentially, constructed from the information stored in the propositional representation or description.

Pylyshyn makes the point that the conscious image is limited in the
objective information it can contain by the information contained in the
propositional structure. At the same time, the conscious image constructed
from the propositional representation may contain more information than
the original stimulus insofar as it includes interpretive information about
the stimulus situation along with information about its objective characteristics. For example, the conscious memory image of a recent encounter
with a colleague may include information about the quality of the interaction (friendly, brusque, hostile) that clearly goes beyond the information
that could be included in a simple pictorial copy of the objective situation.
In other words, information about the qualitative aspects of the interaction
can be stored propositionally in the same way as information about its
objective characteristics.

The arguments for each position are considerably more elaborate than
the preceding summary indicates, and the debate continues in full force
(Anderson, 1978; Kieras, 1978; Kosslyn, 1975; Kosslyn & Pomerantz, 1977;
Paivio, 1976). The presentation in this chapter is limited to the preceding
summary, and turns now to a discussion of the implications of the propositional position for the therapeutic use of imagery.

Therapeutic Implications. Peter Lang has explored some of the therapeutic implications of these ideas about propositional representation (Lang,
1977). Specifically, he has used the propositional idea to analyze the images
used in desensitization and flooding. He proposes that the imagery used in
these procedures can be thought of as propositional networks with units that
refer to features of the environment (stimulus propositions) and to features
of the person's behavior and feelings (response propositions). Lang proposes
that scene descriptions that are loaded with response propositions will
generate more emotionality than those that emphasize stimulus propositions. For maximum effectiveness in evoking emotional arousal, Lang
assumes that the scene description should include response propositions that
refer to the types of response classes that are involved in fear: motor
responses, physiological responses, and thinking responses. With this type of
information included in the imaginary scene, Lang states that it may be
more accurate to think of the imaginal activity as a preparatory set to
respond in the described way than as an internally constructed perception.

Scene descriptions used in flooding contain many aspects of the client's
behavior, thoughts, and feelings. According to Lang's analysis, these

descriptions should elicit greater physiological arousal than the descriptions used in desensitization which are limited to brief definitions of the stimulus situations. Lang (1977) refers to a study in which imagery instructions loaded with response propositions generated greater physiological arousal in subjects than instructions emphasizing stimulus elements.

In Lang's view the therapeutic effectiveness of an image depends on its affective intensity and its vividness. He defines affective intensity by measures of autonomic arousal and self-report. With respect to the vividness of images, Lang offers the following interesting definition:

> Vividness is determined by the completeness of the evoked propositional structure. Thus, subjects reporting vivid images can generally describe them in exquisite detail, providing a large catalog of discriminable stimulus elements. (Lang, 1977, p. 872)

In other words, vividness of imagery can be defined in terms of the amount of relevant detail included in the description of the imagery experience.

A final point that has treatment implications is Lang's idea of the prototypical fear image. Briefly, he assumes that a given fear is represented in long-term storage as a basic propositional network that describes the essential components of the fear situation and response. In a sense, this propositional network is schematic in that it specifies the type of elements involved but does not specify a particular instance of the situation. Therapeutic attempts to work with this fear will be successful to the extent that they succeed in matching the elements of this prototypical proposition. To the extent that a scene description fails to include the key elements, the procedure will be proportionately less effective.

The propositional theorists' characterization of the representational form of imagery-based information suggests a different approach to the assessment of imagery ability. Following Lang's definition of vividness of imagery, imagery ability could be thought of as the relative amount of information or detail that a person can generally pull out of his imagery experience. This could be assessed by coding subjects' descriptions of their imaginal productions in response to a set of standard test scenes, and deriving scores that reflect the overall complexity of the description. This type of measure might be a more direct means of assessing the functionally important dimensions of imagery (i.e., ability to include relevant detail) than the traditional self-report, spatial abilities, and questionnaire approaches, which have not been consistently related with treatment outcomes (Kazdin, 1975; McLemore, 1972).

In summary, the idea of propositional representation of information suggests that therapeutic uses of imagery may achieve their effects by the influence they have on informational structures that are at a deeper, more abstract level than phenomenal imagery. In some cases, the therapeutic goal may be to modify a prototypical fear representation; in others, it may be to establish a new prototype for a more adaptive response pattern. In either case, the effects of imaginal techniques may depend on the extent to which the imagery includes sufficient, relevant information to either engage or establish the appropriate propositional structure.

Ulric Neisser: Images as Schemata

In his book *Cognition and Reality*, Ulric Neisser (1976) proposes a model of perceptual processes that emphasizes the interaction of cognitive, behavioral, and environmental factors. Neisser places special emphasis on the nature and function of the cognitive structures, which he calls schemata. To understand his conception of imagery and imagining, it is necessary to begin by briefly reviewing his model and the function that schemata fulfill in it.

Neisser (1976) conceives of the perceptual process as a continuously active cycle or feedback loop. Schemata are defined as the parts of the cycle that are inside the person. They exist as cognitive structures whose form at any given moment is determined by the past experience of the person. Functionally, schemata anticipate the general form of information to be perceived; they are "readinesses" to apprehend certain configurations in the environment. According to Neisser, schemata serve not only this anticipatory function but they also direct or guide exploratory behavior. Exploratory behavior, the second phase of the cycle, can include everything from ocular movements to gross motor movements. The purpose of the behaviors is to sample, or to obtain information from the environment. The information that is obtained, and especially any information about deviation from the anticipated form, is fed back to the schema. The schema is then modified by the feedback, and the entire cycle of anticipation, exploration, and feedback is set in motion again. Perception is thought of as the cycle in its entirety.

While many of his examples are in terms of visual perception, Neisser stresses that perception in all sensory modalities is structurally the same. The process of obtaining information through the different senses still involves anticipatory schemata that direct exploratory behavior and are modified by feedback.

Schemata may exist at different levels of generality. One could meaningfully speak of a schema for a chair, of a schema for the room in which the chair sits, of a schema for the house of which the room is a part, and of a schema for the neighborhood in which the house is located. Neisser uses the term cognitive maps to refer to the broadest, most extensive schemata, and he thinks of the more specific schemata as being embedded within them in a hierarchical manner. Normal perception is thought of as involving an interaction on all of these levels, with the more specific schemata being determined and motivated, in a sense, by the more general ones. Neisser's analysis of the hierarchical arrangement of schemata, as well as of their anticipatory nature, has close parallels with George Kelly's (1955) theory of personal constructs.

Within this model of the perceptual process, Neisser understands images and imaginings as the exercise of the anticipatory schema without the pickup of new perceptual information. In other words, imagining is the experience of using an anticipatory schema that is detached from the rest of the perceptual cycle. Thus, according to Neisser (1976), "the experience of having an image is just the inner aspect of a readiness to perceive the imagined object, and differences in the nature and quality of people's images reflect differences in the kind of information they are prepared to pick up" (p. 131). He goes on to say that "a description of a visual image is a description of what one is ready to see" (p. 168).

A most important implication of this conception is that the most effective image or imaginal experience is the one that most accurately anticipates the information in the environment for which this schema is attuned. The better it fulfills this task, the more efficiently and smoothly the perceptual cycle will operate. Thus, the quality of any image or visualization should be reflected in the amount of relevant information it contains. Introspective reports of images are understood, then, as descriptions of potentially observable situations, and can be differentiated on the basis of the amount and kind of information they contain.

Supportive evidence for Neisser's view of the functional value of imagery is found in the work of Roger Shepard and his colleagues. Shepard (1978) assumes that perception and imagery share essentially the same neurological pathways, and that consequently, "to imagine a particular object is to place oneself in a unique state of readiness for the actual perception of that particular object" (p. 132). He cites evidence from reaction time experiments to support his position. Subjects who formed appropriate images of a stimulus rotated to a specified orientation identified the match or mismatch between their image and stimuli presented at differing orientations more quickly and accurately than subjects who formed inappropriate anticipatory images.

Therapeutic Implications. To begin with, the conception of imagery offered by Neisser and Shepard suggests that imaginal rehearsal techniques may contribute to change through the modification and improvement of a person's anticipatory routines. Imaginal rehearsal of more adaptive response patterns may be equivalent to the development of new anticipatory schemata that prepare a person to attend to different environmental and personal cues and meanings than he previously did, and from which flow different behavior patterns. As a result of the imagery procedure, the person more efficiently anticipates and identifies these new cues, which then facilitate the smooth execution of the new pattern. This is consonant with Klinger's analogy between fantasy segments and integrated response sequences. This interpretation of imagery effects has the most direct relevance for imagery-based techniques that emphasize the imaginal rehearsal of new responses. This group of techniques includes coping imagery and stress inoculation training, covert modeling and reinforcement, systematic rational restructuring, and anxiety management training.

The uses of dream and fantasy imagery in psychodynamic therapies are also consistent with Neisser's model, although in a different sense than is the case for the behaviorally oriented procedures. By thinking of images as anticipatory schemata detached from the perceptual cycle, dreams and fantasies then become windows to a person's orientation toward his world. The hierarchical arrangement of schemata that Neisser posits would suggest that the dream and fantasy imagery could be used to identify schemata at different levels of generality, from those for specific events or situations to those that are more comprehensive and pervasive and are concerned with the perception of meaning rather than the form of objects. Again, the similarity to the positions of Singer and Klinger should be noted. Hence, in the psychodynamic therapies, spontaneous dream and fantasy imagery productions can be thought of as being used to identify a person's existing anticipatory schemata, while in the behaviorally oriented imagery procedures, deliberate imagery rehearsal can be thought of as contributing to the establishment of new anticipatory schemata.

Finally, similar to the implications of the propositional position, Neisser's model suggests that people's imagery might be qualitatively differentiated on the basis of the information that they can identify in it. Neisser's position suggests the importance of the *kind* of information rather than the *amount* of information. This is consistent with his emphasis on the anticipatory function of imagery and schema. It seems reasonable to assume that both variables could be important. The amount or complexity of the anticipated information might be thought of as the vividness of the image, and the kind of information might determine the functional value of the imagery (for emotional arousal, location, meaning, etc.). In a given situation, imagery that anticipates the proper kind of information and does so in sufficient detail would be more useful than imagery that anticipates either detailed but irrelevant information, or sketchy but relevant information.

CONCLUSIONS

From this admittedly selective review of the therapeutic applications and theoretical models of imaginal thought, the following summary statements are offered. There are four principle therapeutic functions for which imaginal thought has been found useful. First, samples of naturalistic, or spontaneous, imaginal thinking such as dreams and fantasies are used as a means of identifying a patient's important emotional themes, patterns, and conflicts. This use of imagery is typical of the psychodynamic approaches, but a similar version also occurs in the rehearsal phase of Meichenbaum's stress inoculation training. In addition, interpretations of the theoretical positions of Klinger and Neisser suggest that dreams and fantasies also could be used to identify aspects of patients' basic anticipatory routines.

Second, several different therapy techniques rely on imaginal thinking to elicit the cognitive and physiological components of emotional arousal to situations that are impractical to recreate objectively in therapeutic settings. With some approaches, the goal is to recreate aversive emotional states, and with others, it is to develop pleasurable feelings and to deepen relaxation. Some techniques use imagery for this purpose so that the appropriate emotional conditioning can occur (desensitization, implosion, flooding, covert conditioning techniques). Other procedures (anxiety management training, stress inoculation training) use it for this purpose as a means of training patients to identify cues to their own maladaptive arousal, and of exposing them to mild stresses so that they can rehearse coping skills. In addition, psychodynamic approaches use the arousal potential of imaginal thinking as a means of helping patients express and work through emotional conflicts.

The third purpose for which imaginal thinking has been used is to aid in the learning and consolidation of new behavior patterns. In this respect, a conditioning model would emphasize the importance of the emotional arousal capacities of imagery in fostering new learning. A more cognitively oriented model might point to the effects of imaginal rehearsal on memory for the response elements of the new behavior pattern, and on the formation of more adaptive anticipatory schema.

Fourth, imaginal thinking has been used as a means of distracting people from painful stimulation. As noted earlier, this function of imaginal thinking is at a different level than the other uses. In this case, imaginal thinking *is* the new behavior being developed, rather than the *means* to developing a new behavior.

Another area concerning which some summary statements can be made includes the conceptions of the nature and function of imaginal thinking that are represented in this review. One approach is typified by the continuity assumption, as discussed by Mahoney (1974). This approach asserts that images and other forms of thought are simply covert, quasi-sensory copies of environmental stimuli and overt responses that can be manipulated according to the same conditioning principles that are presumed to hold for overt behavior. Techniques that are based on this conception include systematic desensitization and Cautela's covert-conditioning procedures. Another conception of the nature and function of imagery assigns it a role as one of the basic forms of mental representation that is especially adapted for memory functions. Rivaling this interpretation of the nature of imagery is the propositional approach, which views imagery as only an expression of the processing of more abstract informational structures. Yet another conception of the nature and function of imagery is found in the ideas of Singer, Klinger, and Neisser regarding the naturalistic role of imaginal thinking. All three of these theorists point to the potential antici-patory functions of imagery. Klinger and Neisser argue for interactional models that incorporate cognitive, behavioral, and environmental feedback elements and in which imaginal thinking serves an anticipatory role. There are intriguing parallels between these models and Bandura's recent dis-cussion of the role of the self-system in reciprocal determinism (Bandura, 1978).

Finally, this summary concludes with some recommendations for direc-tions of future work in the area. To begin with, much of the conceptual confusion about the different therapeutic uses of imagery is related to the lack of a generally accepted model of the nature and function of imagery. And, in some ways, such a model awaits the development of a more comprehensive model of the relationship between cognition and behavior. The interactional models of Neisser, Klinger, and Bandura referred to in the previous paragraph represent promising steps in the direction of such a model. Each of these was originally designed to account for a different aspect of behavior. Klinger's model helped explain fantasy processes; Neisser was concerned with explaining perceptual processes; Bandura was originally concerned with analyzing the causes of overt behavior. An integration of these models might be an important step in the development of a more comprehensive interactional model that would help clarify the ways in which imaginal thinking contributes to therapeutic change.

Additional topics concerning the role of imagery in therapeutic tech-niques that need further conceptual and empirical work include the follow-ing. The problem of how to most usefully conceptualize and assess the qualitative aspects of a client's imaginal thinking—imagery vividness and ability—is still unresolved. Some suggestions were made in the chapter for a new method of imagery assessment derived from the propositional approach. Another area requiring considerable work is that of identifying the processes through which imagery manipulations contribute to change. For example, research in cognitive psychology has shown imagery to be use-ful in improving performance on memory and perceptual tasks. Does imaginal rehearsal, as used therapeutically, contribute to behavior change through its effects on these two processes? Finally, as Kazdin (1977) has suggested, research is needed on identifying the proper role of imagery rehearsal techniques in our therapeutic armamentarium, and in particular, on their relationship to overt behavior rehearsal techniques.

REFERENCES

Anderson, J. Arguments concerning representations for mental imagery. *Psychological Review*, 1978, *85*, 249–278.

Anderson, J., & Bower, G. *Human associative memory.* Washington, D.C.: Winston, 1973.

Anderson, M. P. *Imaging as a self-control response to enhance voluntary tolerance of an aversive stimulus.* Unpublished doctoral dissertation, University of Texas, 1975.

Antrobus, J., Coleman, R., & Singer, J. Signal-detection performance by subjects differing in predisposition to daydreaming. *Journal of Consulting Psychology*, 1967, *31*, 487–491.

Bandura, A. *Principles of behavior modification.* New York: Holt, Rinehart & Winston, 1969.

Bandura, A. Psychotherapy based upon modeling principles. In A. Bergin & S. Garfield (Eds.), *Handbook of psychotherapy and behavior change.* New York: Wiley, 1971.

Bandura, A. Self-efficacy: Toward a unifying theory of behavioral change. *Psychological Review*, 1977, *84*, 191–215. (a)

Bandura, A. *Social learning theory.* Englewood Cliffs, N.J.: Prentice-Hall, 1977. (b)

Bandura, A. The self system in reciprocal determinism. *American Psychologist*, 1978, *33*, 344–359.

Bandura, A., & Jeffery, R. Role of symbolic coding and rehearsal processes in observational learning. *Journal of Personality and Social Psychology*, 1973, *26*, 122–130.

Bandura, A., Jeffery, R., & Bachicha, D. Analysis of memory codes and cumulative rehearsals in observational learning. *Journal of Research in Personality*, 1974, *7*, 295–305.

Barber, T., & Hahn, K. Experimental studies in "hypnotic" behavior: Physiological and subjective effects of imagined pain. *Journal of Nervous and Mental Disease*, 1964, *139*, 416–425.

Borkovec, T. Effects of expectancy on the outcome of systematic desensitization and implosive treatments for analogue anxiety. *Behavior Therapy*, 1972, *3*, 29–30.

Boulougouris, J., & Marks, I. Implosion (flooding): A new treatment for phobias. *British Medical Journal*, 1969, *2*, 721–723.

Cautela, J. R. Covert sensitization. *Psychological Reports*, 1967, *20*, 459–468.

Cautela, J. R. Covert negative reinforcement. *Journal of Behavior Therapy and Experimental Psychiatry*, 1970, *1*, 273–278. (a)

Cautela, J. R. Covert reinforcement. *Behavior Therapy*, 1970, *1*, 33–50. (b)

Cautela, J. R. Covert extinction. *Behavior Therapy*, 1971, *2*, 192–200. (a)

Cautela, J. R. *Covert modeling.* Paper presented to the Association for the Advancement of Behavior Therapy. Washington, D.C., 1971. (b)

Cautela, J. R. Covert conditioning: Assumptions and procedures. *Journal of Mental Imagery*, 1977, *1*, 53–65.

Danaher, B., & Thoreson, C. Imagery assessment by self-report and behavioral measures. *Behaviour Research and Therapy*, 1972, *10*, 131–138.

Davis, D., McLemore, C., & London, P. The role of visual imagery in desensitization. *Behaviour Research and Therapy*, 1970, *8*, 11–13.

Ellis, A., & Harper, R. *A new guide to rational living.* Englewood Cliffs, N.J.: Prentice-Hall, 1975.

Gerst, M. Symbolic coding processes in observational learning. *Journal of Personality and Social Psychology*, 1971, *19*, 7–17.

Goldfried, M. *Therapist manual for rational reevaluation of test anxiety in a group setting.* Unpublished manuscript, State University of New York at Stony Brook, 1977.

Goldfried, M., & Davison, G. *Clinical behavior therapy.* New York: Holt, Rinehart & Winston, 1976.

Goldfried, M., & Goldfried, A. Cognitive change methods. In F. Kanfer and A. Goldstein (Eds.), *Helping people change.* New York: Pergamon, 1975.

Goldfried, M., Decenteo, E., and Weinberg, L. Systematic rational restructuring as a self-control technique. *Behavior Therapy*, 1974, *5*, 247–254.

Grossberg, J., & Wilson, H. Physiological concomitants accompanying the visualization of fearful and neutral situation. *Journal of Personality and Social Psychology*, 1968, *10*, 124–133.

Hiscock, M. Imagery assessment through self-report: What do imagery questionnaires really measure. *Journal of Consulting and Clinical Psychology*, 1978, *46*, 223–231.

Holt, R. Imagery: The return of the ostracized. *American Psychologist*, 1964, *12*, 254–264.

Jacobs, A., & Wolpin, M. A second look at systematic desensitization. In A. Jacobs and L. Sachs (Eds.), *The psychology of private events*. New York: Academic, 1971.

Jacobson, E. *Progressive relaxation*. Chicago: University of Chicago Press, 1938.

Jeffery, R. The influence of symbolic and motor rehearsal in observational learning. *Journal of Research in Personality*, 1976, *10*, 116–127.

Kazdin, A. E. Covert modeling and the reduction of avoidance behavior. *Journal of Abnormal Psychology*, 1973, *81*, 87–95.

Kazdin, A. E. Covert modeling, model similarity, and the reduction of avoidance behavior. *Behavior Therapy*, 1974, *5*, 325–340. (a)

Kazdin, A. E. The effect of model identity and fear-relevant similarity on covert modeling. *Behavior Therapy*, 1974, *5*, 624–635. (b)

Kazdin. A. E. Covert modeling, imagery assessment, and assertive behavior. *Journal of Consulting and Clinical Psychology*, 1975, *43*, 716–724.

Kazdin, A. E. Research issues in covert conditioning. *Cognitive Therapy and Research*, 1977, *1*, 45–59.

Kazdin, A. E., & Wilcoxon, L. Systematic desensitization and nonspecific treatment effects: A methodological evaluation. *Psychological Bulletin*, 1976, *83*, 729–758.

Kelly, G. *The psychology of personal constructs*. New York: Norton, 1955.

Kieras, D. Beyond pictures and words: Alternative information-processing models for imagery effects in verbal memory. *Psychological Bulletin*, 1978, *85*, 532–554.

Klinger, E. *The structure and functions of fantasy*. New York: Wiley, 1971.

Kosslyn, S. Information representation in visual images. *Cognitive Psychology*, 1975, *7*, 341–370.

Kosslyn, S., & Pomerantz, J. Imagery, propositions, and the form of internal representations. *Cognitive Psychology*, 1977, *9*, 52–76.

Lang, P. J. Imagery in therapy: An information processing analysis of fear. *Behavior Therapy*, 1977, *8*, 862–886.

Lazarus, A. Crucial procedural factors in desensitization therapy. *Behaviour Research and Therapy*, 1964, *2*, 65–70.

Lazarus, A., & Abramovitz, A. The use of "emotive imagery" in the treatment of children's phobias. *Journal of Mental Science*, 1962, *108*, 191–195.

Mahoney, M. J. *Cognition and behavior modification*. Cambridge, Mass.: Ballinger, 1974.

Mahoney, M. J., & Arnkoff, D. Cognitive and self-control therapies. In S. L. Garfield & A. E. Bergin (Eds.), *Handbook of psychotherapy and behavior change*. New York: Wiley, 1978.

Mathews, A. Psychophysiological approaches to the investigation of desensitization and related procedures. *Psychological Bulletin*, 1971, *76*, 73–91.

McLemore, C. W. Imagery in desensitization. *Behavior Research and Therapy*, 1972, *10*, 51–57.

McLemore, C. W. Factorial validity of imagery measures. *Behaviour Research and Therapy*, 1976, *14*, 399–408.

Meichenbaum, D. Cognitive modification of test anxious college students. *Journal of Consulting and Clinical Psychology*, 1972, *39*, 370–380.

Meichenbaum, D. *Therapist manual for cognitive behavior modification*. Unpublished manuscript, University of Waterloo, 1973.

Meichenbaum, D. *Cognitive-behavior modification: An integrative approach.* New York: Plenum, 1977.

Meichenbaum, D., & Turk, D. *The cognitive-behavioral management of anxiety, anger, and pain.* Paper presented at the 7th Banff International Conference on Behavior Modification, Alberta, Canada, 1975.

Morganstern, K. Implosive therapy and flooding procedures: A critical review. *Psychological Bulletin,* 1973, *79,* 318–334.

Neisser, U. *Cognition and Reality: Principles and implication of cognitive psychology.* San Francisco: Freeman, 1976.

Paivio, A. Imagery and language, In S. Segal (Ed.), *Imagery: Current cognitive approaches.* New York: Academic, 1971. (a)

Paivio, A. *Imagery and verbal processes.* New York: Holt, Rinehart & Winston, 1971. (b)

Paivio, A. A theoretical analysis of the role of imagery in learning and memory. In P. Sheehan (Ed.), *The function and nature of imagery.* New York: Academic, 1972.

Paivio, A. Images, propositions, and knowledge. In J. M. Nicholas (Ed.), *Images, perception, and knowledge. The Western Ontario series in the philosophy of science.* Dordrecht, The Netherlands: Reidel, 1976.

Paivio, A., Yuille, J., & Madigan, S. Concreteness, imagery, and meaningfulness values for 925 nouns. *Journal of Experimental Psychology,* 1968, *76,* (1, Pt. 2).

Pylyshyn, Z. What the mind's eye tells the mind's brain: A critique of mental imagery. *Psychological Bulletin,* 1973, *80,* 1–22.

Rachman, S. *Phobias: Their nature and control.* Springfield, Ill.: Charles C Thomas, 1968.

Rehm, L. Relationships among measures of visual imagery. *Behaviour Research and Therapy,* 1973, *11,* 265–270.

Richardson, S. The meaning and measurement of memory imagery. *British Journal of Psychology,* 1977, *68,* 29–43.

Richardson, F. Anxiety management training: A multimodal approach. In A. Lazarus (Ed.), *Multimodal behavior therapy.* New York: Springer, 1976.

Rimm, D., & Bottrell, J. Four measures of visual imagination. *Behaviour Research and Therapy,* 1969, *7,* 63–69.

Rimm, D., & Masters, J. *Behavior therapy: Techniques and empirical findings.* New York: Academic, 1974.

Segal, S. (Ed.). *Imagery: Current cognitive approaches.* New York: Academic, 1971.

Sheehan, P. (Ed.). *The function and nature of imagery.* New York: Academic, 1972.

Shepard, R. N. The mental image. *American Psychologist,* 1978, *33,* 125–138.

Singer, J. L. *Daydreaming.* New York: Random, 1966.

Singer, J. L. *Imagery and daydream methods in psychotherapy and behavior modification.* New York: Academic, 1974.

Singer, J. L. *The inner world of daydreaming.* New York: Harper and Row, 1975.

Singer, J. L., & Antrobus, J. Daydreaming, imaginal processes, and personality: A normative study. In P. Sheehan (Ed.), *The function and nature of imagery.* New York: Academic, 1972.

Sipprelle, C. N. Induced anxiety. *Psychotherapy: Theory, Research, and Practice,* 1967, *4,* 36–40.

Stampfl, T., & Levis, D. Essentials of implosive therapy: A learning theory-based psychodynamic behavioral therapy. *Journal of Abnormal Psychology,* 1967, *72,* 496–503.

Steffy, R., Meichenbaum, D., & Best, A. Aversive and cognitive factors in the modification of smoking behavior. *Behaviour Research and Therapy,* 1970, *8,* 115–125.

Suinn, R., & Richardson, F. Anxiety management training: A non-specific behavior therapy program for anxiety control. *Behavior Therapy,* 1971, *4,* 498–511.

Turk, D. *An expanded skills training approach for the treatment of experimentally induced pain.* Unpublished doctoral dissertation, University of Waterloo, 1976.

Watson, J., & Marks, I. Relevant and irrelevant fear in flooding—A crossover study of phobic patients. *Behavior Therapy*, 1971, *2*, 275–293.

Wilkins, W. Desensitization: Social and cognitive factors underlying the effectiveness of Wolpe's procedure. *Psychological Bulletin*, 1971, *76*, 311–317.

Wolpe, J. *Psychotherapy by reciprocal inhibition*. Stanford, Calif.: Stanford University Press, 1958.

Wolpe, J. *The practice of behavior therapy* (2nd ed.). New York: Pergamon, 1973.

Wolpe, J. Cognition and causation in human behavior and its therapy. *American Psychologist*, 1978, *33*, 437–447.

Yuille, J., & Paivio, A. Abstractness and the recall of connected discourse. *Journal of Experimental Psychology*, 1969, *82*, 467–471.

Imaginal Processes

A Glimpse of the Promised Land

ERIC KLINGER

This brief comment begins with a general highly favorable critique of the preceding chapter, considers some omissions and some implications of the way imagery is viewed, and suggests outlines of general principles concerning imaginal processes that appear to emerge from the material reviewed by Anderson as well as from some not reviewed.

GENERAL CRITIQUE

Merrill Anderson has written a most important chapter. It is important for a number of reasons. First, there is the sheer variety of imaginal approaches compressed into one brief space. It still comes as something of a surprise that so many different kinds of practitioners and theorists have moved into this area, which was not so long ago beyond the pale of respectability in American psychology. They have arrived, like a polyglot encampment, to discover that they are in strange and unexpected company. It will take a period of exchanging observations and of conceptual sorting

ERIC KLINGER • Department of Psychology, University of Minnesota, Morris, Minnesota 56267.

out before we can fully consolidate the possibilities offered by this variety. The kind of integrative mutual introduction represented by Anderson's chapter is an essential part of the process.

Second, there is the care and clarity with which Anderson has portrayed different theoretical positions. The pressure for brevity has apparently helped him to set the main features of each position in bolder relief. I regard his exposition of my own position as nothing less than masterful in its lucid, balanced articulation of central themes and in its sensitivity to subtle but essential distinctions. So far as I can tell, he has been equally canny in his exposition of the other major positions.

Third, his review sets theoretical structures side by side in a way well calculated to reveal as clearly as possible common themes and researchable issues. The heuristic gain is potentially enormous.

Emphases

With a chapter already straining at its editorial limits, it seems almost out of place to speak of material omitted or underplayed. A chapter such as this is a feat of selectivity. Nevertheless, the reader ought to be aware that Anderson has devoted space as a rough function of the experimental and academic-theoretical contributions made by the various approaches. One notes with regret the omission of specific academic theorists or of various specific investigators. But most of all, Anderson's understandable tilt toward academic psychology perpetuates an academic neglect (to which I have also contributed!) of the clinically observed unfolding and continual transformation of imaginal forms reported by the "European" investigators and by a good many Americans, including Shorr, Rossi, Reyher, and many others. The work of some major contributors in this area—Desoille, Leuner, and Fretigny and Virel—is mentioned in a fraction of the space accorded to the single influential technique of systematic desensitization. The work thus compressed has largely (though not entirely) remained at the level of clinical report. It is hard to systematize and is vulnerable to the suspicion of case reports endemic among well-socialized American academics. To present it adequately requires, if anything, even more space and care than the presentation of experimental data. Anderson refers the reader to the summary of this work in Singer's 1974 book. What is lost to this chapter is the fine grain of important observations concerning the moment-to-moment flow of imagery, and thereby a whole sector of the phenomena under consideration.

The Operative Dimensions of Imagery. One of the very valuable functions of Anderson's chapter is to bring together current cognitive work on imagery with the use of imagery in therapy. Anderson deftly extracts significant implications for therapy from writers such as Neisser, Shepard, Paivio, and Bandura. He also points out the debate still raging over the place of images in cognitive function, and he expresses some discomfiture over the weakness of the evidence linking the "vividness" of imagery with its therapeutic effectiveness. This problem may, however, lead us to a more developed view of imagery.

There is a tendency to think of imagery primarily in visual terms. This seems natural enough given the prominence of the visual modality in imagery. Among one group of college students whose thoughts were sampled both in the laboratory and at unpredictable intervals during the course of a normal day, none rated the visual component of their images as less prominent than the auditory component (Klinger, 1978). (The instructions explicitly defined spoken words as auditory images.)

Nevertheless, there is reason to suppose that there is a good deal more to images than their visual or other sensory representations in consciousness. In the investigation just cited, the students rated each of their images on a number of scales. Factor analysis of the ratings based on within-student correlations (statistically eliminating individual differences) yielded two orthogonal factors related to the cluster of variables one might normally think of jointly as representing "vividness." I interpreted one of these factors to represent the clarity of the image and the second to represent its sensory saturation (Klinger, 1978–1979). The dimension of clarity contains high loadings for specificity (versus vagueness) of the image and at least moderate loadings for the amount of detail in the image. The implication is that images can vary in clarity independently of the extent to which they are judged intensely visual or auditory. If we recall that under the "constructivist" view images are efferent events—mental *acts*—we might speculate that for at least some purposes the functional usefulness of the image lies in the process of constructing the image, regardless of how saturated it turns out. Perhaps the typical measures of imaging ability have confounded the two factors—ability to construct and ability to saturate—or have focused too heavily on saturation, and have therefore failed to find relationships with clinical utility.

For instance, in our data (Klinger, 1978, 1978–1979), the subjects' Betts QMI Vividness of Imagery Scale scores correlated interindividually most heavily with the mean detailedness ratings of their images, which loaded intraindividually on both the clarity and the sensory saturation factors. (The two factors were not differentiated in interindividual-correlational data.) Thus, studies employing Betts scores or their close correlates to measure imaging ability are confounding the two factors.

SOME PRINCIPLES IN SILHOUETTE

The imaginal therapies have mostly emerged out of Pavlovian, Skinnerian, Freudian, and Jungian frameworks. None of these frameworks adequately encompasses the rich phenomena the imaginal therapists have encountered. It is time to develop a new set of principles that must in part, as Anderson rightly points out, rest on a more general understanding of "the relationship between cognition and behavior" but can in part be formulated only through careful study of the imaginal process itself. Some such principles can already be seen taking shape. Others are still represented only by awareness of a specific gap in our knowledge. They vary greatly in the detail with which they can now be envisioned. What follows is a tentative list of them.

1. Imagining is an efferent process of constructing perceptual schemata in the absence of actual sensory representations. Tomkins (1962) advanced an early argument for this principle, and the positions of Neisser and Shepard have developed in agreement with it. We still need to spell out the specifics and the enormous implications of this principle.

2. The imaginal stream carries with it affective responses to both the internal and external cues present at the time. Anderson points out the central place of this principle as regards imaginal cues in the theoretical underpinnings for desensitization, implosion, and other methods. Creating something in imagination constitutes creating a large part of the psychological reality of the thing. When therapists harness the imaginal stream, they are harnessing a substantial part of the whole psychological apparatus.

3. The thematic content of the imaginal stream shifts in lawful ways that reflect the impact of internal and external cues in relation to the person's current concerns (Klinger, 1977a,b, 1978). The principle needs much filling in, but a start has been made.

4. The representational forms—the specific objects and events—of the imaginal stream undergo lawful transformations. These have been considered from Freud (1900/1961) to Foulkes (1978) in the case of dreams, but work with the "waking dreams" of clients in guided imagery therapy suggests similar transformations in the imaginal stream during at least some waking states. The ways in which forms appear, divide, fuse, change, and interact with one another have not been specified well enough, for either sleeping or waking mentation, to permit substantial prediction. The phenomena involved require observation over sufficient time to enable transformations to emerge, a condition rarely provided in the systematic work reviewed by Anderson.

5. Focusing attention on an image or on one of its parts often results in a spontaneous transformation of the thing—in the amount of detail, in its form, or in the effect it evokes. This principle underlies a number of behavioral techniques for eliminating anxiety as well as a number of particular guided daydream techniques. Some images, however, seem to resist change (e.g., Ahsen, 1977). We need to know which images can be expected to change, in what ways, and under what conditions.

6. Guided waking dreams seem able to generate therapeutic effects without the need for interpretation on the part of the therapist or for intellectual insight on the part of the patient (e.g., Leuner, 1970). Reports such as this call not only for rigorously conducted outcome studies but also for detailed examination of how such therapeutic effects are produced.

7. The imaginal stream tends to circumvent resistances and self-deceptions by representing both (or all) sides of a conflict. The evidence here is largely but not altogether clinical (e.g., Reyher, 1977).

8. Fantasy solutions, especially when rehearsed, seem to generalize outside the therapy situation. Anderson has mentioned some of the best systematic evidence for this, and the clinical case literature suggests additional possibilities.

REFERENCES

Ahsen, A. Eidetics: An overview. *Journal of Mental Imagery*, 1977, *1*, 5–38.

Foulkes, D. *A grammar of dreams*. New York: Basic Books, 1978.

Freud, S. *The interpretation of dreams*. New York: Wiley, 1961. (Originally published, 1900).

Klinger, E. *Meaning and void: Inner experience and the incentives in people's lives*. Minneapolis: University of Minnesota Press, 1977. (a)

Klinger, E. The nature of fantasy and its clinical uses. *Psychotherapy: Theory, Research and Practice*, 1977, *14*, 223–231. (b)

Klinger, E. Modes of normal conscious flow. In K. S. Pope & J. L. Singer (Eds.), *The stream of consciousness: Scientific investigations into the flow of human experience*. New York: Plenum, 1978, pp. 225–258.

Klinger, E. Dimensions of thought and imagery in normal waking states. *Journal of Altered States of Consciousness*, 1978–1979, *4*, 97–113.

Leuner, H. Das katathyme Bilderleben in der Psychotherapie von Kindern und Jugendlichen. *Praxis der Kinderpsychologie und Kinderpsychiatrie*, 1970, *19*, 212–223.

Reyher, J. Spontaneous visual imagery: Implications for psychoanalysis, psychopathology, and psychotherapy. *Journal of Mental Imagery*, 1977, *1*, 253–273.

Singer, J. L. *Imagery and daydream methods in psychotherapy and behavior modification*. New York: Academic, 1974.

Tomkins, S. S. *Affect, imagery, consciousness* (Vol. 1). New York: Springer, 1962.

Chapter 9

Biomedical and Health Factors in Psychotherapy

LINDA WHITNEY PETERSON AND
TERRY J. KNAPP

The recognition of physical as contrasted with psychological causes of aberrant behavior and patient distress has always been of critical concern to the practicing psychotherapist. Historically, and contemporarily, the clinical psychologist has devoted much time and effort to the development of assessment devices aimed at identifying and locating focal brain lesions, thus assisting the physician in separating brain disease and dysfunction from psychiatric disorder and mental illness. The ethical guidelines under which clinical psychologists practice, and many of the state certification and licensing laws under which they work, make specific provisions for medical supervision or consultation, apparently in acknowledgment of the variety of ways in which physical illness and disorder may present. Currently, the psychologist's desire to be recognized and accepted as an independent private practitioner clearly requires that he or she know when to refer and defer to allied health professionals.

Pellagra is an excellent prototypical illustration of the concerns reflected in these considerations. During the early part of this century, pellagra accounted nationally for 10% of the patients in state mental hospitals, and in the southern region of the country for as much as one-third to

LINDA WHITNEY PETERSON • Department of Pediatrics, Medical School, University of Nevada, Reno, Nevada 89557. TERRY J. KNAPP • Department of Psychology, University of Nevada, Las Vegas, Nevada 89154.

one-half of all admissions (Roe, 1973). Mental dysfunction and behavioral disturbance were frequently associated with pellagra; hence, it was often seen and treated as a psychiatric disorder. With the discovery of the nutritional etiology of the illness (niacin and protein deficiency), its physical treatment became possible, and as a consequence pellagra became rare in the United States. Currently it is found only among chronic alcoholics, food faddists, or those with the genetic disorder of Hartnup's disease (Lipton & Kane, 1977).

Nevertheless, the history of pellagra needs periodic recounting least we in the psychotherapeutic community forget that psychological signs and symptoms may have largely physiological and biochemical origins. Our sensitivity to such possibilities should be further heightened by public awareness and argument to the effect that nutritional and exercise considerations are paramount in psychological well-being. Popular works with titles such as *Psychochemistry* (Gillette & Hornbeck, 1974), *Diet Away Your Stress, Tension, and Anxiety* (Palm, 1977), or *Psycho-Nutrition* (Fredericks, 1976) have resulted in many a client asking his or her psychologist whether problems in living might not be a simple matter of what one is eating or not eating. Earlier anecdotal accounts (Rossman, 1963), reviews (Hollender & Wells, 1975), and a recent careful medical screening of psychiatric patients (Hall, Popkin, Devaul, Faillace, & Stickney, 1978) point to a high incidence (9.1%) of medical disorders masquerading as psychological symptoms.

We would be remiss if the reader concluded that psychological, or for that matter physical signs and symptoms, may ever be regarded as of purely psychic or physical origin. As we have said in another context: "Physical medicine has long recognized the biobehavioral nature of pain and of somatic disorders in general. The bedside manner of Marcus Welby and the entire specialty of psychosomatic medicine testify to the interface between physical illness and the behavioral milieu in which it occurs" (Knapp & Peterson, 1976, p. 264). Such an approach to conceptualizing the interface between medical and behavioral science is further validated by the emergence of what might be termed life style disorders (e.g., coronary heart disease) as the principle cause of early death in America. We have discussed the impact of behavior therapy on such "somatic" disorders elsewhere (Knapp & Peterson, 1977); in this chapter we hope to raise the consciousness of psychotherapeutic practitioners to the impact of biochemical and health factors on behavioral disorder and well being.

THE PROBLEM: CASE ILLUSTRATIONS

The following four case studies serve to illustrate the variety of ways in which patients may present with psychological signs and symptoms (behaviors) traceable to physiological and biochemical causes.

Case 1. A 27-year-old nurse complained of lightheadedness, tremor, breathlessness, headache, and daily, but sporadically, irregular heartbeats (premature ventricular contractions, PVCs). The attending internist offered a prescription for the PVCs and a referral to the outpatient psychiatric service with a diagnosis of "anxiety reaction," which he suggested was related to the possible transfer of her husband to Vietnam. The patient, not satisfied with the professional opinion, conducted her own search for the cause of the distress, finally discovering that the symptoms had begun shortly after she purchased a fresh-drip coffee maker. Greden (1974) who reported this case, noted that she was consuming about 10 to 12 cups of coffee a day, or in excess of 1,000 mg of caffeine. Within 36 h following withdrawal of the coffee consumption, "virtually all symptoms had disappeared." Greden twice challenged her with dosages of caffeine, and on each occasion was able to reproduce both the subjective symptomatology and the PVCs. During a two-year follow-up in which she abstained from excessive caffeine intake, no symptoms reappeared. Additional case studies reported by Greden (1974) describe patients treated by both physicians and psychiatrists for as long as two years without success. In each instance excessive caffeine intake was the relevant controlling variable.

Case 2. A 28-year-old married woman had just delivered her first child.[1] She experienced considerable prenatal and postpartum bleeding. Public health nurses reported during home visits that she was listless and apathetic. When her baby cried, she frequently seemed unconcerned. The child was not fed on demand and was often found lying in a urine-soaked bed. During the prenatal period, she had looked forward to childbearing and had kept her home neat and decorated a nursery, but she was now withdrawn, cried excessively, and complained of fatigue. Her physician hospitalized her on the psychiatric unit and designated a diagnosis—postpartum depression. After several weeks of no improvement with psychotherapy, a young medical student was assigned to the unit. In the course of his duties, he performed a physical examination and took blood samples which revealed a hemoglobin level of 3 g (a hemoglobin below 12 g is suspect of anemia). With treatment, she was soon out of the hospital, caring for her infant appropriately.

Case 3. The junior author of this chapter, during his internship period, saw a 21-year-old male who complained of chronic pain associated with a back injury, and revealed during early assessment a pattern of depressive thoughts and a low-activity level of some months duration. Concurrent with behavioral treatment, the patient was receiving Prednisone (a corticosteroid) for a condition diagnosed by a general practitioner as Crohn's disease. The attempted suicide of the patient was preceded not only by a deterioration in the patient's home life, but also by a physician-prescribed increase in the dosage of Prednisone, a compound which ranks as number one in producing

[1] Our gratitude to Barbara Bishop, R.N., M.N., for this illustration.

adverse reactions of a psychiatric nature (Shader, 1971). Undoubtedly, the depression would have worsened simply as a function of the deteriorating home environment; however, the added effects of a steroid with depressive side effects may well have placed the patient at suicidal risk.

Case 4. Our final case for consideration is based upon the work of Parker and her colleagues (Parker, Deibler, Feldshuh, Frosch, Lauereano, & Sillen, 1976) at the Geriatric and Evaluation Service unit of Bellevue Hospital in New York. An elderly lady was twice admitted to the hospital; in each instance the diagnosis was originally "cerebral arteriosclerosis" (CA), a common category for the elderly who may present in part with complaints of memory loss and confusion. In the first admission, a more thorough medical history by the geriatrics staff revealed recent and acute behavior change, as well as the presence of pneumonia. After successful treatment she was released and lived independently at home for one year, when she was again brought to the emergency room, and again diagnosed as CA. A subsequent workup revealed a fracture produced by a recent fall. In a careful medical workup of 116 newly admitted geriatric patients referred to the psychiatric unit, over 61% were found to have treatable, medical disorders which were producing their psychological disturbances. Parker *et al.* (1976) emphasize the need for a thorough medical history in the assessment of such patients, with attention to recent events, and if necessary, supplementing the history with that of neighbors, relatives, and friends.

Although this chapter addresses the ambulatory adult population, one should also keep biological factors in mind for children. How certain are you that the child who has been shifting in his desk seat in the classroom is just "hyperactive" and not infested by pinworms and experiencing anal itching? Was scabies ruled out, before the label hyperactive was given?

Each of these case studies describes a different form of biochemical or physiological involvement, and suggests different levels of knowledge required on the part of the examiner in order to rule out physical causation. The skills necessary to detect such cases, whether rare or frequent in one's practice, are dependent on certain structural aspects of the intake interview and on certain prerequisite knowledge on the part of the interviewer. This chapter focuses on the former, while attempting to provide a preliminary introduction and suggested references to the latter.

THE HEALTH HISTORY: PRELIMINARY ISSUES
AND ETHICAL DILEMMAS

Should a health history[2] be a part of the general psychological intake interview? Unless the client's chief concern is a specific physical symptom

---

[2] The term *health* rather than *medical* history has been used to designate the focus on wellness

such as chest pain, with referral from a physician stating there is no organic cause for the condition, does the psychologist have any business going into a review of other systems, lab data, or the physical exam? Is it appropriate to designate baseline parameters of physical as well as psychological symptoms in order to assess the progress of the client in therapy?

Emotional health and physical health are so interwoven that to neglect the physical is to give inadequate coverage of the emotional. As was evident in the introduction, vague or subtle symptoms that manifest themselves as emotional may in fact have a specific biological etiology. *A physical workup by a physician is no guarantee that all physiological causes have been ruled out.* A client who fears confirmation of a physical disorder may mask or distort his symptoms. Furthermore, the sheer amount of time spent by a busy physician may lead to a situation where some health-related issues are missed. The setting in which the interview takes place influences the degree of self-disclosure by patients. Many medical practitioners incorporate history taking concurrently with the physical exam. Consider the female client undressed, being examined for a pelvic examination, while the physician takes a sexual history, versus the same client dressed in the office of an unhurried clinical psychologist.

If it is true that a psychological assessment should include health-related questions, which assessments should be performed and how? How many psychologists feel prepared for such an endeavor? How much preparation does the psychologist receive related to biological factors that may present as psychological symptomatology? How many incorporate health-related questions in the intake exam? How many could, at the end of the intake, write a physical description of the client seen? How many could interpret the range of normal for physical assessment or common laboratory values? If the psychologist accepts the "why" of health assessment and understands "how," what is to prevent him from being accused of practicing medicine? Is this role complementary or competitive with allied health professionals?

Incorporating health history questions in the psychological intake is an area open to scrutiny and deliberation by practitioners in the field. There exists at present no universally ascribed format or approval for such an endeavor. Psychologists as a group are particularly vulnerable to being accused of practicing medicine if health-related issues are pursued. It is curious that physicians are not accused of "practicing psychology" when most current health histories incorporate major sections that review the sociological system, or developmental and psychological data.

---

in the social, developmental, and psychological context of daily living rather than a stylized disease-oriented history characteristic of medical history in which a differential diagnosis is sought.

What seems a primary consideration is the attitude of the interviewer. There is a vast difference between the *collection* of health data and the ability to perform a differential diagnosis from that data. It is completely within the providence of psychology to collect health data, record it, and work in collaboration with a physician who may make a medical differential diagnosis. The psychologist might selectively gather data in those systems most directly correlated with psychological disorders (Martin, 1975), i.e., the central nervous system (CNS), gastrointestinal (GI) system, and endocrine system to a greater extent than the pulmonary, cardiovascular, hematopoietic, and musculoskeletal system (except in advanced disease). Similarly, it is fully within the context of psychology to utilize the physical assessment technique of inspection in a systematic fashion, reserving auscultation, palpation, and percussion to medical colleagues. In this context, after interview, inspection, or acknowledgment of lack of progress in therapy, the psychologist may refer a client to a physician for a repeated physical examination or extended laboratory work. Patients such as those described in the introduction provide the rationale for such a collegial relationship between the primary physician and the practicing psychologist.

A final major difference between the psychologist's and the physician's pursuit of medical data is related to the psychologist's interest in health and the prevention of disease versus the physician's attempt to detect and diagnose disease. With these concepts in mind, how can psychologists prepare to collect health data?

HEALTH ASSESSMENT: PREPARATION OF THE PSYCHOLOGIST

One of the most accessible ways to increase one's knowledge of health assessment with emphasis on wellness is to read some of the literature written by physicians encouraging the lay self-help medicine movement. *How to Be Your Own Doctor Sometimes*, by Sehnert (1975) for the adult, or *Childhood Illness*, by Shiller (1972) for the child, are classics in physical assessment and intervention with specific guidelines as to when to call a physician. The *Well Body Book* by Samuels and Bennett (1973) is a simplified formula for taking one's own health history. A practical, quantifiable, health assessment form that could be given to clients prior to the psychological intake examination is included in Ardell's *High Level Wellness* (1977). This form adapts well to the psychological aspects of health care. Positive, specific behaviors are assessed which involve one's life style related to self-responsibility, nutritional awareness, stress management, physical fitness, and environmental sensitivity. Excerpts from this form are presented in Table I.

TABLE I. Wellness Inventory[a]

Self-responsibility	Yes	No	Nutritional awareness	Yes	No
Would you question a physician who prescribes a drug or medicine as to whether it is really necessary? If not persuaded that it is essential, would you ask for nonmedical alternatives, seek another doctor, or simply disregard his advice and not buy the drug?	—	—	Do you read all labels on all packaged foods?	—	—
Do you wear seat belts when you drive, and do you require the same of children who ride with you?	—	—	Do you conscientiously attempt to reduce your sugar intake?	—	—
			Is your breakfast larger than your lunch, and is your lunch in turn larger than your dinner (and any snacks thereafter)?	—	—
Are there values which you place before promotion, prestige, profits, and success? And, do you reflect on these other motivators in your day-to-day existence?	—	—	Do you take food supplements (vitamins) regularly?	—	—
Do you feel well-acquainted with your body? Do you know what your extremities look like?	—	—	Are you careful to maintain a high-roughage diet?	—	—
			Physical fitness		
			Are you comfortable with and proud of your body?	—	—
Are you generally aware of the way in which your body processes food, what physiological events take place when you are stressed, and what happens during strenuous exercise?	—	—	Do you exercise vigorously at least 30 minutes nearly every day (i.e., five out of seven days)?	—	—
Can you laugh at yourself?	—	—	Do you include some flexibility and stretching exercises in your daily routine?	—	—
Environmental sensitivity			*Stress management*		
If you have a meeting one mile away and about 15 minutes to get there, are you likely to walk or bike rather than motor?	—	—	Do you meditate or otherwise try to center, balance, or quiet your mind on a regular basis?	—	—
			Do you respect your own accomplishments?	—	—
			Are you free, most of the time, from tension, frustration, insecurity, aimlessness, and dissatisfaction with your work and vocation?	—	—
			Have you taken at least two weeks of vacation in the past year?	—	—

[a]From Ardell, 1977, pp. 67–84. The above represents selected questions from a more extensive inven-

Many professionally oriented texts are available for reference (Bernstein, Bernstein, & Dana, 1974; Troelich & Bishop, 1972; Yarnall & Wakefield, 1972). The authors prefer, however, the comprehensive *Health Assessment* (Malasanos, Barkauskas, Moss, & Stoltenberg-Allen, 1977) for beginning medical and clinical psychology practitioners who are learning to assess the health status of the client by obtaining a health history and performing a physical exam.

Numerous other works can serve as useful references. Among the essential ones is the *Physicians' Desk Reference* (1979), which provides detailed information on prescription drugs, their use, contraindications, dosage, and possible side effects and adverse reactions. The *Merck Manual of Diagnosis and Therapy* (Holvey, 1972) is a condensed handbook organized by bodily systems and listing major disorders, their etiology, signs and symptoms, diagnosis, and prognosis and treatment. The latter part of the book contains a description of common drug categories, laboratory tests, and normal values. Two more comprehensive works of this kind are *Current Medical Diagnosis and Treatment*, edited by Krupp and Chatton (1977), and *Current Therapy*—1979, edited by Conn. Finally, the U.S. Department of Health, Education and Welfare (HEW) has an excellent brief introduction (Felton, Perkins, & Lewin, 1969) to medical terminology and specialties, the medical examination, and common disorders and diseases. Although the book is intended for rehabilitation counselors, it is an excellent reference work for clinical psychologists. Klein (1977) has a good book on medical tests.

It goes without saying that access to such sources doesn't make or imply the knowledge of a doctor of medicine, but instead provides background for intelligent discussion with the medical practitioner. The axiom for this section is keep humble! Contrary to popular belief, there are many unknowns in medicine, and numerous ways of handling different conditions—which at present is the prerogative of the client's physician.

HEALTH HISTORY: WHEN?

Health assessment can be accomplished prior to or during the initial psychological intake interview. The clinician needs to decide whether to use a precounseling assessment form or incorporate health history questions into his psychological interview, or both. One way to use a form for health assessment would be to introduce the subject of health, including your rationale during the first interview, asking the client to complete the forms before the second session.

Whether or not the initial health history elicits significant problem areas may have little significance. Perhaps none exist. Perhaps the client needs time to trust the therapist engaging in this new practice before a long-standing secret is revealed. This kind of early involvement may pay off when a physical problem does arise in conjunction with therapy. The client may initially express his concerns to a psychologist and later be directed to an appropriate medical professional.

HEALTH HISTORY: HOW?

An opening statement might be:

"As your psychologist I will be asking you some questions about your health and daily activities as I interview you. There are several physical factors that influence how people feel and, of course, how we feel influences how we take care of our bodies. The area of health assessment has been relatively neglected in the past by psychologists. It is becoming clear that if we are to help people we can no longer separate the mind and the body. Typically there are certain subjects that raise questions or cause concerns. These include how much and the quality of sleep we get, the amount and kind of food we eat, what kind and how much exercise we get. Whatever we discuss is confidential, as are all other aspects of your psychological history. It is my preference to work with your physician as a partner if anything should arise that would require knowledge of your medical status such as laboratory test results. This helps us provide you with total care."

Each clinician will generate his own explanation. The foregoing is offered as one model.

An axiom of interviewing is the "ubiquity" question. Questions are introduced with the assumption that most people have had experience with the situation in question. We ask: When did you last have a complete physical exam, including testing of your blood and urine? (rather than, Did you have a physical in the last ten years?), and How did you find a source for your medical care (rather than, Did you call a physician before you were ill?) Or after the preliminary statement, Many people experience difficulty finding a family physician, the interviewer follows with, What has been your own experience?

The interview style for health history proceeds from the use of open-ended questions to determine the chief concern to direct questions about specific systems. An example of the open-ended question is, What is your main reason for seeking help today? A direct question is, Are you taking birth control pills?

Another axiom is proceeding from "less sensitive to more sensitive" areas. The typical health record, for example, has a place where biographical data is first elicited. Questions regarding the client's genetic history or sexual history are reserved until greater rapport has been established.

A final axiom is the use of language geared to that of the client. Dsypnea, diuresis, and anorexia may be familiar to the therapist and suitable for some patients, whereas difficult breathing, sweating, and loss of appetite will communicate more effectively to others.

HEALTH HISTORY FORMAT

The primary objective is to determine the client's chief concern (cc). What is his reason for seeing you? What does he want specifically to work on today? The chief concern should reflect the client's own words. It is his perception of his problem.

"Anxiety and dizziness three hours after eating. First noticed one month ago."

"Tired, don't care about anything since birth of baby."

Thus, the chief concern is not a diagnostic statement. It is not your diagnosis of the condition or the "real" underlying reason for the visit (Bockar, 1976).

Once the chief concern has been determined, the psychologist must again make a critical decision depending on the setting (inpatient or ambulatory and the degree of severity of presenting symptoms). When a patient is experiencing acute psychosis, the medical interview may be short and direct. Bockar provides such an example when she writes, "The three major tasks in the first interview are to ascertain the chief complaint, decide on a working diagnosis and formulate what you are going to do about it." (Bockar, 1976, p. 50)

A somewhat different approach may be taken by the psychologist working in an ambulatory health clinic or private practice. The open-ended interview espoused by Enlow and Surisher (1972), although more time consuming, may yield more knowledge about health care practices and be incorporated into the psychological intake interview in so subtle a fashion the client may not differentiate between psyche and soma.

The format used by the writers is similar to that utilized in formula writing.[3] "Tell me about your . . ., How was it a year ago? . . . What are you doing about it?" The intake incorporates information about sleep patterns, elimination, diet, exercise, and drugs. The past medical and family history is reviewed to ascertain patterns of recurring health problems or specific fears the client might have about a specific disease or disability. The client's perception of self- or other responsibility for his or her health is determined. That is: Who do you feel is most responsible for maintaining your health? Your physician? Your spouse? Yourself?

[3] The authors wish to acknowledge the assistance of Marjorie K. Tsuda, M.S., R.N.C., in the preparation of this section.

PRESENT HEALTH PRACTICES

Sleep. Lack of sleep (under four hours) or excessive sleep (over ten hours) or interrupted sleep can result in a host of psychological symptoms, including chronic fatigue, irritability, paranoia, and lassitude. The following questions are asked: Tell me about your sleeping patterns this week. What do you have to do to go to sleep? When do you wake up? What do you do when you wake up in the middle of the night and can't go back to sleep?[4] How is this sleep pattern different from a year ago? Your sleep 10 years ago? How does your environment affect your sleep (ambient noise)? What have you tried to do to change your sleeping pattern?

Diet. How's your appetite? What is your weight now? A year ago? When you were 20? Tell me about your eating habits (how often, what, how fast, where). Tell me what you ate yesterday starting with your first meal of the day. If this area is of concern a three-day diet history form is sent home and the client is asked to return it. Types of foods are scrutinized (kinds of seasoning used, amount of refined sugar in the diet, amount of fat).

Elimination. The clinical psychologist has long been familiar with the fact that peptic ulcers, colitis, and GI pain of nonorganic origin is frequently due to psychological factors. Persons without a diagnostic designation can also display subtle psychological symptoms from a change in bowel or bladder habits. Constipation has been associated with headaches, diarrhea with weakness, irritability, and fatigue. Very frequent urination may be associated with diabetes, itching or painful urination with infection. As a way of questioning, the interviewer asks: Tell me about your urination pattern (how often, how much, color). What was it a month ago? Tell me about your bowels. What was your elimination pattern this week? A month ago? Last year?

Diversional Activities. The degreee to which a person can laugh at himself or absorb himself in hobbies or nurture himself by time out from work is a measure of wellness and reflective of life style habits. The interviewer asks, What do you do for fun? or What did you do for yourself this week? A year ago? When you were 20? How much vacation time do you have on the books? How do you spend your vacation? What did you notice about yourself on vacation as opposed to being "on the job"?

Physical Exercise. It has long been recognized that many physiological advantages accrue from physical exercise. Food can be properly digested and metabolized, bowel regularity is improved, the lungs process more air with less effort, blood vessels increase in size and number and saturate

---

[4] If the client urinates more than two times a night, or if he or she awakens short of breath, or needs two or more pillows to sleep, physician consultation is indicated. If the client awakens with night sweats and dizziness relieved by eating, hypoglycemia may be present. The same symptoms, when not relieved by eating, may have a cardiovascular-respiratory origin.

tissue with oxygen (including the brain). Psychological changes are often reported in studies of exercise physiology and include: increased self-confidence, increased energy levels, increased sense of well-being and decreased depression (Gomez, 1973). Assessing and considering exercise as an adjunct in treating psychological problems seems pertinent. The interviewer might ask: Are you comfortable and proud of your body? How much exercise did you get this week, last year, and at the age of 20? Are you motivated to exercise for the pleasure of it or for the joy of winning or for the excitement of risking defeat? Persons may lose some of the benefits of exercise if they must win or risk defeat.

MEDICAL ILLNESS: PAST AND PRESENT

One way to make transition to this topic is to ask: How many sick days did you have to use this past year? A year ago? When you were 20?

The writers prefer to look at the pattern of illness and injury from infancy to present by inquiring: What were you told about your health as a baby (colicky, allergies, physical defects)? How was your health as a preschooler (allergies, accidents, common childhood contagious diseases)? How much time did you miss in your school years due to illness or injury? What health problems have bothered you as an adult? Such questions give an overview of the life cycle, thus revealing which systems seem to be most vulnerable to stress (e.g., respiratory for the person with asthma, GI for the person with peptic ulcer). Such questions may document accident-prone persons, or persons who have experienced the trauma of hospitalization. In this context, the interviewer inquires as to how the person copes with illness and who the person thinks is responsible for maintaining health (self, physician, spouse, other).

PRESCRIBED AND SELF-MEDICATION

The interviewer asks: What drugs have you taken this week? Last year? When you were 20? What medications has your doctor prescribed this year? Do you use aspirin, birth control pills, or laxatives? What other forms of self-medication do you use? (If they are not mentioned, ask about allergy shots.) Many people have trouble taking the medication at the time or in the amount prescribed by their physician. How would you describe *yourself* in that regard? Many people experiment with drugs or alcohol. What kinds of experimenting have *you* done?

To determine the client's perception of drug reaction or action the interviewer asks: What have you noticed about yourself since you first started taking the drug (body image, sexuality, food habits, memory, concentration, hallucination, sleep, diversional activities)? These questions frequently elicit specifics not noted before (e.g., impotence is frequently a side effect of hypertensive drugs and is often the reason men stop taking the medication.)

FAMILY HISTORY

Knowledge of the medical history of family members may reveal genetic or familial health problems that deserve attention. It is not essential that the psychologist check off a list of common diseases. One might simply ask, What diseases or illnesses stand out in your mind as having affected members of your family? If the client does not answer an open-ended question one might ask directly: Do you know if anyone presently experiences, or has experienced in the past, any problems with heart or lung diseases, sugar diseases, cancer, alcoholism, drug abuse, mental illness, etc. One might also say: Many people experience the fear that either they or someone in their family might get a certain type of disease. Is there a specific disease that you worry most about getting? Such a question might lead to specific fears, such as a disability or disclosure of additional symptoms, that the client did not bring up earlier.

PHYSICAL ASSESSMENT

Few activities have enjoyed the awe of the physical exam. Sense extenders, such as the stethoscope, opthalmoscope, proctoscope, pelvic speculum, have explored dark, hidden places of the human body, which to most people remain mysterious only because they have not been seen. Much of this mystique is being challenged by the self-help medical classes that teach adults, as well as children, how to use these instruments.[5] In addition, some women's health collectives have gone as far as teaching women to perform a self-pelvic exam with the rationale that unless a woman has explored her entire body, she can not fully claim responsibility for herself.

Given the ever increasing knowledge and skill of lay persons in physical assessment, one might question the appropriateness of teaching clinical psychologists some basic skills if only to undergird their knowledge of the range of normal. At present the use of physical assessment, other than inspection of a client, is not acceptable psychological practice. Inspection, however, is the most basic assessment tool and may yield much data, even

[5] A newsletter summarizing much of the medical self-help literature is edited by T. Ferguson, M.D., Box 717, Inverness, California 94937.

though auscultation, palpation, and percussion are not performed. As an example, although the clinical psychologist may not use a stethoscope to detect heart sounds, his visual appraisal that a person has clubbing in the fingers, an ash-grey to cyanotic skin, or puffy edematous ankles would lead to a suspicion that a cardiovascular-respiratory disorder exists.

There are three axioms that are helpful to keep in mind when making a physical appraisal. Systematically view the person: (1) from the broad overall body presentation to the more specific, (2) proceed in a cephalocaudal (head to toe) direction, and (3) observe for symmetry. Symmetry is as basic to physical assessment as frequency is to behavior. Does one side of the body look the same or different from the other? Given the wide range of normal, the intricacy of physical assessment is in the ability to compare and contrast presenting features. The previously cited assessment references provide great detail with respect to the critical features requiring inspection, as does a new lay introduction to the topic (Rosenfeld, 1978).

COMMON CAUSES OF ANXIETY AND DEPRESSION

In this concluding section, we shall review for illustrative purposes three common causes of physiologically induced psychological disturbance. These are by no means the only sources of biochemical influence with which clinical psychologists should be familiar. A wide range of medical problems may present as behavioral symptoms (see Martin, 1975). For example, though rarely discussed in psychological textbooks, pancreatic carcinoma may present as depression, and only be diagnosed otherwise in thorough workups or in advanced stages. Similarly, hyperthyroidism is frequently seen as anxiety, although of a hot-sweaty rather than cold-sweaty kind. Thus, anxiety and depression are common behavior patterns associated with a wide range of physical disorders in addition to the three reviewed here.

Caffeinism. Case 1, in the introductory section of this chapter, illustrated the manner in which moderate-to-large dosages of caffeine can produce symptoms of anxiety that are likely to be diagnosed as of psychological origin. A dosage of 250 mg is regarded as "large" (Truitt, 1971), and may produce CNS stimulation effects of agitation, headache, hyperexcitability, ringing in the ears, visual flashes of light, sleep onset insomnia and sleep disruption, and tremor, among others (Greden, 1974). The reaction to caffeine appears to be individualistic, however, and clients may vary considerably in their presenting symptoms.

Greden and his colleagues at the University of Michigan have made the most thorough studies of caffeinism. In a recent study (Greden, Fontaine, Lubetsky, & Chamberlin, 1978), they examined by questionnaire 83 psychiatric inpatients of two different hospitals. Employing a daily dosage level of 750 mg of caffeine (the equivalent of about 6 cups of coffee), they found that 22% of the inpatients exceeded this intake dosage, while 42% were in the moderate range (250–749 mg/day), and 36% in the low range (0–249 mg/day). It should be recalled, however, that even a dosage as low as 250 mg is regarded as likely to produce psychopharmacological effects. In examining these patients with the State-Trait Anxiety Index and the Beck Depression Scale, clinical symptoms of both state and trait anxiety, and self-reported depression increased as caffeine intake increased, and in each case the heavy consumers were statistically discriminable from the low consumers.

While drawing their conclusions conservatively, the Michigan researchers caution that: (1) Patients should be routinely questioned at intake concerning their caffeine consumption (Table II provides a list of common sources). (2) Patients with anxiety or depression symptoms are likely to be large consumers of caffeine. (3) Abrupt withdrawal of caffeine may produce headache, lethargy, and other adverse reactions. (4) Among high con-

TABLE II. Some Common Sources of Caffeine[a]

Source	Approximate amounts of caffeine per unit
Beverages	
Brewed coffee	100–150 mg per cup
Instant coffee	86–99 mg per cup
Tea	60–75 mg per cup
Decaffeinated coffee	2–4 mg per cup
Cola drinks	40–60 mg per glass
Prescription medications	
APCs (aspirin, phenacetin, caffeine)	32 mg per tablet
Cafergot	100 mg per tablet
Darvon compound	32 mg per tablet
Fiorinal	40 mg per tablet
Migral	50 mg per tablet
Over-the-counter analgesics	
Anacin, aspirin compound, Bromo Seltzer	32 mg per tablet
COPE, Easy-Mens, Empirin compound, Midol	32 mg per tablet
Vanquish	32 mg per tablet
Excedrin	60 mg per tablet
Pre-Mens	66 mg per tablet
Many over-the-counter cold preparations	30 mg per tablet
Many over-the-counter stimulants	100 mg per tablet

[a] From Greden, 1974.

sumers, night sleep does not appear to be impaired, although caffeine will lessen the effectiveness of hypnotics and other psychopharmacological agents. (5) Finally, caffeine should not be a part of the psychiatric regimen, either as an agent to reduce the drowsiness brought on by psychotropic medication, or as a recreational drink.

Psychiatric Effects of Nonpsychiatric Drugs. Case 3 demonstrates the necessity of knowing what prescription (and nonprescription) drugs a client may be taking, at what dosages, and with what possible adverse reactions.[6] A perusal of the *Physicians' Desk Reference* would lead one to believe that almost any drug can produce almost any kind of side-effect. Fortunately, the recent work of the Boston Collaborative Drug Surveillance Program (1971) has narrowed the range somewhat. This group has collected data on more than 90,000 drug exposures in over 8,000 patients. Table III is a list of the ten most frequent drugs that produced adverse psychiatric reactions. These may range from agitation, anxiety, depression, and fatigue to hallucinations and delusions. The reader should be cautioned that the results listed in Table III were gathered among inpatients and may not accurately reflect the likely reactions seen in an adult ambulatory patient.

However, these are all commonly prescribed drugs. For example, Prednisone is often used with patients experiencing various kinds of GI difficulties. Aldomet is employed in managing hypertensive patients and can produce impotence in the male. Lasix is a diuretic that could produce disturbances in fluid and electrolytic balance. Variations in sodium, potassium, and magnesium level can produce psychological signs and symptoms. A detailed discussion of the psychiatric effects of nonpsychiatric drugs may be found in a monograph by that title edited by Shader (1971).

Hypoglycemia. The diagnosis and consequences of low blood sugar are hotly debated. Some authors (Fredericks & Goodman, 1969) have provided a list of signs and symptoms associated with hypoglycemia, which is so extensive as to apply to virtually any patient who may request psychotherapy; other writers (Levine, 1974) have claimed that the condition is quite rare, and infrequently a serious problem when it does occur in the reactive (following food ingestion) form. Similarly, there is little agreement on what the patient must display to be diagnosed hypoglycemic. Levine (1974) writing for the *Journal of the American Medical Association* claims that the patient's blood sugar level on the six-hour glucose-tolerance test (GTT) must fall below 45 mg. Other researchers (Fredericks & Goodman, 1969) consider the relative change for the individual as more critical to diagnosis than the absolute glucose level. Still other investigators (Fabrykant, 1955) have diagnosed their clients based upon the reproduction of symptom-

---

[6] Obviously clinical psychologists also need to be familiar with psychotropic medication. Several excellent introductions are available (Bockar, 1976; Honigfeld & Howard, 1973; van Praag, 1978).

TABLE III. Ranking of Observed Rates of Moderate-to-Severe Psychiatric Adverse Reactions; Ten Most Frequent Drugs With Four or More Adverse Reactions[a]

Drugs	Moderate psychiatric adverse reactions	Severe psychiatric adverse reactions	Rates per 100 patients exposed
Prednisone	9	9	2.6
Isoniazid	1	5	1.9
Methyldopa (Aldomet)	4	0	1.9
NPH Insulin	6	0	1.7
Sol Insulin	4	0	1.3
Diazepam (Valium)	15	0	1.3
Furosemide (Lasix)	9	2	1.2
Phenobarbital	10	1	1.2
Chlordiazepoxide (Librium)	11	2	0.8
Aminophylline	6	0	0.7

[a]From Boston Collaborative Drug Surveillance Program, 1971.

atology in the course of the GTT and relief of symptoms when diet therapy was instituted. It is evident that there is no clear set of criteria uniformly agreed upon to differentiate a state of hypoglycemia from the normal physiological process that maintains sugar balance. The term hypoglycemia may itself be a misnomer in that unusual symptoms can occur at normal (55 mg%) glucose levels.

What we can assure the clinician, as others have (Bockar, 1976; Martin, 1975; Mowrer, 1979), is that low blood sugar must be ruled out as a physiological cause of at least the four most commonly cited symptoms: exhaustion, depression, insomnia, and anxiety. A six hour GTT with concurrent recording of symptomatology is a good starting point, but may not be sufficient. Recent work by the senior author (Peterson, 1978) has explored the use of neurometric electroencephalogram (EEG) as an additional assessment technique. In the course of this research, one patient's data, depicted in Figure 1, showed a drastic drop in plasma glucose following a 100 gm glucose loading dose, and concurrent alterations in radial pulse rate and EEG frequency ratio (power function ratio of Delta + Theta/Alpha + Beta). During the first two hours of testing, the patient was alert, articulate, and cooperative. During the third to fourth hour, he complained, "I'm at the mercy of everyone." "I've got to get out of here." "I might hurt someone." In addition, he had slurred speech and could not speak in complete sentences; later, his voice became almost inaudible. By the fourth hour the symptoms subsided and he stated, "I can make it now." This patient was clearly hypoglycemic, yet he had been undergoing treatment for depression by a forty-dollar-an-hour marriage and family counselor. We clearly need to

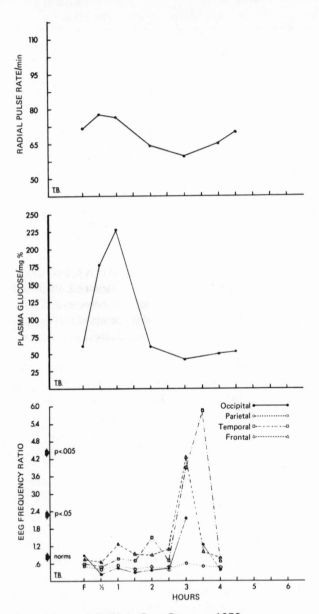

FIGURE 1. From Peterson, 1978.

acquire better skills at separating the physiological from the psychological. This patient showed dramatic improvement and remission of depression when placed on a proper diet (Peterson, 1977).

The three physiologically induced disturbances just reviewed are part of a larger number of cases in which clients have, with or without intention, placed a substance in their body that produces an adverse reaction. Discounting drugs, we might regard the cases as a matter of nutrition, and consider the fact that mere absence of signs and symptoms is an unworthy goal. As noted earlier, health is the general consideration, and psychologists may be useful in promoting good nutritional habits, regular exercise, and health maintenance life styles. The relationship between nutritional considerations and psychological well-being is at once an obvious one (Serban, 1975), but one which is wrought with controversy.

The popular trade book market suggests that whatever one's difficulty, there is a diet to cure it. Food fadism (Alfin-Slater & Aftergood, 1977; Robson, 1977) has emerged as a concern among practitioners, and well it should, given the recent reports of deleterious effects produced by some diets. The issues are complex, and exceed the capabilities of a mere chapter. Two excellent references, however, are the recent exchange of papers on learning disabilities and food additives (Preston, 1977) and a newly published text by Schneider, Anderson, and Coursin (1977).

In addition to acquainting themselves with the basic issues, and being sensitive to possible nutritional involvement in behavior disorders, clinical psychologists would do well to assist nutritional authorities in developing appropriate methodologies for discerning the impact of dietary regimens on behavior disorder and well-being.

The case studies and topics reviewed in this chapter suggest that clinical psychologists need to increase their knowledge of possible biochemical and health factors in psychotherapy. In addition, it may be necessary to develop congenial working relationships with physicians. This is the topic with which we close.

WORKING WITH PHYSICIANS

One of the most difficult aspects of working with physicians as colleagues is finding time to meet with them. Psychologists commonly bemoan the fact that even if they have the interpersonal skills for working with doctors, they are frequently "stood up" because of an emergency or the over-busy office schedule. The writers suggest that if this is your problem, talk to the office nurse about what is the most likely time to see the physician or talk to him or her by phone. Each has his or her own idiosyncrasies. One physician sees the senior author over his lunch hour, another after 5 P.M., a third takes the psychologist on hospital rounds or meets after rounds for coffee.

Most physicians are *not* accustomed to sharing medical records or laboratory results with psychologists. Such collaboration will need to be worked out individually and with client consent. This is a changing area. The proponents of self-help medicine consider it imperative that patients demand and expect access to their medical records. Complaints by physicians about such an innovation include: "People don't know enough to read and interpret their records," or "Patients don't really want to know that information." Other concerns involve fear of retribution and medicolegal problems from such "openness." With the advent of the problem-oriented record, such legal problems have been shown to decline markedly. With the advent of the professional team approach to health and the lay self-help medical movement, such interchange seems more likely.

It goes without saying that all the communication skills inherent in the field of psychology may come into play in developing professional, equal, collegial relationships with physicians. Typically, the physician has been the "head of the team." Initial contacts may proceed more smoothly if one recognizes the physician's expertise and asks questions, asks for assistance, and asks for clarification as to why a test was not run. Ask for another test or the repeat of a physical "because progress in therapy has not been forthcoming" (i.e., this "saves face" for the physician who may have deleted a lab test, such as hemoglobin, or simply rules out for the psychologist any physical problem that may have come up since the last physical exam). In the experience of the authors, psychologists who seem to have the best rapport with physicians subscribe to the format used when physicians consult with each other, that is, they write up summaries of client contact and report progress at several different time intervals. They may call or write to express appreciation for shared information, respect the time constraints of physicians by being prompt and staying for short intervals (15–30 min), are direct and prepared for information desired, and use appropriate sources other than physicians for "norms" such as lab values (books or laboratory technologists) or drug actions and reactions.

Communication can be further facilitated between psychologist and physician by adaptation of similar recording forms. The problem-oriented medical record (POMR) first designed by Lawrence Weed (1970) is particularly adaptable to the work of the behavioral psychologist. A problem list is generated and serves much as does an index to a book, as an index to the client's record. The "SOAP" format provides a method of clearly delineating the specifics of each problem. The S refers to the patient's *subjective* appraisal of his problem. For example, "I'm uptight at work, I can't concentrate." The O is *objective* data. This represents the psychologist's appraisal of what he observes about the patient's appearance and behavior.

A recording of objective data might include: Client wrings hands, diverts eye contact when discussing sexuality, talks in a high-pitched, rapid voice. A refers to the clinical psychologist's *assessment* of the problem at present, based on information obtained in S and O. Often this is a "provisional" or working diagnosis. It can be as broad as "anxiety reaction specific to school performance" or as specific as "conversion hysteria." The P is for *plan* and is the place where the therapist rules out other possible causes for symptoms, incorporates a tentative treatment program and includes initial client education. The psychologist might consider: DX refers to further diagnostic tests that should be performed to rule out (R/O) physiological causation. In this chapter we have alluded to the similarity of presenting symptoms in caffeinism, hypoglycemia, and anemia. A person with such presenting symptomatology who has not seen a physician or who has seen a physician but for whom the following tests have not been completed, should consider:

DX: R/O hypoglycemia: GTT
     R/O low hemoglobin: Blood tests
     R/O caffeinism: Record frequency of cups of coffee
                              drunk over three-day period

TX refers to treatment at present. Some clinicians prefer to delay treatment until tests have been run in order to specifically tailor treatment to diagnosis.[7] In such a case, TX might read: None til test results obtained. Other clinicians may engage in temporary treatment strategies: i.e., TX: Increase amount of rest; decrease refined sugar intake; increase exercise. Note that these are all wellness strategies that would not modify physical test results. The treatment is palliative until further diagnosis is forthcoming.

In the patient education (PT/ED) section you report to your colleagues the extent to which you have *informed* the client of your working hypothesis, the need for further tests, and suggestions for treatment at present. A typical entry might be:

> PT/ED: Mrs. J. was told that several factors could be accounting for her present problem. Due to interrelationship of psyche and soma there is a need to check some possible medical contributing factors. Requested consent to discuss her problem with her physician and schedule some laboratory tests. Session scheduled. 11/15.

Other references provide additional detailed information on the POMR (Hurst, 1971; Weed, 1968) and its possible use by psychologists (Katz & Wolley, 1975).

---

[7] A lay introduction to medical tests is provided by Evans (1976) and Klein (1977).

REFERENCES

Alfin-Slater, R. B., & Aftergood, L. Food fads. In H. A. Schneider, C. E. Anderson, & D. B. Coursin (Eds.), *Nutritional support of medical practice*. Hagerstown, Md.: Harper & Row, 1977.

Ardell, D. B. *High level wellness: An alternative to doctors, drugs and disease*. Emmaus, Pa.: Rodale Press, 1977.

Bernstein, L., Bernstein, R. S., & Dana, R. H. *Interviewing: A guide for health professionals* (2nd ed.). New York: Appleton-Century-Crofts, 1974.

Bockar, J.A. *Primer for the nonmedical psychotherapist*. New York: Spectrum, 1976.

Boston Collaborative Drug Surveillance Program. Psychiatric side effects of non-psychiatric drugs. *Seminars in Psychiatry*, 1971, *3*, 406–420.

Conn., H. F. (Ed.). *Current therapy*. Philadelphia: Saunders, 1979.

Enlow, A. J., & Surisher, S. *Interviewing and patient care*. New York: Oxford University Press, 1972.

Evans, D. M. D. *Special tests and their meanings*. London: Faber and Faber, 1976.

Fabrykant, M. The problem of functional hyperinsulinism or functional hypoglycemia attribute to nervous causes: II. Dietary and neurogenic factors, diagnostic and therapeutic suggestions. *Metabolism*, 1955, *4*, 480–490.

Felton, J. S., Perkins, D. C., & Lewin, M. *A survey of medicine and medical practice for the rehabilitation counselor*. Washington, D.C.: U.S. Government Printing Office, 1969.

Fredericks, C. *Psycho-nutrition*. New York: Grossett & Dunlap, 1976.

Fredericks, C., & Goodman. H. *Low blood sugar and you*. New York: Grosset & Dunlap, 1969.

Gillette, P. J., & Hornbeck, M. *Psychochemistry*. New York: Warner, 1974.

Gomez, J., *How not to die young*. New York: Pocket Books, 1973.

Greden, J. F. Anxiety or caffeinism: A diagnostic dilemma. *American Journal of Psychiatry*, 1974, *131*, 1089–1092.

Greden, J. F., Fontaine, P., Lubetsky, M., & Chamberlin, K. Anxiety, depression, and caffeinism among psychiatric inpatients. *American Journal of Psychiatry*, 1978, *135*, 163–166.

Hall, R. C. W., Popkin, M. K., Devaul, R. A., Faillace, L. A., & Stickney, S. K. Physical illness presenting as psychiatric disease. *Archives of General Psychiatry*, 1978, *35*, 1315–1320.

Holvey, D. N. *The Merck manual of diagnosis and therapy*. Rahway, N.J.: Merck, 1972.

Hollender, M. H., & Wells, C. E. Medical assessment in psychiatric practice. In A. M. Freedman, H. I. Kaplan, & B. J. Sadock (Eds.), *Comprehensive textbook of psychiatry*. Baltimore: Williams & Wilkins, 1975, pp. 716–782.

Honigfeld, G., & Howard, A. *Psychiatric drugs: A desk reference*. New York: Academic, 1973.

Hurst, J. W. Ten reasons why Lawrence Weed is right. *New England Journal of Medicine*, 1971, *284*, 51–52.

Katz, R. C., & Wolley, F. R. Improving patients records through problem orientation, *Behavior Therapy*, 1975, *6*, 119–124.

Klein, A. E. *Medical tests and you*. New York: Grosset & Dunlap, 1977.

Knapp, T. J., & Peterson, L. W. Behavior management in medical and nursing practice. In W. E. Craighead, A. E. Kazdin, & M. J. Mahoney (Eds.), *Behavior modification: Principles, issues, and applications*. Boston: Houghton Mifflin, 1976, pp. 260–288.

Knapp, T. J., & Peterson, L. W. Behavior analysis for nursing of somatic disorders. *Nursing Research*, 1977, *26*, 281–287.

Krupp, M. A., and Chatton, M. J. *Current medical diagnosis and treatment*. Los Altos, Calif.: Lang Medical, 1979.

Levine, R. Hypoglycemia. *Journal of the American Medical Association*, 1974, *230*, 462.

Lipton, M. A., & Kane, F. J. Psychiatry. In H. A. Schneider, C. E. Anderson, & D. B. Coursin (Eds.), *Nutritional support of medical practice*. Hagerstown, Md.: Harper & Row, 1977, pp. 463-476.

Malasanos, L., Barkauskas, V., Moss, M., & Stoltenberg-Allen, K., *Health assessment*. St. Louis, Mosby, 1977.

Martin, M. J. Psychiatry and medicine. In A. M. Freedman, H. I. Kaplan, & B. J. Sadock (Eds.), *Comprehensive textbook of psychiatry*. Baltimore: Williams & Wilkins, 1975, pp. 1737-1748.

Mowrer, O. H. *Are "behaviorists" really objective and scientific*. Unpublished manuscript, 1979.

Palm, J. D. *Diet away your stress, tension, and anxiety*. New York: Pocket Books, 1977.

Parker, B., Deibler, S., Feldshuh, B., Frosch, W., Lauereano, E., & Sillen, J. Finding medical reasons for psychiatric behavior. *Geriatrics*, 1976, *31*, 87-91.

Peterson, L. W. *Self control strategies for persons with reactive hypoglycemia*. Unpublished manuscript, 1977.

Peterson, L. W. *Brain neurophysiology in persons with reactive hypoglycemia*. Unpublished doctoral dissertation, Union Graduate School West, 1978.

Physicians' Desk Reference. Oradell, N.J.: Medical Economics Co., 1979.

Preston, J. B. (Ed.). Special symposium: Are the new therapies effective? *Academic Therapy*, 1977, *13*, whole issue.

Robson, J. R. K. Food faddism. *Pediatric Clinics of Northern America*, 1977, *24*, 189-201.

Roe, D. A. *A plague of corn—the social history of pellagra*. Ithaca, N.Y.: Cornell University Press, 1973.

Rosenfeld, I. *The complete medical examination*. New York: Simon & Schuster, 1978.

Rossman, P. L. Organic diseases simulating functional disorders. *General Practitioner*, 1963, *28*, 78-83.

Samuels, M., & Bennett, H. *The well body book*. New York: Random, 1973.

Schneider, H. A., Anderson, C. E., & Coursin, D. B. (Eds.). *Nutritional support of medical practice*. Hagerstown, Md.: Harper & Row, 1977.

Sehnert, W. *How to be your own doctor (sometimes)*. New York: Grosset & Dunlap, 1975.

Serban, G. (Ed.). *Nutrition and mental functions*. New York: Plenum, 1975.

Shader, R. I. (Ed.). Psychiatric effects of non-psychiatric drugs. *Seminars in Psychiatry*, 1971, *3*, 401-508.

Shiller, J. G. *Childhood illness: A common sense approach*. New York: Stein and Day, 1972.

Troelich, R. E., & Bishop, F. M. *Medical interviewing: A programmed manual* (2nd ed.). St. Louis: Mosby, 1972.

Truitt, E. B. The xanthines. In J. R. Dipalma (Ed.), *Drill's pharmacology in medicine* (4th ed.). New York: McGraw-Hill, 1971, pp. 533-556.

van Praag, H. M. *Psychotropic drugs: A guide for the practitioner*. New York: Brunner/Mazel, 1978.

Weed, L. L. Medical records that guide and teach. *New England Journal of Medicine*, 1968, *278*, 593-599, 652-657.

Weed, L. L. *Medical records, medical education and patient care*. Cleveland: Cleveland Press and Case Western Reserve University, 1970.

Yarnall, S. R., & Wakefield, J. S. *Acquisition of the history data base* (2nd ed.). Seattle, Wash.: Medical Computor Services Association, 1972.

Treating the Whole Patient

The Psychologist as a Member of the Health Team

YOLANDA F. HALL

The authors of Chapter 9 perform a valuable service by focusing on the interface between medical and behavioral science, stressing the basic unity of emotional and physical health. They conclude that in order to treat the whole patient effectively the psychologist must avail himself of vital health-related information. This conclusion is well supported and not debatable in my view.

Several major concerns are treated:

1. How can the therapist avoid misdiagnosis and inappropriate therapy by learning to identify the patient who presents with psychological symptoms which in fact can be traced to physical or biochemical causes? Case studies highlight the kinds of issues which might be encountered.

2. What are the legitimate needs of the psychologist or behavioral counselor for health-related information and how can these concerns be differentiated from "practicing medicine"? Sensible answers are given to these questions.

3. Given an affirmative answer to the question of *why* take a health history, suggestions for the *what*, *when*, and *how* of doing so are described in a

YOLANDA F. HALL • Department of Preventive Medicine, Rush–Presbyterian–St. Luke's Medical Center, Chicago, Illinois 60612.

straightforward, common sense manner. As a guide to practice, it is undoubtedly useful.

4. How can the counselor draw on the resources of preventive health and self-help approaches to make a unique contribution to the achievement of optimal health for the patient? The importance of nutrition and physical activity to a feeling of well-being and health are discussed.

5. The final section, concerning how to work with the physician in situations where the psychologist functions as an independent professional in settings usually removed from other health and medical care providers, focuses on tactics for bridging the gap. This discussion illustrates quite accurately what currently exists. It is apparent that today, in the majority of situations, the psychologist is less than a full-fledged member of the health team. Helpful suggestions for functioning in this situation are given. But the question is never asked: Is this desirable? Should this remain the outlook and goal for the future? My viewpoint is that a much stronger case can and should be made for reorganizing health care so that the psychotherapist can become a member of a multidisciplinary health team. The current state of fragmented care is not necessarily desirable and in the patient's best interest; perhaps some directions for change should be charted.

Does taking a health history expose a psychologist to the charge of "practicing medicine"? Where does one draw the line? Certainly the behavioral counselor cannot ignore potentially useful, even vital, information that can assist in diagnosis and effective treatment. It is crucial for the therapist to rule out disease states and to be alert for signs which might point to physiological or biomedical disorders, although this function must eventually be viewed as a shared responsibility with the physician and the patient. Precisely because of the complex way in which human social and psychological factors interdigitate with physiological and medical conditions, pertinent data must be explored in a unified way. However, we must recognize that in a comprehensive health care setting these data would be more readily available for sharing and evaluation.

Should the taking of a dietary history open one to the charge of practicing in the province of the clinical nutritionist? It certainly might be argued that a more complete nutritional assessment might result if done by the nutritionist or dietitian trained to identify a wide variety of nutritional problems. On the other hand, recent programs have found it desirable to combine the skills of behaviorists and nutritionists to accomplish desired changes in eating behaviors (Barlow & Tillotson, 1978). Again a team approach might be the preferred way, providing an opportunity for the psychologist to consult as needed.

There is a recognition that many patients are susceptible to faddist notions about diet and lifestyle changes. Note should also be taken of the fact that the literature in areas such as "wellness" and "prevention" often contains questionable advice. The psychologist, as well as other health professionals, must constantly distinguish reliable information supported by research from the dramatic solutions derived primarily from individual case studies or small uncontrolled experiments on highly selected populations. Regular review of reputable publications which use peer review procedures such as the *New England Journal of Medicine, Nutrition Reviews, Preventive Medicine,* and others can keep the therapist current as he moves into the broader areas of preventive medicine.

Although the authors note the controversy surrounding the diagnosis of hypoglycemia, their discussion may tend to reinforce a widely held misconception that this disorder is relatively common. Hypoglycemia has in recent years become a very popular "disease." It has been blamed for a diversity of mankind's ailments. By far the most common cause is the use of hypoglycemic drugs (insulin, sulfonylureas) for the treatment of diabetes. This condition is readily identified and treated by the physician managing the diabetic patient. Other causes are extremely rare (Service, 1975). In contrast, drug reactions are correctly identified as an area of major concern when dealing with underlying causes of anxiety and depression. Increased attention should also be given to the problems of nutrient–drug interactions and the role of even moderate alcohol consumption (Schneider, Anderson, & Coursin, 1977).

In the context of current practice, the psychologist is given the following guidance for dealing with medical and health-related issues:

1. Enlist patient consent and cooperation to obtain recent medical evaluation from the physician and encourage the patient with no recent examinations to get one. By stressing the continuity of physical and mental health and their interrelationship, the therapist can lay a foundation for cooperation with the professionals involved in medical care.

2. Gather health-related information selectively using both interview and questionnaires as appropriate, with the focus on those areas most commonly associated with psychological symptoms.

3. Share information and findings with the physician using the problem-oriented record and periodic progress summaries; refer the patient for further medical evaluation if there is a lack of progress under treatment.

4. Stress preventive care. Involve the patient in self-help and self-responsibility activities aimed at the achievement of an optimal life style. Thus, behaviors or conditions identified with high risk of chronic disease and which interfere with maximal well-being may be discussed as appropriate. Habits such as cigarette smoking, high alcohol consumption, sedentary life style, and ingestion of a diet high in calories, fat, sugar, and salt may be identified by the patient as dysfunctional with the goal of

optimal health. Further guidance may be given to responsive patients by acquainting them with appropriate publications (Farquhar, 1978; Mahoney & Mahoney, 1976).

The above goals are certainly desirable and in the patient's best interest. How likely is it that they will be followed by the average practitioner? As indicated, the effort to establish "congenial working relationships" with physicians requires considerable initiative and responsibility on the part of the psychotherapist. However, there is also a need for the medical community to assume greater responsibility for working toward the goal of integrating the psychotherapist into the health team.

REFERENCES

Barlow, D. H., & Tillotson, J. Behavioral science and nutrition: A new perspective. *Journal of the American Dietetic Association*, 1978, *72*, 368–371.

Farquhar, J. *The American way of life need not be hazardous to your health.* New York: Norton, 1978.

Mahoney, M. J., & Mahoney, K. *Permanent weight control.* New York: Norton, 1976.

Schneider, H. A., Anderson, C. E., & Coursin, D. B. (Eds.). *Nutritional support of medical practice.* Hagerstown, Md.: Harper & Row, 1977.

Service, F. J. Hypoglycemias. *Comprehensive Therapy*, 1975, *2*, 27–31.

Chapter 10

Toward Specifying the "Nonspecific" Factors in Behavior Therapy

A Social-Learning Analysis

G. TERENCE WILSON

Behavior therapy has a defining characteristic, a commitment to scientific method, measurement, and evaluation. This scientific orientation dictates that treatment be consistent with both the substance and the method of psychology as a broadly based experimental behavioral science. Therapeutic techniques must be described with sufficient precision to be measured objectively and replicated across different situations. The experimental evaluation of theoretical concepts and treatment outcome is fundamental (e.g., Bandura, 1969; Kazdin & Wilson, 1978). Partly as a consequence of the scientific emphasis that influences the description and application of behavioral techniques, behavior therapy is often criticized as clinically naive or even sterile. The conceptual bases of behavior therapy are said to be theoretically unable to accomodate the nuances of the therapeutic process, particularly the subtleties of the therapist–patient relationship. Successful applications have frequently been ascribed to the role of factors inadvertently inherent in the therapeutic relationship rather than to the specific behavior change techniques employed (e.g., Marmor, 1971).

G. TERENCE WILSON • Graduate School of Applied and Professional Psychology, Rutgers University, Piscataway, New Jersey 08854.

Characterizations of behavior therapy as a simplistic, symptomatic approach derive from basic misconceptions about the field (cf. Goldfried & Davison, 1976; O'Leary & Wilson, 1975). In part, the mechanistic view of behavior therapy that is shared by many nonbehavioral professionals is attributable to the way in which some proponents of behavior principles and procedures have described their use. Applied behavior analysts who eschew all mediating variables in their single-minded preoccupation with overt behavior inevitably overlook many of the interpersonal intricacies and subjective factors that are an integral part of successful therapy. Symbolic processes or private events are dismissed as epiphenomenal or irrelevant in this needlessly truncated conception of psychological functioning (Bandura, 1977b; Mahoney, 1974; Wilson & O'Leary, 1980). Alternatively, among the more theoretically liberal behavior therapists who have been engaged in clinical practice, it has been customary to designate therapeutic factors associated with relationship experiences as "nonspecific" influences (cf. Lazarus, 1961). Although usually recognized as significant, viewing the therapeutic relationship as a nonspecific influence relegated it to a position of secondary importance (e.g., Wilson & Evans, 1977). Traditionally, the role of placebo influences, therapeutic expectations, demand characteristics, trust, empathy, and rapport were all subsumed under the accommodating rubric of nonspecific influences. As "nonspecifics," they were de-emphasized and held in sharp contrast to specific behavioral techniques derived from learning theory, such as systematic desensitization, aversion conditioning, or token reinforcement programs.

Scientific advances within psychology and psychotherapy are characterized by increasing specificity in the types of questions that are asked and the procedures developed to answer them. As I have argued elsewhere (Wilson, 1977b), a comprehensive yet useful theoretical framework is essential in guiding the search for answers to these questions. Aside from making explicit the conceptual biases within a particular approach and facilitating the formulation of testable hypotheses, a scientific theory influences which facets of human behavior will be studied and which will be ignored. The view taken here is that by conceptualizing behavior therapy within a broader social-learning framework (Bandura, 1977b)[1] as opposed to earlier S–R conditioning theories (Eysenck, 1964; Wolpe, 1969), nonspecific influences can be seen as an integral part of behavior therapy. It would be realistic, therefore, to propose that, although many nonspecific influences still remain to be specified, they are neither intrinsically

[1] The term "social-learning theory" was used earlier by Rotter (1954), who has been deservedly credited as an important historical influence on the development of a cognitive-behavioral approach (cf. Mahoney & Arnkoff, 1978). However, Bandura's (1977a,b) social-learning theory is distinctly different and there should be little conceptual confusion between the two.

unspecifiable nor qualitatively very different from other independent variables involved in the treatment of clinical disorders (cf. Wilson & Evans, 1976).

The purpose of the present chapter is to indicate how so-called nonspecific therapeutic influences can be usefully conceptualized within a social-learning analysis. Specifically, such a theoretical integration has important consequences for both research in and the practice of behavior therapy. In terms of research, a social-learning analysis of nonspecific factors is important for the conduct and evaluation of process and outcome studies of therapeutic efficacy. The informed use of attention–placebo or pseudotherapy control groups rests heavily on one's conceptualization of the nature of nonspecific influences. With respect to treatment, social-learning theory provides a means of sharpening our conceptual focus and identifying increasingly fundamental therapeutic issues. Embracing as it does a broader yet specifiable range of psychological variables than traditional conditioning accounts, a social-learning approach to clinical practice makes it less likely that behavior therapy will ignore potentially powerful therapeutic influences that have been recognized although not conceptualized well by other therapeutic systems. Finally, by recognizing the therapist–client relationship as a legitimate and often essential aspect of the influence process, behavior therapy can be seen as a more sophisticated and sensitive approach than some critics acknowledge.

A DEVELOPMENTAL PERSPECTIVE

Before proceeding to an analysis of some of the nonspecific factors in contemporary behavior therapy, it may be useful to place emphasis on specifying an increasingly wide range of therapeutic influences within a developmental perspective. It is important to point out that little more than 20 years have passed since Wolpe (1958) completed his singularly influential book, *Psychotherapy by Reciprocal Inhibition*, which in many ways provides a convenient landmark for the modern origins of behavior therapy. During the relatively brief intervening period, behavior therapy has rapidly grown more complex. Exponentially expanding research activity has resulted in the modification of earlier techniques and the development of more effective methods. Theoretical formulations of behavior therapy have progressed from the early neo-Hullian and operant-conditioning models of Wolpe (1958) and Skinner (1953) to the more comprehensive and sophisticated social-learning framework detailed by Bandura (1969, 1977b). In the remarkable development of the clinical and experimental foundations of behavior therapy over the past two decades, many previously nonspecific variables have been specified and incorporated into the mainstream of routine behavioral treatment.

The modern, multifaceted nature of behavioral intervention programs is often a far cry from the early emphasis on circumscribed methods based upon unnecessarily narrow conceptions of traditional conditioning theories. For example Eysenck and Rachman (1965) were able to describe Stevenson and Wolpe's (1960) treatment of two homosexuals through the modification of relevant nonsexual behavior using systematic desensitization, assertion training, and environmental manipulation as "nonspecific behaviour therapy." "Specific" treatment in that early stage of development of the field would have consisted of the simple use of aversion-conditioning procedures aimed at directly suppressing homosexual behavior. Today, the ethical and clinical propriety of attempting to change a client's homosexual orientation is seriously questioned and behavioral procedures have been used to facilitate homosexual adjustment, including enhanced sexual functioning, *per se* (cf. Kohlenberg, 1974; Wilson & Davison, 1974). Electrical aversion conditioning is definitely contraindicated, even with those homosexuals seeking heterosexual readjustment. In cases such as these, the application of methods designed to enhance interpersonal skills, reduce heterosexual anxiety, and develop heterosexual arousal is dictated by a complete behavioral assessment of the full range of variables that maintain the unwanted behavior. Multifaceted treatment of complex problems is now commonplace and quite specific in nature. Anything less would be bad behavior therapy.

Another example of the important theoretical and practical consequences that attach to the specification of what was once described as a nonspecific variable concerns the nature of self-monitoring. Some years ago, McFall and Hammen (1971) labeled patient motivation, treatment structure, and self-monitoring as nonspecific factors which, they suggested, could account for the apparent lack of treatment-specific effects in most behavior modification programs for cigarette smoking. With the increasing conceptual and methodological sophistication of behavior therapy, self-monitoring has been investigated as an assessment and behavior change procedure in its own right. A good deal is now known about the parameters of self-monitoring, including the conditions under which it is most accurate as an assessment procedure (cf. McFall, 1977; Nelson, 1977). One of the early findings was that self-monitoring was reactive in certain instances irrespective of its accuracy. Initial research on this reactivity of self-monitoring produced inconsistent findings and premature conclusions. The problem was the manner in which the question was formulated. Is self-monitoring reactive or not? was too general and simplistic a question. The more specific and meaningful question, as Sieck and McFall (1976) have recently noted, is "What effects occur, under what conditions, in what behaviors, with what subjects, as a function of what specific self-monitoring procedures?" (p. 958).

Consider, for example, the importance of the specific behavior that is the target of self-monitoring. In the treatment of obesity, Mahoney (1974) found that instructing clients to self-monitor what were presumed to be the determinants of eating, such as what, when, and with whom they ate, failed to produce significant weight loss. However, subsequent research that was more analytical in nature demonstrated that self-monitoring of caloric content, as opposed to the circumstances under which eating took place, reliably produced significant reductions in weight (cf. Green, 1978; Romanczyk, Tracey, Wilson, & Thorpe, 1973). Similarly, with respect to cigarette smoking, Abrams and Wilson (1979) showed that self-monitoring of estimated tar and nicotine content of each cigarette smoked was more effective in reducing smoking than the more molar procedure of recording mere number of cigarettes smoked. These findings bear on *what* the target behavior is. *When* the behavior is self-monitored is another parameter with potential applied significance. Contrary to previous research that suggested that self-monitoring of food-related behavior prior to eating was more effective in producing weight loss than self-monitoring after eating (Bellack, Rozensky, & Schwartz, 1974), a well-controlled study by Green (1978) showed that self-monitoring caloric content before or after eating had the same reactive effect on weight reduction. Importantly, independent estimates of subjects' adherence to treatment instructions indicated that self-monitoring prior to consumption resulted in lower rates of adherence. Given the practical importance of prescribing therapeutic procedures that are both effective and acceptable or feasible for clients (Wilson, 1979a), postprandial self-monitoring would appear to be the preferred method in the treatment of obesity.

Initial interpretations of the reactive effects of self-monitoring stressed its function of providing discriminative stimuli that signal the ultimate reinforcing consequences of the behavior in question (Kazdin, 1974). In terms of social-learning theory, self-monitoring results in self-evaluative reactions with respect to an individual's performance standards. Perceived discrepancies between performance and self-prescribed goals or standards creates a negative self-appraisal that motivates corrective changes in behavior. Self-monitoring of personally significant behavior such as eating, drinking, or smoking inevitably will be associated with self-evaluative processes that constitute an important cognitively based source of motivation in social-learning theory (Bandura, 1977b). One of the advantages of social-learning theory is that it generates specific predictions about self-regulatory processes in behavior change. For example, it is not assumed that goals or external incentives automatically trigger self-evaluative processes. As Bandura and Simon (1977) have observed,

The degree to which goal setting creates incentives and guidelines for performance is partly determined by the specificity of the goals. Explicitly defined goals regulate performance by designating the type and amount of effort required to attain them, whereas general intentions provide little basis for regulating one's efforts or for evaluating how one is doing. (p. 178)

It is also predicted that specific subgoals will be more likely to motivate behavior than long-term goals. In a study comparing self-monitoring of eating behavior, obese subjects who monitored their behavior and set specific subgoals for each of four time periods during each day showed significantly greater weight loss than subjects who simply self-monitored eating behavior or who set more delayed, weekly goal limits.

Finally, this increasingly specific analysis of the nature and effects of self-monitoring has implications for the evaluation of commonly used behavioral techniques. Covert sensitization, for instance, is frequently used in the treatment of obesity, among other behavior disorders. Yet contrary to the interpretation of the technique in terms of aversion conditioning (Cautela, 1972), several well-controlled studies have shown that whatever success is achieved is attributable to nonspecific factors such as placebo or therapeutic expectations and not conditioning (Diament & Wilson, 1975; Elliot & Denney, 1975; Foreyt & Hagen, 1973). It may well be that the nonspecific agent of change inherent in the procedure is self-monitoring. Thus, Cautela (1972) has emphasized that the administration of covert sensitization entails instructing the client "to write down everything he eats including the time and place and exact amount. He is also asked to indicate the *amount of calories and grams of carbohydrates for each food item*" (p. 211) [emphasis added]. Unsuccessful applications of the technique might result from the failure to emphasize this instruction in favor of a misplaced focus on the discredited aversion-conditioning aspect of the method.

NONSPECIFIC FACTORS IN TREATMENT OUTCOME RESEARCH

Virtually all forms of psychological therapy involve the influence of factors such as the relationship between therapist and client, including therapist attention, interest, and warmth; expectations of improvement; the provision of a therapeutic rationale that places the client's problem within a particular theoretical framework; suggestion; and other so-called placebo influences (Frank, 1961). In their attempts to conduct controlled investigations of the specific treatment outcome effects, behavioral researchers designated these potentially therapeutic influences that are common to most therapies as nonspecific factors (Paul, 1966). With the emergence of innovative research strategies for studying therapy outcome, treatment control groups were designed to rule out these nonspecifics as explanations of treatment effects obtained with specific behavioral techniques. These control groups have variously been referred to as nonspecific, attention placebo, or pseudotherapy control groups. In general, these terms have denoted those variables that the experimenter has not specified as the critical or active ingredients of the particular treatment method under consideration (cf. Kazdin & Wilson, 1978).

With Paul's (1966) landmark study serving as a blueprint, it became common practice to include an attention placebo or nonspecific control group in treatment outcome research, particularly in the case of laboratory-based investigations of systematic desensitization. Recently, however, it has become clear that nonspecific treatment effects may not be as easily controlled as originally thought and that many nonspecific control groups have not necessarily been adequate for their intended purpose (cf. Borkovec & Nau, 1972). For example, it has been shown that in some studies the control group did not create expectations of therapeutic success commensurate to the favorable expectations generated by the specific behavioral technique of systematic desensitization. Nor was the perceived credibility of the control treatment rationale the equal of the rationale for systematic desensitization. Accordingly, it was argued that differences in treatment effects between systematic desensitization and nonspecific control treatments were difficult to interpret unambiguously. In a comprehensive review of the massive research literature on systematic desensitization, Kazdin and Wilcoxon (1976) concluded that only five studies included treatment control groups that had been empirically shown to account for credibility and expectations of therapy change. Their conclusion is a provocative one:

> Overall the five studies do not support the proposition that desensitization includes a specific therapy ingredient beyond expectancies for improvement. The relative paucity of studies showing that desensitization is superior to an equally credible control group would seem to weaken the usual statements made about desensitization as a technique with specific therapeutic ingredients. The alternative explanation, that the therapeutic effects are due to nonspecific treatment effects, at least at the present time, cannot be ruled out. (p. 745)

As I have suggested elsewhere (Franks & Wilson, 1977), such a conclusion appears to be extreme and tends to overlook evidence that clearly attests to the specific efficacy of the specific procedural ingredients of specific techniques such as systematic desensitization and flooding over and above the therapeutic influences collectively consigned to the nonspecific dumping ground. Nonetheless, this sort of searching methodological analysis points up one of the problems in previous treatment outcome research, namely, the failure to specify what has been referred to as nonspecific influences so that their precise effects can be evaluated and appropriate control groups devised. A most useful set of guidelines for the specification of nonspecific treatment control factors is discussed by Jacobson and Baucom (1977). In brief, these authors suggest that two major classes of variables need to be kept constant across treatment and control groups. The first consists of stylistic variables. These include therapist presence and attention, the activity levels of both therapist and subject, and the directiveness of the therapist. The second class is referred to as procedural variables. These include the presentation of a therapeutic rationale, the giving of homework assignments to equate for "effortfulness" of therapy, and other procedures that serve as the context for the specific active ingredients of treatment. The degree to which equating these variables across treatment and control groups creates comparable expectations of success and credibility ratings and expectations of treatment success should be assessed independently. Of course, it should be emphasized that highly specific and rigorous control of this nature is possible only in laboratory-based research. O'Leary and Borkovec (1978) point out the ethical considerations and methodological complexities that often make it impossible to institute such control in more applied investigations. As Kazdin and Wilson (1978) emphasize, "the applied clinical arena may be less the place to isolate specific mechanisms of behavior change than the place for demonstrating the efficacy of laboratory-tested methods" (p. 61).

COGNITIVE PROCESSES IN BEHAVIOR THERAPY

Clinical behavior therapy initially developed as a neobehavioristic $S-R$ approach based on the application of conditioning principles and procedures (Wolpe, 1969). Within this context, the role of cognitive processes was viewed essentially as a form of nonspecific influence that was subordinate to conditioning techniques. As Wolpe (1969) put it, "Behavior therapists, by contrast [to cognitive therapists], regard rational corrections as, in most instances, merely a background to the specific reconditioning or reactions that usually belong to the autonomic nervous system" (p. 131). Although Wolpe (1976) has continued to downgrade the significance of cognitive processes in behavior change, behavior therapy has, in general, increasingly "gone cognitive" (cf. Franks & Wilson, 1973, 1974, 1975, 1976, 1977, 1978). Indeed, what is referred to as cognitive behavior therapy is the most recent of the major conceptual approaches within the broadly defined field of behavior therapy (cf. Beck, 1976; Mahoney, 1974; Meichenbaum, 1977).

There is no need to detail the defining characteristics of cognitive behavior therapy here, as they are described by Mahoney, Beck, and Goldfried in their contributions to this volume. Nor is it necessary to elaborate my own view of the significance of the emergence of cognitive behavior therapy (Wilson, 1978). In short, I have suggested that the recent advances in cognitive-behavioral therapy are best seen as important extensions and clinically significant applications that are consistent with the existing conceptual model and empirical foundations of social-learning theory (Bandura, 1969, 1977b). The latter is a comprehensive yet testable framework that integrates the seminal importance of cognitive-mediating processes with the behavioral regulatory systems in which behavior therapy has always been rooted. Suffice it in this chapter to mention a few examples of how an explicit focus on cognitive-mediating influences in psychological functioning has greatly facilitated the specification of what were once undifferentiated and underemphasized factors in behavior therapy.

Insight, stripped of its surplus psychoanalytic meaning, has always been one of the nonspecifics of behavior therapy. An effective means of gaining insight or developing awareness about one's psychological functioning is self-monitoring. Specific thoughts and feelings can be monitored in addition to overt behaviors. These private events can then be consciously reflected upon or evaluated in terms of one's reciprocal interaction with the social environment. Another means of promoting insight is self-instructional training (Meichenbaum, 1977), one of the forms of cognitive restructuring that distinguishes cognitive behavior therapy. Unlike psychodynamic talk therapies in which "insight" is often a nebulous, overinclusive concept, self-instructional training involves clearly specified behavioral procedures to teach more adaptive patterns of self-talk. These procedures include client self-monitoring of maladaptive thought (self-statements); modeling of more appropriate verbal behavior, such as self-instructions that guide graded task performance, stress personal adequacy, and counteract worry over failure; and self-reinforcement for successful performance.

An important feature of social-learning theory is that while cognitive mechanisms are increasingly used to explain the acquisition and regulation of behavior, the most potent methods of therapeutic change appear to be those that are performance based. It would be difficult to overemphasize the significance of this distinction. The continuing neglect of cognitive variables by strict behaviorists needlessly restricts the scope and efficacy of their treatment methods. The tendency on the part of some cognitive therapists to focus on *symbolic* instead of *behavioral* methods runs the risk of returning therapy to a verbal, interview-based model of treatment which the introduction of behavior therapy did much to improve upon. An excellent example of a cognitive mechanism that is hypothesized to explain different fear reduction treatment methods is Bandura's (1977a) self-efficacy theory that is discussed more fully below. In essence, this theory holds that fear reduction methods are effective to the extent that they increase the client's sense of personal efficacy in coping with threatening situations. Specific predictions are generated by this theory that promise to shed light on hitherto imperfectly understood phenomena.

It is now well-established, for example, that exposure methods such as *in vivo* desensitization, flooding, and participant modeling are extremely effective in treating phobias and compulsive disorders (Leitenberg, 1976; Rachman & Hodgson, 1980). However, the process mechanisms responsible for this success have yet to be explained. Particularly puzzling has been the frequently marked variability in performance under similar conditions of exposure. According to self-efficacy theory, this variability is due to the fact that similar exposure conditions create efficacy expectations that differ in terms of strength and generality. Ordering the effects of diverse treatment methods in terms of the levels of self-efficacy that are induced will presumably reduce variability in treatment outcome and greatly enhance predictive power. Bandura (1977a) refers to the specification of the mechanisms of treatment-produced change along these lines as microanalyses. In similar fashion, microanalyses of specific efficacy expectations bid fair to explain the generalization of behavior change that cannot be accounted for solely on the basis of behavioral cues or stimulus similarity. If subsequent research bears out the encouraging initial findings obtained with this fine-grained cognitive analysis of therapeutic process and outcome, enormous progress will have been made.

Some of the strategies of cognitive behavior therapy have evolved independently of behavior therapy. Others represent the refinement or elaboration of procedures commonly used in behavior therapy but lacking conceptual definition. Thus, Mahoney and Arnkoff (1978) identify coping skills and problem-solving therapies as two of the major forms of cognitive behavior therapy. It is not difficult to conceptualize techniques such as assertion training and behavior rehearsal as strategies designed to increase coping skills and improve problem-solving abilities. Allied to the cognitive therapy emphasis on coping skills is the importance attached to the client's perceived control over his or her functioning. Those engaged in clinical practice have always recognized the significance of the client's appraisal of his or her problem and the logic of the therapy received. Regardless of the techniques ultimately used, the appropriate therapeutic groundwork has to be completed before specific treatment interventions will be successful. For instance, even a relatively simple and straightforward procedure as progressive relaxation training can founder if administered inappropriately. Many a novice behavior therapist has experienced difficulty in teaching clients to relax because of their apprehension about the sense of losing personal control. Clients may have to be reassured that in the ultimate analysis they are always in control. Relaxation training is not a form of therapeutic influence that is imposed on clients but a self-regulated process that clients choose to engage in. Clients are given the rationale that they are actually

acquiring greater personal control over their emotions by deliberately let-
ting go and relaxing themselves. The frequent results of this therapeutic
intervention are the enhancement of perceived control on the part of clients
and a greater willingness to confront anxiety-eliciting sources of their problems.

Clinical considerations of this sort were all too often confined to what
Goldfried and Davison (1976) have called the "therapeutic underground."
Serious theoretical analysis of concepts such as perceived control and
attributional processes were derailed in the late 1960s as a result of the simplistic and unsuccessful application of attribution theory to the modification
of avoidance behavior by directly altering the cognitive labeling of emotional distress through deception. Happily, analyses of the role of cognitive
appraisal in behavioral change are back on the tracks by virtue of a social-
learning framework in which cognitive processes such as attributions are
firmly tied to observable action (Wilson, 1979b). Perceived control appears
to be therapeutic only if it is at least partly based on actual control of
threatening situations. This underscores the value of performance-based
treatment procedures (cf. Bandura, 1977a). This relationship is not iso-
morphic and behavioral competence does not ensure emotional tranquility.
Cognitive processing of coping adequacy must be reasonably accurate and
this is one of the main objectives of Beck's (1976) cognitive therapy.
However, illusory or purely perceived control is rapidly disconfirmed in most
real-life situations and such disconfirmation frequently aggravates the individual's distress.

A final word on the behavioristic objection to the current focus on
cognitive processes is in order. (More detailed discussions of the inadequacy
of the nonmediational operant condition model are provided elsewhere: cf.
Mahoney, 1974 and Wilson, 1979a.) Briefly, the view that an operant
analysis is more precise, more specific, and less inferential than a cognitive-
mediational model of behavior is highly questionable. The operant-conditioning model is avowedly inferential (Rachlin, 1977) and current cognitive
influences on behavior are reinterpreted as the person's "history of environmental interaction." However, a regressive dependence on the loose
construct of "reinforcement history," which, for all practical purposes, is
not observable, tends to obscure the identification of specific regulatory
variables in behavior.

THERAPEUTIC EXPECTATIONS

Reflecting what surely must be a consensus among therapists of all
theoretical persuasions, Frank (1961) concluded that "part of the success of
all forms of psychotherapy may be attributed to the therapist's ability to

mobilize the patient's expectation of help" (pp. 70–71). Behavior therapy is no exception to this fundamental tenet of clinical lore (e.g., Klein, Dittman, Parloff, & Gill, 1969). However, caution should be exercised in uncritically accepting this assumption. In a recent review of expectancy factors in applied settings, Wilkins (1978) concluded that "very little evidence exists to support the popular assumption that therapist expectancies play a contributory role in causing therapeutic change" (p. 350). A major difficulty in investigating the effect of therapist expectations on therapeutic change has been the failure to carry out sufficiently specific analyses. Expectations do not operate independently but interact with other factors such as the type of treatment method, therapist behavior, client characteristics, and the particular outcome measure employed. In many behavioral studies, clients' expectations have been uncritically lumped together with other nonspecific influences as part of the background against which specific conditioning techniques were implemented. To the extent that further theoretical and experimental analysis of therapeutic expectations did take place, expectations were pitted against conditioning mechanisms in an oversimplified and misleading dichotomy in disputes over the effective agent of change in systematic desensitization (e.g., Marcia, Rubin, & Efran, 1969). More recently, however, the role of expectancy in behavioral change has been increasingly recognized, and it is important to attempt a theoretically consistent integration of the expectancy effect with the more formal techniques of behavior therapy.

Expectations and Systematic Desensitization

Much of the research on the relationship between expectancies and behavioral techniques has involved investigations of the active ingredients of systematic desensitization. It appears reasonable to conclude that induced expectancies can enhance the technique's therapeutic effects (cf. Emmelkamp, 1975; Franks & Wilson, 1976; Lick & Bootzin, 1975), although the precise manner in which expectancies contribute to fear reduction is still unclear.

Lick and Bootzin (1975) have proposed five possible mechanisms. First, positive expectancies may engender feelings of hope and optimism which facilitate counterconditioning. Consistent with this view are Borkovec's (1974) findings that therapeutic instructions resulted in significantly lower heart rate during treatment sessions than nontherapeutic instructions. Similarly, Rosen (1974) has suggested that positive expectancies help clients to relax, thereby facilitating nonreinforced exposure to the threatening situations. Second, therapeutic instructions might enhance compliance with the treatment procedures, such as symbolic representation of aversive events, practice in relaxation, and homework assignments (Bandura, 1969). Third, therapeutic instructions might serve a motivational rather than a counterconditioning function. Having experienced a "convincing therapy," subjects may be encouraged to engage in reality testing in the natural environment such that *in vivo* extinction occurs (Leitenberg, 1976). An important aspect of this hypothesis is that *in vivo* extinction is facilitated by the fact that subjects are motivated to look for improvement in their behavior in a persistent fashion. One of the advantages of this interpretation is that it plausibly accounts for what has been called the "transfer gap" in systematic desensitization, i.e., the incomplete generalization from imaginal to *in vivo* stimuli. Fourth, therapeutic instructions function as demand characteristics for improvement. Borkovec (1973), however, has demonstrated that demand characteristics of this sort modify the behavior only of mildly fearful but not genuinely phobic clients. Fifth, therapeutic instructions may modify cognitive processes which reduce fear responding directly. There is little compelling evidence for this view (cf. Davison & Wilson, 1973). For example, false feedback designed to induce favorable cognitions about decreased fear arousal has been shown to be ineffective in reducing fear or avoidance in very fearful subjects.

Self-Efficacy Theory

In his recent self-efficacy theory of behavioral change, Bandura (1977a) has proposed the most sophisticated and far-reaching analysis of the relationship between expectations and more formal behavioral techniques. An important conceptual distinction is drawn between outcome expectations, that is, the individual's belief that a specific action will result in a particular outcome, and efficacy expectations, that is, the belief that one is capable of performing the behavior necessary to produce the desired outcome. The investigations of the role of expectations in systematic desensitization have been limited almost exclusively to outcome expectations. However, efficacy expectations that reflect a sense of personal mastery and determine whether the client will initiate coping behavior, what degree of effort will be devoted to that behavior, and how long it will be maintained in the face of obstacles, appear to be more crucial in elucidating the mechanisms of therapeutic change. In addition to this conceptual distinction, Bandura (1977a) points out that expectations have usually been assessed in an inadequate global manner at a single point in time (e.g., at the beginning or end of therapy) as though they represented a static dimension of influence. In keeping with the conceptual bases of social-learning theory, specific assessments of the magnitude, generality, and strength of expectations need to be made at repeated points in the change process.

Self-efficacy theory permits the specification of how efficacy expectations are influenced by information derived from behavioral performance (e.g., participant modeling), vicarious experience (e.g., symbolic modeling), emotional arousal (e.g., systematic desensitization), and verbal persuasion (e.g., traditional psychotherapy). In comparative studies of different behavioral methods, independent assessments of subjects' self-efficacy expectations proved to be significantly superior to past behavioral performance in predicting subsequent behavior in different situations. As mentioned earlier, self-efficacy expectations seem to account for variability in outcome among subjects receiving the same type of treatment. Furthermore, self-efficacy theory has specific implications for the analysis of one of the most important yet curiously neglected aspects of therapy, namely, the maintenance of treatment-produced change.

Expectations and the Maintenance of Behavior Change

One of the major problems common to all forms of therapy has been the conspicuous lack of convincing demonstrations of the long-term efficacy of psychological treatment methods. Rejecting the traditional quasi-disease or psychodynamic model in which treatment outcome is described in terms of the molar concepts of "cure" and "relapse," the behavioral approach has emphasized the necessity of explicit maintenance strategies in order to ensure lasting therapeutic change. A distinction is drawn among the initial induction of change, its generalization to real life settings, and its maintenance over time. This more molecular analysis of the therapeutic enterprise is required by the fact that the different phases of treatment might be governed by different variables and call for different intervention strategies at different points in time (cf. Bandura, 1969; Kazdin & Wilson, 1978). Yet, despite this improved conceptual framework, relatively little systematic research has been devoted to developing effective maintenance strategies (see Franks & Wilson, 1978, for a fuller discussion of these issues). For the most part, thinking and research on the maintenance of behavior change has been dominated by an emphasis on reinforcement contingencies in the natural environment. This operant dictum has been simple—change the external environment if you wish to support newly developed behavioral changes (e.g., Atthowe, 1973). Cognitive variables were given short shrift. More recently, however, cognitive-behavioral formulations emphasizing the importance of self-efficacy theory and attributional processes have been proposed that may prove helpful in increasing our understanding and management of the phenomena of relapse (Marlatt, 1978; Wilson, 1979a).

Briefly, in addition to the necessary coping skills and personal incentives, these cognitive-behavioral conceptualizations of the relapse process emphasize the significance of the person's cognitive appraisal of a "slip" or transgression following an initial period of successful treatment. Take the case of a client who entered therapy because his behavior was out of control, e.g., an exhibitionist who cannot control the urge to expose himself, the alcoholic who cannot refrain from drinking, the cigarette smoker who cannot quit, the gambler who is unable to stop, and numerous other examples. It treatment is successful, the client desists from his previously self-defeating activity. His deviant (or addictive or compulsive) behavior is under control, albeit precariously in all too many instances. After three months of complete abstinence, the client transgresses and engages in the proscribed behavior. According to Marlatt's (1978) and Wilson's (1979a) social-learning analyses, a critical determinant of whether the client returns to the treatment program and abstinence or loses control and catapults mindlessly into excessive problem behavior is how the client construes the transgression. It is not so much the errant act *per se* but the meaning that attaches to it that will influence subsequent actions.

Consider the treatment of alcoholism. Based upon the assumptions of the prevailing disease model of alcoholism, the alcoholic is usually led to believe that he or she is qualitatively different from nonalcoholics, uniquely vulnerable to the addicting properties of alcohol, and unable to exercise control over drinking once it has started. As a result, any deviation from abstinence is assumed to produce the loss of voluntary control that is the hallmark of alcoholism. Recast in terms of social-learning theory, the person's efficacy expectations about coping with alcohol are deliberately minimized, and the outcome expectations that are inculcated stress the certainty of a return to uncontrollable alcohol abuse in the event of any subsequent consumption, regardless of the specific sociopsychological circumstances under which that drinking occurs. Together, these efficacy and outcome expectations are part of a social-learning analysis that can plausibly explain subsequent relapse phenomena without resorting to the biological inevitability of a return to alcohol abuse following any consumption of alcohol.

Studies designed to test this formulation of the relapse process directly have yet to be conducted. However, there is compelling evidence of the influence of expectations in determining the effects of alcohol consumption in both alcoholic abusers (Marlatt, Demming, & Reid, 1973) and alcohol users (Wilson, 1977a). Research on the maintenance of the reduction of cigarette smoking has yielded interesting correlations between outcome expectations and maintenance success (Colletti & Kopel, 1978; Schlegel & Kunetsky, 1977). Lastly, Marlatt and Marquis (1977) and Green (1978) have reported correlations between crude measures of personal efficacy and treatment outcome in heavy drinkers and obese clients, respectively.

Specific treatment and maintenance strategies derive from this social learning analysis (cf. Marlatt, 1978; Wilson, 1979a). To summarize, treatment would be geared to developing effective coping skills and maximizing efficacy expectations based on authentic personal control under conditions that were associated with alcohol abuse in the past. Maintenance strategies would include symbolic rehearsal of coping reactions to high-potential, high-risk situations and the possibility (likelihood?) that the client will transgress from time to time. Meichenbaum's (1977) stress inoculation training is especially useful in this regard and Lazarus (1978) has described what he calls "emotional fire drills" for precluding or at least attenuating the untoward impact of "future shock." Marlatt (1978) has gone as far as to suggest the use of a "programmed relapse" to enhance coping skills and instill realistic efficacy expectations.

Most of the ideas discussed above will not be unfamiliar to behavioral and other practitioners. However, instead of being confined to the therapeutic underground, it is important that such views surface and the psychological processes involved be progressively specified within the framework of a formal theoretical analysis.

THE THERAPIST–CLIENT RELATIONSHIP

The last example I wish to discuss in order to illustrate the progress that is being made in specifying important therapeutic influences that were once slighted as nonspecific factors is the therapist–client relationship. Although still a topic that receives scant attention in the behavioral literature, recent references to the therapist's contribution to treatment outcome are apparent (cf. Alexander, Barton, Schiavo, & Parsons, 1976; Jeffery, Wing, & Stunkard, 1978; Levitz & Stunkard, 1974; Mathews, Johnston, Lancashire, Munby, Shaw, & Gelder, 1976; Stuart & Lott, 1972). The following is by no means an attempt to provide a full analysis of the therapist–client relationship within a social-learning framework (see Wilson and Evans, 1976, 1977, for a more detailed analysis of this area). Rather, the focus is on a few selected aspects of the therapeutic relationship, which are beginning to be clarified.

Considerable conceptual and practical progress has been made in specifying the therapist's influence on the selection of treatment goals. Interested readers may consult Stolz and associates (1978) and Wilson and Evans (1977) for a review of the relevant issues in this fundamentally important and frequently controversial area. Suffice it to state that while the client has decision-making primacy in determining the goals of treatment in behavior therapy, it would be naive to imagine that in practice the therapist does not influence this process. In principle, behavior therapists are encouraged to assist the client by generating alternative courses of action and attempting to analyze their likely consequences. In doing so, it is crucial that the therapist's personal biases be recognized and honestly declared. Particular care should be exercised in helping the client differentiate between advice and information having some empirical basis and that which largely reflects the therapist's own values. Performing this delicate task obviously demands self-knowledge and self-understanding on the part of the therapist. There are no guidelines for assuring or assessing these personal qualities. The same applies to the interpersonal skills and social sensitivity of the therapist, which are as vital in behavior therapy as they are in any other form of therapy. Simply requiring that therapists themselves undergo therapy does not guarantee that personal requirements will be met.

The interview is a major vehicle for obtaining information about the nature of the client's problems and for initiating corrective therapeutic experiences. Accordingly, it is vital that the client come to trust the therapist. Interpersonal communication and the ability to give honest feedback is facilitated by higher levels of trust. Trust is a classic example of a nonspecific that was always taken for granted in behavior therapy without any formal attempt to specify procedures that would facilitate the development of a trusting relationship. Recently, Johnson and Matross (1977) have specified an operational model for building trust in a cooperative problem-solving situation such as behavior therapy. In response to the client's disclosing problems, the therapist shows warmth, accurate understanding, and cooperative intentions. The next step in promoting trust involves reciprocity of self-disclosure by the therapist with respect to his or her perceptions of the client. Davis and Skinner (1974), for example, found that self-disclosure by an interviewer was significantly more effective in producing self-disclosure by the interviewee than either exposure to a self-disclosing model or simple requests to self-disclose. However, intimacy of client disclosure can be reduced by self-disclosure from high-status figures such as professional therapists (Chaikin & Derlega, 1974). Self-disclosure of personal information should be done cautiously. The guiding principles should be whether the therapist's disclosure provides useful information for the client to model and whether the disclosure helps clarify the therapeutic situation so that the client's experiences may be more carefully structured and focused (Mahoney, 1974).

Modeling is increasingly used as a specific treatment technique in the modification of phobias and compulsions, teaching assertive behavior and social skills, language acquisition, and other problems (Rosenthal & Bandura, 1978). Less frequently recognized is the fact that modeling may occur implicitly and sometimes haphazardly during therapy interactions. Addressing himself to the latter, Mahoney (1977a) has advocated viewing the therapist as a personal role model for the development of broadly based coping skills and problem-solving competencies. According to Mahoney, modeling of behavioral, affective, and cognitive reactions—including appropriate self-disclosure by the therapist of his or her own coping strategies — may be a valuable function of the therapeutic relationship. In the cognitive realm, for example, Mahoney suggests that the therapist provide problem-solving expertise by "thinking out loud." Some empirical support for the efficacy of this strategy is provided by Meichenbaum's (1971) finding that a model who verbalized thoughts and feelings during the performance of a behavioral task exerted more influence on observers than a model who did not. The latter model is self-confident and totally competent from the outset in effortlessly performing the behavioral task. The coping model appears far more effective in producing behavioral change than a mastery model (Kazdin, 1973; Meichenbaum, 1971). In line with this analysis, Mahoney (1977b) has reported the preliminary use of "co-counseling" in which the therapist and his superviser formed dyads in which they alternated the roles of counselor and client. Co-counseling is described as a way to practice clinical methods as well as an opportunity for personal counseling. It is based on a coping self-disclosing model of supervision.

THE THERAPEUTIC RELATIONSHIP AND TREATMENT ADHERENCE

Client compliance or adherence with therapeutic prescriptions—be they medical or behavioral—has become the focus of recent research attention, particularly in the area of behavioral medicine (cf. Blackwell, 1976; Dunbar & Stunkard, 1979). Adherence refers to a client's premature termination of therapy as well as the incomplete implementation of therapeutic instructions. The relevance of adherence to behavior therapy or any other directive therapy is especially great since most behavioral methods involve asking the client to *do* something. Until recently, client cooperation in complying with the therapist's instructions was another nonspecific factor in therapy. The only specific behavioral strategy in this respect was contingency contracting, in which clients would be penalized for failing to engage in the agreed-upon behavior. Although unquestionably useful in many instances (Hagen, Foreyt, & Dunham, 1976), contingency contracting is only a single technique that must be conceptualized within the broader context of reciprocal social influence. Many operant-conditioning formulations of the therapeutic relationship suggested that the therapist could automatically "shape" desired behavior in the client using differential social reinforcement, assumptions reflected in unfortunate metaphors that depicted the therapist as a "social reinforcement machine" or as a "behavioral engineer." However, contrary to the unidirectional model of causal processes that characterizes radical behaviorism, unilateral therapist control over the client is largely a myth (Bandura, 1978). Interpersonal behavior is reciprocally determined, and the client can effectively resist or neutralize the therapist's attempts at influence (cf. Bandura, 1977b; Wilson & Evans, 1976). As a result, successful behavior therapy depends in large part on securing the active cooperation and participation of the client in the behavior change process.

Several specific therapeutic influences help determine adherence to treatment. The therapist's attitudes and behavior are significant factors. In their review of adherence to medical regimens, Dunbar and Stunkard (1979) conclude that "better adherence tends to be elicited by the clinician who is warm and empathetic, engages in social conversation . . . (and) active interchange, gives specific and individualized instructions, shows continuing interest . . . and demonstrates genuine concern." Blackwell (1976) cites evidence from a child guidance clinic in which the problems of clients who remained in therapy were similar to those of clients who terminated prematurely. Clients who remained in therapy were differentiated by the fact that their therapists' affective responses were consistently more positive. Other findings indicate that nonadherence to taking medication is increased if clients sense that their physician does not have much confidence in drugs. That this probably holds true for behavior therapy is illustrated by the following example.

In the course of conducting a workshop for therapists on the behavioral treatment of addictive behaviors, one of the participants expressed considerable skepticism in response to my enthusiastic advocacy of self-monitoring of daily caloric intake as a useful treatment technique. Accordingly, I had her role-play an interaction with one of the group members in which she asked him to self-monitor as a homework assignment. At the end of this scene, the "client" offered the observation that if he were one of her clients, he would come away from the session feeling that his therapist was only lukewarm about self-monitoring and that it would not matter much if he neglected to carry out the assignment she had given him. It seemed clear to me—and other members of the group—that the way in which this therapist presented the rationale and request for self-monitoring was implicitly self-defeating. Indeed, it proved to be the case that this therapist had a common misconception about the nature and purpose of self-monitoring that led her to present it in a very mechanistic manner rather than emphasizing its role in providing insight and self-knowledge. Her consequent lack of success was almost certainly due to her clients' nonadherence to the monitoring procedures.

Other therapist factors that affect the probability of the client cooperating with treatment instructions include the therapist's personal attractiveness to the client and social reinforcement for adherence. Personal attractiveness depends more on what the therapist does than on preexisting interpersonal characteristics. Specific strategies for enhancing therapeutic attractiveness and hence adherence are outlined by Goldstein, Heller, and Sechrest (1966) and Johnson and Matross (1977). Social reinforcement is not the automatic strengthener of behavior it has often been depicted as in operant-conditioning formulations of the therapeutic interaction, and its results depend on the client's awareness of what is being reinforced and whether he or she wishes to comply with the therapist's direction (Wilson & Evans, 1977). However, it may serve as a source of information and incentive that assists in maintenance of desired behavior.

Clients' expectations, already discussed in some detail above, also contribute to treatment adherence in different ways. Since efficacy expectations partly determine the persistence with which coping behavior will be sustained, they have obvious relevance for adherence. By developing realistic outcome expectations of ultimate success, the therapist may help to bridge the often formidable-looking gap between the short-term, often-demanding behavior required and eventual improvement (Mischel, 1974). Behavior is more readily regulated by immediate rather than delayed consequences, yet the treatment of numerous disorders rests on the success of the treatment in shifting regulation of behavior to delayed or long-term influences.

Clients enter treatment with expectations not only of outcome but also of what the therapeutic process will entail. Incongruities between what they expect and what they receive could impede progress or cut down on adherence (Baekelund & Lundwill, 1975). In their review, Dunbar and Stunkard (1979) observe that adherence is lowered in those patients whose expectations about their medical treatment program are not congruent with their experience of it. Specific practical suggestions for fostering congruent expectations are offered by Goldfried and Davison (1976). Related to this point is the desirability of adequately structuring the treatment experience for the client. Ideally, clients should be given an explanation of the development and treatment of their problem, a rationale for the type of therapy used, and a precise description of their own responsibilities in actively participating in treatment. Again, Dunbar and Stunkard (1979) indicate that this structuring of relevant information improves adherence rates.

No discussion of adherence would be complete without mention of the concepts of "resistance" or "countercontrol." Strict behavioristic approaches have overlooked this phenomenon in their overly narrow and often unproductive reliance on external contingencies. Thus, contingency contracting is acceptable and effective with some clients while others find it unacceptable and coercive. Even if clients agree to contingency contracting, it is not always effective. Social-learning analysis of resistance and some specific strategies for overcoming it have been presented by Davison (1973), Mahoney (1974), and Wilson and Evans (1976). However, these are sketchy at best, and this area of behavior change remains murky and far from understood. Specification of the nature and modification of client resistance is one of the more important tasks facing research-minded clinicians. In this connection, Kiesler, Bernstein, and Anchin (1979) have described a communication theory of the therapeutic relationship that provides many useful leads. This communication theory goes beyond current social-learning theory in emphasizing the role of nonverbal and connotative relationship influences in interpersonal interaction. The multilevel nature of the messages exchanged in the therapeutic relationship is emphasized. As such, this communication theory has relevance for the development of trust, congruent expectations, and structuring the therapeutic process.

CONCLUSION

Unlike most other forms of psychotherapy, behavior therapy has emphasized the development and application of a wide range of specific techniques based upon social-learning principles. Moreover, it appears that many of these techniques have been effective even when administered by therapists differing widely in personal style and background. The efficacy of behavior therapy techniques has been further highlighted by successful self- or client-administration, thereby enhancing self-regulated improvement in naturalistic settings (cf. Kazdin & Wilson, 1978). As a result, behavior therapy has been identified as more mechanistic than traditional verbal therapies that lacked specific intervention techniques and centered on the transference relationship between therapist and client. Behavior therapists contributed to this view by indiscriminately lumping together as nonspecifics such important influences as cognitive mediating processes, the development of therapeutic expectations, and the therapeutic relationship itself. These so-called nonspecifics were usually relegated to a position of secondary importance compared to the more formal behavioral techniques.

The present chapter has taken the position that these nonspecifics are potentially specifiable. It asserts that their specification will result in the more effective practice of behavior therapy. Fundamental to this development is the adoption of a broader, more flexible social-learning approach as opposed to the narrow strictures of earlier conditioning conceptualizations of behavior therapy. Some of the progress that has been made in this connection is briefly illustrated.

Behavior therapy is an often intricate and challenging approach to behavior change, and requires considerable therapeutic skill, social sensitivity, and clinical acumen for effective application. The theme of this paper—that nonspecific variables are extremely important and that they can be fruitfully conceptualized and integrated into the social-learning formulation of behavior therapy—is in fundamental disagreement with the view that is held in some behavioristic quarters that therapists are really only skilled technicians and that, therefore, only formal procedures should be evaluated. This view reveals a limited understanding of the essence of behavior therapy, which does not lie merely in a set of techniques.

REFERENCES

Abrams, D., & Wilson, G. T. Self-monitoring and reactivity in the modification of cigarette smoking. *Journal of Consulting and Clinical Psychology*, 1979, *47*, 243–251.

Alexander, J. F., Barton, C., Schiavo, R. S., & Parsons, B. Systems-behavioral intervention with families of delinquents: Therapist characteristics, family behavior, and outcome. *Journal of Consulting and Clinical Psychology*, 1976, *44*, 656–664.

Atthowe, J. M. Behavior innovation and persistence. *American Psychologist*, 1973, *28*, 34–41.

Baekelund, F., & Lundwill, L. Dropping out of treatment: A critical review. *Psychological Bulletin*, 1975, *82*, 738–783.

Bandura, A. *Principles of behavior modification.* New York: Holt, Rinehart & Winston, 1969.

Bandura, A. Self-efficacy: Towards a unifying theory of behavior change. *Psychological Review*, 1977, *84*, 191–215. (a)

Bandura, A. *Social learning theory.* Englewood Cliffs, N.J.: Prentice Hall, 1977. (b)

Bandura, A. The self system in reciprocal determinism. *American Psychologist*, 1978, *33*, 344–358.

Bandura, A., & Simon, K. M. The role of proximal intentions in self-regulation of refractory behavior. *Cognitive Therapy and Research*, 1977, *1*, 177–194.

Beck, A. T. *Cognitive therapy and the emotional disorders.* New York: International Universities Press, 1976.

Bellack, A. S., Rozensky, R. H., & Schwartz, J. A comparison of two forms of self-monitoring in a behavioral weight reduction program. *Behavior Therapy*, 1974, *5*, 523–530.

Blackwell, B. Treatment adherence. *British Journal of Psychiatry*, 1976, *129*, 513–531.

Borkovec, T. D. The role of expectancy and physiological feedback in fear research: A review with special reference to subject characteristics. *Behavior Therapy*, 1973, *4*, 491–505.

Borkovec, T. D. Heart-rate process during systematic desensitization and implosive therapy for analog anxiety. *Behavior Therapy*, 1974, *5*, 636–641.

Borkovec, T. D., & Nau, S. D. Credibility of analogue therapy rationales. *Journal of Behavior Therapy and Experimental Psychiatry*, 1972, *3*, 257–260.

Cautela, J. R. The treatment of overeating by covert conditioning. *Psychotherapy: Theory, Research, and Practice*, 1972, *9*, 211–216.

Chaikin, A. L., & Derlega, V. J. *Self-disclosure.* Morristown, N.J.: General Learning Press, 1974.

Colletti, G., & Kopel, S. A. *Maintaining behavior change: An investigation of three maintenance strategies and attributional processes in the long-term reduction of cigarette smoking.* Unpublished manuscript, State University of New York at Binghamton, 1978.

Davis, J. D., & Skinner, A. E. G. Reciprocity of self-disclosure in interviews: Modeling or social exchange? *Journal of Personality and Social Psychology*, 1974, *29*, 779–784.

Davison, G. C. Counter-control in behavior modification. In L. A. Hammerlynck, L. C. Handy, & E. J. Mash (Eds.), *Behavior change: Methodology, concepts and practice.* Champaign, Ill.: Research, 1973.

Davison, G. C., & Wilson, G. T. Processes of fear reduction in systematic desensitization: Cognitive and social reinforcement factors in humans. *Behavior Therapy*, 1973, *4*, 1–21.

Diament, C., & Wilson, G. T. An experimental investigation of the effects of covert sensitization in an analogue eating situation. *Behavior Therapy*, 1975, *6*, 499–509.

Dunbar, J. M., & Stunkard, A. J. Adherence to medical regimen. In R. Levy, B. Rifkind, B. Dennis, & N. Ernst (Eds.), *Nutrition, lipids, and coronary heart disease.* New York: Raven, 1979.

Elliot, C. H., & Denny, D. R. Weight control through covert sensitization and false feedback. *Journal of Consulting and Clinical Psychology*, 1975, *43*, 842–850.

Emmelkamp. P. M. G. Effects of expectancy on systematic desensitization and flooding. *European Journal of Behavioural Analysis and Modification*, 1975, *1*, 1–11.

Eysenck, H. J. *Experiments in behaviour therapy*. Oxford: Pergamon, 1964.

Eysenck, H. J., & Rachman, S. *The causes and cures of neurosis*. London: Routledge and Kegan Paul, 1965.

Foreyt, J. P., & Hagen, R. L. Covert sensitization: Conditioning or suggestion? *Journal of Abnormal Psychology*, 1973, *82*, 17–23.

Frank, J. D. *Persuasion and healing*. Balitmore: Johns Hopkins University Press, 1961.

Franks, C. M., & Wilson, G. T. *Annual review of behavior therapy: Theory and practice* (Vol. I). New York: Brunner/Mazel, 1973.

Franks, C. M., & Wilson, G. T. *Annual review of behavior therapy: Theory and practice* (Vol. II). New York: Brunner/Mazel, 1974.

Franks, C. M., & Wilson, G. T. *Annual review of behavior therapy: Theory and practice* (Vol. III). New York: Brunner/Mazel, 1975.

Franks, C. M., & Wilson, G. T. *Annual review of behavior therapy: Theory and practice* (Vol. IV). New York: Brunner/Mazel, 1976.

Franks, C. M., & Wilson, G. T. *Annual review of behavior therapy: Theory and practice* (Vol. V). New York: Brunner/Mazel, 1977.

Franks, C. M., & Wilson, G. T. *Annual review of behavior therapy: Theory and practice* (Vol. VI). New York: Brunner/Mazel, 1978.

Goldfried, M. R., & Davison, G. C. *Clinical behavior therapy*. New York: Holt, Rinehart & Winston, 1976.

Goldstein, A. P., Heller, K., & Sechrest, L. B. *Psychotherapy and the psychology of behavior change*. New York: Wiley, 1966.

Green, L. The temporal and stimulus dimensions of self-monitoring in the behavioral treatment of obesity. *Behavior Therapy*, 1978, *9*, 328–341.

Hagen, R. L. Foreyt, J. P., & Durham, T. W. The dropout problem: Reducing attrition in obesity research. *Behavior Therapy*, 1976, *7*, 463–471.

Jacobson, N. S., & Baucom, D. H. Design and assessment of nonspecific control groups in behavior modification research. *Behavior Therapy*, 1977, *8*, 709–719.

Jeffery, R. W., Wing, R. R., & Stunkard, A. J. Behavioral treatment of obesity: The state of the art in 1976. *Behavior Therapy*, 1978, *9*, 189–199.

Johnson, D. W., & Matross, R. Interpersonal influence in psychotherapy. In A. S. Gurman & A. M. Razin (Eds.), *The therapist's contribution to effective psychotherapy: An empirical approach*. New York: Pergamon, 1977.

Kazdin. A. E. Covert modeling and the reduction of avoidance behavior. *Journal of Abnormal Psychology*, 1973, *81*, 87–95.

Kazdin, A. E. Reactive self-monitoring: The effects of response desirability, goal setting, and feedback. *Journal of Consulting and Clinical Psychology*, 1974, *42*, 704–716.

Kazdin, A. E., & Wilcoxon, L. Systematic desensitization and nonspecific treatment effects: A methodological consideration. *Psychological Bulletin*, 1976, *83*, 729–773.

Kazdin, A. E., & Wilson, G. T. *Evaluation of behavior therapy: Issues, evidence, and research strategies*. Cambridge, Mass.: Ballinger, 1978.

Kiesler, D. J., Bernstein, A. B., & Anchin, J. C. *Interpersonal communication*. New York: Psychological Dimensions, 1979.

Klein, M. H., Dittman, A. T., Parloff, M. B., & Gill, M. M. Behavior therapy: Observations and reflections. *Journal of Consulting and Clinical Psychology*, 1969, *33*, 259–266.

Kohlenberg, R. J. Treatment of a homosexual pedophiliac using *in vivo* desensitization: A case study. *Journal of Abnormal Psychology*, 1974, *83*, 192–195.

Lazarus, A. A. Group therapy of phobic disorders. *Journal of Abnormal and Social Psychology*, 1961, *63*, 504–512.

Lazarus, A. A. *In the mind's eye*. New York: Rawson, 1978.

Leitenberg, H. *Handbook of behavior modification and behavior therapy*. Englewood Cliffs, N. J.: Prentice-Hall, 1976.

Levitz, L. S., & Stunkard, A. J. A therapeutic coalition for obesity: Behavior modification and patient self-help. *American Journal of Psychiatry*, 1974, *131*, 424–427.

Lick, J., & Bootzin, R. Expectancy factors in the treatment of fear: Methodological and theoretical issues. *Psychological Bulletin*, 1975, *82*, 917–931.

Mahoney, M. J. *Cognition and behavior modification*. Cambridge, Mass.: Ballinger, 1974.

Mahoney, M. J. Personal science: A cognitive learning therapy. In A. Ellis & R. Grieger (Eds.), *Handbook of rational psychotherapy*. New York: Springer, 1977. (a)

Mahoney, M. J. *Therapist liberation*. Unpublished manuscript, The Pennsylvania State University, 1977. (b)

Mahoney, M. J., & Arnkoff, D. Cognitive and self-control therapies. In S. L. Garfield & A. E. Bergin (Eds.), *Handbook of psychotherapy and behavior change* (2nd Ed.). New York: Wiley, 1978.

Marcia, J. E., Rubin, B. M., & Efran, J. S. Systematic desensitization: Expectancy change or counter-conditioning. *Journal of Abnormal Psychology*, 1969, *74*, 382–387.

Marlatt, G. A. Craving for alcohol, loss of control, and relapse: A cognitive-behavioral analysis. In P. E. Nathan, G. A. Marlatt & T. Løberg (Eds.), *Alcoholism: New directions in behavioral research and treatment*. New York: Plenum, 1978.

Marlatt, G. A., & Marquis, J. K. Meditation, self-control, and alcohol use. In R. B. Stuart (Ed.), *Self-management: Strategies, techniques and results*. New York: Brunner/Mazel, 1977.

Marlatt, G. A., Demming, B., & Reid, J. Loss of control drinking in alcoholics. *Journal of Abnormal Psychology*, 1973, *81*, 233–241.

Marmor, J. Dynamic psychotherapy and behavior therapy. *Archives of General Psychiatry*, 1971, *24*, 22–28.

Mathews, A. M., Johnston, D. W., Lancashire, M., Munby, M., Shaw, P. M., & Gelder, M. G. Imaginal flooding and exposure to real phobic situations: Treatment outcome with agoraphobic patients. *British Journal of Psychiatry*, 1976, *129*, 362–371.

McFall, R. M. Parameters of self-monitoring. In R. B. Stuart (Ed.), *Behavioral self-management*. New York: Brunner/Mazel, 1977.

McFall, R. M., & Hammen, C. Motivation, structure, and self-monitoring: Role of non-specific factors in smoking reduction. *Journal of Consulting and Clinical Psychology*, 1971, *37*, 8–86.

Meichenbaum, D. Examination of model characteristics in reducing avoidance behavior. *Journal of Personality and Social Psychology*, 1971, *14*, 298–307.

Meichenbaum, D. *Cognitive behavior modification. An integrative approach*. New York: Plenum, 1977.

Mischel, W. Processes in the delay of gratification. In L. Berkowitz (Ed.), *Advances in experimental social psychology* (Vol. 7). New York: Academic, 1974.

Nelson, R. O. Methodological issues in assessment via self-monitoring. In J. D. Cone & R. P. Hawkins (Eds.), *Behavioral assessment*. New York: Brunner/Mazel, 1977.

O'Leary, K. D., & Borkovec, T. D. Placebo groups: Unrealistic and unethical controls in psychotherapy research. *American Psychologist*, 1978, *33*, 821–830.

O'Leary, K. D., & Wilson, G. T. *Behavior therapy: Application and outcome*. Englewood Cliffs, N. J.: Prentice-Hall, 1975.

Paul, G. L. *Insight versus desensitization in psychotherapy*. Stanford, Calif.: Stanford University Press, 1966.

Rachlin, H. A review of *Cognition and Behavior Modification* by M. J. Mahoney. *Journal of Applied Behavior Analysis*, 1977, *10*, 369–374.

Rachman, S., & Hodgson, R. *Obsessive-compulsive neuroses*. Englewood Cliffs, N.J.: Prentice-Hall, 1980.

Romanczyk, R. G., Tracey, D. A., Wilson, G. T., & Thorpe, G. L. Behavioral techniques in the treatment of obesity: A comparative analysis. *Behaviour Research and Therapy*, 1973, *11*, 629–640.

Rosen, G. M. Therapy set: Its effect on subjects' involvement in systematic desensitization and treatment outcome. *Journal of Abnormal Psychology*, 1974, *83*, 291–300.

Rosenthal, T. L., & Bandura, A. Psychological modeling: Theory and practice. In S. L. Garfield & A. E. Bergin (Eds.), *Handbook of psychotherapy and behavior change* (2nd Ed.). New York: Wiley, 1978.

Rotter, J. B. *Social learning and clinical psychology*. Englewood Cliffs, N.J.: Prentice-Hall, 1954.

Schlegel, R. P., & Kunetsky, M. Immediate and delayed effects of the "five-day plan to stop smoking" including factors affecting recidivism. *Preventive Medicine*, 1977, *6*, 454–461.

Sieck, W. A., & McFall, R. M. Some determinants of self-monitoring effects. *Journal of Consulting and Clinical Psychology*, 1976, *44*, 958–965.

Skinner, B. F. *Science and human behavior*. New York: Macmillan, 1953.

Stevenson, I., & Wolpe, J. Recovery from sexual deviations through overcoming non-sexual neurotic responses. *American Journal of Psychiatry*, 1960, *116*, 737–742.

Stolz, S. B. *Ethical issues in behavior modification*. San Francisco, Calif.: Jossey-Bass, 1978.

Stuart, R. B., & Lott, L. A. Behavioral contracting with delinquents: A cautionary note. *Journal of Behavior Therapy and Experimental Psychiatry*, 1972, *3*, 161–169.

Wilkins, W. Expectancies in applied settings. In A. Gurman & A. Razin (Eds.), *Effective psychotherapy: A handbook of research*. New York: Pergamon, 1978.

Wilson, G. T. Alcohol and human sexual behavior. *Behaviour Research and Therapy*, 1977, *15*, 239–252. (a)

Wilson, G. T. The importance of being theoretical: Comments on Bandura's "Self-efficacy: Toward a unifying theory of behavioral change." In H. J. Eysenck & S. Rachman (Eds.), *Advances in behaviour research and therapy*. New York: Pergamon, 1977. (b)

Wilson, G. T. Cognitive behavior therapy: Paradigm shift or passing phase? In J. P. Foreyt & D. Rathjen (Eds.), *Cognitive behavior therapy: Research and application*. New York: Plenum, 1978.

Wilson, G. T. Cognitive factors in life-style changes: A social-learning perspective. In P. Davidson (Ed.), *Behavioral medicine*. New York: Brunner/Mazel, 1979. (a)

Wilson, G. T. Perceived control and the theory and practice of behavior therapy. In L. C. Perlmuter & R. A. Monty (Eds.), *Choice and perceived control*. Hillsdale, N.J.: Lawrence Erlbaum, 1979. (b)

Wilson, G. T., & Davison, G. C. Behavior therapy and homosexuality: A critical perspective. *Behavior Therapy*, 1974, *5*, 16–28.

Wilson, G. T., & Evans, I. M. Adult behavior therapy and the therapist–client relationship. In C. M. Franks & G. T. Wilson (Eds.), *Annual review of behavior therapy: Theory and Practice* (Vol. IV). New York: Brunner/Mazel, 1976.

Wilson, G. T., & Evans, I. M. The therapist–client relationship in behavior therapy. In A. Gurman & A. Razin (Eds.), *Effective psychotherapy: A handbook of research*. New York: Pergamon, 1977.

Wilson, G. T., & O'Leary, K. D. *Principles of behavior therapy*. Englewood Cliffs, N.J.: Prentice-Hall, 1980.

Wolpe, J. *Psychotherapy by reciprocal inhibition*. Stanford Calif.: Stanford University Press, 1958.

Wolpe, J. *The practice of behavior therapy*. New York: Pergamon, 1969.

Wolpe, J. Behavior therapy and its malcontents—II. Multimodal eclecticism, cognitive exclusivism and "exposure" empiricism. *Journal of Behavior Therapy and Experimental Psychiatry*, 1976, *7*, 109–116.

Catalyzing the Integration of Social-Learning Theory and Behavior Therapy

THEODORE X. BARBER

In its early years of development, the behavior therapy movement was guided by a limited behavioristic outlook which de-emphasized mediational variables and social-interactional variables while it focused on stimulus-response variables and conditioning concepts. In line with the broad changes in psychology occurring in recent years, the behavior therapy movement is now rapidly breaking out of traditional boundaries; and this process of broadening is fueled by the conceptions and viewpoints that derive from social-learning theory (e.g., Bandura, 1977). The present chapter by G. Terence Wilson is another important step in utilizing social-learning conceptions to expand the scope of behavior therapy.

Dr. Wilson demonstrates in a useful way, within a social-learning framework, how factors previously viewed as "nonspecific," such as self-monitoring, sense of personal efficacy, expectations of help, and the client–therapist relationship, can also be viewed as important independent variables in their own right which can produce therapeutic gains. The social-learning approach stimulates us to reevaluate how these variables "work"; for example, it predicts that self-monitoring will be effective in producing

THEODORE X. BARBER • Proseminar Institute, Research Division, Cushing Hospital, Framingham, Massachusetts 01701.

behavior change if and when it leads clients to perceive incongruous discrepancies between their goals and the observed target behaviors (smoking, eating, drinking alcoholic beverages, etc.).

As Dr. Wilson also noted, the social-learning framework sensitizes us to the importance of how clients appraise a transgression or "slip" which comes after they have succeeded in stopping smoking, stopping alcohol intake, or reducing food consumption. What happens after a relapse appears to depend on how the clients perceive the "failure". If they are guided by the therapist to perceive it as a temporary relapse that need not interfere with subsequent abstinence, it need have no untoward consequences. On the other hand, if the client is guided to view any "slip" or relapse as indicating a total loss of control—as often happens in alcohol reduction programs, for example—an iatrogenic treatment failure would probably be produced.

Dr. Wilson has also usefully summarized Bandura's self-efficacy theory which postulates that procedures which aim to reduce anxiety or fear are effective to the extent that they enhance the individual's sense of personal efficacy in handling threatening situations. This aspect of social-learning theory has broad implications for behavior therapy and also for other therapies. For instance, it can be hypothesized that modern hypnotic suggestive techniques that are useful in alleviating chronic and acute pain are effective to the extent that they provide the clients with something *they can do* to affect their discomfort and suffering. Instead of suffering helplessly with no means of controlling their fate, individuals in pain are taught a variety of techniques that can be used to control the pain—e.g., techniques involving relaxation, self-distraction, dissociation and imagined numbness (Barber, Spanos, & Chaves, 1974, Chapter 8; Hilgard & Hilgard, 1975). These techniques can reduce discomfort and suffering by removing the feelings of helplessness and giving the client a feeling of control, regardless of whether they also actually produce relaxation, distraction, dissociation, or numbness (Chaves & Barber, 1976).

In brief, Dr. Wilson's chapter is helpful in catalyzing the integration of social-learning theory and behavior therapy. This integration, in turn, will stimulate further thinking and new evaluations of hitherto neglected variables which were viewed as "nonspecifics" from the traditional $S-R$ conditioning approach but which are now seen, from the social-learning perspective, to be important independent variables that need to be rigorously evaluated.

REFERENCES

Bandura, A. *Social learning theory.* Englewood Cliffs, N.J.: Prentice-Hall, 1977.
Barber, T. X., Spanos, N. P., & Chaves, J. F. *Hypnosis, imagination and human potentialities.* Elmsford, N.Y.: Pergamon, 1974.

Chaves, J. F., & Barber, T. X. Hypnotic procedures and surgery: A critical analysis with applications to "acupuncture analgesia". *American Journal of Clinical Hypnosis*, 1976, *18*, 217–236.

Hilgard, E. R., & Hilgard, J. R. *Hypnosis in the relief of pain.* Los Altos, Calif.: William Kaufmann, 1975.

Chapter 11

Rhetoric and Psychotherapy

SUSAN R. GLASER

This chapter describes the application of rhetorical analysis to the content of therapeutic dialogue. Rhetorical analysis as a method of analyzing verbal influence processes has been developed over a period of 2000 years and provides a rich framework for analyzing these processes. The majority of analyses of psychotherapeutic interactions have failed to provide a content-oriented basis for analyzing therapeutic interchanges. Rhetorical maneuvers in therapy have not been explicated. If we can develop an empirical approach for analyzing therapeutic transactions, we may be better able to identify effective therapist maneuvers and to subsequently teach them. This paper offers rhetorical concepts as hypotheses for explaining therapeutic impact. We have selected those rhetorical behaviors that on the basis of rhetorical theory seem relevant to the psychotherapeutic situation. Our purpose is to explicate specific therapist verbal behavior that might have influential effects on client behavior. The relationship between these rhetorical concepts and therapeutic outcome may later be tested empirically.

SUSAN R. GLASER • Department of Speech, University of Oregon, Eugene, Oregon 97403.

THERAPY AS A RHETORICAL SITUATION

Rhetoric, according to Aristotle, is the art of discovering in any given case all the available means of persuasion. More simply, the study of rhetoric focuses on the things people say and how they affect other people. Rhetoric is traditionally associated with public discourse where one person, the rhetor, stands before an audience and attempts to modify its beliefs or behavior. The rhetorical critic, based on 2000 years of rhetorical theory, analyzes such public messages to ascertain the rhetorical resources available or absent; an attempt is made to discover the potential impact of the discourse. More recently, nonpublic interpersonal transactions have been examined as rhetorical situations (Glaser & Glaser, 1976; Glaser, 1977; Knapp, 1978). In analyzing private, everyday discourse, rhetorical scholars focus on the persuasive elements that affect the outcome of interpersonal episodes.

Psychotherapy is a rhetorical process; perhaps it constitutes the most basic rhetorical act. Therapists, as certainly as politicians, advertisers, or intimates, are in the business of belief and behavior change. Therapists use the spoken word to alter their clients' thoughts, feelings, and behavior in direct, deliberate ways. The therapist's talk is rhetorical because "it is a response to a situation of a certain kind" (Bitzer, 1968, p. 3). It is a "personalized request for adherence to some proposition or position" (Arnold, 1974, p. 12). Its purpose is to "render the audience different in belief, in attitude, in feeling, or conduct as a direct result of the discourse" (Oliver, 1968, p. 12). Its basic function is the "use of words by human agents to form attitudes or induce actions in other human agents" (Burke, 1969, p. 41). It is the "art of motivation, . . . of instilling, activating, or directing in another individual . . . a belief or a type of conduct" (Oliver, 1968, p. 10). "It functions ultimately to produce action or change. [It is] a mode of altering reality . . . by the creation of discourse . . . introduced into the situation . . . to bring about the significant modification of a thing which is other than it should be . . ." (Bitzer, 1968, pp. 3–4, 6–7). It contains the "strongly practical, deliberate, suasory . . . instructional qualities that are associated with the 'rhetorical'" (Arnold, 1974, p. 5). Psychotherapeutic discourse, then, appears to be rhetoric which "functions ultimately to produce action or change" in the client-audience by the use of words to "form attitudes or induce actions."

For decades, advocates of varied forms of psychotherapy have argued the effectiveness of their particular method. That all are able to flourish simultaneously despite wide differences in approach suggests that each has something which clients find acceptable and helpful. This supports Frank's contention that there are characteristics common to all types of therapy, which probably contribute as much to their effectiveness as the features that differentiate them (Frank, 1973, p. 23). If these common characteristics are rhetorical processes it may be possible to uncover some major components of therapist potency, which until now have remained elusive.

Much of what happens in the therapeutic transaction is shaped by the interactions between client and therapist (Lennard & Bernstein, 1960). This makes the therapeutic situation a rhetorical event in which the psychotherapist assumes the burden of change agent. If change-inducing talk is somewhere important in therapy transactions, it becomes critical to find out where it occurs, how, and what its characteristics are and ought to be. Rhetorical activity, then, may be viewed as fundamental to the process of psychotherapy. Clients enter therapy because they are distressed about some aspect of their behavior, thoughts, and feelings. The therapist as helper is expected to lead the client to change. In order to facilitate this change, the therapist must *influence* the client to behave, think, and feel differently. Regardless of therapeutic mode, therapists sometimes succeed in this influencing and sometimes they fail. There are times when clients accept the therapist's directives, suggestions, assignments, language, reframing of events, and analysis of past history. But there are times when they do not. It is this critical element of the therapeutic chain that rhetorical analysis seeks to explain.

Viewing psychotherapy as a persuasive process is not original to this work. Freud was probably the first to recognize the relationship between persuasion and therapy (Abroms, 1968, p. 1214). As we review how more current psychotherapeutic writers define and describe their profession, it becomes apparent that there are increasing numbers who view therapy primarily as an influence process in which therapists engage in verbal maneuvers designed to achieve a desired end state from a given beginning state (Gillis, 1974, p. 92; Strong & Matross, 1971, p. 20). There has been an increased emphasis on the procedures by which therapeutic change occurs and on how the influence process can be most effectively utilized to promote client change (Haley, 1963, pp. 2, 16, 137–149; Watzlawick, Weakland, & Fisch, 1974, p. xvi).

The psychotherapeutic positions reviewed above, then, support Frank's contention that what is shared by therapists may be as therapeutic as what is unique, the common element being persuasion. Now, we must consider the structure and content of these persuasive elements, for it is not particularly relevant to call psychotherapy an influence process unless we can explicate particular therapist acts that are influential. It is here that a large body of rhetorical literature may provide direction and focus. If rhetorical components are discovered in divergent modes of therapy, we may agree with Frank that "features common to all types of psychotherapy probably contribute as much, if not more, to their effectiveness than the characteristics that differentiate them . . . any specific healing effects of different methods would be overshadowed by therapeutically potent ingredients shared by all" (Frank, 1973, pp. 2, 23).

RHETORICAL ANALYSIS OF THERAPEUTIC DISCOURSE

Derived from a review of rhetorical theory, this section will present the basic components of rhetorical analysis that seem relevant to therapeutic exchanges. The framework offered in this section should be viewed as tentative hypotheses generated from rhetorical theory. The proof of such a system would be found by conducting empirical analyses of therapeutic processes. What follows, then, is designed to objectify acts that could be influential in therapeutic transactions. The next step will be to test whether therapists engaging in these acts are more influential than those who do not. The purpose is to crystalize those therapist behaviors that affect client change. Table I provides a description and illustration of each rhetorical device discussed below. The discourse offered to clarify each rhetorical operation should be viewed as an illustration of the concept—not as empirical evidence.

Therapist rhetorical potency, defined theoretically as "the capacity of therapist discourse to influence," appears in all probability to be multidimensional in nature, depending on the following four devices: (1) extent of *ethos* appeals, (2) extent of logical appeals, (3) extent of tension release mechanisms, (4) extent of stylistic devices. Each of these rhetorical variables will now be discussed. First, each concept will be operationalized, then specific segments of therapeutic dialogue will be presented to illustrate how the device functions as a rhetorical resource.

Extent of Ethos Appeals

Ethos was originally described by Aristotle as the most potent means of persuasion:

> The character (*ethos*) of the speaker is a cause of persuasion when the speech is so uttered as to make him worthy of belief; for as a rule we trust men of probity more . . . we might almost affirm that his character (*ethos*) is the most potent of all the means of persuasion . . . the sources of our trust in [speakers] are three . . . intelligence, character, and good will . . . the speaker who is thought to have all these qualities has the confidence of his hearers. (Aristotle, 1960, pp. 8–9, 91–92)

The findings from a series of investigations concerning therapy as an influence process help us to delineate three components of therapist *ethos* strikingly similar to those Aristotle described: perceived expertness, trustworthiness, and attractiveness. Strong defines expertness as the "perception of a communicator as a source of valid assertions" (Strong, 1968, p. 216). He contends that this perception is influenced by "(a) objective evidence of specialized training, such as diplomas, certificates, and titles, (b) behavioral evidence of expertness, such as rational and knowledgeable arguments and confidence in presentation, and (c) reputation as an 'expert'" (Strong, 1968, p. 216).

Strong and Matross argue that therapists can increase their perceived expertness by certain behaviors, such as referring to specific areas of expertise. For example, they suggest that a therapist can begin an attempt at influence with, "I have dealt with this problem many times and in my therapy experience it means..." (Strong & Matross, 1971, p. 19). Torrey suggests that the naming process is another means by which therapists are able to offer behavioral evidence of their expertness:

> The very act of naming [what is wrong with the client] has a therapeutic effect. The patient's anxiety is decreased by the knowledge that a respected and trusted therapist understands what is wrong. (Torrey, 1973, p. 16)

Schmidt and Strong, after studying perceived expertness in therapists, report the following behaviors as indicative of expertise:

> The expert ... treats [the client] as an equal ... asks direct and to the point questions ... moves quickly to the root of the problem ... points out contradictions and suggests possible solutions. (Schmidt & Strong, 1970, p. 116)

A second component of therapist *ethos* is perceived trustworthiness which, Strong concludes, affects the extent to which the therapist is able to influence opinion in the client (Strong, 1968, p. 219). Frank contends that certain attitudes of therapists must be communicated to the client if trust is to be established. These include "a steady, deep interest, an optimistic outlook, and a dedication to the patient's welfare" in addition to the assurance of confidentiality, which tells the client there are no selfish or devious motives involved (Strong, 1968, p. 222).

Based on the research of Strong and his associates, the third component of therapist *ethos* appears to be perceived attractiveness. "A communicator's attractiveness is based on his perceived similarity to, compatibility with, and liking for the influence recipient" (Strong, 1968, p. 216). Perceived similarity is often associated with interpersonal attraction (Berscheid & Walster, 1969; Schmidt & Strong, 1970), and interpersonal attraction increases the probability of acceptance of influence (Brock, 1965; Strong & Dixon, 1972):

> A therapist develops ... power by bringing to the client's attention similarities in values, opinions, and experiences. This requires that the therapist reveal himself to the client. (Strong & Matross, 1971, p. 11)

TABLE I. Rhetorical Resources

Rhetorical resource	Rhetorical resource operationalized	Example of rhetorical resource
Ethos appeals	Therapists may directly refer to their own expertise and experience in a given matter.	I'm what's generally called eclectic; I'm going to try and find out what really is at issue with you and then, with you, try to find the best means to alleviate that situation. And if that means employing analytic notions or rational emotive therapy or some form of desensitization, I could do that.
	Therapists may indirectly demonstrate their expertise by labeling or naming what is wrong with the client.	There are some common themes running through this—one of perfection striving.
	Therapists may make recommendations and suggest possible solutions.	I think you're setting it up to be easy for Bob to play this game . . . by being so cooperative about it . . . he doesn't really have to make a choice as long as you're quite willing to go down there with him and to get out of the way when he wants to be with Barbie . . . that makes it easy for him not to have to make any decisions.
	Therapists may communicate an interest and concern for the client's welfare as well as an optimistic outlook.	It sounds to me like your head is very well together in terms of the way you're looking at this. I like the way you're handling it.
	Therapists may assure clients of confidentiality.	I want you to know that anything you say here in our sessions is completely confidential.
	Therapists may reveal values, opinions, experiences which they share with the client.	One of the reasons I enjoy talking to you . . . not only because I like you, but because I've had some experiences that parallel yours, partly in terms of the perfectionism . . . and I share the physical fitness thing.

	Therapists may communicate understanding of the client.	She could call you a lot of things, but I suspect that "uptight" and "selfish" would be the two that would totally rack you up. You would sit there for hours worrying about whether this was the case.
	Therapists may communicate high esteem for the client.	If you run down the characteristics which in our culture theoretically should make you an ecstatic person, you're in the upper 10% of the distribution in almost everything.
Logical appeals	Supporting examples are presented: these examples may be drawn from past and present client behaviors, other relevant cases, other persons' behaviors.	You're in the upper 10% of the distribution in almost everything: you're in good physical condition, obviously intelligent, physically attractive, you don't have any trouble attracting the opposite sex, you're successful in athletics, you've been successful in school, prestigious occupation.
	Statistics are presented: therapists may provide numerical evidence to support claims.	In the last 5 or 6 years, 30–40% of the clients that I see present similar problems.
	Citations from authority are presented: therapists may quote relevant authorities or professional literature.	Judging from some of the research in the clinical field, there are some common themes running through this.
	Analogies are presented: therapists may support claims through comparisons: analogies often compare present to past behavior, client behavior to other behavior.	So when you're attacked on that [belief] it's like attacking a Christian on his belief in Christ.
Tension release mechanisms	Discourse describes the client's situation as being hopeful, solvable.	And again all of that is a reflection of the kinds of standards you set which is something we can work on if you want to.

(Continued)

TABLE 1 (continued)

Rhetorical resource	Rhetorical resource operationalized	Example of rhetorical resource
	Discourse reconceptualizes the client's problem in more manageable, less traumatic terms.	You never arrive . . . you never get there . . . and it's the realization that you never get there that's getting there; it's always a journey rather than a destination; and I think it's going to have tremendous benefits to you when you realize that you're never going to get there . . . that you're never going to arrive.
	Discourse suggests that change is already taking place, progress is being made.	I can't believe the movement you've shown in the short period of time already . . . you're a therapist's dream in terms of a client . . . I think that's a sign of . . . partly in terms of independence and partly that you're willing now to look at some things that in the past were taboo to even consider.
	Discourse offers direct solutions.	It seems that in terms of where to go from here, an important exercise or thing to do would be to monitor on a daily basis what's going through your head and to decide whether, number 1: if life continues like it did last week, would you be happy with it or, number 2: if you would not be happy with it, is it because there's something missing that you wish were there or is it because there's something present that you wish weren't?
Stylistic devices	Balances refer to verbal patterns which put ideas in pairs, in a series, or in other parallel constructions.	If you are jealous, you are jealous, and if you're feeling rejected, you're feeling rejected.
	Antitheses involve ideas that are marked by their contrast or opposition with each other.	We are liberal; we are not uptight.

Metaphors are stylistic devices in which a term or phrase is applied to something to which it is not literally applicable.	To be accused of being "uptight" is to be accused of being a traitor to your clan.
Sensory images are all words and phrases that direct listeners to think of anything they could feel, hear, taste, smell, or see.	Good physical condition; undergoing surgery; somebody said: "gee, this is terrific!"; feeling jealous.

Strong and Matross contend that if therapist and client discover strong similarities in world views, the client is more likely to "adopt therapist interpretations, attitudes, and reactions" (Strong & Matross, 1971, p. 10). Strong argues that when counselors communicate their understanding of a client, even if it is derived from theoretical knowledge, such understanding is likely to enhance the client's perception of similarity and compatibility with that therapist (Strong, 1968, p. 222).

Based on this discussion of therapist *ethos*, this variable may be operationalized by eight different behaviors that a therapist might perform. It is contended that if therapists behave in any of the following ways, their *ethos* is likely to be enhanced:

1. Therapists may directly refer to their own expertise and experience in a given matter.
2. Therapists may indirectly demonstrate their expertise by labeling or naming what is wrong with the client.
3. Therapists may make recommendations and suggest possible solutions.
4. Therapists may communicate an interest and concern for the client's welfare as well as an optimistic outlook.
5. Therapists may assure clients of confidentiality.
6. Therapists may reveal values, opinions, and experiences which they share with the client.
7. Therapists may communicate understanding of the client.
8. Therapists may communicate high esteem for the client.

In the following segments of therapeutic discourse, the therapist's talk has the potential to heighten his *ethos* in a number of ways:

1 *T:* It sounds to me that your head is very well together in terms
2 of the way you're looking at this. . . . You're not shitting on
3 yourself and saying, "I'm responsible for what happened with Joan."
4 I like the way you're handling it by saying, "I'm going to take a
5 breather from this relationship and I'm not going to make any
6 commitments or plans for what I do within the next week or month."
7 On the other hand your perception of yourself—speaking as profes-
8 sional to professional for a minute—is not atypical. In the last
9 5 or 6 years I would say about 30 to 40 percent of the clients that
10 I see present situations where . . . well if you run down the char-
11 acteristics which in our culture theoretically should make you an
12 ecstatic person, you're in the upper 10% of the distribution
13 in almost everything: you're in good physical condition, you're
14 obviously intelligent, physically attractive, you don't have any
15 trouble attracting the opposite sex, you're successful in athlet-
16 ics, you've been successful in school, prestigious occupation. Yet,

17 in spite of the fact that from someone else's perspective you seem
18 to have everything going for you and you have no reason to feel
19 badly about yourself or complain about your life situation, your
20 perception of yourself is quite a bit different than that. Even
21 though at a cognitive level, at a rational level, you can agree to
22 all this; you can say, "Yes, I'm in good physical shape. I'm
23 intelligent. I'm attractive. I'm good in athletics. I'm a tal-
24 ented professional." . . . even though you can give these relatively
25 rational responses, at a gut level you still feel relatively inse-
26 cure about yourself. Judging from some of the research in the
27 clinical field there are some common themes running through this:
28 one of perfection striving. One of the reasons you have been good
29 as an athlete and in your profession is that you seek perfection.
30 You don't just want to be better than the group, you want to give
31 it everything you've got and be as good as is humanly possible.
32 That obviously has advantages. If I'm undergoing surgery that's
33 the kind of surgeon I'd want. The problems that arise are when
34 those standards start to carry over to your evaluation of yourself.

First, there is considerable talk about this therapist's professionalism, his knowledge, and his ability as a therapist. In lines 7–10, for example, the implicit message is: I have been doing therapy for a long time; I have had many clients; I can spot trends. Lines 26–28 point to his familiarity with the research of his field. Thus, on several occasions, the therapist has provided an opportunity to heighten his *ethos* with talk that explicitly suggests he is a competent and experienced professional. Another opportunity for credibility enhancement by this therapist is provided by talk that suggests his high esteem for the client. Lines 10–16, for example, indicate this positive regard. In addition, on several occasions the implicit message of the therapist's words is: You're moving in a positive direction and that is something to be proud of.

248 *T:* I can't believe the movement you've shown in the short period
249 of time already. . . . You're a therapist's dream in terms of a
250 client . . . in terms of being very much into what you're thinking
251 and where you're going. . . . Are you aware of how differently
252 you're coming across now than three or four weeks ago?

253 *C:* I feel differently.

254 *T:* I wish I had saved the tapes so that you could listen to your
255 self or see yourself. . . . That's very different from the way
256 you were coming across then.

Although this talk is not directly aimed at heightening the therapist's professional image, it has the capacity to raise his *ethos* by communicating high esteem for the client as well as an optimistic outlook.

Extent of Logical Appeals

This variable focuses on what Aristotle called *logos*, the content or logical argument of speech. Toulmin offers a perspective that clarifies how we may estimate the potential strength of a given argument:

> A man who makes an assertion puts forward a claim—a claim on our attention and to our belief . . . its merits depend on the merits of the argument which could be produced in its support . . . we can, that is, demand an argument; and a claim need be conceded only if the argument which can be produced in its support proves to be up to standard. (Toulmin, 1958, pp. 11–12)

The notion of argument seems particularly relevant to client–therapist transactions. Because of the nature and purpose of psychotherapy, clients in all likelihood perceive the therapist's talk as intended to change them in some way. Strong and Matross define "influence attempts" in therapy as: "therapist remarks which the client perceives to imply that he change his actions, feelings, or thoughts" (Strong & Matross, 1971, p. 18). Arnold's adaptation of Toulmin's formulations provides insight into and clarification of the audience as judge of arguments:

> The respondent perceives the utterance as one meant to modify his experience. He knows he has the right to challenge if the grounds for claims seem perplexing or insufficient. He functions as judge on questions of relevance, significance, and sufficiency. (Arnold, 1974, p. 49)

The persuasiveness of reasoned argument is confirmed by studies conducted by Brehm and Lipsher (1959). They examined the effects of providing supporting reasons in general attempts to persuade and discovered that communication accompanied by supporting arguments was more likely to result in opinion change than communication without support. But what, exactly, does it mean to "support an argument?" Most simply, it refers to the provision of evidence which makes claims appear more reasonable. In analyzing therapist discourse, the following may be considered to be evidence of support:

1. Supporting examples are presented. These examples may be drawn from past and present client behaviors, other relevant cases, and other persons' behaviors.
2. Statistics are presented. Therapists may provide numerical evidence to support claims.
3. Citations from authority are presented. Therapists may quote relevant authorities or professional literature.
4. Analogies are presented. Therapists may support claims through comparisons. Analogies often compare present to past behavior, client behavior to other behavior.

Examining the first therapist's discourse in lines 6–33 on pages 322–333, the claim appears to be: Your problems arise from perfection striving, setting standards that are unrealistically high. The likelihood of the client's accepting this claim is increased by the large amount of evidence offered to answer the client's possible question: What have you got to go on? In fact, most of the 27 lines of talk provides evidence encouraging acceptance of the major claim. The evidence consists of examples, statistics, and authority references. The following evidence is provided to indicate perfection striving in the client's life:

Statistics:

You're in the upper 10 percent of the distribution in almost everything.

Examples:

Good physical condition, obviously intelligent, physically attractive, don't have any trouble attracting the opposite sex, successful in athletics, successful in school, prestigious occupation.

Yet, on a gut level you still feel relatively insecure.

The warrant for accepting the therapist's general claim is implicit: If a person has so much going for him and still feels insecure, it is reasonable to believe his standards are too high.

To make the client's acceptance of this claim even more likely, the therapist offers statistics and authority as further support. The extensive use of numbers and percentages adds to the scientific sound of the therapist's evidence:

Statistics:

In the last 5 or 6 years, 30–40 percent of the clients I see present similar problems.

Authority

Judging from some of the research in the clinical field . . . there is a theme of perfection striving running through this.

The implication appears to be: According to scientific research, perfection striving is a real problem, and the data don't lie.

Extent of Tension Release Mechanisms

This variable appears especially important in therapeutic rhetoric, for one of the main reasons a client enters into a therapeutic situation is to achieve relief from tension and anxiety. Arnold emphasizes the importance of tension release mechanisms:

> To the degree that problems are vivified and anxieties intensified, tension-releasing solutions must come from *somewhere*, else communication ends in producing unfocused feeling and/or general frustration. Generally speaking, failure to give clear directions for releasing tensions is a faulty rhetorical practice. (Arnold, 1974, p. 77)

This is not intended to suggest that it is incumbent upon a therapist to provide solutions to every problem a client generates. It does mean, however, that when a problem is vivified—either by the client or therapist—ways of alleviating it need to be located, either directly or indirectly. It is the case in therapeutic situations, as in general rhetorical situations, that: "Only where situational or other data assure a critic that frustration or vague euphoria was aimed at, or that tension release mechanisms were clearly known to the listeners, should he [a critic] suppose non-releasing rhetoric fulfilled its aims" (Arnold, 1974, p. 77). In therapeutic transactions, we may consider any of the following to be tension release mechanisms:

1. Discourse which describes the client's situation as being hopeful, solvable
2. Discourse which reconceptualizes the client's problem in more manageable, less traumatic terms
3. Discourse which suggests that change is already taking place, progress is being made
4. Discourse which offers direct solutions

Examining the first therapist's discourse in lines 6–34 on pages 322–323, it is clear that a problem is vivified by him. The implicit message from the therapist seems to be:

> You are feeling anxious and tense because you seek perfection; unless you modify your standards of self-judgment, you will continue to feel insecure.
> (see lines 6–34 on pages 322–323)

The question now becomes: If the client accepts these problem claims, is he offered a way out of the accompanying anxiety and tension?

After spending considerable time vivifying the problem of perfection striving, the therapist concludes by offering his client a release from that tension by describing the client's situation as hopeful, solvable, and by reconceptualizing the client's problems in more manageable, less traumatic terms:

67   and I guess one of the reasons I enjoy talking to you . . . not only
68   because I like you, but because I've had some experience that par-

69   allels yours, partly in terms of the perfectionism . . . about how I
70   feel about myself . . . I've had to work on that. . . . I've had
71   to work a lot about how I feel about . . . what my standards are.
72   . . . I share the physical fitness thing. . . . And I guess one
73   of the things that was most important in my feeling good about me
74   was realizing . . . I was always waiting for the day when I would
75   wake up and say: "I'm there. I've got my shit together." And the
76   thing that was most missing from me was something that will come
77   across a lot in my speculations with you and that is that you never
78   arrive . . . you never get there. . . . And it's the realization
79   that you never get there that's getting there. It's always a jour-
80   ney rather than a destination. You never hear the whistle and say,
81   "This is the stop." Because you're always moving . . . always
82   rolling with the punches. I think that part of the empty feeling
83   that I had and some of what's coming across as part of the
84   feeling that's missing is that you haven't gotten anyone either
85   from the outside or the inside to say, "You're there. You've
86   arrived." And I think it's going to have tremendous benefits to
87   you when you realize that you're never going to get set . . . that
88   you're never going to arrive. . . . And so it's not playing the
89   game to win, it's playing the game to stay in.

In this segment, the therapist discloses that he, too, had problems and anxieties similar to those of the client, which he has been able to resolve. This has the potential to provide some release from tension. Further release is offered in lines 73–79. Here, the therapist offers his client a new way of conceptualizing his problems and anxieties. If the client accepts the notion that "you never arrive, because life is a journey and not a destination," he cannot feel as anxious about "not getting there." Thus, the therapist first vivifies a problem of perfection seeking, and then offers his client several avenues leading to tension release.

Extent of Stylistic Devices

In examining this component of therapist rhetorical potency, we shall be looking for the extent of balances, antitheses, metaphors, sensory images, and their capacity to intensify the content of therapist discourse. Although these four components of communicative style have not been empirically tested, each of them does have normative acceptance in rhetorical theory (Arnold, 1974, pp. 168– 169). Balances refer to verbal patterns which put ideas in pairs, in a series, or in other parallel constructions. Rhetorical critics argue that these balanced groupings have the capacity to make what is said seem more completely true, important, and impressive. Antitheses, although usually balanced in some way, involve ideas that are asserted to be marked by their contrast or opposition with each other. By emphasizing differences and by suggesting conflict, antithetical constructions argue that the contrast or conflict suggested linguistically is actually true in fact. Metaphors are stylistic devices in which a term or phrase is applied to something to which it is not literally applicable, in order to influence the listener to perceive a resemblance. Based on the lore of ancient and modern rhetorical theory, it is contended that unless metaphors are confusing, distasteful, or hackneyed, they are likely to make communication appear more interesting and colorful, as well as to argue in favor of the relationships they portray (Arnold, 1974, p. 168). For the last of these assertions there is considerable modern, theoretical argument and some empirical evidence (Bowers & Osborn, 1966, pp. 147–155). Sensory images are all words and phrases that direct listeners to think of anything they can feel, hear, taste, smell, or see. Presumably, sensory images encourage listeners to experience messages vicariously; to the extent that this occurs, listeners are more likely to become personally, experientially involved in the speaker's message (Arnold, 1974, p. 183).

In conducting an analysis of speakers' styles, the verbal forms described above are pulled out of their context and listed by class. To illustrate the use of stylistic analysis, let us examine the second therapist as she attempts to convince her client that her fear of being perceived as "uptight" is a function of her Berkeley peer group, among whom "uptight" behavior is considered a severe violation of norms. The therapist attempts to convince her client that human feelings are different from theoretical principles and that any feeling is legitimate—including feelings that might be labeled "uptight" by the Berkeley group. The client's response to this discourse indicates her verbal acceptance of the therapist's message: "I think I would. Yeah. . . . I do . . . ooh. I had't ever thought of it . . . right . . . it's true . . . right. Yeah." An examination of the therapist's stylistic devices shows us that choice of language was a rhetorical resource available to the therapist. Following are the lines of therapist discourse from which stylistic features were compiled:

214   *T:* My guess is that it would be a heavy attack on you because of
215   what looks like a substitution of Berkeley for your family.
216   Is that

217   *C:* Explain that.

218   *T:* In needing a family you used Berkeley as a family. And so it's
219   very important for you to live up to their principles, just as it
220   is to somebody who is still very attached to their family to live
221   up to their family principles.

222   *C:* Uh.

223   *T:* And one of those principles is not being uptight. Right?
224   (*Laughter.*) Its probably A #1 principle is "We are liberal.

225 We are not uptight." And to be accused of being "uptight" is
226 to be accused of being a traitor to your clan.

227 *C:* Ooh. I hadn't ever thought of it.

228 *T:* (*Interrupting.*) This is a basic accusation that is very, very
229 hard to handle when it hits at: that's the thing that makes me
230 a part of the group that is most important to me. Mine is a
231 group where people are not uptight, where they are liberal and
232 can stand nonnuclear families and can look at life in broader
233 terms and can be loving, and you know, all those things are
234 part of that, a, that folklore that makes your group a group.
235 So, when you are attacked on that, it's like attacking a Christian
236 on his belief in Christ.

237 *C:* Right. In fact, we call it our mythology. (*Client laughs.*)

238 *T:* Yeah. Right.

239 *C:* And there's that kind of "this is ridiculous but." Yeah, it's
240 true.

241 *T:* And the difficulty is that human feelings are human feelings
242 whether you happen to believe in being liberated or in being a
243 Christian or whatever you happen to believe in. You know if
244 you are jealous, you are jealous, and if you're feeling re-
245 jected, you're feeling rejected.

246 *C:* Right. Yeah.

Balances

uptight and selfish
to be accused of . . . is to be
    accused of
when you are . . . it's like
human feelings are human feelings
happen to believe in . . . happen
    to believe in

they are . . . and can . . . and
    can . . . and can . . .
believe in being . . . in being
if you are jealous, you are jealous
if you're feeling rejected, you're
    feeling rejected

Antitheses

she could call . . . but I suspect
where people are not . . . where
    they are

We are . . . we are not
Whether you . . . or . . . or . . .

Metaphors

totally rack you up
heavy attack
attached to their family

traitor to your clan
it hits at . . . the thing that makes
    me a part

very hard to handle   you are attacked
look at life
attacking a Christian

Sensory Images

call you a lot of things   accused of being a traitor
uptight (repeated)   a group where people are not
Berkeley (repeated)   uptight
family (repeated)   nonnuclear families
needing a family   be loving
accused of being uptight   being liberated
feeling jealous   being a Christian
                                       feeling rejected

The therapist's uses of balance, antithesis, metaphor, and sensory images have the capacity to intensify the content of her talk. Let us now consider more specifically how this is accomplished. The balanced constructions are likely to make the ideas appear more "sweepingly true," "impressive," "important" (Arnold, 1974, p. 168). They also have the capacity to make the therapist seem more "logical" to her client. The content of the array of balanced constructions is striking; each balance contributes to the impact of one of three therapeutic messages:

1. You have substituted Berkeley for your family.
2. Being perceived as uptight is extremely difficult for you to handle because it goes against one of Berkeley's most important principles.
3. Human feelings are all legitimate—even if they are indications of being "uptight."

The therapist also employs antithesis to argue by emphasizing contrasts. By contrasting "We are liberal" with "We are not uptight" the therapist emphasizes the extremes of the Berkeley philosophy and the implicit impact these contrasting ideas have had on her client's values. The therapist also employs antithesis as she attempts to convince her client that any feeling is legitimate, even though it may be perceived as less than liberal on the Berkeley hierarchy of values. By focusing the client's attention on contrasting belief systems ("Whether you happen to believe in being liberated or in being a Christian or whatever you happen to believe in"), the therapist is able to emphasize her residual message: Even in diverse belief systems, human feelings are human feelings—they are always legitimate. In short, by setting ideas against each other in antithetical constructions, the therapist increases the likelihood that she will influence her client.

The therapist's abundant metaphors, in addition to adding color and interest, also seem to function argumentatively. Most bring into figure a message of: It is because you have substituted Berkeley for your family that you find it difficult to handle being perceived as uptight. Thus, the metaphors, like the balances and antitheses, focus on a prominent therapeutic message.

The possibility of the client becoming "experientially hence feelingly" involved in the therapist's talk is enhanced with the abundance of sensory images (Arnold, 1974, pp. 168–69). In addition, these sensory images appear to work together to alter the client's feelings toward "uptight" behavior. "Uptight" images are contrasted with "liberated" images thereby serving as an antithesis-generated argument. Once more a stylistic device focuses the client on Berkeley's hierarchy of values as the source of her distress. The therapist's sensory images also have the capacity to evoke and sustain feelings and impressions that are vital to her argument. This examination of style, then, illustrates how a therapist's use of balance, antithesis, metaphor, and sensory images can represent rhetorical resources that have the capacity to focus client attention on ideas central to the therapeutic message, and to make those ideas appear more legitimate and believable.

LIMITATIONS AND CONCLUSIONS

Delineating aspects of therapist verbal behavior that might have influence on clients, this chapter has illustrated how the key features of rhetorical analysis can be operationalized to apply to the study of therapeutic transactions. By analyzing the content of therapist verbal behavior, we are able to understand it as rhetoric in process. With it demonstrated that rhetorical activity is fundamental to therapeutic practice, we are in a position to begin exploring the relationships of various rhetorical strategies, or lack of them, to outcomes. The opportunity is present, then, for the therapist to ask questions *before* the fact, much as the critic does *after* the fact. This is already done in public speaking situations; there is no reason to believe it cannot be done in private therapeutic transactions.

The most significant limitation of the rhetorical approach described is its lack of an empirical base. For 2000 years, rhetoric has been approached as an artistic rather than scientific inquiry. Rhetorical critics make supported artistic judgments about the rhetorical potency of a given piece of discourse. They do not isolate and manipulate variables to predict outcome. All of this can be remedied, however, through objective procedures developed in the behavioral sciences. The four components of therapist rhetorical potency described in this chapter can be stated as hypotheses that can be further operationalized and tested. That such research has utility is strongly implied by Mahoney:

> We have devoted invaluable human skills and material resources in efforts to change beliefs about the relative merits of deodorants and political candidates. Meanwhile, our clinics, hospitals, and homes are inhabited by individuals whose existence and daily well-being are painfully jeopardized by dysfunctional beliefs. . . . Had we devoted as much time and concerted research effort toward refining the techniques of therapeutic belief change as we have invested in marketing research, the pervasiveness of contemporary thought disorders might have been dramatically reduced. Needless to say, our priorities are in need of re-examination. (Mahoney, 1974, p. 238)

Toward this end, coding procedures could be developed which reliably discriminate rhetorical acts. Such coding procedures have been developed in other contexts, and there is no reason to assume that they could not be developed for this purpose (Hops, Wills, Patterson, & Weiss, 1971). In addition, outcome studies could be conducted to clarify the relative contributions of specific rhetorical acts to change in client behavior. In order for such outcome studies to proceed, however, we must first define therapeutic influence, what a client might do or say to indicate that a therapeutic effect has been produced. So far we have been examining independent variables—those behaviors that a therapist might engage in to influence clients. Before an outcome study can be undertaken, the dependent variable, therapeutic change, must be further delineated. Given that "mental health" as an abstraction is not a particularly helpful measure of therapeutic outcome, we must further specify those ways in which a client can be affected, changed by a therapist. Shall we look for changes made within the therapeutic hour, compliance with a treatment regimen, changes in problematic behavior occurring outside the therapy session, verbal acceptance of therapist directives, changes in relationships with others, changes in self-talk? It is possible that rhetorical analysis is useful only in predicting differences in client verbal behavior within the context of therapy, but has no predictive value with regard to client extra-session behavior. In any case, before we can more fully understand the relationship between therapist talk and client change, we must first delineate specific independent variables and their effects on specific dependent variables. As indices of therapeutic outcome, we should explicate and evaluate specific client behaviors and avoid global measures of psychological functioning (Biglan & Kass, 1977).

If psychotherapy is a rhetorical process, examining its rhetorical components may reveal why and how it succeeds and fails, thereby allowing therapists to maximize the occurrence and maintenance of therapeutic improvement, and allowing rhetoricians to understand better the processes by which individuals are persuaded by other individuals. Therapists would gain access to a body of rhetorical literature with potential for improving therapeutic effectiveness. Rhetorical scholars, by studying the theory and procedures of psychotherapy, could receive insight into the process by which behavior, thoughts, and feelings are changed or modified through talk.

REFERENCES

Abroms, G. M. Persuasion in psychotherapy. *American Journal of Psychiatry*, 1968, *124*, 9.

Aristotle. *The rhetoric*. (Lane Cooper, Ed.). New York: Appleton-Century-Crofts, 1960.

Arnold, C. C. *Criticism of oral rhetoric*. Columbus, Ohio: Merrill, 1974.

Berscheid, E., & Walster, E. *Interpersonal attractions*. Reading, Mass.: Addison-Wesley, 1969.

Biglan, A., & Kass, D. J. The empirical nature of behavior therapies. *Behaviorism*, 1977, *5*, 25–26.

Bitzer, L. The rhetorical situation. *Philosophy and Rhetoric*, 1968, *1*, 3.

Bowers, J. W. & Osborn, M. M. Attitudinal effects of selected types of concluding metaphors in persuasive speeches. *Speech Monographs*, 1966, *33* (2), 147–155.

Brehm, J. W., & Lipsher, D. Communicator-communicatee discrepancy and perceived communicator trustworthiness. *Journal of Personality*, 1959, *27*, 350–361.

Brock, P. C. Communicator-recipient similarity and decision change. *Journal of Personality and Social Psychology*, 1965, *1*, 650–687.

Burke, K. *A rhetoric of motives*. Berkeley, Calif.: University of California Press, 1969.

Frank, J. *Persuasion and healing*. Baltimore: The John Hopkins University Press, 1973.

Gillis, J. S. The therapist as manipulator. *Psychology Today*, December 1974, 92.

Glaser, S. R. *Rhetorical criticism of psychotherapeutic discourse*. Paper presented at the Western Speech Communication Association Convention, Phoenix, 1977.

Glaser, S. R., and Glaser, P. A. *Rhetorical criticism of interpersonal discourse*. Paper presented at the Western Speech Communication Association Convention, San Francisco, 1976.

Haley, J. *Strategies of psychotherapy*. New York: Grune & Stratton, 1963.

Hops, H., Wills, T., Patterson, G., & Weiss, R. *Marital interaction coding system*. University of Oregon, unpublished manuscript, 1971.

Knapp, M. *Nonverbal communication in human interaction*. New York: Holt, Rinehart & Winston, 1978.

Lennard, H. L., & Bernstein, A. *The anatomy of psychotherapy: Systems of communication and expectation*. New York: Columbia University Press, 1960.

Mahoney, M. *Cognition and behavior modification*. Cambridge, Mass.: Ballinger, 1974.

Oliver, R. T. *The psychology of persuasive speech*. New York: McKay, 1968.

Schmidt, L. D., & Strong, S. R. Expert and inexpert counselors. *Journal of Counseling Psychology*, 1970, *17* (2), 115–118.

Strong, S. R. Counseling: An interpersonal influence process. *Journal of Counseling Psychology*, 1968, *15* (3), 215–224.

Strong, S. R., & Dixon, D. N. Expertness, attractiveness, and influence in counseling. *Journal of Counseling Psychology*, 1971, *18* (6), 562–570.

Strong, S. R., & Matross, R. P. Change processes in counseling and psychotherapy. *Journal of Counseling Psychology*, 1973, *20* (1), 25–37.

Torrey, E. F. *The mind game, witchdoctors and psychiatrists*. New York: Bantam Books, 1973.

Toulmin, S. E. *The uses of argument*. New York: Cambridge University Press, 1958.

Watzlawick, P., Weakland, J., & Fisch, R. *Change: Principles of problem formation and problem resolution*. New York: Norton, 1974.

Aristotle as Psychotherapist

JEROME D. FRANK

The insight that the psychotherapeutic interview, as a powerful influencing situation, is suitable for rhetorical analysis is so illuminating, once it is stated, that one marvels that so few people have thought of it. The similarities of rhetorical and therapeutic interventions are indeed striking. The author's cogent analysis is in itself a valuable contribution by showing that Aristotelian categories of rhetoric can be applied to features of therapeutic interactions, thereby opening up a new and exciting domain of study.

The paper also well describes some potential limitations and problems involved in the rhetorical analysis of the psychiatric interview. In attempting to apply categories derived from one realm of discourse to phenomena of another, questions of goodness of fit inevitably arise. To mention an example, the rhetorical category of tension release subsumes both labeling and inspiring hope. From the standpoint of psychotherapy, it is useful to distinguish at least two types of tension release—reduction of anxiety and arousal of hope. Although overlapping, they are not identical. I would regard labeling primarily as a means of reducing anxiety by dispelling ambiguity, whereas the therapist's optimism primarily inspires hope.

JEROME D. FRANK • Department of Psychiatry, The Johns Hopkins University School of Medicine, Baltimore, Maryland 21205.

Furthermore, certain important phenomena of psychotherapy may completely elude the rhetorical analyst's net because of some major differences between the psychotherapeutic interview and the kinds of situation from which the categories of rhetorical analysis were derived. Two are especially striking. The first is that the target of the rhetoric is already strongly predisposed to accept the therapist's influencing attempt by virtue of being a sufferer who expects relief from the therapist.

Dependence on the therapist for help creates the second difference, namely that the power of the therapist is much greater than that possessed by the rhetorician in most situations. If the patient remains in therapy, this in itself indicates acceptance of the therapist's ethos. By the act of coming repeatedly, the patient shows that he or she considers the therapist to be a trustworthy expert with a world-view that the patient typically either already shares or regards as superior to his or her own. It also implies that the patient hopes to gain relief from therapy.

As a result, the therapist can directly control the patient's behavior and, to some extent, thinking, by instruction or advice. Moreover, based on this power, the therapist can use strong influencing techniques, some of which are aimed at deliberately increasing tension to a level beyond that sought by the rhetorican before reducing it. Thus the therapist may forbid the patient to carry out certain tension-relieving activities such as performing a compulsive ritual, or require the patient to perform a feared act such as entering a situation about which he or she is phobic. Other examples of therapists' influencing maneuvers that may not be encompassable by the categories of classical rhetoric are taking control of symptomatic acts by encouraging or commanding the patient to perform them (Haley, 1963) or insisting that the patient voluntarily produce a symptom he fears such as fainting—termed "paradoxical intention" (Frankl, 1973), Not knowing the field, I can only ask whether instruction, advice-giving, paradoxical intention and the like can be fitted into categories of rhetoric. To the extent that they cannot be, this limits the applicability of classical rhetorical analysis to psychotherapy.

The author is suitably cautious about attempting to apply rhetorical analysis to outcome research. For one thing, although of potential theoretical interest, search for regularities between therapist interventions and patient's responses within an interview can have little practical relevance. Evaluation of therapeutic outcome, whether from the standpoint of the patient, the patient's social unit, or society, depends solely on changes in the patient's behavior and subjective state outside the therapeutic interview. It is highly unlikely that changes in these could be related to specific rhetorical maneuvers within the interview. More promising might be a more macroscopic approach. It could well be that such features as the therapist's overall skill in carrying out rhetorical maneuvers or the level of intensity or frequency of these maneuvers, regardless of their specific nature, would prove to be related to outcome.

In any case, this paper has aroused my hopes that rhetorical analysis of psychotherapy will prove to be a fruitful enterprise, in itself persuasive evidence for the author's rhetorical skill.

REFERENCES

Frankl, V. F. *The doctor and the soul*. New York: Vintage, 1973.
Haley, J. *Strategies of psychotherapy*. New York: Grune & Stratton, 1963.

Chapter 12

Psychotherapy from the Perspective of Cognitive Theory

DIANE B. ARNKOFF

The "cognitive revolution" in psychology is having a profound impact on the concerns and practices of clinical psychology. Cognitive phenomena such as expectancies and self-verbalizations are routinely invoked as essential elements in clinical theory and practice. To date, however, there has actually been little cross-fertilization between clinical and cognitive psychology. While some clinicians have attempted to sketch a cognitive model for clinical work (e.g., Mahoney, 1974; Meichenbaum, 1977), clinicians have not been extensively influenced thus far by cognitive theorizing.

A systematic exchange between clinical and cognitive perspectives could be of great benefit to both fields. An adequate theory of cognition would provide direction and a framework for explanation for clinical psychology. Attention by cognitive psychologists to clinical phenomena, in turn, would provide a significant opportunity for development and testing of cognitive theory.

This chapter will introduce an approach to clinical phenomena derived from the positions of a group of cognitive theorists. A cognitive framework

DIANE B. ARNKOFF • Department of Psychology, The Pennsylvania State University, University Park, Pennsylvania 16802.

for viewing clinical events will be created that will provide a perspective from which to view the process of psychotherapy. The ultimate goals for clinical psychology are both a better understanding of clinical phenomena and a coherent basis from which to direct future research and practice.

THE INDIVIDUAL'S MODEL OF THE WORLD

The basis of the perspective to be presented is that each individual creates a model of the structure of the world. The model is a map, or set of structural relations, which constitute the framework from which the individual interprets events and determines actions to be taken. The model both guides behavior and provides a structure for inferring the meaning of events. In fact, the model *creates* events, in that it determines what will be perceived in the individual's internal and external environment.

The notion of a model of the world is not new in clinical theorizing, of course. For example, the idea of a guiding set of principles or assumptions is central to the work of both Kelly (1955) and Frank (1961). To understand how the idea of a model is being used here, it will be informative to consider the perspective taken by Hayek (1952).

According to Hayek, the primary function of the nervous system is *classification*. An object or event is recognized, or classified, by virtue of the pattern of neural impulses that it evokes. Events which frequently occur together produce changes in brain functioning—i.e., the organism learns. As Hayek says:

> A system of connexions will be formed which will record the relative frequency with which in the history of the organism the different groups of internal and external stimuli have acted together. Each individual impulse or group of impulses will on its occurrence evoke other impulses which correspond to the other stimuli which in the past have usually accompanied its occurrence. We shall call this bundle of secondary impulses which each primary impulse will set up through these acquired connexions the *following* of the primary impulse. It will be the total or partial identity of this following of the primary impulse which makes them members of the same class. (1952, p. 64)

According to Hayek, new events are classified by virtue of the similarity of their pattern of impulses to existing patterns. An essential implication is that our knowledge of a particular event depends on a *prior* classification rule. Hayek calls this aspect of his theory the "primacy of the abstract" (1969). The abstract must be prior to the particular. In fact, particular events cannot be known directly. To know particulars would entail being able to know the infinite ways in which particulars differ from each other. This in turn would require an infinitude of complexity in the finite brain. The conclusion must be drawn that the individual knows concrete events only through their similarity to an abstract model of structural relations among events (Weimer, 1975).

Hayek (1952) calls this pattern of semipermanent structural relations the individual's *map* of the world. The map is not a static mirror of those relations. It will be imperfect in that the infinite ways in which events can vary cannot be represented in the finite brain. However, the map will not be insensitive to changes in events. It will be continuously and gradually modified as events change.

A consequence of the concept of the map is that an event or relation between events cannot be understood at all if it cannot be assimilated to an existing classification. As Hayek says, the map is not unchanging; it is not insensitive to external events. But an event or relation which falls totally outside the current perspective must be passed by as if it did not exist—because it does not exist for that individual. A model is a set of spectacles through which to view the world, much as is a scientific theory (Weimer, 1973). If the spectacles screen out a certain pattern of inputs because there is no classification for it, the pattern cannot be known.

Clinically, the application of the idea of models is obvious. Our clients as well as ourselves have structures with which to know both our experiences and the nonmental realm. Since we manage to survive as individuals and as a species, our models must be more or less adequate mappings of at least some of the real structural relations among events. Individuals' models will differ depending on their experiences, especially the early experiences through which the basic structure of the model is established.

Some aspects of our models vary considerably from person to person. For example, people differ greatly in their beliefs about interpersonal relationships, and yet the differences usually pose no threat to survival. Models formed in early childhood can therefore remain essentially the same until they are vigorously undermined—as in psychotherapy. But as Hayek argues, change in the model cannot take place if the individual is not "ready" for it—if he or she has no existing classification for the new events. In such cases the new input would not be recognized at all. It is not sufficient for the therapist who has labored to identify the client's problems simply to say to the client that everything would be much better if only the client would see X, Y, and Z. As every novice therapist who has tried this has learned, the client, without careful priming, *cannot* see X, Y, and Z at all. What this priming entails, of course, is the basic issue in psychotherapy process.

It was noted above that models are similar to scientific theories in being spectacles through which to see the world. A brief digression into the nature of scientific theory will suggest some interesting implications for therapy. Weimer (1977b) has argued that the inference schema of science is not the if–then of Aristotelian logic, but that of "since–necessarily": *"Since my theory is true, the world is necessarily this way"* (Weimer, 1977b, p. 10). Espousing a scientific theory is a matter of seeing phenomena in only one way. Once the world is seen in the way dictated by the theory, certain consequences necessarily follow—it cannot be any other way.

Similarly, the models that clients present in therapy have a "since–necessarily" character: since the world is this way, I necessarily act and feel a certain way. Clients often do not realize that their model is only one of many possible theories of the world—their perspective appears both natural and inevitable to them. Changing his or her model involves persuading the client to take on another model. This may first require persuasion that another perspective is even possible. The shift to another model is not a matter of choosing among "if–then" alternatives in logical discourse, but persuasion to another, very different mode of seeing—to another theory with its own "since–necessarily" force.

CONSTRUCTIVE AND MOTOR THEORIES

It has been strongly implied in the above arguments that individuals construct their own experience. Constructive theories of cognition stand in opposition to those that hold that knowledge of the external world comes directly, in an immediate fashion. The point of view being put forth here is a *constructive* one, in that the meaning of an event or patterning of inputs is constructed by the individual.

Constructive theories predominate currently in cognitive psychology. Neisser's (1967) text was a landmark in the development of an influential type of constructive theory known as information processing. Bower (1978) has recently written on the implications of such a theory for clinicians. As he states, information processing uses the metaphor of the computer as its basis for cognition, borrowing such terminology as input, memory storage, programs, and so on. The computer metaphor is an improvement over stimulus–response theories in that it allows for the study of the mental processes intervening between stimulus and response (Bower, 1978; Neisser, 1976). However, the computer as a metaphor for the mind is ultimately unsatisfactory, especially from a clinical point of view. The image it evokes is of a *passive* organism, receiving sensory input and then processing the sensory information through the system. Information-processing models are inadequate from a clinical perspective because clients are *active creators*, not passive receivers or automatic transformers of stimuli.

Weimer (1977a) calls these information-processing models "sensory" theories, because they focus on the channeling of sensory information. He argues instead for a *motor* theory of the mind, one in which the individual *creates* his or her own input. Neurophysiological work reviewed by Eccles (1973) and Pribram (1971) demonstrates that a passive theory is inadequate. The most striking aspect of cognition is its generative nature. For example, no sensory, passive theory could hope to explain my ability to create (and your ability to comprehend) the novel sentence "The gold-speckled epileptic hippopotami danced in the ancient space station." Only an active, motoric theory, one which makes creativity its starting point, can be adequate to the task.

The conception of memory is also different in a motor theory as opposed to a sensory theory. Bransford and his associates argue that the usual concept of memory is inadequate because it implies static storage (Bransford & McCarrell, 1974; Bransford, McCarrell, Franks, & Nitsch, 1977). The problem of remembering is inseparable from understanding. Rather than storage, remembering is the *use* of information. New events are incorporated into an already-established pattern (Hayek's map), and remembering is the use of the pattern in a particular context.

The motor conception of remembering and understanding is consistent with the idea of the individual modeling the environment. To say that clients generate their own input as well as their behavior fits well with most clinicians' perceptions of how their clients structure their world. It is commonplace to hear clinicians say that their clients "see what they want to see" and that clients generate the situations they get into, which then "feed into" their own biases. For example, clients who expect to be continually rejected will in fact experience rejection. They will create this outcome both by constructing situations that can lead to no other conclusion, and by viewing events so that they appear to mean rejection even when no such meaning is intended. The belief that individuals construct their world is an accepted part of clinical lore.

The idea that memory is the use of information in context also coincides with the model of clinical events that most clinicians have. The meaning of events for clients (and even their recall of them) are greatly affected by the current work being done in therapy. For example, the memory of a childhood event can be completely different when the client has changed perspectives during therapy. Consider the case of a depressed client who described her childhood as one in which she had a great deal of responsibility for siblings at an early age. She initially remembered feeling proud as a child of her maturity and related incidents of family and others remarking favorably on her sense of responsibility. When asked about missing out on childhood and adolescent activities, she replied that she occasionally felt lonely but, in general, did not enjoy the immature interests of her peers. As therapy progressed, it became apparent to the therapist and client that her model of interpersonal relationships involved the belief that the only means of feeling worthwhile was to sacrifice for others. Irresponsibility and selfishness were loaded words for this client. She began tentatively to express the belief that her own needs were at least as important as those of others. In a highly charged therapy session, she then remembered her childhood as a time when unwanted responsibility was thrust on her. She was continually angry at being cheated out of the opportunity to do what she wanted; but that anger was decisively punished by her parents. She came to believe that she was proud of her "maturity" and did not want what she could not have. Yet the desires and the anger never really disappeared. From then on in the therapy she frequently referred to that new understanding of her childhood as profoundly important. The new memory both encompassed the old one and changed its meaning. Neither memory was more correct than the other; a match against some objective standard of what "really" occurred is not important. It is clear from this example that memory is an ongoing and living process, not the retrieval of static bits from cold storage.

DEEP STRUCTURE

To this point the clinical implications of the cognitive ideas presented are, if not obvious, at least reasonably commonplace. But it may not be so obvious to say that the model the individual has is to a large extent not part of conscious awareness. Much knowledge an individual has of the world is *tacit* (Polanyi, 1966). Tacit knowledge is knowledge of which we are not explicitly aware. Polanyi's favorite example is that of recognizing a face: we can do it, but we cannot give an adequate explicit account of how we do it. Our tacit knowledge demonstrates the truly abstract, structural nature of our classification systems: we know more than we ever could have learned (Weimer, 1973). Our ability to generate unique and grammatical English sentences even if we explicitly know no grammar is an example of tacit knowledge in action (e.g., Reber & Lewis, 1977).

The tacit knowledge concept is intimately related to the deep-structure–surface-structure distinction due to Chomsky in linguistics. But its ramifications extend far beyond the study of language (Weimer, 1973, 1974). To demonstrate the distinction, the surface structure of a sentence is the actual words and phrases as they are written or heard. It may bear little overt resemblance to the deep structure, the abstract ordering which determines the meaning of the sentence. For example, the sentences "I am going to the store today" and "It is to the store today that I am going" have the same deep-structure meaning in spite of having different surface structures. The deep structure consists of the abstract underlying forms from which surface structure can be generated. Here, as earlier, it is asserted that the abstract is prior to the particular.

The tacit deep-structure rules determine the meaning of surface structure. Meaning is a deep-structure problem, but we can have only surface-structure evidence of it. It is essential for us to remember that these surface-structure entities are not necessarily identical to or even closely related to the underlying tacit structure (Franks, 1974). An example was given above of two sentences with different surface structures but identical deep structure. The sentence "Flying planes can be dangerous" is an illustration of one surface structure with at least three possible deep-structural meanings. It is not sufficient to investigate surface structure only; meaning is ambiguous when observables alone are considered.

The same conclusion must be drawn in clinical practice. The same surface structure, or observable behavior, can have more than one meaning for the client. An example is a client who is unassertive, passively avoiding expression of needs or beliefs in any situation in which there could be a conflict with someone else. Often underlying the acquiescence is the belief that the client would lose friends if he were assertive. To the client, being passive is preferable to being alone. Another possible deep structure, however, is the belief that the client is so worthless that his needs should not take precedence over anyone else's. Being assertive is appropriate for other people, but being a doormat is in keeping with his assessment of his own value. Standard assertiveness training aims at reducing anxiety associated with the consequences of being assertive. This form of treatment may well be successful only with the first deep-structural interpretation. Experienced clinicians are well aware of the dangers of confusing surface structure with deep structure in this way, even if they do not use these linguistic terms. They speak instead, for example, of the necessity for taking a careful history, or for doing a complete behavior analysis.

The same deep structure or meaning may also be manifested in more than one surface structure. An example is a client's fundamental belief in her worthlessness. As described above, one surface structure consistent with this deep structure is lack of assertiveness. Severe evaluation anxiety is another surface structure that could have the same underlying meaning: the client has managed to be judged as competent to this point, but she lives in fear that her worthlessness will be "found out" if someone looks at her performance carefully. "Worthlessness" is the deep-structural meaning underlying both of the problem behaviors described.

Bandler and Grinder (1975) have used the deep-structure–surface-structure distinction to propose a procedure for psychotherapy. They see the task of the therapist as twofold: to help the client change surface-structure utterances to make them coincide with the richer deep structure; and to change the deep structure to make it reflect more accurately the experience available to the client. They suggest some verbal and nonverbal methods aimed at achieving these goals.

INVARIANTS AND TRANSFORMATIONS

What constitutes the model that the individual has of the environment? It consists of the abstract rules (principles of classification) that set forth the unvarying aspects of the individual's experience. Every event is unique in some fashion from every one in the past or future. Yet there are some invariant aspects. These *invariants* are the rules which govern perception and conception. For example, a small child learns under what circumstances his mother will be kind, and under what circumstances she will be angry. Each incident varies considerably in details from each other, yet the child creates an abstract rule (probably tacitly) that sets forth the conditions for each category. Thus, the child learns how to act to get the reaction he wants from his mother.

The concept of invariance is a central one for Gibson (1966). He argues that it is not the particulars of an event but the invariants in the environment that are perceived. Gibson conceives of perception as the pick-up of information over time. As the organism moves or the object moves, there is inevitably transformation—an object is quite different when viewed at a closer range or from a different angle. Yet there are invariant aspects, and Gibson argues that the invariant aspects constitute meaningful information for perception. Events share invariants that *afford* a certain meaning. For example, a chair affords sitting, a pen affords writing. Although Gibson conceives of perception as an environment–organism interaction, he has devoted his energy to specifying the nature of the ecological *environment* only—the information in the environment of value to the organism. He treats the organism, in fact, as a receiver of information rather than a perceiver—perception is direct for Gibson and not constructed.

Since organisms do generally manage to survive in their environments, it is reasonable to accept Gibson's notion of information available in the environment and the task of specifying that information as a part of cognitive psychology. In fact, Neisser's (1976) decision to modify his cognitive perspective to incorporate Gibson testifies to the power of Gibson's ecological theory to deal with real-life phenomena. However, Gibson's idea of direct perception—the organism as an information receiver—is in conflict with a motor theory of the organism as structuring its own input. A motor theory incorporating Gibson's ecological approach asserts that *potentially* meaningful information is available in the environment, but that *meaning* is constructed by the individual (Weimer, 1977a).

Clinical experience supports a Gibsonian analysis of information within a constructive theory. The Gibsonian analysis of invariants and affordances is useful in describing aspects of the self-concept. For example, certain consistent events may "afford" a negative self-evaluation. Though the events inevitably differ in their particulars, they share certain invariant properties that lead in this case to the classification "I am an inadequate person."

The Gibsonian analysis may easily be extended to psychotherapy. The therapist doing an assessment prior to treatment engages in the attempt to discover the *invariant properties* of the events leading to the client's negative self-evaluation. The clinician in turn has his or her own classifications in which to interpret the client's world. For example, the clinician may use the classification "Oedipal complex." He or she would look for (and, of course, tend to see) invariants in the client's world which "afford" the conclusion that the negative self-evaluation occurs in the situations sharing (the invariant of) an authority figure. Such an assessment would be likely for an analyst since the Oedipal concept is central in the psychoanalytic model. A behavior therapist would be less likely to search for the cause of a negative self-evaluation in dealings with authority figures. Even if the behavior therapist did see such an invariant, he or she would recreate the learning history as involving reinforcement patterns rather than an Oedipal conflict. It is clear that clinicians with different classifications for abnormal behavior would evaluate and therefore treat a client in different terms.

SYMMETRY AND ASYMMETRY

It is central to the perspective being presented that the model the individual has of the world is constructed. This is a model of structural relations among events, but since it is constructed, it need not accurately reflect the actual patterns in the world. The extent to which a client's model is *symmetrical* with the "real world" is described by a number of terms in clinical work, including "reality testing." A seriously discrepant picture of the world is maladaptive: the model is not serving its adaptive function of providing the direction for actions that will be successful in the world.

The idea of the symmetry between the model and the world has been elaborated by Shaw, McIntyre, and Mace (1974). The term symmetry is used in science in the following manner: "a thing is symmetrical if there is something we can do to it so that after we have done it, it appears the same as it did before" (Shaw *et al.*, 1974, p. 276, italics deleted). In other words, symmetry involves invariance. Shaw and his co-workers postulate that an organism is adapted to its environment to the extent that it is in dynamic equilibrium (a form of symmetry) with that environment. To the extent that a change in one is reflected in a change in the other, the organism is adapted.

Although Shaw *et al.* do not discuss it, since symmetry is possible, then *asymmetry* must be possible. When asymmetry occurs, the organism's classificatory model of the world is not adequate (or is at least less adequate) to the task of adaptation. Maladaptive behavior would be likely to result.

It should not be concluded from the concept of symmetry that there can be an objective standard of accuracy. It has been asserted here that our knowledge of the world is of structural relations only, and is always an imperfectly constructed map rather than a mirror. Further, as was noted above, it is possible for adults to have quite distorted maps (especially of interpersonal relationships) and still survive in a literal sense. From this perspective, what constitutes psychological adaptation becomes a complex issue. As therapists we have a sense that a particular client changes in a positive fashion—that is, that his or her model becomes more symmetrical with the real world. This sense of progress may be illusory; yet we feel that we can judge (at least tacitly) the adequacy of models. How we judge progress in psychotherapy is an interesting problem of tacit knowledge worthy of investigation. Several clinical perspectives that may be cast in the symmetry-asymmetry framework will be discussed below. Nevertheless, it must be kept in mind that symmetry is a matter of judgment from the perspective of one imperfect model about another imperfect model.

A number of clinical approaches in the new cognitive trend use the idea of an asymmetry between the model and the real world. For example, Bandler and Grinder (1975), in their language analysis of therapy, describe three types of asymmetry. They are generalization, in which a part is taken for the whole of experience; deletion, in which we selectively attend to only parts of the available array; and distortion, in which events are misclassified.

Beck (1976) has performed a compelling analysis of what he calls the cognitive content of emotional disorders. He summarizes the idiosyncratic thinking pattern of each of the neurotic patterns. In an anxiety neurosis, for example, the thinking pattern found is that of perceived danger to the individual's domain. In each case the idiosyncratic "thought disorder" may be conceived as an *asymmetry* between the classificatory structures of the individual and the information available in the environment. To take the anxiety neurotic as an example once more, the classification "this is a dangerous situation" is the construction placed on too many events, at least from the therapist's perspective. The invariant "danger" is perceived when in fact there is no danger; either the rules that determine danger are too broad, or danger means something different for the client than for most people. Each of the neurotic disorders may be conceptualized in this fashion.

Beck's (1967, 1976) analysis of the thought disorder in depression is that the individual experiences a devaluation of his or her domain. More specifically, Beck describes the cognitive triad of depression: "a negative view of his world, a negative concept of himself, and a negative appraisal of his future" (Beck, 1976, pp. 105–106). There are four logical errors involved in the triad: arbitrary inference, selective abstraction, overgeneralization, and magnification or minimization (Beck, 1967). Each may be interpreted from the point of view of an asymmetrical relationship between the information available in the depressed individual's world and the classification system the individual uses. Magnification or minimization, for example, are processes in which an individual misjudges the significance of an event. Experimental evidence suggests that depressed individuals estimate receiving a lower rate of reinforcement and a higher rate of punishment than nondepressed individuals (Nelson & Craighead, 1977). Recalling the caution stated above regarding symmetry, it is interesting that in the case of punishment, it was the nondepressed subjects whose rating was asymmetrical with the actual rate of punishment. From the point of view of classification, it appears that depressed persons do perceive the invariants that afford failure, but they attach a different meaning to success than do nondepressed individuals. In this case, therapy would require not a simple increase in reinforcement, but a shift in the meaning of success.

In the the next section, some further implications of the viewpoint presented will be drawn for the theory and practice of psychotherapy. This cognitive perspective does not demand a radically new type of therapy. Rather, it can serve to categorize the communalities across all successful therapies and to suggest what types of future work in therapy may be more fruitful than others.

PSYCHOTHERAPY AS DEEP STRUCTURAL CHANGE

The individual's model of the world undergoes constant change. The question to be asked is not why change occurs: change is, so to speak, the stable aspect of the system. It is more profitable to ask the question of what type of change occurs under what circumstances. Psychotherapy would appear to involve both change in the individual's model and in the environment. The most successful treatments would be those in which both the model changes and the individual creates the environment to fit the model.

What is involved in altering a model? It is a change in *deep-structural rules*, the rules regarding the invariants and transformations among events. For change to be maintained and generalized, the deep structure must be altered. This idea is, of course, known by other vocabularies in therapy writings—for example, for Frank (1961), it involves a change in assumptive worlds, for Ellis (1962), the replacement of irrational ideas by rational ones.

If change comes about in only one fashion, how can diverse types of therapy be successful? The answer which follows involves another application of the surface–deep distinction: perhaps all effective therapies, while differing in surface structure, have an identical deep structure. There is probably some truth to this statement. Studies that find new differences between therapies, such as the Sloane, Staples, Cristol, Yorkston, and Whipple (1975) comparison of behavior therapy and dynamic therapy, lend credence to the view that there are deep-structural similarities. But by itself the statement of similarity is not sufficient. Not all therapies are equally effective in all cases. It would be the height of folly to refer a snake phobic to a psychoanalyst, or a person in an existential crisis to an operant-behavior modifier. Every clinician has some implicit idea of which clients to match with which therapists or therapies.

Differences among techniques should be explored for their influence on different types of clients. Therapies differ, for example, in their scope. Most behavior therapy techniques aim at using specific means to induce change in a specific behavior. The aim of psychoanalysis or client-centered therapy, on the other hand, is broader, as is reflected in terms like reeducation and congruence between self and ideal concept. If the techniques are consonant with the aims, the type of deep-structural changes these therapies would induce would surely differ.

Related to differences in scope are differences in focus. Behavior therapists (at least of the traditional variety) would like to deal only with observables. Psychoanalysts believe that the overt actions are merely the key to the more interesting material, and that therapy aims at uncovering the unconscious. Both can be seen to be limited from the perspective presented in this chapter. The error of the behaviorists is glaring: surface structure is not deep structure. In fact, it is impossible to deal only with observables—any description of overt behavior is ambiguous unless there is a deep-structural analysis available to disambiguate it (Weimer, 1974). This is related to the point made repeatedly above: there are no particulars without prior reference to abstract structures. There can be no unambiguous specification of an observed behavior without abstract meaning. In attempting to deal only with topographically similar events, the radical behaviorist commits an error in believing that behaviors can be understood without inference. By attempting to focus only on surface structure, the behaviorist ignores the ultimate issue, that of *meaning* (Weimer, 1975).

The criticism just expressed of behavior therapy is similar to a point made by Wachtel (1977) in discussing strengths and weaknesses of behavior therapy and psychoanalysis. A strength of psychoanalysis in relation to behavior therapy lies in its emphasis on the meaning of behavior to the individual—its focus on the deep-structural rules. But psychoanalysis is guilty of another type of error, which is equally serious for the success of therapy. To put Wachtel's idea into the present framework, psychoanalysis is guilty of ignoring the importance of surface structures since it assumes that the deep structure must be dealt with through the layers of the past. The present is too unimportant to analysts. Even transference only stands for the real issue, that of the past. A behavior therapist, in focusing on the present, could decide to teach social skills to a client who has no heterosexual experience and could achieve success. With the same client, the analyst would spend years working on the client's anger toward his mother and wonder why the client still was not dating, ignoring his present predicament of having no idea of what is involved in interpersonal relationships. The analyst's map from surface to deep structure therefore is faulty. Deep structure involves the present, even though it arose out of the past.

Changing the deep-structural rules means shifting the pattern of relations seen in the world. A temporary shift in surface structure may be easily achieved, as evidenced by the initial success of many types of therapy. Maintenance or generalization of that shift is a much more difficult matter. Change in deep structure entails what Hayek calls a change in the "following," or a shift in the patterning of neural events that constitute classification. The analytic term "working through" suggests the same type of process. In other words, the *meaning* of events changes for the client.

There is, of course, a vast array of techniques available to initiate deep-structure change. Some are particularly interesting in relation to the idea of a shift in the ongoing pattern. The use of metaphor as a therapeutic technique is one such example. Metaphor is a creative act in which a similarity is expressed "in the midst of difference" (Billow, 1977, p. 82). The use of verbal metaphor allows exploration of the similarities and differences. For example, a therapist may say to a withdrawn and fearful client that he is like a spectator at a football game. The metaphor can then be examined for its range of similarities to the client's situation. In addition to the idea of passivity, being a spectator allows for enjoyment without the danger of being in a conflict, etc. Metaphor is not, however, solely a verbal process. For example, Haley (1976) suggests that a client with chronic headaches may be using her body as an instrument to express metaphorically that people close to her give her a headache. Haley also describes Erickson's technique of indirectly improving a couple's sexual relationship by teaching them to act considerately toward each other in nonsexual situations.

The power of metaphor is in the expansion of a conceptual framework: "When we use metaphor the original concept we apply to the new situation *is itself transformed* . . . we tend to 'see' the events differently" (Price, 1972, pp. 12–13). Metaphor stretches the individual's model. Other techniques which may be seen to involve a shift in the individual's characteristic pattern include paradoxical techniques and humor. Along with the standard armamentarium that therapists use, these techniques invite study as inducing change in deep-structural rules.

A change in model or deep-structural rules involves moving from one way of understanding the world to another. As the therapist assists the client in moving through the layers of the old model, in some fashion a new one takes its place. The new perspective may encompass the old—or it may be a radically new way of seeing. The analogy to revolutions in science is interesting. According to Kuhn (1970), anomalies in the old scientific paradigm set the stage for its overthrow. The current way of seeing the world will not be overturned, however, until there is a new paradigm to take its place. "The decision to reject one paradigm is always simultaneously the decision to accept another" (Kuhn, 1970, p. 77). In psychotherapy, it may or may not be the case that overthrowing an old way of seeing can occur only when there is a new one to take its place. It is clear, however, that in psychotherapy there need not be an *explicit* new model available before the old is overthrown (Mahoney, 1978). When their old perspective no longer works, some clients feel they have no basis now for directing their life; they may voice despair over the possibility of ever finding another way. A new, *tacit* set of deep-structural rules may well be in operation before the client abandons the old rules. But if this is the case, it is clear that explicit knowledge follows (if at all) only later for some clients—often when they notice themselves acting differently. The comparison with science is another illustration that the analysis of change in psychotherapy requires the concept of deep-structural rules or tacit knowledge.

THE THERAPEUTIC RELATIONSHIP

If the goal of therapy is to alter deep-structural rules, the major question is how this is accomplished. Examining the role of the therapeutic relationship would appear to be a key factor. The role of the therapist is just beginning to be recognized in behavior therapy. It has, of course, always played a central role in the theorizing of schools such as psychoanalysis and client-centered therapy.

The essential preconditions on the part of the therapist for successful psychotherapy have been variously called emphathy, unconditional positive regard, and so on. The function of empathy is most intruiging. Lesswing (1976) has analyzed empathy, following Cassirer, as *direct* knowledge of the other when the subject (therapist) and object (client) are not distinguished.

He refers to Freud's dictum to the therapist not to bias what is obtained from the client, but to maintain an attitude of "equally hovering attention" (Freud, 1924, p. 324).

The analysis of empathy may be assisted by considering Bertrand Russell's distinction between knowledge by acquaintance and knowledge by description. Knowledge by acquaintance is "direct" knowledge or phenomenal experience. The only knowledge by acquaintance that we have is of our own mental processing (Weimer, 1973). Knowledge by description is inferential or nondirect knowledge; all the rest of our knowledge, including that of science, is knowledge by description. The function of empathy for the therapist may be to provide material about the client in the therapist's acquaintance. This phenomenal knowledge may then be analyzed by description. The experience during empathic communication would provide much richer material than would be the case if the client had not been understood empathically.

The question remains as to what empathy accomplishes for the client and also how it facilitates therapeutic change. I suggest that empathy fosters therapy from the client's point of view by providing the client with conditions for restructuring his or her model of the world. The therapist almost certainly embodies an attitude to the client which is different from that of anyone else in the client's life. There is no one else in the client's life whose interest comes so close to coinciding with that of the client. Through demonstrating empathy, the therapist shows that he or she knows the client's model and accepts it—yet the therapist plainly sees the world from a different model. The therapist simultaneously both knows and knows beyond the client's perspective.

In the early stages of therapy, as Rogers (1951) describes it, the client finds it unnecessary to be as defensive in therapy as outside it. The client learns to classify the communication with the therapist as not dangerous and as valuable. A description of motivation on the client's part, or the capacity to profit from therapy, would seem to be that the client's cognitive structures must be initially permeable enough to be able to characterize the therapeutic relationship in this manner.

The therapeutic alliance appears to function to establish conditions for the therapist to influence change in the client's structuring of experience. Johnson and Matross (1977) describe the process of influence in therapy. Rather than locating power in characteristics of the client or therapist, they propose that influence is a function of the therapeutic relationship. Influence is fostered by the therapist's timely expression of his or her resources. Factors such as trust and the establishment of mutual goals set the stage for the client to change. In the terms of the motor theory, the relationship between client and therapist prepares the client to change the deep-structural rules by which events are structured.

The therapist structures the therapeutic experience so that the client is comfortable in trying out new rules for organizing events. As noted above, because of the therapist's unique influential position, the new rules are either those of the therapist, or those that the therapist sanctions. The therapist provides the standard of what would constitute symmetry with the environment. Clinicians surely allow a wide latitude of behavior that would be considered adequately adaptive, yet they also determine when there is asymmetry. The clinician cannot claim that *any* direction the client took would be acceptable (as many Rogerians, for example, claim). In fact, unless his or her own classificatory structures were asymmetrical in the same fashion as the client's, the clinician could not avoid perceiving—if not acting upon—the asymmetry in the client's world view. It is for this reason that psychoanalysts must undergo analysis themselves—to guard against their own asymmetrical models intruding destructively in therapy. However, in contrast to analytic theory, the proper role for the therapist, from the perspective espoused here, would usually *not* be to be as invisible as possible. The vigorous challenge necessary for deep-structural change would appear to require more active intervention than infrequent interpretations (Wachtel, 1977).

AFFECT

Affect in therapy has a central place, emphasized from Freud to Perls. And no theory of cognitive psychology can ignore affect; it should be a part of the purview of cognitive psychology. To date, however, there has been little discussion of affect in the writings of those discussed here (save Pribram, 1971). Nevertheless, no discussion of psychotherapy can afford to ignore it. In fact, to describe the perspective I have outlined as a cognitive theory can be dangerous—if by cognitive the reader understands a theory which deals only with cold, intellectual processes.

Just as it is dangerous to think of cognition as being affectless, so it is misleading to think of affect as an independent system. Affect would appear to be a necessary component in Hayek's "following of the primary impulse." Some early remarks by Freud are interesting along these lines. In the long-neglected "Project for a Scientific Psychology," Freud ties affect to memory (Freud, 1895/1966; see also Pribram & Gill, 1976). He postulates that memory is a process by which nervous tissue is altered by experience. When an impulse is conducted through nervous tissue, a "facilitation" occurs, so that a similar conduction has less resistance on the next occasion. When the memory trace or facilitation is activated by a similar experience to the original, affect is experienced through the release of endogenous energy by "'secretory' neurones" (Freud, 1895/1966, p. 320).

When affect is experienced, "the releasing idea itself gains in intensity" (Freud, 1895/1966, pp. 357–358). The similarity to Hayek's theorizing on physiological memory is striking. The picture of affect is thus of a process inseparably tied to memory, indicating the quality of the experience.

Current neurophysiological work on affect (e.g., MacLean, 1975; Sigg, 1975) suggests that the sympathetic and central nervous system pathways implicated in affect have complex connections with both perceptual and cortical structures. Consistent with Freud, affect appears to be closely tied to memory (MacLean, 1975). Memory, from the perspective taken in this chapter, is the physiological representation of previous experience, engaged and modified when new experiences are assimilated. The conclusion must be that any experience that would result in significant alteration of the individual's model (or memory) would inevitably involve affect. Conversely, the inference can be made that arousal of affect can facilitate a change in model since affect serves as a signal of significant events. Affect, therefore, would be an inevitable component of deep-structural changes.

These remarks are only suggestive of the work that needs to be done on affect. The role of affect in psychotherapy is an area in most urgent need of careful thinking and research.

SELECTED APPLICATIONS AND IMPLICATIONS

There have been innumerable attempts to characterize the nature of change in psychotherapy. One such effort which is certain to be highly influential in behavioral approaches is that of Bandura (1977). According to Bandura's analysis, "psychological procedures, whatever their form, alter the level and strength of self-efficacy" (p. 191). Self-efficacy expectation is "the conviction that one can successfully execute the behavior required to produce the outcomes" (p. 193).

Much of Bandura's analysis can be aligned with the present perspective. For example, he views reinforcement not as an automatic strengthener of behavior but as providing information on appropriate behavior. In the terms of our framework, reinforcement functions to specify the invariants of actions that will be adaptive. Part of the meaning of those actions is that they bring about a desired outcome.

Bandura's paper will be influential, particularly with behavior therapists. Since his analysis deals with deep-structural rules rather than with surface-structure manifestations only, the influence will be positive. But there are certain limitations to Bandura's approach from the cognitive perspective taken here. When he uses the concept of self-efficacy, for example, it is unclear whether he intends to create a model of the effects of therapy for all types of disorders, or only for fearful and defensive behavior.

The distinction becomes important when a disorder such as depression is considered. Are self-efficacy considerations fundamental in depression—or, as Beck (1976) would have it, is devaluation of the self the core?

A second difficulty arises in Bandura's discussion of the most appropriate procedures to alter behavior. He argues that the most effective procedures to effect a change in self-efficacy are "performance-based" rather than symbolic. However, if all behavior change is achieved by a "common cognitive mechanism" (Bandura, 1977, p. 191), as Bandura asserts, the deep-structural difference between the two types of procedures is elusive. Is participant modeling less "cognitive" than modeling? Both apparently operate through "cognitive" means. The surface-structure differences between the two types of therapies are obvious; in modeling, the client just watches a model, while in participant modeling, the client also practices the behaviors. There may be deep-structural differences, as well, but they will have to be sought rather than assumed.

A final problem with Bandura's analysis results from an interaction of the type of disorder with type of treatment. When discussing symbolic techniques, Bandura (1977) mentions only modeling, systematic desensitization, and covert modeling. These procedures may adequately cover the field when the disorders in question are fear and defensive behavior. But to analyze the treatment of other disorders like depression, other "symbolic" techniques such as verbal psychotherapy must be considered for comparison with "performance-based" techniques. The inclusion of verbal psychotherapy is important since verbal procedures may result in better generalization of change than participant modeling—at least when the scope of the disorder is broad, as in depression.

The first and third problems discussed may be eliminated by restricting the scope of the self-efficacy proposal to fear and defensive behaviors only. (The second problem, that of the difference between symbolic and performance-based techniques, remains.) If the proposal is limited in this way, Bandura's concept of self-efficacy is compatible with the perspective being presented here. In the cognitive vocabulary, self-efficacy concerns would be the deep-structural rules underlying fear and defensive behavior. The most effective form of therapy would involve an alteration in situations evoking the conclusion "I can't do this." The change would come about through altering the perceived invariants of situations evoking that reaction. The deep-structural rules would become more symmetrical with the individual's actual capabilities. For example, the invariants of situations evoking a belief of incapability would shift from all interactions with snakes to only those in which a real threat obtained.

The deep-structure idea can be fruitfully applied to other aspects of psychotherapy. It is apparent that generalization of therapeutic effects must entail deep-structural similarity rather similarity of surface structure. For example, suppose a young man goes into therapy complaining of impotence.

Suppose also that potency with a surrogate partner is easily established. Generalization of therapeutic gain would ordinarily be measured by performance with a nonsurrogate partner. But it is possible that the problem was due to a conflict over the morality of sex with "virtuous" women, and the young man did not consider the surrogate to be virtuous. Then generalization to a nonsurrogate (virtuous) partner would be unlikely—in spite of the surface-structure similarity among women.

Since the deep-structural rules which constitute a model are generally tacit, it is misguided to expect an individual to be able to voice them without careful analysis. One type of therapy that is seen in a different light when tacit knowledge is considered is *self-instructional training* with neurotics (Meichenbaum & Cameron, 1974). This is an example of the "cognitive behavior therapy" movement. The procedure of self-instructional training is as follows: the therapist analyzes the client's behavior from the viewpoint of maladaptive self-statements, and persuades the client that the things he or she is saying covertly are detrimental. Together they design replacement self-statements, and the client rehearses them both in therapy and through homework assignments. A related procedure is stress inoculation, which involves the additional procedure of stress induction (e.g., through imagery) and practice with relaxation and self-statements to control the anxiety.

Beck (1976) and others speak of the "automaticity" of certain self-thoughts, saying that clients must *return* the thoughts to conscious awareness—where they presumably arose originally. From a motor theory point of view, it is more reasonable to consider the constructions that are maladaptive as arising from *tacit* knowledge classes. In self-instructional training, it would appear that persuasion and/or the use of adaptive self-statements in action leads to a reconstruction of the individual's theory of the environment. The therapist, in persuading the client that he or she has been using automatic self-thoughts, may possibly *create* the self-thoughts for the client—but the covert statements do reflect the underlying deep-structure relations. The new "replacement" self-statements apparently alter the deep-structure relations. The rehearsal of self-statements can be seen to encourage the restructuring of the client's classification scheme. This may be particularly relevant in stress inoculation, in which an emotional situation is created for rehearsal of coping behavior. Presumably when the client generates a similar context—a similar emotional situation—outside therapy, the adaptive effects of the rehearsal of coping are also recreated. This is consistent with the analysis presented above of memory.

EXCLUSIONS

In order for a theoretical perspective to be meaningful, it must be specific enough to declare certain ideas to be contrary to its viewpoint. If nothing can be excluded, the theory is vacuous and can truly explain nothing. Therefore this final section will examine some ideas which the cognitive-clinical framework denies.

A constructive cognitive position rules out Gibsonian direct perception as the mechanism of perception. Gibson's (1966) idea of there being an "affordance structure" of events, or potentially meaningful information available in the environment, is reasonable. Certainly from an evolutionary point of view it is more likely than the extreme constructivist position that everything is constructed: most organisms do manage to function in their environment, making it likely that they are using some real basis for their constructions. But Gibson's implication that meaning resides in the environment rather than in the individual must be rejected. "One can argue with Gibson that the *information* is directly there in the stimulus array, but it is clear that our *experience* is not. All perceptual experience must be a construction" (Weimer, 1977a, p. 305). As Hayek (1952) argued, our experience of the qualities of sensation is not directly mirrored from the environment. So while there is information in the environment, the meaning of that information is constructed.

The clinical counterpart to Gibsonian direct perception may be found in those clinicians who see as the goal of healthy functioning the ability to experience and understand events directly (e.g., Rogers, 1961). While experience, or knowledge by acquaintance, may be direct, once it is classified, it is neither acquaintance nor direct. The only communicable knowledge of the nonmental realm is structural knowledge. We can never communicate the particulars of our experience—even to ourselves. The goal of the adaptive organism is not direct knowledge of events but a relatively symmetrical model of the structural relations among events. To know the world descriptively in an unmediated fashion is, from this perspective, impossible.

Finally, the Freudian idea (from Freud's later writings) that dynamic change requires that the unconscious become conscious must be ruled out from this cognitive framework. There is a similar disagreement with those cognitive behavior therapists who see change as being achieved only through conscious thought. The current perspective denies that conscious awareness is necessarily a precursor to change. This was implied above in the discussion of Kuhn and paradigm shifts. The model's deep-structural rules are generally tacit; they may change without the explicit knowledge of the individual. Consciousness is certainly not irrelevant to change, however. If an individual becomes aware of the deep structure underlying his or her surface-structure actions, further change and integration of that change will probably be facilitated. Conscious thought surely has an adaptive function, that of modeling reality (Craik, 1943). Consciousness is not essential to change, but it is facilitative of change.

The cognitive behavior therapy movement improves on behavior therapy by utilizing conscious awareness. But it would be misguided from the present perspective to assume that *all* important change processes are conscious. An example of such a belief is stated by Meichenbaum: "I believe that if we are going to change a behavior then we must think before we act" (Meichenbaum, 1977, p. 210, italics deleted). Cognitive behavior therapists restrict themselves both in theory and technique if they conceive of all change as being conscious. Awareness is facilitative of change, but we will always know more than we can tell.

No one approach to therapy stands out within the framework adopted. The most successful method in any given case would be that which resulted in the widest ranging change in the deep-structural organization. But any technique can, of course, deal directly only with surface structure. It is ultimately an empirical question, albeit with theoretical overtones, as to which method best brings about the desired change.

The framework developed in this chapter is clearly just the beginning of a theory of cognition and psychotherapy. Only a few bricks have been laid in the structure. Important issues yet to be investigated include the actual process of change in therapy, and the discovery of which techniques should theoretically maximize change in a given case. The ultimate test of the theory will be the extent to which it fosters a more adequate understanding of the process of psychotherapy. A theory of psychotherapy will be successful to the extent that it both coincides with the tacit and explicit knowledge that clinicians have, and simultaneously expands and transforms that knowledge into a new way of seeing.

Acknowledgments

The author wishes to thank Kathryn Mahoney, Michael Mahoney, Carolyn Mazure, Alvin Rosenthal, and Debra Wallett for their helpful comments on earlier drafts of the manuscript, and she is especially grateful to Walter Weimer for his teaching and encouragement.

REFERENCES

Bandler, R., & Grinder, J. *The structure of magic I: A book about language and therapy*. Palo Alto, Calif.: Science and Behavior Books, 1975.

Bandura, A. Self-efficacy: Towards a unifying theory of behavioral change. *Psychological Review*, 1977, *84*, 191–215.

Beck, A. T. *Depression: Clinical, experimental, and theoretical aspects*. New York: Harper & Row, 1967.

Beck, A. T. *Cognitive therapy and the emotional disorders*. New York: International Universities Press, 1976.

Billow, R. M. Metaphor: A review of the psychological literature. *Psychological Bulletin*, 1977, *84*, 81–92.

Bower, G. H. Contacts of cognitive psychology with social learning theory. *Cognitive Therapy and Research*, 1978, *2*, 123–146.

Bansford, J. D., & McCarrell, N. S. A sketch of a cognitive approach to comprehension: Some thoughts about understanding what it means to comprehend. In W. B. Weimer & D. S. Palermo (Eds.), *Cognition and the symbolic processes*. Hillsdale, N.J.: Lawrence Erlbaum, 1974.

Bransford, J. D., McCarrell, N. S., Franks, J. J., & Nitsch, K. E. Toward unexplaining memory. In R. Shaw & J. Bransford (Eds.), *Perceiving, acting, and knowing: Toward an ecological psychology*. Hillsdale, N.J.: Lawrence Erlbaum, 1977.

Craik, K. J. *The nature of explanation*. Cambridge, England: Cambridge University Press, 1943.

Eccles, J. C. *The understanding of the brain*. New York: McGraw-Hill, 1973.

Ellis, A. E. *Reason and emotion in psychotherapy*. New York: Stuart, 1962.

Frank, J. D. *Persuasion and healing*. Baltimore: Johns Hopkins Press, 1961.

Franks, J. J. Toward understanding understanding. In W. B. Weimer & D. S. Palermo (Eds.), *Cognition and the symbolic processes*. Hillsdale, N.J.: Lawrence Erlbaum, 1974.

Freud, S. *Collected papers* (Vol. 2). (J. Riviere, Trans.). London: Hogarth, 1924.

Freud, S. *Project for a scientific psychology*. In S. Freud, *Standard edition* (Vol. 1) (J. Strachey, Ed. and trans.) 1966. (Originally written, 1895.)

Gibson, J. J. *The senses considered as perceptual systems*. Boston: Houghton Mifflin, 1966.

Haley, J. *Problem solving therapy*. San Francisco: Jossey-Bass, 1976.

Hayek, F. A. *The sensory order*. Chicago: University of Chicago Press, 1952.

Hayek, F. A. The primacy of the abstract. In A. Koestler & J. R. Smythies (Eds.), *Beyond reductionism*. New York: Macmillan, 1969.

Johnson, D. W., & Matross, R. Interpersonal influence in psychotherapy: A social psychological view. In A. S. Gurman & A. M. Razin (Eds.), *Effective psychotherapy*. New York: Pergamon, 1977.

Kelly, G. A. *The psychology of personal constructs*. New York: Norton, 1955.

Kuhn, T. S. *The structure of scientific revolutions* (2nd ed.). Chicago: University of Chicago Press, 1970.

Lesswing, N. J. *Implications of selected issues in epistemology and philosophy of science for psychotherapy theory, research, and practice*. Unpublished doctoral dissertation, The Pennsylvania State University, 1976.

MacLean, P. D. Sensory and perceptive factors in emotional functions of the triune brain. In L. Levi (Ed.), *Emotions: Their parameters and measurement*. New York: Raven, 1975.

Mahoney, K. Personal communication, May 1978.

Mahoney, M. J. *Cognition and behavior modification*. Cambridge, Mass.: Ballinger, 1974.

Meichenbaum, D. *Cognitive-behavior modification: An integrative approach*. New York: Plenum, 1977.

Meichenbaum, D., & Cameron, R. The clinical potential of modifying what clients say to themselves. In M. J. Mahoney & C. E. Theoresen (Eds.), *Self-control: Power to the person*. Monterey, Calif.: Brooks/Cole, 1974.

Neisser, U. *Cognitive psychology*. New York: Appleton-Century-Crofts, 1967.

Neisser, U. *Cognition and reality: Principles and implications of cognitive psychology*. San Francisco: Freeman, 1976.

Nelson, R. E., & Craighead, W. E. Selective recall of positive and negative feedback, self-control behaviors, and depression. *Journal of Abnormal Psychology*, 1977, *86*, 379–388.

Polanyi, M. *The tacit dimension*. Garden City, N.Y.: Doubleday, 1966.

Pribram, K. H. *Languages of the brain*. Englewood Cliffs, N.J.: Prentice-Hall, 1971.

Pribram, K. H., & Gill, M. M. *Freud's 'Project' reassessed*. New York: Basic, 1976.

Price, R. H. *Abnormal behavior: Perspectives in conflict*. New York: Holt, Rinehart & Winston, 1972.

Reber, A. S., & Lewis, S. Implicit learning: An analysis of the form and structure of a body of tacit knowledge. *Cognition*, 1977, *5*, 333–361.

Rogers, C. R. *Client-centered therapy*. Boston: Houghton Mifflin, 1951.

Rogers, C. R. *On becoming a person*. Boston: Houghton Mifflin, 1961.

Shaw, R., McIntyre, M., & Mace, W. The role of symmetry in event perception. In R. B. MacLeod & H. L. Pick, Jr. (Eds.), *Perception: Essays in honor of James J. Gibson*. Ithaca, N.Y.: Cornell University Press, 1974.

Sigg, E. B. The organization and functions of the central sympathetic nervous system. In L. Levi (Ed.), *Emotions: Their parameters and measurement*. New York: Raven, 1975.

Sloane, R. B., Staples, F. R., Cristol, A. H., Yorkston, N. J., & Whipple, K. *Psychotherapy vs. behavior therapy*. Cambridge, Mass.: Harvard University Press, 1975.

Wachtel, P. L. *Psychoanalysis and behavior therapy: Toward an integration*. New York: Basic Books, 1977.

Weimer, W. B. Psycholinguistics and Plato's paradoxes of the *Meno*. *American Psychologist*, 1973, *28*, 15–33.

Weimer, W. B. Overview of a cognitive conspiracy: Reflections on the volume. In W. B. Weimer & D. S. Palermo (Eds.), *Cognition and the symbolic processes*. Hillsdale, N.J.: Lawrence Erlbaum, 1974.

Weimer, W. B. The psychology of inference and expectation: Some preliminary remarks. In G. Maxwell & R. M. Anderson, Jr. (Eds.), *Induction, probability, and confirmation. Minnesota studies in the philosophy of science* (Vol. 6). Minneapolis: University of Minnesota Press, 1975.

Weimer, W. B. A conceptual framework for cognitive psychology: Motor theories of the mind. In R. Shaw & J. Bransford (Eds.), *Perceiving, acting, and knowing: Toward an ecological psychology*. Hillsdale, N.J.: Lawrence Erlbaum, 1977. (a)

Weimer, W. B. Science as a rhetorical transaction: Toward a nonjustificational conception of rhetoric. *Philosophy and Rhetoric*, 1977, *10*, 1–29. (b)

Three Cognitive Psychologies and Their Implications

ULRIC NEISSER

What does cognitive theory have to offer a psychotherapist? The question is less straightforward than it sounds, because "cognitive theory" is not a single coherent set of ideas. It is hardly even a family of theories sharing common assumptions; at least, the family is deeply divided against itself. In the last few years it has become clear that there are at least three different approaches to the study of cognition, with quite different assumptions and implications. They are (1) the attempt to model cognition as a series of information-processing stages; (2) the "constructive" approach described and advocated by Arnkoff in the preceding article; (3) the hypothesis of perceptual realism first put forward by J. J. Gibson (1966, 1979). It is too early to say whether their differences will prove irreconcilable. I recently tried to reconcile (2) and (3), for example (Neisser, 1976), but I am not sure whether my attempt was successful. Whatever the ultimate outcome, there is no doubt that the present differences among cognitive psychologists are deep and serious. No review of the implications of cognitive theory can be complete without taking these differences into account.

ULRIC NEISSER • Department of Psychology, Cornell University, Ithaca, New York 14853.

Paradoxically, the most popular of the three views may be the one with the least to offer a clinically oriented reader. The information-processing approach, whose goal is the detailed experimental analysis of perception, memory, and thought, has curiously little to say about the kinds of experiences that bring patients to therapists. It is easy to understand why Arnkoff gave such short shrift to information processing in her review, and I have been tempted to ignore it here as well. Nevertheless it deserves at least a brief mention, simply because it dominates cognitive psychology today by every practical criterion: the number of its advocates, the profusion of relevant courses and textbooks, and the amount of published research. A reader of this volume who becomes interested in cognitive psychology and looks for new insights in contemporary cognitive journals will probably be disappointed. *Cognitive Psychology*, *Memory and Cognition*, *Cognitive Science*, and the several subseries of the *Journal of Experimental Psychology* include relatively few references to the construction of reality. Instead, they contain studies of short-term memory, visual information storage, list learning, recall of brief neutral paragraphs or stories, puzzle solving, and the like. In the great majority of these studies, the dependent variable is reaction time, measured in milliseconds. Their aim is to analyze the human cognitive system, conceived as a series of stages like those executed by a computer in the course of running a program. Typical theories of information processing include such stages as stimulus registration, very brief sensory persistence, short-term memory, and long-term memory; the stages are thought to be connected by various recoding processes and special strategies.

How is this hypothetical mechanism related to fear, fantasy, or insight? To life in society, human relations, achievement and failure, love and hate? These questions do not come up for information-processing psychology. It does not even address seemingly relevant problems like *repression* or *motivated perception*—an omission that Erdelyi and Goldberg (1979) find so striking as to demand a clinical explanation. And indeed, such an unswerving determination to model processes rather than to understand human nature must strike most outsiders as an odd substitute for doing psychology. There is no space here to speculate on the reasons for the current popularity of this enterprise. I can only say that while it will surely lead to a better understanding of the mechanisms of short-term memory sooner or later, it is unlikely to offer any significant insights into the human condition.

The status of the second approach to cognitive psychology is very different. The notion that individuals construct a model of reality and then are guided by that model makes immediate contact with every psychotherapist's experience. As Arnkoff says, it is "an accepted part of clinical lore." The notions of "deep structure," (at the rather casual metaphorical level employed by Arnkoff), "tacit knowledge," "asymmetry," and "paradigm" are equally easy to assimilate to clinical experience, and for that matter to Freudian conceptions of repression and defense. The current interest of some cognitive psychologists in the "schemata" from which people reconstruct remembered stories (e.g., Mandler & Johnson, 1977) or the "scripts" we have for frequently occurring events (Bower, Black, & Turner, 1978) would probably strike many clinicians as reasonable. They might wonder why the stories used in these experiments are so dull, the events so banal, and the analysis so empty of serious meaning, but perhaps those faults are temporary. The enterprise itself can hardly fail to find favor in their eyes, for it extends to all mankind the assumptions they already make about their own patients. When one has daily encounters with delusion, projection, hallucination, and denial, there seems little reason to dispute the constructive account of cognition.

As a former constructive theorist myself (Neisser, 1967), I am particularly aware of the easy rapport between that position and the traditional clinical assumptions. My own version of the claim that perceiving is "constructive" may have enjoyed a modest popularity among clinicians for that reason. I found this popularity gratifying at first, but my enthusiasm soon began to wane. For one thing, the cognitive notion of "construction" seemed to add very little to what clinicians already believed; it served more often as a rationalization than as a source of new insights. Moreover, it lends itself very readily to a kind of radical relativism, in which every perception and thought is as good as every other. If everyone's percepts are constructed, why are the therapist's constructions any more valid than the patient's? How can we distinguish sanity from insanity, truth from falsehood, or good from evil if all knowledge is of models in our heads rather than of the world itself? Of course no general theory can make such decisions for any particular case, but shouldn't there be some way to make them in principle?

The third approach to cognitive psychology may offer a solution to this dilemma. James J. Gibson (1966, 1979) has long insisted that perception is not a matter of processing, constructing, or recoding at all. The perceiver detects, or picks up, information that is objectively available to him. The "optic array" of structured light directly specifies what the environment is like, how it is laid out, and what possibilities for action it affords. Our perceptual systems have evolved so that they can pick up this objectively available information, just as our motor systems have evolved so they can move us around on the objectively existing terrain. Given the concept of evolution, how could it be otherwise? The organism does not need to "add meaning" to what it perceives, because the meaning of events is among their objective characteristics. A nearby object looks "reachable" because available information specifies that it is in fact within reach; a tiger looks dangerous because aspects of his appearance and movement objectively specify dangerousness, and these aspects are visible. To be sure, not all perceivers pick up all the available information; they could not, for it is infinite. Information pickup requires appropriate sensory systems and adequate perceptual skill; it is never complete. Nevertheless what *is* picked up is veridical, because the optic array specifies the real characteristics of the environment.

At first glance, Gibson's theory seems to be almost a mirror image of the constructive view presented before. Where that account had no way of describing truth, this one seems to leave no room for error; where constructivism gives the same account of hallucination as of perception, Gibson would make hallucination impossible and perception perfect. What can such a theory offer the psychotherapist? Very little, I think, if perception is taken as the model of all mental activity. If we treated all thinking, imagination, and fantasy as weak examples of objective information pickup, we would make no advance over the vague generalities of constructive theory. Indeed, we would be stuck with a much less plausible metaphor. Gibson himself sometimes talks as if he intended to generalize his theory in this unpromising way, but he may not mean it; in any case, we need not follow him so far.

Let us consider the hypothesis that perception and imagination are fundamentally different. Perceiving is a matter of picking up objectively available information that actually specifies something about the environment (e.g., that your father is angry). Imagination and fantasy grow out of perception (see Neisser, 1976, 1978 for details); they involve a readiness to perceive but no information pickup. Thus they can be, and often are, entirely inappropriate guides for action. You can *imagine* your father as angry when there is no objective basis for it at all. Now we see what therapists might do for patients: they can try to open their eyes, to substitute perception for imagination, information pickup for fantasy, adaptation for neurosis.

This is a more complicated account of cognition than either constructivism or perceptual realism taken alone. It brings up issues of truth and error: not all the patient's claims (or the therapist's) are on the same footing any more. Some may be based on accurate information pickup, others are pure fantasy, still others are complex combinations. It is always going to be difficult to sort them out, and even more difficult to help the patient so he can do more seeing and less imagining. (Of course I do not mean that all imagination is unhealthy—far from it. I am only considering the kinds of thinking that patients bring to therapy.) Difficult or not, however, it is necessary. Cognitive psychologists can afford the luxury of broad and sweeping claims, can insist that all cognition is constructive or alternately that it all consists of information pickup. Therapists and other people in real interpersonal situations have to make finer distinctions. It is only after we have distinguished construction from information pickup that we can hope to replace one with the other when it is appropriate to do so, and thus make Freud's prophecy come true: "Where Id is, there ego shall be."

REFERENCES

Bower, G. H., Black, J. B., & Turner, T. J. Scripts in memory for text. *Cognitive Psychology*. 1979, *11*, 177–220.

Erdelyi, M. H., & Goldberg, B. Let's not sweep repression under the rug: Towards a cognitive psychology of repression. In J. F. Kihlstrom & F. J. Evans (Eds.), *Functional Disorders of Memory*. Hillsdale, N.J.: Lawrence Erlbaum, 1979.

Gibson, J. J. *The senses considered as perceptual systems*. Boston: Houghton Mifflin, 1966.

Gibson, J. J. *An ecological approach to visual perception*. Boston: Houghton Mifflin, 1979.

Mandler, J. M., & Johnson, N. S. Remembrance of things parsed: Story structure and recall. *Cognitive Psychology*, 1977, *9*, 111–151.

Neisser, U. *Cognitive psychology*. New York: Appleton-Century-Crofts, 1967.

Neisser, U. *Cognition and reality*. San Francisco: Freeman, 1976.

Neisser, U. Anticipations, images, and introspection. *Cognition*, 1978, *6*, 169–174.

Psychotherapy and Philosophy of Science

Examples of a Two-Way Street in Search of Traffic

WALTER B. WEIMER

Traditional chapters purveying philosophy of science issues to clinical practitioners have been as boring as their influence has been ephemeral. Taking an attitude similar to the missionary bringing "the true religion" to the heathen, the philosopher or methodologist has often preached the gospel of "true scientific method" to the heathen clinician, pontificating in favor of adequate research design and inveighing against devils such as introspection, intuition, empathy, and the N of 1 in order to bring what are assumed to be methodological sinners to the salvation of respectable scientific conduct. For their part, clinicians have followed the time-honored approach of the South Seas islanders who wore flowers (at least on Sunday) to assuage their missionary's desire for clothing (once they had concluded that layers of black linen were not terribly practical in the tropics), both by suffering through their graduate school philosophy course and then dutifully thumbing through the occasional article of philosophical pretension in clinical literature.

And yet despite this, prominent clinicians acknowledge philosophical issues as central to their work. Why should *practicing* clinicans be led to

WALTER B. WEIMER • Department of Psychology, The Pennsylvania State University, University Park, Pennsylvania 16802.

philosophical and methodological problems? Does their therapy and research show a conversion to "true religion," or are the witch doctors learning to starch clerical collars when it "suits" their purposes? Further, why should anyone (specifically, either methodologists or clinicians) care? What can one learn about science by studying clinical practice? What can the clinician learn about therapy from the philosophy of science?

If one begins from the traditional logical empiricist philosophy of science in psychology then one learns nothing from the heathen, because such a philosopher already knows everything, and the only task is to convert; hence, the predominance of proselytizing literature. Alternatively, one might look at clinical practice as a case study in scientific methodology, to see if the methodologist can corroborate his general account or learn something new, and thus enrich a methodological picture so far painted without looking at clinical praxis.

I wish to argue that clinical practice not only instantiates several characteristics of scientific practice, but provides an excellent opportunity for their further study. Further, the clinical practitioner can learn much about his practice by studying recent developments in philosophy of science which repudiate the preachment of "true scientific method" that was so characteristic of logical positivism and empiricism, and one need not go overboard to "touchy feely" existentialism and guru-like humanism to do so. I shall attempt to make that two-sided argument primarily by exploring problems of complexity and tacit knowledge as both methodological and psychological phenomena that constrain our conception of both science and therapy. If we understand the ramifications of complex phenomena upon rationality, and recognize the centrality of tacit knowledge and awareness, then a repudiation of scientistic methodolatry follows automatically. With that done the way is clear to reconceptualize both science and therapy as fundamentally rhetorical processes that are primarily argumentative in nature. Once their communality is clearer the myriad problems facing an adequate conception of both therapy and methodology become more obvious, as does the extent to which the two-way street could profit both clinicians and methodologists if only it had more traffic.

RATIONALIST CONSTRUCTIVISM AND THE PRETENCE OF KNOWLEDGE

Complex Phenomena and the Relocation of Rationality

Seemingly everyone wants to make psychology into an "exact" and "rigorous" science, presumably modeled after (or perhaps even reduced to) physics and, say, molecular biology. These latter fields have achieved considerable success by explaining particular events by subsuming them to covering laws. When faced with increasing complexity of their domains, it has always been possible to refine the account to the point where precise specification, or prediction and control, reemerges. It has become part of the folklore of science that it is always possible to specify the prediction of particular events to any degree desired if one has an "exact" science. *Scientific rationality* has become identified with this quest for certainty and exact specification, and the poor social and behavioral sciences are looked down upon as errant children because they have not "grown up" like physics. Rationality in science is explicit: It has become identified with exact specification of particulars and precise prediction and control. Explanation is taken to be explanation of particular events by deductive subsumption under covering laws. The positivistic attitude has consistently attempted to reduce complex domains and phenomena to exact, rigorous, and explicitly rational specification. It is assumed that all the knowledge necessary for the understanding of a domain can be collected into a single body of laws, and that such information, in conjunction with statements of initial or boundary conditions for a particular situation under consideration both epitomize and exhaust the possibilities of scientific analysis. This position follows from an attitude that F. A. Hayek (1948, 1952a, 1967, 1978), called *rationalist constructivism*. Those of us who work in complex domains such as the psychological and social "sciences" are constantly indoctrinated with our failure to live up to the ideals of constructivist rationalism, and part of the willingness of the clinician to tolerate methodological diatribes is his or her guilt feelings about having "failed" to live up to snuff.

But have we failed, or has rationalist constructivism? I wish to argue that it is the latter, and that what constitutes scientific understanding in complex domains is vastly different from what we have been indoctrinated to desire. The economic and epistemological work of Hayek provides an example (sufficiently unfamiliar to psychologists to be valuable as an interdisciplinary endeavor) that both details failures of the rationalist constructivist account and points toward a more adequate methodology for complex phenomena. It is simply not rational to endorse the ideals of constructivist rationalism for psychology and clinical practice. Consider some of Hayek's arguments in this regard.

Consider first the ideal of explanation of the particular, and the related notion of a law of nature as a relationship between a few phenomena, linked by a simple relation such as cause and effect:

> In general, the physical sciences tend to assume that it will, in principle, always be possible to specify their predictions to any degree desired. . . .
>
> There is, however, no justification for the belief that it must always be possible to discover such simple regularities and that physics is more advanced because it has succeeded in doing this while other sciences have

not yet done so. It is rather the other way around: Physics has succeeded because it deals with phenomena which, in our sense, are simple. But a simple theory of phenomena which are in their nature complex (or one which, if that expression be preferred, has to deal with more highly organized phenomena) is probably merely of necessity false; at least without a specified *ceteris paribus* assumption, after the full statement of which the theory would no longer be simple. (Hayek, 1967, pp. 24–25)

This implies that science cannot be a search for "laws" as we usually assume:

We may well have achieved a very elaborate and quite useful theory about some kind of complex phenomenon and yet have to admit that we do not know of a single law, in the ordinary sense of the word, which this kind of phenomenon obeys. . . . It would then appear that the search for the discovery of laws is not an appropriate hallmark of scientific procedure but merely a characteristic of the theories of simple phenomena. . . . It would probably have saved much confusion if theoretical science had not in this manner come to be identified with the search for laws in the sense of a simple dependence of one magnitude upon another. . . . And the prejudice that in order to be scientific one must produce laws may yet prove to be one of the most harmful of methodological conceptions. (Hayek, 1967, p. 42)

Instead of a search for laws, theoretical science should be concerned with *patterns of regularity*, with explanation of the abstract, underlying principles rather than laws governing particulars. When we reach the levels of complexity exhibited by the evolution of life, the nervous system, social and cultural phenomena such as language, the economic order, and psychological adjustment, all we can hope to achieve is explanation of the principle. To pretend otherwise, that we possess in a single theory or body of knowledge sufficient information to explain particulars in complex systems is "the pretence of knowledge," Hayek's (1978) Nobel lecture theme. The constraints upon the nature of our knowledge of complex systems guarantee that theories in psychology and the social sciences will be argumentative structures that tell us how to see patterns, of abstract regularities, in phenomena. As N. R. Hanson (1970) said:

Scientifically understanding phenomena x, y, and z consists in perceiving what kinds of phenomena they are—how they relate one to the other within some larger epistemic context; how they are dependent upon, or interfere with, one another. Insights into such relations "out there" are generable within our perceptions of the structures of theories; these theoretical structures function vis-a-vis our linguistic references to x, y, and z in a way analogous to how the (artist's) scene stands to the tree and hill "out there" and also to the painted patches on canvas. Thus, I suggest that in contrast to the delineation of theories as "ideal languages" or "Euclidean hypothetico-deductive structures," the important function of scientific theory is to provide such structural representations of phenomena that to understand how the elements in the theoretical

representation "hang together" is to discover a way in which the facts of
the world "hang together." (p. 240)

Thus, "mere" explanation of the principle would appear to be all that
we can achieve for complex phenomena. It is not an accident or an indica-
tion of immaturity that evolutionary theory or, say, economics have not sur-
passed explanation of abstract, underlying principles in favor of explanation
of particulars. As Hayek (1967) noted:

> The theoretical understanding of the growth and functioning of organisms
> can only in the rarest of instances be turned into specific predictions of
> what will happen in a particular case, because we can hardly ever as-
> certain all the facts which will contribute to determine the outcome. . . .
> But we know that, *if* the mechanism is the same, the observed structures
> must be capable of showing some kinds of action and unable to show
> others; and if, and so long as, the observed phenomena keep within the
> range of possibilities indicated as possible, that is so long as our expecta-
> tions derived from the (theoretical) model are not contradicted, there is
> good reason to regard the model as exhibiting the principle at work in the
> more complex phenomenon. . . . Our conclusions and predictions will also
> refer only to some properties of the resulting phenomenon, in other
> words, to a *kind* of phenomenon rather than to a particular event. (pp.
> 33, 15)

If one understands the argument thus far, it becomes obvious that both
the operation of complex phenomena *and our understanding of them* is
much more tacit than the constructivist rationalist account can allow. The
tacit dimension of understanding is fairly obvious in that what we can know
in scientific theory are the abstract principles of determination according to
which a complex system operates while we must remain ignorant of the
details of particular states of the system. This has been easier to
comprehend since the advent of the computer, as it is now well known that
not even the designers or programmers can tell what steps a computer is
taking at a given time. The programmer is perfectly aware of the abstract
principles of determination (the program) governing the computer's solution
to a problem, but the only way to tell the particular state of the machine at
any given time is to "kill" and dissect it. This might be possible in principle
for computers, but it is a moral and practical impossibility for living
organisms (such as clients in therapy). It is interesting to note that in the
domain of the very small, the Heisenberg indeterminacy principle prevents
one from ever specifying the exhaustive particulars of even the (relatively)
simple (in the nonpejorative sense of less complex) physical realm. Thus, the
tacit dimension of the functioning of "physical" systems is well enough
known to require little comment.

The tacit dimension of *social* systems is another issue, however. Here
the constructivist rationalist myth is far more powerful, and the idea that
social systems that are consciously (*read*: rationally) planned must

inevitably be superior to spontaneously developed systems is widespread. Modern social, political, and economic philosophers have assumed that man could consciously and explicitly create a better system (social, political, or economic) than could possibly arise tacitly (*read*: by chance). The result has been the rise of socialism and collectivism, with the guiding notion that centralized planning is superior to and can correct the insufficiencies in spontaneously developed systems. Although cruder earlier forms of such doctrines (such as Marxist historicism) are acknowledged to be deficient, this is clearly the era of "planned" interventionism (and the bigger, seemingly, the better) in all phases of social life, as instanced in Keynesian economics, labor unions, party politics, even (and especially) governmental regulation of employment and education, etc. The idea of intervention (and now is the time to remember that therapy is universally regarded as intervention) is directly based upon the constructivist rationalist ideal of the superiority of planned control by centralized, rational agents. It is time to ask whether that ideal is worthy of our efforts, and not surprisingly, the answer is "No."

Consider Hayek's alternative:

> That we should not be able fully to shape human affairs according to our wishes went much against the grain of generations which believed that by the full use of his reason man could make himself fully master of his fate. It seems, however, that this desire to make everything subject to rational control, far from achieving the maximal use of reason, is rather an abuse of reason based on a misconception of its powers, and in the end leads to a destruction of that free interplay of many minds on which the growth of reason nourishes itself. True rational insight seems, indeed, to indicate that one of the most important uses is the recognition of the proper limits of rational control. . . . Since our whole life consists in facing ever new and unforeseeable circumstances, we cannot make it orderly by deciding in advance all the particular actions we shall take. The only manner in which we can, in fact, give our lives some order is to adopt certain abstract rules or principles for guidance, and then strictly adhere to the rules we have adopted in our dealing with the new situations as they arise. Our actions form a coherent and a rational pattern, not because they have been decided upon as part of a single plan thought out before hand, but because in each successive decision we limit our range of choice by the same abstract rules. (1967, pp. 93, 90)

To put the problem in another framework, the problem with centralization is its authoritarian basis, and this leads to a justificationist position in either philosophy or social theory. In order to be more effective than the spontaneous factors it is to supersede, the central authority must inevitably take on the role of an ultimate—either epistemological or social—foundation of knowledge, power, and authority, and the well-known problem of a retreat to commitment in one or another *ad hoc* results. As Bartley (1962) noted, we must change the political question from "Who should rule? to:

How can we best arrange our political institutions so as to get rid of bad rulers when they appear, or at least restrict the amount of harm they can do?" (pp. 136–137). The answer Hayek proposed is that we must be governed by the abstract rule of law rather than the whim of momentary legislation directed to a particular problem. Hayek's master work of political philosophy is the three volumes of *Law, Legislation, and Liberty* (1973, 1976, in press). His main theme may be (drastically) simplified to the catch phrase that liberty is obtainable only by our willingness to be governed by the abstract rule of law rather than specific legislation. When legislation of particulars (red tape) rules, chaos and the loss of freedom and liberty results.

Let me develop the point in yet a third manner. Hayek reasons analogously to Polanyi (especially, 1966) in arguing for the primacy of tacit knowledge and organization both within the individual and in the organization of society. Just as our psychological abilities are always tacit in origin, and the conscious control we sometimes exert over them a thin veneer over unconscious principles of determination, the very nature of social phenomena is tacit:

> Any social processes which deserve to be called "social" in distinction to the action of individuals are almost *ex definitione* not conscious. Insofar as such processes are capable of producing a useful order which could not have been produced by conscious direction, any attempt to make them subject to such direction would necessarily mean that we restrict what social activity can achieve to the inferior capacity of a single mind. (Hayek, 1952a, pp. 87–88)

Thus, collectivization and centralization of particulars can, paradoxically, lose the information that is available in a social system: "The fact that no single mind can know more than a fraction of what is known to all individual minds sets limits to the extent to which conscious direction can improve upon the results of unconscious social processes. Man has not deliberately designed this process and has began to understand it only long after it had grown up" (Hayek, 1952a, p. 100).

But what exactly is the problem that constructivist rationalist planning and centralization was to address, and what alternative mechanisms are available for its solution? The problem is how to maximally utilize our resources. This is really a matter of how all the possible momentary "knowledge of the particular" possessed by individuals can be most effectively used. Since no single authority or locus of control can possess enough knowledge of the particular in a complex system to succeed, Hayek argues for *individualism over collectivism:*

> A successful solution can, therefore, not be based on the authority dealing directly with the objective facts, but must be based on a method of utilizing the knowledge dispersed among all members of society, knowledge of

which in any particular instance the central authority will usually know
neither who possesses it nor whether it exists at all. It can, therefore, not
be utilized by consciously integrating it into a coherent whole, but only
through some mechanism which will delegate the particular decisions to
those who possess it, and for that purpose supply them with such information about the general situation as will enable them to make the best use
of the particular circumstances of which only they know.

    This is precisely the function which the various "markets" perform.
(Hayek, 1952a, p. 99)

The problem of maximal utilization of information can be handled by
the market because it is a knowledge transmitting system, "an instrument
for communicating to all those interested in a particular commodity the
relevant information in an abridged and condensed form. . . . (Markets)
help to utilize the knowledge of many people without the need of first
collecting it in a single body" (Hayek, 1952a, p. 99). Thus, the market functions as a social system precisely because it decentralizes decisions and
militates against any single locus of control. The problem that it has arisen
to solve (*not*: was designed to solve) concerns how we may make maximal
use of our tacit and particular knowledge and skill, *not* how to make the
tacit component explictly rational: "The problem is precisely how to extend
the span of our utilization of resources beyond the span of the control of
any one mind; and, therefore, how to dispense with the need of conscious
control and how to provide inducements which will make the individuals do
the desired things without anyone having to tell them what to do" (Hayek,
1952a, p. 88).

Let us take stock for a moment. I have been arguing that the
rationalist constructivist ideals of scientific practice, specifically the quest
for "exact" explanation of the particulars, the superiority of consciously
(rationally) controlled and centralized planning, and the "explicit" conception of scientific rationality, are unobtainable in those domains that deal
with complex phenomena. To foist those ideals upon the social and
psychological sciences in the name of "rigorous science" is to confuse scientific methodology with scientistic methodolatry.

In arguing for methodological individualism and nonjustificational
research methodologies one argues both for and against various positions.
One caveat that should be noted at this point is that we can argue against
scientism and inappropriate methodologies in psychology without automatically endorsing the traditional "muddle-headed" and "soft" alternatives to "hard-headed" positivistic positions. Specifically, the alleged
alternatives represented in the "rigorous humanism" of Rychlak (1977), the
phenomenological perspective associated with the Duquesne series (Georgi,
1970), and the various ephemeral fashions in existentialist approaches are if
anything more glaringly deficient and self-stultifying than their behavioristic
opposition. To state why in terminology that is fully spelled out elsewhere
(Weimer, 1979), these "soft" approaches, despite their laudable concern for

and attempt to reintroduce humanism and personal values into psychology, are inevitably skeptical justificationist alternatives to "positive" justificationism rather than repudiations of the metatheory itself. What the clinician needs to be made cognizant of is that there is an alternative available to both the traditional hard- and soft-headed positions that glut the literature. One need neither suffer under clerical collars nor suffer sunburn from naked frolic on the sand.

Excursus: Scientism, Rationalist Constructivism, and Methodolatry in the Study of Man

Let me be very explicit in noting the pervasive presence and power of the conception of rationality and scientific method that Hayek and I oppose. It is the "received view" doctrine in virtually every area of modern thought. Constructivist rationalism affects social science methodology and research praxis in a double-pronged manner; first by asserting that no system is rational or scientific unless it is subject to explicit rational control and conscious direction, and second, by asserting that science has a method, or a means of acquiring knowledge (so called inductive method or hypothetico-inductive method) which leads to a sufficient knowledge of particular circumstances to ensure that the constructivist rationalist ideal is met (i.e., to ensure that we possess enough knowledge to predict and control in the particular instance). Scientific understanding of a domain is equated with the achievement of the constructivist rationalist ideal of explicit predictive ability and knowledge of particulars that seemed to be available in classical physics. Thus Bertrand Russell (1931), to many the epitome of 20th century scientific philosophy, was merely echoing the folklore of scientific man when he said "no society can be regarded as fully scientific unless it has been created deliberately with a certain structure to fulfill certain purposes" (p. 211).

This sentiment is now common place in psychology. B. F. Skinner, perhaps the loudest advocate of "The Scientific Method," often claims that "man is able, and now as never before, to lift himself up by his own bootstrap" (1955–1956, p. 49). Anyone familiar with *Beyond Freedom and Dignity* and his recent writings for the popular press can think of examples which carry this theme of explicit control and conscious planning of man and society into areas that George Orwell never dreamed of. Similarly, Kenneth B. Clark (1971) in his APA presidential address, called for psychology to live up to the ideal of constructivist rationalism by creating a crash program to develop "that kind of scientific, biochemical intervention which could stabilize and make dominant the moral and ethical propensities of man and subordinate, if not eliminate, his negative and primitive behavioral tendencies" (pp. 10).

Even though it smacks of arguing against apple pie, motherhood, and above all, the great American way of doing things, I must point out that even if the constructivist rationalist's goals were achievable (which, thankfully, they are not), the results would be disastrous rather than beneficial. Such views exhibit what Hayek called "the pretense of knowledge" rather than an understanding of science, an *abuse* of reason rather than the use of it. They epitomize, in other words, what he called *scientism* (Hayek, 1952a) rather than science. The traditional philosophy and methodology of research that is available to clinicians proposes *scientistic methodolatry* instead of an adequate scientific methodology for complex phenomena, and it is the implicit understanding of the inadequacy of scientism that results in the clinician wearing flowers like the South Seas natives.

Scientism is "an attitude which is decidely unscientific in the true sense of the word, since it involves a mechanical and uncritical application of habits of thought to fields different from those in which they have been formed. The scientistic as opposed to the scientific view is not an unprejudiced but a very prejudiced approach which, before it has considered its subject, claims to know what is the most appropriate way of investigating it" (Hayek, 1952a, pp. 15–16). It is the tresspass of scientism into the study of society which Hayek regards as *the counterrevolution of science*, the attempt to make the complex phenomena of man and society fit the model of science which the positivists assumed was represented by classical physics. Scientism literally is an *attitude*, very prevalent in technologically minded culture, "to prefer a deliberately created orderly arrangement to the results of spontaneous growth" (Hayek, 1978, p. 295). It is an attitude that attempts to distill the essence of things into as few preformed categories as possible, to ignore the richness and variability of individual circumstances in favor of common features which can be subtracted from them. In practice, it leads to ignoring anything which cannot be easily quantified, and to reliance upon statistical instead of theoretical understanding.

Scientism invariably originates from and returns to the metatheoretical framework I have stigmatized as justificationism (see, e.g., Weimer, 1979). Scientism simply *assumes* that definite knowledge is obtainable by specifiable procedures that, when followed, yield justified assertions. Unfortunately, that assumption is erroneous: justificationist knowledge, and hence its conception of rationality and testability in science, cannot be obtained; the system is self-stultifying, leading inevitably to either skepticism or abject conventionalism (both of which deny the possibility of informative scientific knowledge). This is why those theorists who are very scientistic and postivistic in their explicit methodology invariably are led to despair in the few candid instances when they reflect upon the rationality of their particular methodology—according to their own criteria they have no rational defense, and endorse their position fideistically, as a matter of dog-matic faith, in what Bartley (1962) aptly called a *retreat to commitment* (see Weimer, 1979, especially, pp. 28–31).

Methodologically, the first insuperable problem is that there is no justified logic of scientific inference. No one has succeeded in rescuing inference procedures (scientific "methods") from the skeptical doubts of Hume. The positive method that was assumed to be the glory of classical physics has been chimerical for two centuries, since David Hume devastated the attempts to justify induction (see Popper, 1959; Maxwell, 1975; Weimer, 1975). Unfortunately, this has not been a sufficient time for the information to filter down to the social sciences, and we are still faced with the vestigial remains of the most scientistic methodology ever proposed: Skinnerian behaviorism. Fortunately, there has been renewed interest, both in philosophy and psychology, in alternatives to justificationist conceptions of science, and the views of, e.g., Karl Popper (1959, 1963) and Thomas Kuhn (1970, 1977) are beginning to counteract the excesses of positivism and scientism. Some psychologists have even suggested that we could look at scientists and their practice as objects of psychological inquiry (e.g., Mahoney, 1976), to perhaps begin a theory of concept formation and knowledge acquisition rather than to pontificate in advance about what science must be like. When such studies are seriously undertaken, there will be little likelihood that the field will continue to be taken in by the scientistic substitution of exactness and symbolic precision, and the chimerical quest for a "rigorous" and "exact science" of psychology will be seen for what it is: the confusion of scientism for science.

One thing to note is that the clinician, in virtue of his or her familiarity with the problems of working with clients as individuals, is in a unique position to contribute to the understanding of science by studying the scientist. One of the most familiar problems of contemporary methodology is the discrepancy between preachment and practice in a scientist's behavior. The conscious, *ex post facto* rationalization which a scientist provides in answer to the query "How do you do science?" often bears only faint resemblance to his or her research practice. A background in clinical practice would be invaluable for a methodologist interested in unraveling the tacit knowledge which guides a researcher's practice. A similar study of the successful clinical practitioner by the methodologist would be equally invaluable.

THE TACIT DIMENSION IN SCIENCE AND SOCIETY

Tacit Knowledge in Science and Psychology

Ordinarily, science proceeds as a skilled performance in which the practitioner is unaware of the particulars of his or her behavior. Performance is regarded as skilled to the extent that it is practiced, and thus tacit and automatic rather than conscious and explicit. Paradoxically, it is the *breakdown* of skilled performance which is associated with explicit awareness and conscious control, and the conscious self that we normally regard as "rationally" arranging our performances is not the *planner* of skilled action but rather an *improvisor* engaged in after the fact adjustment and rationalization.

Such improvisation by the conscious self, even if it produces a successful adjustment, may not provide any information about the underlying tacit organization that produced it. This is one reason why the history of science is full of highly skilled scientists whose explicit methodological prescriptions are totally incapable of accounting for their own skilled performance. The classic example is Newton, who not only fudged data to make it square with his expectations but sincerely believed his famous "Hypotheses non fingo."

Skilled performance, whether in the practice of science or in everyday life (such as Polanyi's 1958, 1966 example of recognizing a face, or a clinician recognizing a problem in a client) presents the same problem: we possess skills that our explicit awareness and rationality are utterly incapable of explaining, describing to others, or improving upon. Such performance by the individual, like that of the marketplace, is the result of human action but not design. To the constructivist rationalist, such phenomena, no matter how skillful, must be regarded as "unscientific" and "irrational."

When more charitably construed, such performances are labeled paradoxical, as witness the historical furor raised by Plato's paradoxes of learning and remembering in the *Meno* (see Weimer, 1973). The marketplace presents a similar paradoxical situation. The mere presence of a buyer (who wants to purchase for the lowest possible price) in the market tends to drive prices upward (because of increased demand), while the presence of a seller (who wants the highest possible price) lowers the price (due to increasing the supply). Thus, both buyers and sellers work against their own interests in entering the marketplace. Or do they? Quite likely not, for unless both buyers and sellers change their demands to meet the momentary market conditions, both will go home empty handed, with no sale taking place. The paradox results more from a false rationalist constructivist premise (that the individual, rather than the market, is the ultimate determiner of gain or loss) than any flaw in the dynamics of the marketplace.

A comparable "paradox" has fascinated me in clinical praxis. Good therapy can be done by clinicians whom we would assess as being at least as poorly adjusted as their clients. How could it be that someone who is not well-adjusted themselves could aid others to adjust? What may be an alternative formulation of the same situation is the observation that clinicians who are skilled practitioners rarely can explain to others how they achieve their results, and good "academic" clinicians seem to be poor performers in actual therapy. It appears that either one can be highly skilled in therapy praxis and not know explicitly what one is doing, or one can be skilled theoretically (in explicit, or after the fact, rationalization) and fail in practice.

What such situations demonstrate is the enormous gulf between explicit knowledge and rationality, on one hand, and the infinitely more skilled tacit substratum that underlies explicit awareness. The problem faced in understanding scientific practice, clinical treatment, and indeed the nature of the client, therapist, and scientist is all the same: we must characterize the abstract principles of determination that constitute the tacit organization of the nervous system, and then relate that deep structural theory of the organism to the behavior we observe at the surface level. We need a theory of the complex phenomenon that is man, one capable of acknowledging that we can occasionally be explicitly conscious and rational even though our primary mode of organization is implicit and tacit. We need to understand what Hayek has called the primacy of the abstract in not only social affairs but also the organization of the individual.

The Primacy of the Abstract

Recent developments in several fields have clarified the nature of the cognitive apparatus of man, what we commonly call "mind," and its manner of functioning. Although their particular form varies from field to field certain issues recur throughout the psychological and social sciences, and the commonality of recent accounts has forced an acknowledgment of what may be called the primacy of the abstract in each. Persistent problems in linguistics, psychology, even philosophy have emphasized the primacy of tacit rules of determination that apply general classificatory operations, often recursively, to generate the vast richness of phenomenal experience and diversity of human action. In each case the moral is the same: abstract principles operating at a deep-structural level have an explanatory and indeed ontological primacy over surface-structure particulars.

Consider the revolution in linguistics occasioned by Chomsky's development of transformational grammar. In order to account for the productivity or creativity of language, the ability to make infinite use of finite means in the production and comprehension of novel utterances, Chomsky was forced to postulate the presence of generatively very powerful principles of determination operating at an abstract level from which the surface structure of language is derived. Transformational grammars emphasize the primacy of the abstract by making the surface–deep distinction, focusing upon the recursive or iterative nature of the application of rules in the generation of behavior, and by the conceptual argument against the adequacy of any surface mechanism or analysis to account for the senses in which language is a productive system. These arguments are now well enough known to require only casual mention, and Bandler and Grinder (1975) have made beginning application of these ideas to clinical practice.

In physiological psychology the picture is similar. The brain's control of motor activity is in terms of abstract underlying functional properties of the *consequences* of actions rather than in the determination of particular muscular activities. The cortex is totally ignorant of the specifics of behavior—it is concerned only with abstract action patterns that could be realized equally well by an indefinite number of muscular activities. A massive literature, partially summarized in Eccles (1973), Pribram (1971a,b) and Turvey (1977), details the extent to which the central nervous system (CNS) is concerned only with broad patterns of behavior, dispositions to respond rather than responses, specifiable only in terms of the functions which the acts effect. As Pribram (1971b) summarized, "the brain need not keep track of the rhythms of contraction and relaxation of individual muscles necessary to achieve an act any more than the thermostat needs to keep track of the turnings on and off of the furnace, the encoding problem is immensely simplified—only end states need to be specified" (pp. 16–17).

The same story reappears in cognition: perception and memory, the two areas most thoroughly studied, show that these skills can have the characteristics we observe in them only if they range over fundamentally abstract entities at a deep-structural level, and utilize generative rules of determination that are never visible at the surface level. Our perceptual knowledge, for example, is based upon abstract rules of "seeing" that pick up the invariant aspects of our environment and the group theoretic transformations that are applicable to them (see Weimer, 1977a). Memory, especially as studied by Bransford and his associates (see Bransford & McCarrell, 1974; Bransford, McCarrell, Franks, & Nitsch, 1977) is a matter of the active, ongoing modulation of information rather than the retrieval of particulars. All of what we refer to as cognition appears to depend upon the operation of tacit, abstract rules that determine what we can perceive, conceive, or do according to functional specifications that have been laid down for us in advance by the evolutionary development of our species and our cultural matrix. The "motor theory" approach to cognition that I have argued for (see Weimer, 1977a) is merely a generalization and exploration of the ramifications of that position.

Even the developments in the philosophy of science that repudiate the inductive inference, learning-from-particulars model so familiar from the positivists can be interpreted in similar fashion. Karl Popper and his associates argue against a logic of induction that would grind out (in what Popper stigmatized as "Sausage Machine Science") scientific theories when fed factual particulars because the very determination of a "fact" presupposes the presence of a theory. Similarly, Thomas Kuhn emphasizes the extent to which learning in science is a matter of assimilating tacit knowledge of great generalizability when the researcher explores exemplary puzzles. Michael Polanyi emphasized the extent to which science depends upon skills that can be demonstrated but not taught by explicit methodology, and that defy explicit analysis. These developments in philosophy point to the same conclusion that arises in psychology: our tacit "heads" are far smarter than and are the source of all the powers of our explicit, conscious heads.

We can sum this up in this passage from Hayek's (1978) essay, from which this section heading is taken:

> The primary characteristic of an organism is a capacity to govern its actions by rules which determine the properties of its particular movements; ... in this sense its actions must be governed by abstract categories long before it experiences conscious mental processes, and what we call mind is essentially a system of such rules conjointly determining particular actions. ... We ought to regard what we call mind as a system of abstract rules of action (each 'rule' defining a class of actions) which determines each action by a combination of several such rules; while every appearance of a new rule (or abstraction) constitutes a change in that system, something which its own operations cannot produce but which is brought about by extraneous factors. (pp. 42–43)

At this point it is incumbent upon the clinician to assimilate the primacy of the abstract into therapy in a more effective manner than the hints that have so far been offered in, e.g., Kelly's (1955) personal construct theory. The chapter in this volume by Arnkoff is one step in this direction, incorporating aspects of Hayek's theoretical psychology (largely in *The Sensory Order*, 1952b), the constructive approach to memory of Bransford, and even rhetoric. Rather than repeat that material here, let me conclude this section by emphasizing one aspect of the primacy of the abstract which debilitates rationalist constructivist accounts, and which forces the redirection of therapy—the inability of conscious direction to form new abstract rules of determination directly. The problem the therapist inevitably faces is "that the formulation of a new abstraction seems *never* to be the outcome of a conscious process, not something at which the mind can deliberately aim, but always a discovery of something which *already* guides its operation (Hayek, 1978, p. 46)." As Leibniz indicated in the *Monadology*, all of what we call knowledge is *a priori*—it consists in our gradual realization of information which is already present in the unconscious processes constituting our tacit mind. If therapy is ever to be effective it must constitute procedures capable of tapping the abstract rules which literally are the client's mind, and redirecting their activity so that a better attunement between the client and his environment results. How this could be done remains a very real problem (one tentative solution is sketched in the next section). Let us conclude this section, however, with a look at the tacit dimension of social organization.

Social Organization and the Implicit Regulation of Behavior

It is a common place that society is filled with regulations and prohibitions that pertain to the conduct of its members. It is also a common desire among rationalist constructivists that these "superstitious" forms of control should be replaced by explicitly rational ones, and that the negatives (inhibitory rules, taboos, or 'thou shalt nots') should give way to positive rules which direct individuals to achieve certain ends. The Skinnerian desire to control behavior by positive reinforcement of rationally approved aims instead of punishing undesirable behavior is a typical example of both attitudes. But what is the relationship between the conduct of individual members and their social structure? Is there a useful function served by those negatives and prohibitions, or can we dispense with them? I wish to argue that in a complex system in which the consequences of action cannot be delimited in advance we cannot dispense with such norms, and that even though our present ones are the result of human action but not design, they nevertheless are more effective than those proposed by the constructivists.

The society in which we live has evolved: the evolutionary selection of rules of conduct operates through the viability of the social order that it produces—if the resultant order is stable and productive, the rules will be selected for survival. Thus, the system of rules of conduct must develop as a whole, and the individual will have little awareness of anything beyond specifics. At each stage of development, the overall prevailing order determines what effect, if any, changes in the individual's conduct will produce. We can judge and modify our conduct only within a framework which, although the product of gradual evolution, remains for us a relatively fixed result of evolution. Thus, in summarizing to ourselves the effects of the social system upon individual conduct, we arrive at a set of particular descriptions of conduct, largely in terms of prohibitions to action, which instantiate abstract rules of which we are unaware either of their formulation, effect, or survival value. We are like the primitive studied by the anthropologist: "the individual may have no idea what this overall order is that results from his observing such rules as those concerning kinship and intermarriage, or the succession to property, or which function this overall order serves. Yet all the individuals of the species which exist will behave in that manner because groups of individuals which have thus behaved have displaced those which did not do so" (Hayek, 1967, p. 70).

What this leads to is an inversion of the cause and effect relationship between the society as a whole and its individual members. The complex structure will exist because the individuals, who were selected by an earlier stage in the complex structure, do what is necessary to secure its continuation. The system is avowedly teleological, even though there is no single creator or designer for whom the system exists. This is the sense in which Adam Smith, in the *Wealth of Nations*, said that man "is led to promote an end which is no part of his intentions" (p. 421). Subsequent writers, assuming that if a man does not promote his own individual ends he must promote those of another agent or planner, misinterpreted this teleological structuring of action into "final cause" accounts that are today rightly in disrepute. One should not interpret the social rules of conduct that result from our actions but not designs either anthropomorphically or animistically.

It is much more plausible to regard the frequent prohibitions to action as a result of our partial knowledge of the regularities of our world in combination with a fear of the unknown. Norms appear to be an adaptation to factual regularities that are relatively dependable only when we obey those norms. (Once such norms are deliberately taught, however, it is almost always in animistic terms, associated with the will of the mentor or some supernatural agency.) We tend to choose between alternatives on the basis of our knowledge of their consequences, preferring those that are known and relatively predictable to those which are unknown, unpredictable, and consequently frightening. As Hayek (1967) remarked,

> Taboos or negative rules acting through the paralyzing action of fear will, as a kind of knowledge of what *not* to do, constitute just as significant information about the environment as any positive knowledge of the attitudes of the objects of this environment. While the latter enables us to predict the consequences of particular actions, the former just warns us not to take certain kinds of action. At least so long as the normative rules consist of prohibitions, as most of them probably did before they were interpreted as commands of another will, the 'Thou shalt not' kind of rule may after all not be so very different from the rules giving us information about what is. (p. 81)

So long as the world in which we live is not completely known to us (and therefore predictable), the culturally transmitted prohibitions to action have considerable survival value both for the individual and society. It would appear that we should attempt to increase our tolerance for ambiguity rather than attempt the replacement of prohibitions merely because we do not understand how they arose or what function they serve. Rather than cultivating an already familiar and secure niche in which there is little possibility of learning anything new, it would be more adaptive if we continued to venture out into the unknown, which although frightening, is the source of whatever progress mankind has made.

SCIENCE AS A RHETORICAL TRANSACTION

Let us attempt to relate some of Hayek's insight into the unique effectiveness of the marketplace as a knowledge transmission and utilization system, the primacy of the abstract and the motor theoretic approach to cognition and tacit knowing, and the methodology of science. What we need to draw out is that both the tacit dimension of scientific creativity and research and the effectiveness of individual knowledge and insight in particular circumstances is better addressed in a framework which construes science as a matter of rhetoric than one which looks for a logic in methodology.

Traditionally, rhetoric was concerned with the persuasive techniques that increase adherence in an audience to discourse that could not be "rigorously" proven to be true by the pure light of logic alone, or logic in combination with scientific "method" (so called dialectic) (see Weimer, 1977b). It was assumed that rhetoric was a second-rate discipline in two respects: first, it was of value only when apodictic proof was unavailable (logical proof, of course, was supposed to make the truth manifest to all who would look upon it, with no need for persuasion or "flattery"), and second, because it dealt with the vicissitudes of adherence and persuasion *in the given case* (rather than applying, as an infallible method, to all cases). Thus, rhetoric was often relegated to the study of persuasion and flattery, and the techniques by which a skilled orator or writer could sway in audience in their favor when "real proof" was lacking.

Rhetoric has lost its second-class citizenship, and gained a central role in both epistemology and methodology, with the realization that knowledge is (both in its nature and its acquisition) a matter of argumentation rather than "proof." It has become clearer that proof in logic and mathematics is only one form of argumentative structure, and that other argumentative structures or patterns of inference are more common in the empirical sciences. This has come about largely as a by-product of the realization that all science is primarily theoretical, even in factual attribution and description. What we do in describing reality "as we see it" is to argue that that is the way it is, and indeed that it must be that way. Our theories are conceptual structures that tell us that nature must be seen (or conceived) in a certain way, and not in others. Scientific revolutions change the conceptual scheme, and normal science, as a puzzle-solving tradition which holds theoretical considerations in abeyance, fleshes out the content according to the dominant vision at the time.

Thomas Kuhn's (1970) monograph, *The Structure of Scientific Revolutions*, can be viewed as an extended argument in favor of the rhetorical nature of science. Kuhn points out that science is intrinsically a social phenomenon, involving the individual researcher in a community of investigators bound together by a shared matrix of values. Insofar as agreement prevails, as in normal science based upon the exploration of exemplary puzzles, it is due to the scientific community's acceptance of the utility and suasory power of a certain vision of nature. When disagreement about fundamentals occurs, as in the conflict of frameworks during a scientific revolution, allegiance to a paradigm becomes explicitly rhetorical, as comments such as this make clear:

> Nothing about that relatively familiar thesis [that theory choice is not susceptible to proof] implies either that there are no good reasons for being persuaded or that those reasons are not ultimately decisive for the group. . . . If two men disagree, for example, about the relative fruitfulness of their theories, or if they agree about that but disagree about the relative importance of fruitfulness and, say, scope in reaching a choice, neither can be convicted of a mistake. Nor is either being unscientific. . . . To understand why science develops as it does, one need not unravel the details of biography and personality that lead each individual to a particular choice, though that topic has vast fascination. What one must understand, however, is the manner in which a particular set of shared values interacts with the particular experiences shared by a community of specialists to ensure that most members of the group will ultimately find one set of arguments rather than another decisive. (Kuhn, 1970, p. 199–200)

The last sentence summarizes the function of rhetoric in science: rhetoric provides a framework for the explanation of decisions that result from the argumentative use of discourse and action, in both revolutionary reconceptualization and in normal science practice. In both cases scientists face arguments, in print and in experimentation, rather than either objective "data" or "proof."

The same point emerges when one considers the relationship of rhetoric and rationality. The *comprehensively critical rationalism* (formulated by Bartley, 1962) that I have defended at length (see especially Weimer, 1979) makes rationality a matter of holding all of one's beliefs subject to critical assessment, and the possibility of modification or wholesale revision, at all times. Rationality is a matter of being critical *whenever necessary*, in the given case. This makes rationality a rhetorical phenomenon, in both its essential formulation and its practical pursuit. Criticism, as the essence of rationality, is a rhetorical process that never seeks final form or ultimate proof. Instead it seeks to articulate and assess the merits of a position within its unique context, and both the nature of the position and the form of criticism are likely to change as a result of that articulation and assessment.

Thus, we have come to realize that argument is fundamental to knowledge. A knowledge claim argues for one possible position to the exclusion of others. Insofar as man is engaged in the acquisition of knowledge (in either science or ordinary life) he is engaged in argumentation and persuasion. Thus *man as knower* is intrinsically a rhetorical creature. As Campbell (1975) put it:

> Unless one is willing to argue that the [scientific] statement includes everything that could conceivably be said, and said from every conceivable vantage point—unless one is willing to argue that—one must grant that what has been told is a partial story. And the partial story told is obviously one that is advocated, for it is senseless to choose a certain story about a certain object/event and to claim at the same time that some other story is preferable. Hence, by definition, the scientific statement is rhetorical. (p. 393)

An analogous argument can be made for the psychological adjustment of the individual to his environment. Unless one wishes to argue that an individual's perspective includes everything that can possibly be said about himself or herself and the environment, then it must be admitted that that perspective is partial, and therefore one advocated by the individual and hence rhetorical. The finitude of the human situation, in other words, makes man a fundamentally rhetorical and suasory animal, not only in science but in daily life as well.

SOME IMPLICATIONS FOR THERAPY

Although the argument thus far has several points of contact for the individual clinician, it is worth emphasizing two major implications of the general framework. First, let me reemphasize that therapy cannot be construed as intervention according to constructivist rationalist principles; second, the social rather than individual or biological nature of adjustment must never be lost sight of. Consider these points in that order.

Therapy as a Rhetorical Transaction Rather Than Constructivist Intervention

One of the most persistent problems of self-doubt and perceived inadequacy in the apprentice clinician arises when a client behaves unexpectedly, i.e., in a manner which the "theory" and praticum experience of the apprentice cannot address. Their training has created in them the impression that there are specific procedures, or algorithms, that will inevitably be effective if only they are skillful enough to recognize when to apply them, and then do so correctly. Being dutiful normal science practitioners, they invariably blame themselves rather than question the brand of therapy they are attempting to practice. Sometimes a few will question some aspect of theory, but none ever get to the point of questioning the rationalist constructivist ideal of therapy as intervention with an algorithm.

But if therapy is viewed as a rhetorical transaction between the therapist and client, in which all the available means of persuasion are to be applied to the situation at hand, it should not be surprising that the therapist will often be confronted with situations for which there is no algorithm (in either diagnosis or treatment). At this point one should not despair the lack of a formula, but rather structure the situation so that tacit knowledge and intuition can be brought to bear. These long forgotten remarks of Freud on how to practice therapy should be kept in mind:

> the technique, . . . disclaims the use of any special aids, even of note taking, as we shall see, and simply consists in making no effort to concentrate the attention on anything in particular, and in maintaining in regard to all that one hears the same measure of calm, quiet attentiveness—or "evenly hovering attention," as I once before described it. In this way a strain which could not be kept up for several hours daily and a danger inseparable from deliberate attentiveness are avoided. For as soon as attention is deliberately concentrated in a certain degree, one begins to select from the material before one; one point will be fixed in the mind with particular clearness and some other consequently disregarded, and in this selection one's expectations or one's inclinations will be followed. This is just what must not be done, however; if one's expectations are followed in this selection there is the danger of never finding anything but what is already known, and if one follows one's inclinations anything which is to be perceived will most certainly be falsified. It must not be forgotten that the meaning of the things one hears is, at all events for the most part, only recognizable later on. (Freud, 1924/1959, p. 324)

Freud's point is well taken as far as it goes, but there is more to therapy than diagnosis. How should we approach the task of changing the client? The answer, at least for the neurotic who is still in possession of a considerable amount of normal competence, may be to take seriously the idea of therapy as a rhetorical transaction. The rhetorical interchange, taking place over time, will create and change the meaning of events and actions for both client and therapist. The result will be a client whose behavior and perspective has been changed as much by his or her own activity as by the intervention of the therapist. Further, it is likely that the final outcome of a successful interaction will be a client that is quite different from any stereotype that the therapist may have envisaged beforehand. The problem of novelty or creativity is as much a factor in therapy as it is in cognition, language, or social phenomena. Since our lives consist in the main of unanticipated occurrences (and we would be incapable of learning anything new if they did not), it is clear that we must adapt to those occurrences by following, as consistently as we are able, abstract rules of conduct. As Hayek noted, "our actions form a coherent and a rational pattern, not because they have been decided upon as part of a single plan thought out beforehand, but because in each successive decision we limit our range of choice by the same abstract rules" (1967, p. 90). The rhetorical approach, with its focus on the given case, appears to be the only way to reconcile the desire for abstract principles of determination at the deep-structural level with the diversity of particulars at the surface level of behavior. We cannot hope to control the particulars in therapy any more than we can explain the details of their occurrence. If we construe therapy as the application of algorithms thought out in advance, then the result must inevitably be frustrated, depressed therapists who regard every case as (at least in part) a failure.

Civilization and Its Discontents: Remarks on the Futility of the Freudian Attitude toward Therapeutic Outcome

Having praised Freud above for acknowledging the role of tacit processes both in the genesis of behavior and in the practice of therapy, let me now damn him for having fostered the constructivist rationalist ideal of the nature and outcome of therapeutic "intervention." It is a commonplace that therapy for Freud was to free man from his culturally acquired repression and inhibition, and to release the culturally blocked "natural drives." Freud impressed upon therapy an implicit rationalist constructivism that has been accepted by virtually all schools of therapy since his time: The idea that the spontaneously developed models of adjustment which incorporate cultural and social rules and wisdom learned through the rise of civilization must be replaced by "rationally determined" patterns of behavior that the therapist, through his midwifery, is to instill upon the client. For the Freudian, the preferred rational behavior consists in the direct expression of innate needs and drives; for the behavior modifier it consists in bits of behavior that are easily quantified on clip boards and susceptible to available contingencies of reinforcement; for the literary mentality that writes Utopian blueprints for the equally enslaved society, it lies in whatever fanciful notions are beyond freedom and dignity in the divine illumination of the central planner in the sky. In all cases it is assumed that omniscient modern man can rationally construct a new social order and individuals that are better adjusted to it than could ever be done by traditional means such as old-fashioned moral values and outmoded concepts like liberty and justice, which require the discipline of cultural and social interaction. Therapy thus assumes that it is not necessary to pass the *burden* of culture to a client in order to render him or her well-adjusted, that one can consciously plan and direct the attunement of the social milieu in which mankind has arisen. Civilization is thus a burden to be overcome rather than the source of man's powers and the hope for his future.

Commentary

Psychotherapy and Science

Impurely Rhetorical

MARY LOU MAXWELL AND GROVER MAXWELL

Professor Weimer's essay is an important contribution, and we applaud his persuasive arguments against "scientistic methodolatry"; indeed, his classification of the twentieth century as an "age of [scientistic] superstition" rings all too true. He rightly emphasizes the centrality of the "tacit dimension" of Polanyi and Hayek in the quest for knowledge, and his reconceptualization of both science and psychotherapy as "rhetorical processes" is a brilliant integrative effort—obviously radical and perhaps somewhat past the mark but undeniably inventive and suggestive.

We agree with Weimer that the excesses of what he (and Hayek) stigmatize as "rational constructivism" (e.g., logical positivism, behaviorism) are due in large part to a gross misapprehension about scientific inquiry. The misapprehension is that there is a unique set of procedures, called "the scientific method," which, if applied assiduously will transform observations, experimental data, etc. into an integrated corpus of "scientific knowledge." Weimer judiciously cites several independent instances of detailed research in both history of science and philosophy of science that

MARY LOU MAXWELL • Department of Psychology, University of Minnesota, Minneapolis, Minnesota 55455. GROVER MAXWELL • Minnesota Center for Philosophy of Science, University of Minnesota, Minneapolis, Minnesota 55455.

clearly demonstrate both that science *does not* operate in such a fashion and that, for logically compelling reasons, it *cannot* so operate. A number of leading theorists (e.g., Einstein and Polanyi) in that hardest of the "hard sciences," physics, have recognized that such a "Method" does not exist even for their discipline. (As has been often noted, this has failed to filter down to most social scientists, including all too many clinical psychologists.) These results pull the rug out from under behavioristic and other scientistic approaches to therapy insofar as they are based on belief in the scientific method and on (the resulting) desire to emulate the hard sciences. Somewhat paradoxically, however, they open the way for recognition of the similarities that Weimer emphasizes between empathetic, creative therapy and creative, critical inquiry in physics and other areas of science.

Several of Weimer's points need clarification, however, and some of them must be challenged. Weimer fails to distinguish between those clinicians who actually practice and are primarily committed to psychotherapy and those who are predominately diagnostically oriented. Far from "wearing flowers and dancing on the beach," all too many in the latter category push the "rational constructivist," scientistic approach with inquisitorial fervor. This may be as much due to the difficulty of doing effective psychotherapy as to the prevalence of scientism. Psychotherapy can be a personally threatening and ambiguous situation, especially for an unskilled practitioner, making it tempting to clutch at "the pretense of knowledge" rather than confess ignorance. Certainly the most difficult task in working with graduate students is to persuade them to discard glib clinical jargon, to face the client as a unique, unpredictable, and basically unknown fellow human being, and to resolutely resist the temptation to try to show the client that they are smarter and better adjusted than he or she. In sum, we (and especially M. L. Maxwell as a clinician) empathize strongly with Weimer's (all-to-brief) characterization of therapy as a tacit and rhetorical interaction rather than an attempt at description and control.

Although science and psychotherapy have crucial rhetorical components, it must be remembered that rhetoric can be used in diverse manners and directed toward different ends. We must therefore take issue with Weimer when he seems to give the impression (perhaps unintentionally) that science and psychotherapy should be nothing but rhetoric (or that they are basically or essentially just rhetorical processes, etc). The goal of science is—or certainly *ought* to be—to discover what the constituents of the universe are, what they are like, what they do, how they are related to each other, etc. In other words, science is in essence, the (systematic, self-critical) search for truth (in the commonsense, straightforward, unproblematic sense of truth—roughly, the "correspondence" sense of truth). This search proceeds by proposing guesses ("theories") as to what there is, what it is like, and then, by testing such proposals in various ways. Although the role of experimental and other observational data in such searching and testing has been disastrously overemphasized and misconstrued by rational constructivists, observational evidence does have a role and, indeed, an indispensable one. It is certainly true that rhetorical transactions can be suggestive and helpful in estimating the relevance and the amount of support a given body of evidence provides a given theory. On occasion, rhetoric even helps determine the meaning of (ostensible) evidence relative to a given theory. Moreover, rhetoric can suggest other (nonevidential) considerations that are important for the critical assessment of proposed theories. But while rhetoric is an important tool, perhaps an indispensable one, we hold that it is a secondary or intermediary one. The primary tools for scientific inquiry are located in the "tacit dimension"; they are (1) the creative ability to propose "fairly decent" theories and (2) the facility for the critical assessment of those that get proposed. The latter includes the ability to recognize a fairly decent theory after it has been proposed and the ability to obtain, recognize, and interpret fairly decent relevant evidence (see, e.g., G. Maxwell, "Induction and Empiricism: A Bayesian–Frequentist Alternative," in G. Maxwell & Robert M. Anderson, Jr., Eds., *Minnesota Studies in the Philosophy of Science*, Vol. 6, Minneapolis, University of Minnesota Press, 1975). It seems to us, thus, that Weimer overestimates the centrality of rhetoric for scientific inquiry and that this, moreover, is at odds with his justified emphasis on the importance, indeed the indispensability, of the tacit dimension.

Rhetoric certainly is important in psychotherapy, but as above, mainly as a device. Moreover, it is not always the most effective device for releasing and facilitating use of the more basic operations of the therapeutic process. Rhetoric is nothing as important, we feel, as careful listening and empathetic, often unspoken understanding. Most therapists talk too much, and even if "discussion and persuasion" were substituted for "diagnosis and control," they would still do better to be silent a greater portion of the time. Freud's "free-floating attention," Reik's "listening with the third ear," and Rogers's "empathetic understanding" are hard to beat as descriptions of effective therapeutic techniques, for it is even more important for the client than it is for the therapist that his tacit dimension be activated and, within reason, given free rein. This is surely necessary if an adequately "deep" understanding of the client is to be obtained, either by the therapist or, much more crucially, by the client him- or herself. Achievement of this happy goal should be sought, we believe, without resorting to "redirection of the client's activity" as Weimer suggests at one point; and once it is reached redirection by the therapist is both unnecessary and undesirable. If empathetic understanding can enable the client to utilize his tacit dimension and thereby come to understand himself, he can then decide whether and how he wishes to redirect his activities. This claim of ours may appear partisan and contentious, but, we believe, it follows from a precept that we share with Weimer, that critical rationalism should be the central guiding principle both in science and in psychotherapy. If Weimer resolves this tension between his allegiance to critical rationalism with its crucial dependence on the tacit dimension and his virtual definition of science and psychotherapy in terms of rhetoric by substantially modifying the latter—as we believe he must—then it seems that his view of psychotherapy would have much more in common with that of the humanistic psychologists than he now cares to admit.

Weimer's interesting de-emphasis of the "specification of particulars" in favor of "underlying [abstract] principles" calls for a note of caution. Sight must not be lost of the fact that principles are exemplified only by particulars and, therefore, must be evidentially tested by particulars. Admittedly, the specification of particulars must often be quite abstract, but overemphasis of abstraction and general principles, especially in psychotherapy, must not be done at the expense of the individual. Weimer's contention that "therapy must tap the abstract rules which literally are the client's mind" is easier said than done. As a client once said to one of us, "Please do not understand me too quickly." Too much haste in formulating abstract rules might harm the client as much as diagnostic rational constructivism.

Finally, it seems to us that Weimer takes a giant leap from his emphasis on the tacit dimension in science and psychotherapy to his defense of "the marketplace" and traditional moral values and practices on the ground that they arose spontaneously without conscious thought and, moreover, have survived by virtue of natural selection. Despite the primacy of tacit knowledge, it is nevertheless one of the important functions of science to transform a good portion of the tacit into the explicit. Otherwise, how can critical rationalism, that is, testing and critical scrutiny, operate? Why should the practices of the marketplace and other traditional values and procedures be immune to such tests and criticism? It will not do to reply that they have survived the tests that natural selection provides. It is true that the marketplace and many other mores have survived for centuries (in some societies), but the same was and in many cases still is true of such things as slavery, witchhunting, bigotry and superstitions, institutionalized cruelty, exploitation of all descriptions—the list is endless. Even if it were the case that some of these played an adaptive role, it must be emphasized that traits that are adaptive in one environment may become harmful and even lethal as the environment undergoes change. Perhaps, for example, matters such as dwindling resources, overpopulation, and accumulating pollution make advisable a very critical reexamination of a totally self-regulating marketplace, however successful it may have seemed to be in the past. Actually, we feel very friendly toward the marketplace (with reservations like those just mentioned); and we believe that many of the results of planned economies have been disastrous and are becoming even more so. Moreover, in raising children up to and through adolescence, we continually find ourselves defending traditional values with a vigor that astonishes us. However, we remain, in principle at least, committed to critical rationalism. Therefore, we hold that such defense, if only we had the time, energy, information, and ingenuity, should be based on critical examination, comparison with alternatives, etc., rather than on the fact that such values and practices arose tacitly and have, so far, survived natural selection.

Due to limitations of space, most of our remarks have been critical. Therefore, we must emphasize that we are in general agreement with most of Weimer's important and innovative essay. We hope that the impetus that he has provided will result in continued fruitful interaction between psychotherapy and philosophy of science.

Index